THOMAS TALLIS

Thomas Tallis

JOHN HARLEY

LONDON AND NEW YORK

First published 2015 by Ashgate Publishing

2 Park Square, Milton Park, Abingdon, Oxfordshire OX14 4RN
52 Vanderbilt Avenue, New York, NY 10017

Routledge is an imprint of the Taylor & Francis Group, an informa business

First issued in paperback 2020

British Library Cataloguing in Publication Data
A catalogue record for this book is available from the British Library

The Library of Congress has cataloged the printed edition as follows:
Harley, John.
Thomas Tallis / by John Harley.
pages cm
Includes bibliographical references and index.
ISBN 978-1-4724-2806-6 (hardcover : alk. paper)
1. Tallis, Thomas, approximately 1505–1585.
2. Composers–England–Biography. 3. Music–England–16th century–History and criticism.
4. Church music–England–16th century. I. Title.
ML410.T147H37 2015
780.92–dc23
[B]

2015017486

ISBN 978-1-4724-2806-6 (hbk)
ISBN 978-0-367-59755-9 (pbk)

Bach musicological font developed by © Yo Tomita

Contents

List of Figures

List of Tables

List of Music Examples

Permission to use copyright material is acknowledged at the end of this list.

Acknowledgements

Grateful acknowledgement is made for consent to the use of the following copyright material. Adaptation, where noted, consists principally of the restoration of reduced note values to those in the original sources.

Example 6.5b is adapted from the Oxenford Imprint edition of Tallis's *Mass Puer natus est nobis* (revised 2009), by permission of the editors, Sally Dunkley and David Wulstan.

Examples 4.1, 6.3a, and 9.1 are adapted by permission of Stainer & Bell Ltd, London, England, from Thomas Tallis, Early English Church Music, volume 12, edited by Leonard Ellinwood, revised by Paul Doe, ©1971 The British Academy.

Example 4.2 is adapted by permission of Stainer & Bell Ltd, London, England, from Thomas Tallis, Early English Church Music, volume 13, edited by Leonard Ellinwood, revised by Paul Doe, © 1971 The British Academy.

Examples 7.1 and 7.2 are reproduced by permission of Stainer & Bell Ltd, London, England, from *The Mulliner book*, edited by John Caldwell, Musica Britannica, volume 1, © 2011 Musica Britannica Trust.

Preface

Writings about Tallis have generally been confined to passages in histories of music, and articles in encyclopaedias and periodicals. Other accounts of the composer and his music have been few. Paul Doe's brief *Tallis* appeared as long ago as 1968 (second edition 1976). The quality of longer and more detailed studies of aspects of Tallis's music, written as theses by Davitt Moroney and John Milsom (1980 and 1983), means that they have since become widely known, as has Penelope Rapson's thesis of 1981 (published 1989), *A technique for identifying textual errors and its application to the sources of music by Thomas Tallis*. More recently Suzanne Cole has surveyed Tallis's posthumous reputation in her valuable *Thomas Tallis and his music in Victorian England* (2008).

The absence of other books about Tallis appears to result partly from the difficulty of dating many of his works, and partly from the lack of an adequate modern collected edition, arising from the problems of reconciling the different versions of pieces presented by early copies. It is problems of the latter kind which Rapson's study addresses, and it will be for future editors to take account of her work. As things stand, no 'complete' edition of Tallis's Latin-texted pieces has been published since 1928, though the need for a new one has in part been met by John Milsom's fine edition of the 1575 *Cantiones* by Tallis and Byrd. I have fortunately found it possible to include a number of references to the Milsom edition (2014), which appeared when the present book was nearing completion.

In spite of the lack of some desirable resources, it has seemed worthwhile attempting to describe what is known of Tallis's life, and to give a largely non-technical account of all his extant music, not least in the hope that it will encourage someone to do it better at some time in the future. When I began work I knew only a limited amount of Tallis's music, but what I have learned since has been a revelation. My admiration for his powers as a composer – and for the man, insofar as it is possible to know him – has grown immensely. If I have adopted a personal view, it is of Tallis as a composer adept at setting words to music, and as a creator of musical patterns. It will certainly be possible for someone to view his music from a different angle and to describe it more fully.

The plan of this book is a compromise between two possibilities, neither of which might have been satisfactory. To describe Tallis's works simply by genre would have concealed what can be deduced about their chronology, while an attempt to describe the music chronologically piece by piece would have been unsuccessful because of the difficulty of dating pieces narrowly. Therefore, although I have not been entirely unmindful that Tallis's music is 'the product of a single creative imagination',[1] I have chosen, in spite of any misconceptions it might engender, to categorize the bulk of Tallis's works within four chronological periods. (I gave up an attempt to fit all but the latest of his instrumental works into this scheme, and they have a separate chapter.) This makes it easier to offer parallel accounts of his music and his life and some of the events he lived through. Even if the division into reigns slightly obscures the fact that all of Tallis's music is the work of one man, it is useful because successive reigns gave rise to new requirements in terms of the language and texts to be set to music, and to different ideas about the kind of music suitable for setting them. Within certain periods, but not all, many of Tallis's works tend to group themselves on the basis of their words, and notwithstanding the risks this brings they are probably more easily described and understood when considered category by category. I nevertheless recognize, and I hope readers will bear in mind, that each new work Tallis wrote was the result of experience gained continuously.

There is another problem of which readers should be aware. Not only is much of Tallis's music hard to date, to put it mildly, but many of the surviving sources were compiled a long time after the music they contain was composed. Furthermore, a number of pieces survive in unique copies, which means that we have to rely on the musical accuracy and the ascription to Tallis of works which they alone preserve. The first of these considerations is especially important in the case of a composer like Tallis, who evidently revised a good many of his works. The sources of Tallis's music present modern editors with formidable difficulties.

I have hardly attempted to answer in detail questions about the attribution of certain pieces to Tallis, though it is as well to remember that they exist. There is a potential problem about the authorship of any piece when there is only one source, or when only one source gives the composer's name. There is an added difficulty when one source names Tallis as the composer, and another source names somebody else, but in general I have not sought to upset the accepted canon. Since several of Tallis's works appear anonymously in some manuscripts, even when he is named as their composer in others, it is possible that some of the music he wrote, particularly in his early years, may exist without his name attached to it in any source; but that is a matter I have not been able to tackle in detail.

For a different reason I have not attempted to describe Tallis's posthumous reputation. In the space available I could not have added anything to Suzanne Cole's account in *Thomas Tallis and his music in Victorian England* and her supplementary articles listed in my bibliography. Another topic I have not

---

1 '[T]here is clearly a pressing need to regard Tallis' surviving music as the product of a single creative imagination, rather than to categorize and discuss it strictly according to liturgical genre; it is essential that we break down the convenient but misleading classification of his career into four monarchical "periods" … and also the distinction between works with English and Latin text' (John Milsom, 'English polyphonic style in transition: a study of the sacred music of Thomas Tallis' (Doctoral thesis, University of Oxford, 1983), vol. 1, p. 127).

attempted to deal with is that of the relationship between Tallis's music and the music that was being written on the Continent in his lifetime. It is an important subject, and I hope that one day somebody will be brave enough to tackle it.

Early manuscript sources of Tallis's music which are mentioned in this book are listed in the index of names and subjects, but I have not tried to provide a complete account of the sources. Readers are referred instead to the EECM Primary Source Database, hosted by Trinity College Dublin, which is readily available online,[2] and to the lists of sources in the editions included in my bibliography,

Acknowledgements

My indebtedness to others is usually indicated in footnotes, though I hope any victim of unacknowledged pilfering will take it as a compliment. A number of people have been kind enough to share unpublished information with me, but without disrespect to others I should like to single out the generosity of Alan Brooks, John Milsom, Ian Payne and Stefan Scott. Members of staff at libraries and archive collections have assisted with a willingness reflecting their belief that being helpful is a natural way of life, though those at the Victoria and Albert Museum's Archive of Art and Design and Jonathan Partington at the Greenwich Heritage Centre deserve special thanks. So does Jenny Bracey, the Church Administrator at St Alfege Church, Greenwich.

I am especially grateful to Richard Turbet and Kerry McCarthy for their kind encouragement and advice, for reading and commenting on my drafts, and in Kerry's case for replying so helpfully to emails seeking information on matters about which she knows more than I do. They assuredly will not have saved me entirely from error, but any mistakes are my own.

I am indebted to all the owners of copyright material which they have very kindly allowed me to include among the figures and examples in this book. Those who have granted permission to reproduce illustrations are noted in the captions. Those who have given permission for the use of musical examples are listed on p. xii.[3]

[2] The EECM Primary Source Database builds on two printed supplements to the Early English Church Music series: Ralph T. Daniel and Peter le Huray, compilers, *The sources of English church music, 1549–1660*, parts I & II (EECM, supplementary volume 1, parts 1 and 2: London, 1972), and May Hofman and John Morehen, compilers, *Latin music in British sources*, c.*1485*–c.*1610* (EECM, supplementary volume 2: London, 1987).

[3] The derivation of other examples is as follows. Example 9.2 has been newly edited from Matthew Parker's *The whole* Psalter (1567?), and Examples 6.1, 6.2, 10.2 and 10.3 have been newly edited from the Tallis–Byrd *Cantiones* of 1575. The *Tudor Church Music* editions of music by Taverner (1923) and Tallis (1927), although outdated in many respects, have proved useful guides in creating further examples, but material they contain has been freshly edited to take account of the original manuscript sources.

Completing this book has been made easier by the prospect of its publication by Ashgate. What has now become a long association makes it appropriate to record my gratitude to the several editors and their colleagues with whom it has been a pleasure to work at one time or another, and to thank them for their patient and friendly help.

John Harley

Note

Abbreviations

The following abbreviations are used in this book:

BL	The British Library
GL	The Guildhall Library
LMA	London Metropolitan Archives
TNA	The National Archives

Spelling

Except in quotations, the customary modern spelling 'Tallis' is used in this book, though Tudor documents frequently have 'Tallys', the form used by the composer himself (assuming it was he who wrote his name in BL Lansdowne MS 763). At least one contemporary document (TNA E115/368/133) uses both these spellings, and others occur elsewhere.

The spelling of English words in quotations, and in the wills of Thomas and Joan Tallis, follows that of the sources (identifiable from the references provided). The expansion of abbreviations and contractions is indicated by italic letters. In presenting or referring to English texts set by Tallis modern spellings have been used. An arbitrary uniformity has likewise been imposed on his Latin texts.

Note Values, Pitch and Key

References to note values are always to those in the original sources, not to those in editions where they are halved.

Musical examples are transcribed at the original written pitch and with the original note values, but (apart from mensural signs) modern notation has otherwise been used, the number of flats in clef signatures has been regularized[1] and ligatures occurring in original copies have not been indicated. Bar lines drawn with dashes are editorial. The spelling and punctuation of English texts has been

1 On clef signatures, flats, sharps and naturals in the Tallis–Byrd *Cantiones* of 1575, see the edition by John Milsom, p. xxxiii.

modernized; and in a few examples the placement of words is editorial where the underlay is unclear or words are missing in the source.

When a note needs to be identified by the octave in which it occurs, an italic letter is used and the pitch is indicated (from the bass) thus: *C* to *B*, *c* to *b*, *c′* (middle C) to *b′*, *c″* to *b″*.

A few keys used by Tallis may be unfamiliar to some readers. For brevity the key note and the number of flats is occasionally indicated thus: G(♭), G(♭♭).

Dates

In Tallis's time the year began on 25 March. Dates from 1 January to 24 March are given in a form combining the old and modern styles of writing the year, for example 1571/2.

Chapter 1
The Reign of Henry VIII: Biographical and Historical Background

Thomas Tallis's date of birth, his family origins, and where he received his education are unrecorded. In Grove's *Dictionary of music and musicians*, William H. Husk wrote that Tallis 'is supposed to have been born in the second decade of the 16th century'.[1] Henry Davey at first thought he was 'probably born about 1510', though he later changed his mind to 'about 1500–10'.[2] Judging by the date when Tallis is known to have been employed at Dover Priory (see below), he is unlikely to have been born much later. In 1928 E.H. Fellowes proposed that the date should be pushed back to 'four or five years earlier' than 1510,[3] and that is where it has remained. The editors of the Tudor Church Music edition of Tallis's Latin-texted music gave it as 'about 1505',[4] though even this may be a little late. Much depends on the dating of his early works, and whether an accomplished piece like *Salve intemerata*, apparently the last of his early antiphons, could have been circulating before he reached his mid-twenties (see p. 30). All that is certain is that Tallis grew up in the reign of King Henry VIII, who was born in 1491 and came to the throne in 1509. He went on to serve not only Henry, but his three children who followed him to the throne. It is an understatement to say that Tallis lived through a period of great change.

Tallis's only known relation, apart from those gained through marriage (see pp. 93–4), is named in his will as his 'Cosen John Sayer dwelling in the Ile of Thanet' in Kent ('cousin' had a range of meanings). Sayer was a common name in Thanet, and during the second half of the sixteenth century it was recorded frequently in parish registers throughout the Isle, but John Sayer appears to have lived at or

---

1 George Grove, ed., *A dictionary of music and musicians* ... (London, 1879–90), vol. 4, p. 52. Husk, who was at one time the librarian of the Sacred Harmonic Society, died in 1887.

2 *Dictionary of national biography*, ed. Leslie Stephen and Sidney Lee (London, 1885–1900), vol. 55, p. 348; Henry Davey, *History of English music*, 2nd edn (London, 1921), p. 132.

3 *Grove's dictionary of music and musicians*, 3rd edn, ed. H.C. Colles (London, 1927–40), vol. 5, p. 256. Fellowes developed the idea in *Grove's dictionary of music and musicians*, 5th edn, ed. Eric Blom (London, 1954), vol. 8, p. 294, and suggested (almost certainly erroneously) that Tallis might have come from Leicestershire.

4 Thomas Tallis, *Tudor church music ... Volume VI: Thomas Tallis c.1505–1585* (London, 1928), p. xii.

near Margate.[5] There is thus some reason for thinking that Tallis may have been born in Kent, where during his lifetime the name Tallis could be found in the registers of places as widely spread as Canterbury, Elham and New Romney.

It is very likely, though of course not certain, that wherever Tallis gained his musical training, it was as a chorister. He would have become familiar with the daily and seasonal devotions of the church and the chants associated with them. As he progressed he undoubtedly learned to play the organ, and perhaps the viol as well. His general schooling, too, was probably of a kind received by choristers.[6] It would be easy to allow speculation to run riot, but one cannot help wondering whether a clue to his training may lie in his early employment by the Benedictine priory at Dover. The priory had a song school, but as nothing is known of it beyond the fact of its existence and that it had a master, it is impossible to say whether Tallis could ever have been one of its pupils. More tellingly, perhaps, Dover Priory was not far from Christ Church, Canterbury, of which it had once been a cell. Christ Church was a larger Benedictine priory, with a cathedral church where Tallis might well have been a chorister.[7] All the same, there is no record of him before 1531, when 'Thomas Tales' was named in the accounts of Dover Priory as

[5] Tallis's origins have most recently been investigated by Ian Payne, in 'A tale of two counties: the biography of Thomas Tallis (*c.*1505–85) revisited', *The Leicestershire Archaeological and Historical Society: Transactions*, vol. 88 (2014), pp. 85–100. He has convincingly identified as Tallis's relations 'four generations of the Sayer family, all apparently property-owning yeomen connected with St John's parish on the Isle of Thanet' (i.e. at Margate), and provided a family tree. The occurrence of the name Sayer elsewhere in the Isle is illustrated by *The register book of St Laurence in Thanet, from 1560 to 1653. Transcribed by Kenyon Wood Wilkie ... completed and indexed by ... Christopher Hales Wilkie* (Canterbury, 1902). This also contains entries for 'Pearc' ('Pierce', etc.), a name which (because of the similarity of 'e' and 'c' in Tudor handwriting) seems sometimes to be confused with 'Peare' ('Paire', etc.), found in the wills of Thomas and Joan Tallis (see pp. 229–33). 'Sayer' appears too in other Thanet registers, e.g. St Mary's, Minster. Queen Mary was to grant Tallis and Richard Bower the lease of the manor of Minster in 1557 (see p. 96). There were Sayers also in the parishes of All Saints', Birchington (where 'Peers' or 'Pierce' occurs again), and St Peter's, Broadstairs. A wider search for these names has not been made.

[6] For brief accounts, see Jane Flynn, 'The education of choristers in England during the sixteenth century', in John Morehen, ed., *English choral practice* (Cambridge, 1995), pp. 180–99; David Allinson, 'The rhetoric of devotion: some neglected elements in the context of the early Tudor votive antiphon' (Doctoral thesis, University of Exeter, 1998), chapter 4, particularly p. 87ff.

[7] Canterbury remained a monastic cathedral until it was refounded with a secular chapter in 1540–41: see Church of England, General Synod, *Talent and Calling. A review of the law and practice regarding appointments to the offices of suffragan bishop, dean, archdeacon and residentiary canon* (GS 1650: London, 2007), Appendix IV. This is available online and provides a useful summary of the history of English cathedrals. An alternative possibility is that Tallis had been a chorister at Rochester Cathedral, another Benedictine priory, but his later connection with Canterbury makes this seem less likely.

its '*joculator* organ*orum*' (organ player). Other sixteenth-century musicians, such as William Byrd, Robert White and Thomas Morley, held cathedral posts in their early or middle twenties, so it is possible that Tallis was no older when he was appointed to his position at Dover. The title he is given in the accounts echoes the description of visiting minstrels like those of the King, Lord Bergavenny and the Lord Warden of the Cinque Ports. Tallis can hardly have been unaware of the songs and tunes these men brought with them, or of those played by the waits of Canterbury, but if he absorbed anything from them there seems to be little trace of it in his own music.[8]

The religious community was small – a dozen or so monks presided over by an abbot – although the priory church appears to have been unusually large.[9] Throughout most of Tallis's employment the prior was William, concerning whom there is almost no information. About 1529 he was succeeded by Thomas Lenham, who was in turn succeeded by John Lambert (or Folkestone), to whom fell the task, completed in 1535, of surrendering the priory to the Crown.[10] By then the priory was not what it had once been. At the end of the fourteenth century it had owned a library of several hundred books, the catalogue of which has been well examined.[11] But when Archbishop Warham made a visitation in 1511, he found the monks' knowledge wanting. He ordered that a teacher should be appointed to instruct them in grammar (presumably Latin), and that the novices among them should attend a grammar school on three days each week.[12] In Tallis's time the community does not seem to have been notably wealthy, and the balance sheet for 1530–31, drawn up by Abbot Thomas, shows an expenditure considerably greater than the income.

Tallis's annual wage of two pounds in 1531 was one mark (13s 4d) less than the wage received by the 'scole mast*er* of the song scole' and the 'scole mast*er* of the grammar scole' at the time of the priory's dissolution.[13] This suggests that the

---

[8] For visiting performers see Charles Reginald Haines, *Dover priory* (Cambridge, 1930), pp. 452–3.

[9] Ibid., pp. 156–7.

[10] Ibid., pp. 303–6. Lenham and Folkestone are Kentish names.

[11] Montague Rhodes James, *The ancient libraries of Canterbury and Dover* (Cambridge, 1903), pp. 407–96; Charles Reginald Haines, 'The library of Dover priory', *The Library*, 4th series, vol. 10 (1927), pp. 73–118; Haines, *Dover priory*, pp. 382–401; William P. Stoneman, ed., *Dover priory* (Corpus of British medieval library catalogues, 5: London, 1999).

[12] For Warham's visitation, see K.L. Wood-Legh, ed., *Kentish visitations of Archbishop Warham and his deputies, 1511–1512* (Maidstone, 1984), pp. 21–5; Haines, *Dover priory*, pp. 484–7 (translation); *The Victoria history of the county of Kent*, ed. William Page (London, 1908–), vol. 2, pp. 135–6 (summary). Monks: David Knowles and R. Neville Hadcock, *Medieval religious houses: England and Wales* (London, 1971), p. 64. Priory church: Haines, *Dover priory*, pp. 156–62.

[13] BL Additional MS 25107, the accounts of the Priory of St Mary the Virgin and St Martin of the New Work (or Newark), Michaelmas to Michaelmas 1530–31, f.5^{r}; and

priory schools provided two levels of education, with boys being taught reading and plainsong before they went on to the serious study of Latin.[14]

One of the schoolmasters, whom Haines supposed to be the master of the song school, was provided with a meagrely furnished room, but an inventory made at the dissolution makes no mention of accommodation for the organist. Tallis's main task at Dover was probably to direct the singing of chants, substituting the organ for voices as required.[15] The priory's connection with the large church of St Martin at Dover, and the existence of its song school, raise the question of whether he may have had unrecorded musical resources at his disposal. So does the likelihood that before he left Dover he had composed several sizeable antiphons (see p. 25). It is difficult to guess how he continued his early training and developed his abilities as a composer. He may have been able to visit the cathedral, talk to its musicians, and hear his music performed by a skilled choir;[16] but it was not the only source of musical expertise in the county. The composer John Dygon, for example, was the prior of St Augustine's Abbey, Canterbury, from 1528 until it was dissolved 10 years later.[17]

This was a period when radical alterations were being made to the relationship between the church in England and the government. The Statute in Restraint of Appeals (April 1533),[18] also called the Ecclesiastical Appeals Act, was passed to prevent Catherine of Aragon, Henry VIII's first wife, appealing to the Pope after Archbishop Thomas Cranmer's annulment of their marriage.[19] The Act made the King in Chancery the final court of appeal, and it was afterwards illegal to accept the authority of the Pope or to follow papal rulings. The first Act of

Valor ecclesiasticus temp. Henr. VIII auctoritate regis institutus (London, 1810–34), vol. 1, p. 54. See also Haines, *Dover priory*, pp. 448 (Tallis) and 419–20 (the masters).

14 For song schools see Nicholas Orme, *Medieval schools from Roman Britain to Renaissance England* (New Haven, Ct, 2006), pp. 61–6, and as indexed. As late as 1584 the instructions given to Thomas Gyles at St Paul's Cathedral envisaged that boy choristers should be 'skilful in musicke' and 'able conveniently to serve in the Churche' before they went on to learne 'the catechisms in Laten which before they learned in Englishe' (John Harley, *The world of William Byrd: musicians, merchants and magnates* (Farnham, 2010), p. 9).

15 Frank Ll. Harrison, *Music in medieval Britain*, 4th edn (Buren, 1980), pp. 214–18; also, for the duties and training of organists, and their special status, see Roger Bray, ed., *Music in Britain: the sixteenth century* (Blackwell history of music in Britain, 2: Oxford, 1995), pp. 212–13.

16 The priory's accounts for 1530–31 record a payment 'in regard' of Master Mills and the boys of the Archbishop's chapel, but it is not explained (Haines, *Dover priory*, p. 452).

17 Dygon is thought to have copied part of a treatise by Franchinus Gaffurius (1451–1522), to which new music examples were added (Trinity College, Cambridge, MS O.3.38). John Baldwin included three pieces by Dygon, possibly extracted from a longer work, in BL MS R.M. 24.d.2.

18 24 Henry VIII, c. 12.

19 The marriage was annulled on 23 May 1533, four months after Henry had secretly married Anne Boleyn.

Supremacy followed in November 1534.[20] In December the monks of Dover Priory acknowledged the King's supremacy in matters of religion, even before he assumed the title of Supreme Head of the Church on 15 January.[21]

Commissioners were appointed in January to assess the value of church properties and revenues (the *Valor Ecclesiasticus*), with a view to completing the work by the end of May. In July Thomas Cromwell, as vicar-general, launched a programme of visitations which included religious houses in the Dover area. On 23 October Cromwell's unpleasantly ambitious agent Richard Layton submitted a report typical of those he supplied. His remarks about Dover Priory were brief and to the point: 'The p*ri*or of Dov*er* and his monk*es* be evyn as other be / but he the worste / sodomites ther is none for they nede not they have no lake of women'.[22] Was it true? One suspects that Layton was not instructed to investigate fully and make a wholly objective report. The priory was surrendered on 16 November 1535.[23] Its buildings fell into long years of disrepair, and Turner's watercolour of about 1793, in the Victoria and Albert Museum, shows what is believed to be the refectory in use as a barn. The surviving buildings are today part of Dover College, founded in 1871. A memorial to Tallis, in the form of a plaque, was installed by the Dover Society at the College gate in 2013.

St Mary-at-Hill

Tallis's whereabouts for the next few months are obscure, and it may be that he was given temporary shelter by the priory at Canterbury until he found a new post. He next became a conduct (singer) at St Mary-at-Hill in London, the largest church in the Billingsgate ward, and one with a strong musical life. Possibly the well-connected Alan Percy, the rector of St Mary-at-Hill from 1521 to 1560, secured Tallis's services for his church, but this is not recorded.[24] Tallis was paid the usual wage of the church's permanent conducts, of whom there appear to have been four at any one time, though other singers might be brought in for special occasions. He received four pounds for half a year in each of the accounting periods 1536–37 and

20 26 Hen. VIII, c. 1.

21 TNA E25/42; Haines, *Dover priory*, pp. 318–19.

22 TNA SP1/98, f.54^v (number at top of leaf); paraphrased in *Letters and papers, foreign and domestic of the reign of Henry VIII* (London, 1864–1932), vol. 9, p. 226 (no. 669).

23 TNA E322/78; Haines, *Dover priory*, pp. 319–21; and p. 111ff on the fate of the priory buildings.

24 Percy was a son of the fourth Earl of Northumberland. Among his appointments, often held simultaneously, was that of Master of the collegiate church of the Holy Trinity at Arundel, where in 1538 he succeeded Edward Hygons (Higgins). See the article on Percy by Malcolm Greenwood in the *Oxford dictionary of national biography*, ed H.C.G. Matthew and Brian Harrison (Oxford, 2004), vol. 43, pp. 676–7, and the article on Edward Higgins by Nicholas Sandon in Grove Music Online.

1537–38. Since the accounts ran from Michaelmas to Michaelmas (29 September), he must have been paid for the year leading up to Lady Day (25 March) in 1538.

It seems likely that, besides singing, Tallis sometimes played the organ, as doubtless did his colleague Richard Wynslate, who became the master of the choristers and organist at Winchester Cathedral (1541–72).[25] The date of Tallis's appointment means he was not at St Mary-at-Hill when Robert Okeland was the organist there (1533–35), but he afterwards found himself serving alongside Okeland as a member of the Chapel Royal.[26] What duties any of the organists may have had in connection with the school attached to St Mary-at-Hill during Tallis's brief employment there is unknown. The school, whose children sang in the church, had been the responsibility of an earlier organist, John Northfolke, though it is not mentioned in the churchwardens' accounts after 1530. However, a note added to the 'brief' version of a certificate prepared in 1548, recording what had been appropriated to the Crown following the dissolution of chantries in London, refers to the organist Ryse William (possibly William Rhys) as the schoolmaster, who had been pensioned off.[27]

The instruments at St Mary's were maintained and repaired by the ubiquitous organ-maker John Howe, and both 'lyttel organs' and 'great organs' appear from time to time in the churchwardens' accounts. The 'lyttel organs' were perhaps the regals mentioned in 1559.[28] Tallis's period at St Mary-at-Hill may have been the time when he taught music to John Harington (*c.*1517–1582), whose son, another John, said his father learned music 'in the fellowship of good Maister Tallis, when a young man'.[29] As the elder Harington came from Stepney, less than two miles from Tallis's place of work, there could have been a brief opportunity for him

---

25 LMA P69/MRY4/B/005/MS01239/001/003 (formerly Guildhall Library MS 1239/1, part 3), ff.681r, 693v; Henry Littlehales, ed., *The medieval records of a London city church (St Mary at Hill) A.D. 1420–1559* (Early English Text Society, original series, 125, 128: London, 1904–05), pp. 375, 376, 380; John Harley, *The world of William Byrd*, pp. 32–3. Wynslate may have compiled the earliest section of BL Additional MS 29996.

26 LMA P69/MRY4/B/005/MS01239/001/003, ff.642r, 653v, transcribed in Littlehales, *The medieval records of a London city church*, pp. 365, 368; Andrew Ashbee, *Records of English court music* (Snodland, *later* Aldershot, 1986–96), vol. 7, pp. 99, 103, 105, 113.

27 TNA E301/88, showing that Ryse received a pension of five pounds a year; C.J. Kitching, ed. *London and Middlesex chantry certificate, 1548* (London Record Society publications, 16: London, 1980), p. 6. Ryse William's previous salary of £8 10s is shown in LMA P69/MRY4/B/005/MS01239/001/003 (formerly GL MS 1239/1, part 3), f.707v, and he is also shown to have received 6s 8d for one quarter when he played daily at Lady Mass; transcribed in Littlehales, *The medieval records of a London city church*, p. 386. In 1547 he seems to have replaced 'Philipp Ryse' (Philip ap Rhys), subsequently the organist of St Paul's cathedral where he may himself have replaced John Redford, who died in that year.

28 LMA P69/MRY4/B/005/MS01239/001/003, f.826r; Littlehales, *The medieval records of a London city church*, p. 411.

29 John Harington, *Nugae antiquae* (London, 1769), pp. 132–3.

to receive lessons. After 1538 Tallis worked at Waltham and Canterbury, and Harington was in the King's service.

Waltham Abbey and Canterbury Cathedral

St Mary-at-Hill had a close connection with the Augustinian abbey of Waltham Cross in Essex, whose abbot's London house was near the church. The abbey enjoyed royal patronage (two chambers were set aside for the King and the Queen), and its size and proximity to London gave it a special importance. Tallis most probably moved to the abbey on leaving St Mary-at-Hill, and was there at its dissolution. On 23 March 1540 the abbot, Robert Fuller, signed a deed of surrender, which was received by Sir William Petre as deputy Vicar-general.[30] An inventory made at the time describes the instruments available to Tallis: 'a lytell payre of organes' in the Lady Chapel, valued at 20 shillings, and in the choir 'a greate large payre of organes above, one the north isle' with 'a lesser payre beneth'.[31] Members of the religious community were treated generously, and payments were made to lay employees not granted the pensions received by the abbey's canons.[32] The sum of 20 shillings was paid to a group of five 'chyldrene of the churche', who may have been Tallis's choristers. Tallis himself received two final payments, each of 20 shillings, for 'wages' and 'rewards'.[33] These were greater than those made to any of the others named. He seems to have carried off with him a manuscript in which (assuming the hand is his) he wrote his signature: 'Thomas Tallys' (p. 8, Figure 1.1).[34] The manuscript is a collection of writings about music, assembled by John Wylde, a former musician of Waltham Abbey.[35] Some are speculative and some are practical, but all belong to a musical world which the manuscript's new owner was long to outlive.

---

30 TNA E322/252.

31 TNA E117/11/24, f.9^{v}, slightly mistranscribed in Mackenzie E.C. Walcott, 'Inventory of Waltham Holy Cross', *Transactions of the Essex Archaeological Society*, [original series] 5 (1873), pp. 257–64. Tallis's connection with Waltham Abbey was first noted by musical biographers about the time when Walcott published the inventory (Suzanne Cole, *Thomas Tallis and his music in Victorian England* (Woodbridge, 2008), pp. 83–4).

32 Seventeen canons to whom pensions were granted in April 1540 are named in *Letters and papers ... of the reign of Henry VIII*, vol. 15, p. 554.

33 TNA E117/11/24, f.20^{v}.

34 BL Lansdowne MS 763; Tallis's signature is on (modern) f.124^{v}. It is not known who added Tallis's name in capitals below the signature, or the other writing on the page. These capitals somewhat resemble the 'S' in the inscription "Sum liber thomae mullineri' on the cover of BL Additional MS 30513 (see p. 68 below), but the book is not not known to have been in Mulliner's possession.

35 Wylde is described in the manuscript as 'precentor' (the canon in charge of liturgical music), amended to 'preceptor' (lay instructor, or master of choristers).

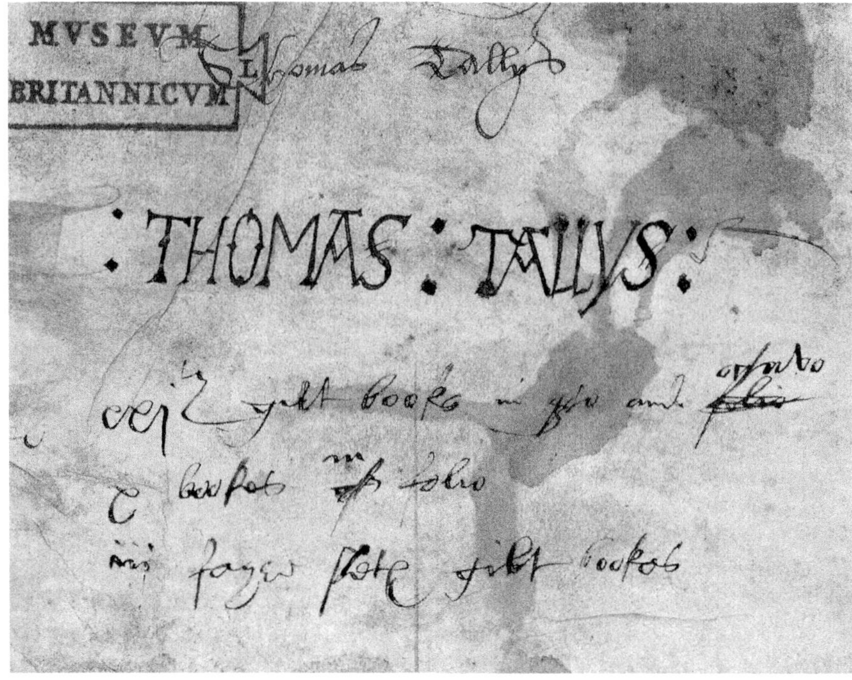

Figure 1.1 A signature, assumed to be Tallis's, at the top of f.124^{v} in a book compiled by John Wylde of Waltham Abbey. It is not known who added Tallis's name in capitals, or the writing below it (Lansdowne MS 763, f. 124^{v}, by permission of the British Library Board)

Tallis must have maintained any connections he may have had with Canterbury, for that was where he was next employed. Cromwell had signed a commission empowering Cranmer, Petre and others to take possession of the city's Benedictine priory, and it was surrendered in March 1539, before the surrender of Waltham Abbey. On 8 April 1541 its cathedral was refounded as a secular institution (one of the 'cathedrals of the new foundation').[36] At the head of a list of 'Vycars' (vicars choral) in 1541–42 is the name of William Selby (or Shelbye), master of the choristers. Although he was not formally appointed organist until five years later he may effectively have held that post.[37] Immediately before its refounding

36 Roger Bowers, *English church polyphony: singers and sources from the 14th to the 17th century* (Variorum collected studies, 633: Aldershot, 1999), article IV, reprinted from Patrick Collinson and others, eds, *A history of Canterbury Cathedral, 598–1982* (Oxford, 1995), pp. 426–9.

37 Canterbury Cathedral Archives, CCA-DCc-DE/164 (unfoliated); Watkins Shaw, *The succession of organists of the Chapel Royal and the cathedrals of England* (Oxford, 1991), p. 44.

the cathedral had possessed 'ij peire' of organs in the choir, and another 'ij peire' in the Lady Chapel.[38]

Tallis's name follows Selby's, on a new page, as the first in a list of 12 vicars (p. 10, Figure 1.2).[39] His annual wage was eight pounds, the amount he had been paid at St Mary-at-Hill. There were also ten choristers. To provide music for the choir of Canterbury's new foundation cathedral shortly after its establishment, the 'Peterhouse' partbooks may have been compiled from music used at Magdalen College, Oxford, where Thomas Bull, who is listed with Tallis as a vicar at Canterbury, had sung in the choir.[40] Among Tallis's other colleagues was Thomas Wood, who had formerly been the master of the cathedral's Lady Chapel choir.

If the position of Tallis's name in the list of vicars choral means that he was the senior among them, after Selby, it may be explained by the experience he had accumulated. His experience may also explain why he was shortly translated to the Chapel Royal, the body of priests and musicians whose principal duties were to serve the personal religious needs of the King, and to enhance his royal splendour in support of his domestic and diplomatic endeavours. During the following two decades the departure of Tallis from Canterbury was followed by that of other singers, creating severe difficulties for the cathedral choir.[41]

Henry VIII's Chapel Royal

It is not known exactly when Tallis took up his new duties, but the earliest document naming him as a Gentleman of the Chapel is a lay subsidy roll of 1543/4.[42] By that time the English court had undergone a transformation. Before Henry VIII's accession it had looked to the Burgundian court as a model; afterwards it came to adopt the style of the French court of François I. Household ordinances drawn up by Wolsey, as Lord Chancellor, were promulgated from Eltham Palace in January 1525/6. A humanistic view of the ideals, education and behaviour desirable in

[38] J. Wickham Legg and W.H. St John Hope, eds, *Inventories of Christchurch Canterbury* (Westminster, 1902), pp. 192–3, from an inventory dated 10 April 1540. Compare the description of the organs played by Tallis at Waltham Abbey (p. 7 above).

[39] Canterbury Cathedral Archives, CCA-DCc-DE/164 (unfoliated); C.E. Woodruff, 'Canterbury Cathedral: a contemporary list of the members of King Henry VIII's new foundation', *Canterbury Cathedral Chronicle*, no. 37 (1941), pp. 9–13.

[40] Cambridge, University Library, Peterhouse MSS 471–4 (formerly 40, 41, 31, 32), tenor part missing. See Paul Doe, 'Latin polyphony under Henry VIII', *Proceedings of the Royal Musical Association*, vol. 95 (1968/69), pp. 81–95, where the Peterhouse books are described (p. 83) as 'a provincial and slightly retrospective anthology'; Nicholas Sandon, 'The Henrician partbooks at Peterhouse, Cambridge', *Proceedings of the Royal Musical Association*, vol. 103 (1976–77), pp. 106–40, at 112–4; Bowers, *English church polyphony*, article IV, pp. 428–9.

[41] Bowers, *English church polyphony*, article IV.

[42] TNA E179/69/36; Ashbee, *Records of English court music*, vol. 7, p. 91.

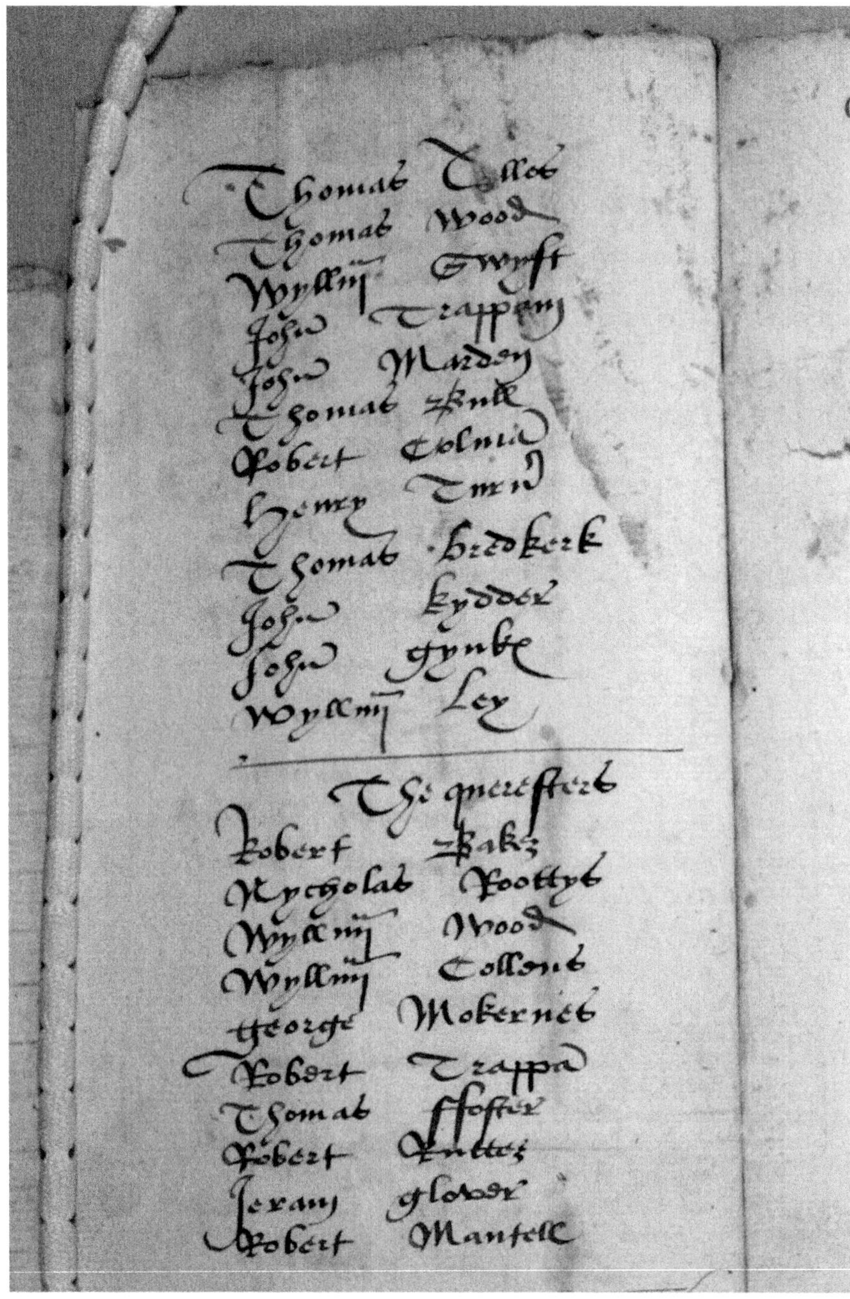

Figure 1.2 Tallis's name appears in an unfoliated list of the vicars choral at Canterbury Cathedral in 1541–42 (Canterbury Cathedral Archives, document CCA-DCc-DE/164, by permission of the Archives)

those through whom royal powers were exercised was set out in Sir Thomas Elyot's *Boke named the Governour*, published in 1531 and dedicated to the King.

Regardless of what Tallis already knew of the court, he must have been excited by the prospect of working so near to the centre of English policy and diplomacy, and of the access his post would give him to what was up to date in the fields of learning, music, and all the arts. He could hardly have avoided awareness of the humanistic and theological knowledge to which the King laid claim, or of his religious and marital concerns, and the rising and falling fortunes of some who served him. He may have known of Holbein (who died in London in November 1543), and perhaps met Antonio Toto, the serjeant-painter, and other artists and craftsmen employed at court. He may have been aware, too, of poets such as his Kentish contemporary Thomas Wyatt, and the somewhat younger Henry Howard, Earl of Surrey. He may even have heard of two books published on the Continent in 1543, which changed mankind's view of itself and the universe it inhabited: Vesalius's collection of anatomical drawings, and Copernicus's mathematical description of the revolution of the heavenly spheres.[43]

Tallis was probably admitted to the Chapel by Thomas Thirlby, who had been appointed as its Dean by July 1540, and who (unless, as often happened, he was busy elsewhere) may have administered an oath promising allegiance to the King, and recognizing his supremacy.[44] Thirlby held the post until he was dismissed by Elizabeth I soon after her accession. He was also successively Bishop of Westminster (1540–50), Norwich (1550–54) and Ely (1554–59), and besides being a churchman he held a variety of secular posts, some of which involved extensive travels abroad.[45] He was already on the Continent in July 1545 when he was made the resident ambassador at the imperial court of Charles V. Since Thirlby had many irons in the fire, the day-to-day running of the Chapel must have been in the hands of successive Subdeans. The first of those known to Tallis was Richard Ward (or Wade), who died in 1546. He was followed by John Donne, Emery Tuckfield (1548–57), and then Edmund Daniel.[46]

The early years of Henry's reign had seen the 'young, athletic and sporting King' much engaged with the riverside house he had inherited at Greenwich (p. 12, Figure 1.3), and it remained a favoured residence even after he had converted and extended houses at Hampton Court and Whitehall which had once been in

---

[43] Andreas Vesalius, *De humani corporis fabrica libri septem* (Basel, 1543); Nicolaus Copernicus, *De revolutionibus orbium coelestium* (Nuremberg, 1543).

[44] The Chapel's records of swearings in are not extant before the reign of Queen Elizabeth (see p. 145).

[45] Timothy Francis Shirley, *Thomas Thirlby* (London, 1964).

[46] Fiona Kisby, 'Officers and office-holding at the English court: a study of the Chapel Royal, 1485–1547', *Royal Musical Association Research Chronicle*, vol. 32 (1999), pp. 1–61, at 32–4; Harley, *The world of William Byrd*, pp. 245–8. The first mentions evidence of a slightly earlier date for Thirlby's appointment than that given in the second.

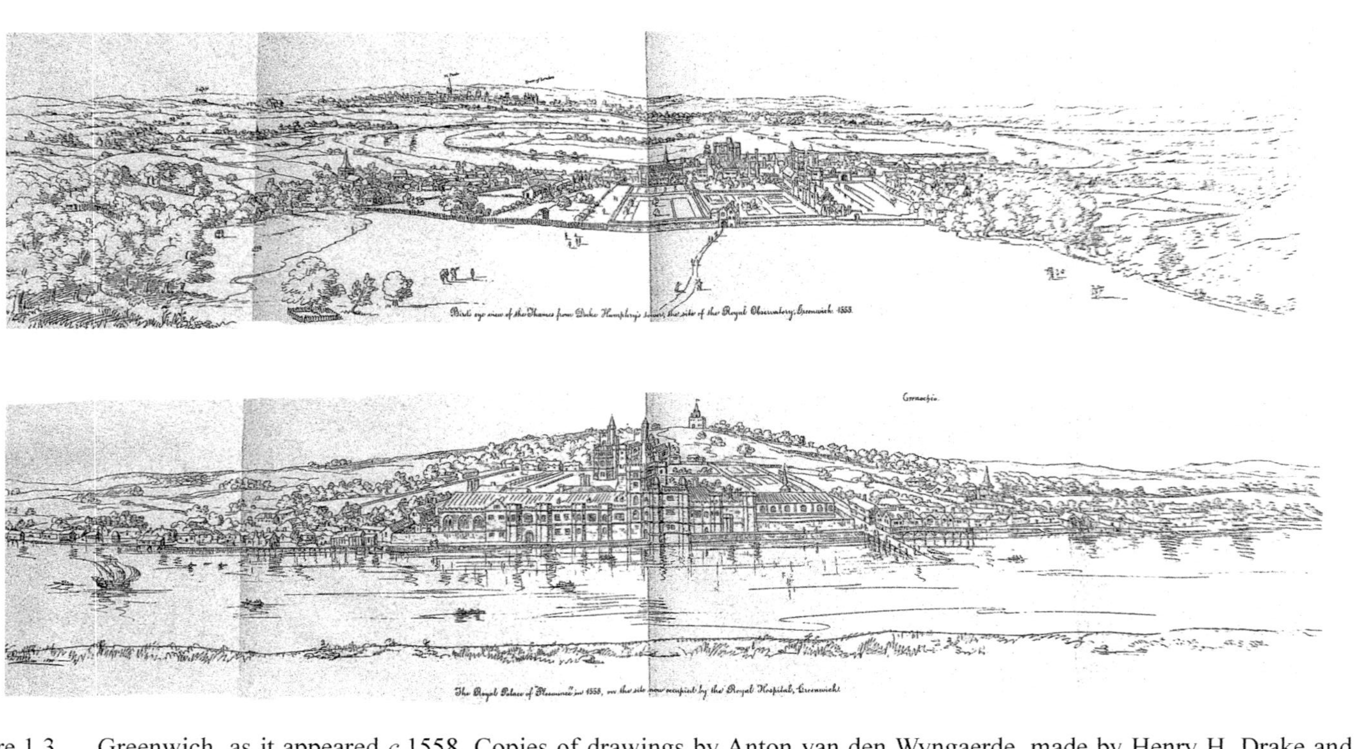

Figure 1.3 Greenwich, as it appeared *c.*1558. Copies of drawings by Anton van den Wyngaerde, made by Henry H. Drake and published in his edition of *Hasted's history of Kent ... The hundred of Blackheath* (London, 1886). St Paul's Cathedral and the Tower of London are labelled at the top of the upper drawing (Author's collection)

Wolsey's hands.[47] Royal musicians might live anywhere which allowed them to be on duty when required (though no doubt lodging at times near any distant palace which the monarch was visiting), and a number settled at Greenwich. Tallis may have lodged there straightaway, and it was where he eventually made his home.[48] It may be no coincidence that at around the time when Tallis began work, 6s 8d was spent on the organ at Greenwich palace.[49]

The Chapel was a sizeable institution. At the end of Henry VIII's reign its personnel numbered 10 clerics besides the Dean, 20 musicians including the Master of the Children, a dozen boy choristers, six vestry staff and a common servant.[50] But its musicians formed a close-knit community, and we are given occasional glimpses of personal friendships: in 1561 Tallis was an overseer of Richard Bower's will (the other overseer was William Roper);[51] and he witnessed Thomas Bury's will, of which Thomas Byrd was an overseer. In joining the Chapel, Tallis joined a group of musicians with many years of experience, though it is not certain how active all its members still were. John Fisher had sung in Henry VII's Chapel in the early years of the century, and in 1520 had been at the Field of the Cloth of Gold. William Crane, recorded as a member of the Chapel shortly after Fisher joined, still held the post of Master of the Children to which he had been appointed some 20 years before. Bury, who had entered the Chapel by 1517, was another who attended the Field of the Cloth of Gold. After his death in 1554, Tallis married his widow (see p. 93). Tallis's association with more recent recruits was to be longer. Thomas Byrd and Richard Bower both lived until 1561, Bower having succeeded Crane as Master of the Children in 1545.[52]

The sums noted beside names in subsidy rolls do not always distinguish salaries from other income, but Tallis's £11 8s, based on a rate of 7½d a day, was the standard yearly wage of a Gentleman of the Chapel Royal at this time (though it appears sometimes to have been recorded simply as £11 or even £10). Certain Gentlemen were valued at a rate which took account of the goods or lands they owned, but Walter Crane's fee of £80 probably included a substantial element for the expenses he incurred in caring and providing for the boys of the choir. The assessment of the Gentlemen may however have been no more than a formality:

47 Simon Thurley, *The royal palaces of Tudor England: architecture and court life 1460–1547* (New Haven, Ct, 1993), p. 49, with Wyngaerde's view of Greenwich *c*.1558. On p. 75 Thurley reproduces a picture of a barge on its way to Greenwich.

48 For the places where royal musicians lived, see Harley, *The world of William Byrd*, p. 112. Robert Parsons should have been added to those living there (ibid., p. 108).

49 Thurley, *The royal palaces of Tudor England*, p. 203.

50 TNA LC2/2.f.33^{r}; Ashbee, *Records of English court music*, vol. 7, pp. 108–9; Kisby, 'Officers and office holding', Table 1 (p. 6).

51 Harley, *The world of William Byrd*, pp. 202–4.

52 Ashbee, *Records of English court music*, vol. 7, p. 96; Andrew Ashbee and David Lasocki, *A biographical dictionary of English court musicians* (Aldershot, 1998), vol. 1, pp. 178–9.

if the customary later practice already prevailed they would have been excused from the payment of subsidies.

The Chapel's routine in the 1540s seems essentially to have been based on the Eltham ordinances, which provided that the whole Chapel was to be with the King when he was at Windsor or other specified residences. And 'when his grace keepeth not his hall and specially in rideing iourneyinge and progresses … the m*aste*r of Children of ye k*inges* chappell w*i*th 6 of the same chyldren & 6 men w*i*th some officers of the vestrie shall give the*ir* contynuall attendance in the kings Co*ur*t and daylie in absence the residue of the Chapell to have a masse of our Lady before noone and on sonday and holle days masse of the day beside our lady masse and an Antheme [antiphon] in the after noone'. The ordinances also list persons who were to enjoy Bouche of Court, including the Dean and Gentlemen of the Chapel and members of the vestry. The Dean was to eat with the Treasurer and the Comptroller of the Household.[53]

Henry VIII's religious observances took place either in his closet, or publicly in the chapel of the palace or house he was occupying. He had built or rebuilt the domestic chapels at Greenwich, Eltham, Hampton Court and Beaulieu by 1530.[54] His private devotions were administered by the Clerk of the Closet and the privy chaplains; public aspects of religion at court were the responsibility of the Chapel Royal. The King's attendance at services in a chapel building (usually at Whitehall or Greenwich in his later years) was limited to Sundays and the numerous feast days and ceremonies occurring throughout the year. On some of these he took part in processions and might be splendidly attired. During the 1530s and 1540s 'continuity with the past was maintained and ceremonies and feast days officially proscribed by statute continued to be celebrated according to the old "popish"

[53] BL MS Harley 610, ff.75–6; Society of Antiquaries, *A collection of ordinances and regulations for the government of the Royal Household, made in divers reigns, from King Edward III. to King William and Queen Mary* (London, 1790), pp. 160–1, 169–70. The residences specified besides Windsor were Beaulieu, Richmond, Hampton Court, Greenwich, Eltham and Woodstock. By the 1540s Whitehall had presumably been added to these. The rules for the Chapel were modified in later reigns, and were restated in the seventeenth century (Andrew Ashbee and John Harley, eds, *The cheque books of the Chapel Royal* (Aldershot, 2000), vol. 1, pp. 96–7, 111–3).

[54] Thurley, *The royal palaces of Tudor England*, pp. 196–205. See also Thurley's *Whitehall Palace: an architectural history of the royal apartments, 1240–1698* (New Haven, Ct, 2003). The remains of the chapel and vestry of Greenwich palace were discovered during work at the Old Royal Naval College in 2005. A report published online by the College (24 January 2006) stated that the original brickwork of the chapel had been found with its tiled floor in place. 'An original Tudor vault supports the high altar platform which is covered in glazed tiles laid in a geometric pattern. Further east, excavation has revealed the Vestry, linked to the Chapel by an anteroom and a fine carved stone doorway.'

tradition in the most public way'.[55] A letter written by John Worth to Lord Lisle on 15 May 1539, before Tallis joined the Chapel, tells how on 'the Holy Thursday eve':

> the King's Grace took his barge at Whitehall, and so rowed up to Lambeth, and had his drums and fifes playing, and so rowed up and down the Thames an hour in the evening after evensong. And on Holy Thursday his Grace went a procession about the Court at Westminster in the Whitehall … And the high altar in the chapel was garnished with all the apostles upon the altar, and mass by note, and the organs playing … And they that be in the King's chapel shewed me, and so did [Benet] Killigrew also, that upon Good Friday last past the King's Grace crept to the Cross from the chapel door upward, devoutly, and so served the priest to mass that same day … and the saying is that the King will remove upon Monday next to Greenwich.[56]

Descriptions of this kind, and of the Chapel's daily routine when Tallis was among its members, are in short supply. There is not much we can do but guess which music was sung. We know that chants formed a large part of the daily work of church choirs during the reign of Henry VIII, but where there was a capable choir, chant might at certain stages of the ritual be combined with or supplemented by contrapuntal music. The riddle is how much of it was new. In 20 years or more since the deaths of Robert Fayrfax and William Cornish, Tallis was the first composer of outstanding ability to join the Chapel, and it would be another five years, at least,

---

55 Fiona Kisby, 'The royal household chapel in early Tudor London, 1484–1547' (Doctoral thesis, University of London, 1996), pp. 129–35, 156–66, 169–71, 178; Kisby, '"When the King goeth a procession": chapel ceremonies and services, the ritual year, and religious reforms at the early Tudor court, 1485–1547', *Journal of British Studies*, vol. 40 (2001), pp. 44–75; Kisby, 'Religious ceremonial at the Tudor court: extracts from the royal household regulations', in *Religion, politics and society in sixteenth-century England*, ed Ian W. Archer and others (Camden, 5th series, 22: Cambridge, 2003), pp. 1–33. The first two include tables referring to Henry VIII's attendance in the Chapel 1538–44, and illustrate the observance or non-observance at court of 'certain superfluous holy days' which were the subject of an injunction in 1536 (C.H. Williams, ed., *English historical documents 1485–1558* (English historical documents, 5: London, 1967), pp. 805–8). Indications of where the court was at any particular time are given by Privy Council, *Acts of the Privy Council. New series, ed. John Roche Dasent* [and others] (London, 1890–1964). and *Letters and papers, foreign and domestic of the reign of Henry VIII* (London, 1864–1932). In the years 1542–47 most meetings of the Privy Council were held at Greenwich, Westminster, or (to a lesser extent) Hampton Court or St James's. Only a few meetings took place elsewhere. From 1541–42, besides being used for occasions demanding particular magnificence, Hampton Court became favoured by Henry as the residence where Christmas and Epiphany were spent (Simon Thurley, *Hampton Court: a social and architectural history* (New Haven, Ct, 2003), p. 64).

56 From the transcription in modern spelling in Muriel St. Clare Byrne, ed., *The Lisle letters* (Chicago, 1981), vol. 5, p. 478 (no. 1415). The custom of creeping to the Cross was not abolished until 1546.

before John Sheppard was recruited.[57] There is very little to show what the Chapel musicians sang during the last four or five years of King Henry's life.

As things stand, we can only suppose that they performed polyphonic music on special days, but were not often called upon to sing anything but the chants of the Sarum Use. An inventory (in effect a probate inventory of King Henry's possessions), drawn up between mid-September 1547 and the end of the following January, shows that several books of chant were kept in the vestry at Whitehall 'in the Charge of Rauffe Tappinge, Sergeaunt of the same'.[58] They included 'xvi Antiphoners' (antiphonaries, containing, chants for the Office), 'xvi graills' (graduals, containing chants for the Mass), 'iii Ordinalls' (detailing the order of services throughout the ecclesiastical year), 'one booke to Singe vers*es* and graills by Children', 'one booke to Singe Collett*es* [collects] on', 'xxiiii processionals' (containing chants for liturgical processions), 'iii Masse book*es* and oon pontificall' (a pontifical set out the offices and duties of a bishop), 'two small bookes for thorganes', 'one graill for thorganes', and 'x prickesonge book*es*' (probably polyphony as distinct from plainsong). The 10 pricksong books bring us close to Worth's 'mass by note', and may have consisted of two sets, each of five partbooks. The list does not look as if it describes a busy choir's up-to-date working library, though it illustrates the kinds of books which must once have existed in abundance. So does the inventory of another collection, in King Henry's library at Westminster and probably never used by the Chapel at all. It includes 'A Pricke songe booke of masses and Anthemes' and 'Bookes of priksong masses. foure'; there were also seven manuscript antiphoners, and a two-volume printed antiphoner.[59]

The organ books that remained in the vestry are slightly less of a puzzle, and may have contained settings used when the choir and organist performed passages alternately. Among those who left such settings was Avery Burton, a predecessor of Tallis in the Chapel.[60] Tallis's appointment may indeed have been a result

---

57 Sheppard was at Magdalen College, Oxford, until 1548; he is not recorded as a member of the Chapel Royal before August 1553.

58 The inventory was prepared by a commission appointed on 14 September 1547. What appears to be the official file copy is now bound in four volumes: BL Additional MS 46348, vols A and B, and BL MS Harley 1419, vols A and B. The books in the vestry are listed in Additional MS 46348B, ff.420^{r-v}. Another copy of part of the inventory is Society of Antiquaries MS 129, printed in *The inventory of King Henry VIII: Society of Antiquaries MS 129 and British Library MS Harley 1419. The transcript*, ed. David Starkey (London, 1998). The vestry also held 'one Legende for men' (a collection of saints' lives), 'one legende for children', and 'one shirmonde [sermon] booke for lente'.

59 TNA E315/160, dated 24 April 1542, ff.108^{v}–109^{r}. See James P. Carley, *The libraries of King Henry VIII* (Corpus of British medieval library catalogues, 7: London, 2000), pp. 38, 40; and Carley, *The books of Henry VIII and his wives* (London, 2004), p. 31 and pl. 22 on p. 32.

60 Both pieces are in BL Additional MS 29996, where an organ Te Deum is attributed to 'Master avere'.

of Burton's death, since they seem to have occurred at around the same time. While it was not until 1575 that Tallis and William Byrd described themselves as 'Gentlemen and Organists in the private Chapel of her Most Serene Majesty, the Queen', it is likely that Gentlemen had often been recruited with an eye to their particular abilities. At a later date the recognized organists, like the other Gentlemen, alternated their periods of duty so that the full Chapel was present only at times of particular significance. It may be that the duty organist was responsible for rehearsing the choir, necessarily in conjunction with the Master of the Children.

Besides their duties in the Chapel, the Gentlemen and children took part in secular celebrations. At Christmas the children might present a play before the King – perhaps an interlude with songs. Payments had been made to William Crane and the children for performances in 1539/40 and 1540/41, and another was made in 1543/4 for 'plaing before the king*es* ma*iestie* this cristm*as*' (the accounts from October 1542 to September 1543 have been lost). In 1539 the children had been paid for singing *Audivi vocem* on All Hallows Day (1 November), and *Gloria in excelsis Deo* on Christmas Day. The Gentlemen too were rewarded each year, 'for there paines taking this cristm*as*' as it was put in 1543/4.[61]

Celebrations of this sort must have introduced Tallis to a wide range of people at court, but it is difficult to name many of Tallis's acquaintances outside the Chapel Royal, even among professional musicians. He might readily have exchanged views and music with the organist John Redford, who was in charge of the choristers at St Paul's Cathedral until his death in 1547, and with Redford's successor Sebastian Westcote, who had some association with the court by Christmas 1545.[62] He must also have been familiar with John Heywood, who held posts at both St Paul's and the court, and had connections with St Mary-at-Hill.[63] But there is no knowing whether, or by what means, he kept in touch with men like his former colleague Richard Wynslate (see p. 6). There was clearly some method of circulating news and music among men in positions like theirs, but there is no record of what it was.

Cranmer's Litany

At about the time when Tallis became a Gentleman of the Chapel Royal, King Henry made clear what he wished his subjects to believe at that stage of his theological evolution. It was set out in 'The King's Book', published in conjunction with a

---

61 BL MS Arundel 97, ff.108^{r}, 164^{v} (1539/40 and 1540/41); BL Additional MS 59900, f.68^{v} (1543/4); Ashbee, *Records of English court music*, vol. 7, pp. 277, 278, 283, 289.

62 BL Additional MS 27404, f.32^{r}, where a partly obscured note may mean that Westcote was collecting money on behalf of John Gamond, or that Gamond had assigned it to Westcote.

63 Harley, *The world of William Byrd*, pp. 40–45.

statute of May 1543.[64] While making plain the King's supremacy, the book was more in line with traditional Catholic doctrine than 'The Bishops' Book',[65] published six years earlier. It may therefore have pleased the conservative Thomas Thirlby, and any Gentleman of like mind. It would have been wise, anyway, not to dispute the King's view of what he described as an 'inclination to sinister understanding of scripture, presumption, arrogancye, carnall liberty, and contention'.

A year later something quite new was set before the members of the Chapel, in the shape of Cranmer's Litany, the first authorized service in the vernacular, printed with a simple and anonymous plainsong setting.[66] Its date (1544) is a reminder that all the major liturgical changes in Tallis's lifetime occurred after he became a member of the Chapel Royal. The text was adapted and severely reduced from the service of supplication forming part of the Sarum processional rite. Cranmer's biographer observes that he 'did a ruthless job in eliminating the possibility of using the litany for saint-worship'.[67] The preface stressed the importance attached to a clear utterance of the words: 'that whiche is printed in blacke letters, is to be sayde or songe of the priest with an audible voyce, that is to saye, so loude and so playnely, that it maye well be understanded of the hearers'. In a subsequent letter to the King, written on 7 October 1544,[68] Cranmer raised the possibility of extending the reform to the other services contained in the *Processionale*. He had tackled other texts in response to Henry's wish, conveyed to him by the Principal Secretary, William Paget, and said, 'I have translated into the englishe tongue, so well as I coulde in so short tyme, certeyne p*ro*cessions to be used upon festivall daies', adding that he had been 'constrayned to use more than the libertie of a translator'. He went on to say that:

> after your highnes hath corrected yt yf your grace com*m*and some devoute and solempne note to be made thereunto (as is to the procession whiche your ma*ies*tie hath alredie set forth in englishe) I truste it woll moch excitate and stirre the hartes of all men unto devotion and godlynes. But in myn opinion, the songe that shalbe made thereunto wolde not be full of notes, but as nere as may be for every sillable a note; so that it may be songe distinctly and devoutly. As be in the matens and evensong, Venite, the Hymnes / Te Deum / Benedictus [/] Magnificat / Nunc Dimittis and all the Psalmes and Versicles. And in the masse, Gloria in

64 *A necessary doctrine and erudition for any Christen man, sette furthe by the kynges maiestie of Englande* (London, 1543); *An Act for the advancement of true religion* (34 & 35 Henry VIII, c. 1).

65 *The institution of a Christen man* (London, 1537), modestly intended, according to the preface, to ensure that 'all errours, doubtes, superstitions, and abuses myght be suppressed, removed, and utterly taken away'.

66 *A Letanie with suffrages to be sayd or songe in the tyme of ... processions* (London, 1544).

67 Diarmaid MacCulloch, *Thomas Cranmer: a life* (New Haven, 1996), p. 329.

68 Dated only 7 October; assigned to 1544 by MacCulloch, ibid., p. 330.

> excelsis, Gloria Patri[,] The crede, The preface[,] The Pater noster and some of the Sanctus and Agnus / As concernyng the Salve festa dies, the Latenn note (as I thinke) is sobre and distincte enough. Wherefore I have travailled to make the verses in Englishe, and have put the latten note unto the same. Nevertheles, thei that be connyng in syngyng, can make a moch more solempne note thereto. I made them only for a profe to see howe Englishe wolde do in songe.[69]

Cranmer was concerned with chant, not polyphony, but there were those who would have regarded what he said as of wider application. Only one note for every syllable was not a new idea, and complaints about ornate music had been made for a long time. Almost 30 years earlier, in an often quoted passage from his commentary on the New Testament, Erasmus had written about the difficulty caused for congregations who could not easily distinguish the words – though this was part of his general dissatisfaction with the overmuch use of 'modern church music'.[70]

[69] TNA SP1/208, f.169; *Letters and papers ... of the reign of Henry VIII*, vol. 20, part 2, pp. 151–2 (no. 539); Thomas Cranmer, *Miscellaneous writings and letters* (Parker Society publications, 24: Cambridge, 1846), p. 412.

[70] *In Novum Testamentum, primum ad Graecam veritatem ... adnotationes Erasmi Roterodami* (Basel, 1516), note on I Corinthians xiv.19. The remarks have been widely quoted, e.g. in John Hawkins, *A general history of the science and practice of music* (London, 1776)., vol. 3, p. 60, and in James Anthony Froude, *Life and letters of Erasmus*, new edn (London, 1894), lecture 7, p. 116, where they are translated as: 'Modern church music is so constructed that the congregation cannot hear one distinct word. The choristers themselves do not know what they are singing ... In college or monastery it is still the same: music, nothing but music'.

Chapter 2
The Reign of Henry VIII: Music with Latin Words

The surviving settings of Latin texts which Tallis made during the reigns of Henry VIII and Queen Mary appear almost entirely to have been composed with church performance originally in view. (One possible exception is *Sancte Deus, Sancte fortis*.) The theatrical nature of religious rites must have been constantly in Tallis's mind while he was writing. Each work was intended to contribute, together with traditional chants and the music of other composers, to a ritual of prayer, adoration and reflection, enhanced by aural, visual and dramatic display. Each may also have had to take its place alongside traditional chants and the music of other composers. But after its initial liturgical function had been fulfilled, a work might begin a new life beyond the church. It was often the copying of pieces for recreational music-making, or simply for interest, which resulted in their preservation.

Probably only a part of Tallis's early music has survived. The loss of sources, which prevents us from knowing fully what Tallis wrote, is not less of a problem in determining the music by other composers which Tallis must have known. All we can really be sure of is that he studied works by Fayrfax and Taverner, because he based pieces of his own upon them.

The forms of worship for which Tallis provided music were those of the Sarum Use. This had evolved in the Salisbury diocese and was followed throughout southern England, including the Canterbury diocese and the royal court.[1]

---

1 A detailed guide to sources prescribing the Use of Salisbury (Sarum) can be found in John Harper, *The forms and orders of western liturgy from the tenth to the eighteenth century* (Oxford, 1991), pp. 202–16. See also Richard W. Pfaff, *The liturgy in medieval England: a history* (Cambridge, 2009). The Gregorian Institute of Canada is in the process of publishing *The Sarum Rite*, containing the full text and music for the breviary Office, the processional, and the missal (online at http://www.sarum-chant.ca). Still very useful is Walter Howard Frere, ed., *Antiphonale Sarisburiense. A reproduction in facsimile of a manuscript of the thirteenth century, with a dissertation and analytical index* (London, 1901–25), published by the Plainsong and Mediaeval Music Society. Concerning printed antiphonaries which would have been known to Tallis, see Magnus Williamson, 'Affordable splendour: editing, printing and marketing the Sarum Antiphoner (1519–20)', *Renaissance Studies*, vol. 26 (2012), pp. 60–87. Editions of Sarum texts are listed in Nigel Morgan, 'The introduction of the Sarum calendar into the dioceses of England in the thirteenth century', in Michael Prestwich and others, eds, *Thirteenth century England VIII: proceedings of the Durham Conference 1999* (Woodbridge, 2001), pp. 179–206, note 1.

The daily round of prayer, excluding the Mass, was the Office, set out in the Sarum breviary.[2] Its constituent services took place at eight times during the day: they were Matins and Lauds; the 'little hours' Prime, Terce, Sext and None; and Vespers and Compline. The sung portions of the Office were contained in the antiphonary (or 'antiphonal' or 'antiphoner'). Mass was celebrated daily in the manner prescribed by the missal. Chants for the Ordinary (unchanging parts) of the Mass were contained in the kyriale; those for the Propers (the parts of the Mass which were changed to suit the occasion) were in the gradual, a book to which the kyriale often formed an adjunct. The order of services and the practices which had come to form an integral part of the rituals were detailed in the Sarum ordinal and customary.[3]

Magnificat

One of the first parts of the Office to be treated polyphonically in England was the Magnificat. Musical settings were perhaps encouraged by the cult of the Virgin, who was thought to have uttered the words of the canticle, so there were many examples Tallis might have followed when he came to make his own. The Eton choirbook (copied 1490–1502) once contained two dozen Magnificats.[4]

A **Magnificat** attributed to Tallis is found only in the retrospective, and probably Elizabethan, 'Gyffard' partbooks,[5] which are also the sole source of several other pieces dealt with in this chapter. There is no easy way of disposing of whatever reservations there may be about the reliability of any copy or attribution transmitted in a single source, but assuming the Magnificat is Tallis's, it must be among the earliest of his surviving works.

Like ten of the Magnificats originally in the Eton choirbook, the piece is for four voices. Tallis followed the convention of setting only the even-numbered verses, leaving the odd-numbered verses to be chanted or played on the organ. (The practice of playing alternate verses is exemplified by an anonymous keyboard

[2] Francis Procter and Christopher Wordsworth, eds, *Breviarium ad usum insignis Ecclesiae ... Juxta editionem maximam pro Claudio Chevallon et Francisco Regnault, A.D. MDXXXI, in alma Parisiorum academia impressam* (Cambridge, 1879–86). For remarks on this edition, see Pfaff, *The liturgy in medieval England*, p. 425ff.

[3] Walter Howard Frere, ed., *The Use of Sarum* (Cambridge, 1898–1901): vol. 1, *The Sarum customs as set forth in the consuetudinary and customary*; vol. 2, *The ordinal and tonal*.

[4] Eton College Library, MS 178. The manner of singing the Magnificat is dealt with in Frere, *The Use of Sarum*, vol. 2, pp. 2, 28–9, 31, 35–6.

[5] BL Additional MSS 17802–5, possibly compiled *c.*1570–*c.*1585: see David Mateer: 'The compilation of the Gyffard partbooks', and 'The Gyffard partbooks: composers, owners, date and provenance', [*Royal Musical Association*] *Research Chronicle*, vols. 26 (1993) and 28 (1995); also the prefaces to David Mateer, ed., *The Gyffard partbooks* (Early English Church Music, 48, 51: London, 2007–09).

setting of Henry VIII's time.)[6] Tallis adopted another common procedure by writing different groups of verses in different mensural notations. The first two polyphonic verses have the signature ⦶, meaning that a 'perfect' breve has the value of three semibreves, each consisting of two minims. The middle two have ₵, meaning that an 'imperfect' breve has the value of two semibreves, each worth two minims; and ⦶ is applied again to the last two polyphonic verses.[7]

Tallis's settings of Office texts are all based on chants contained in the antiphonary, but very often a Magnificat cantus firmus did not use the chant directly. It was a faburden[8] derived from one of the tones (melodic formulae) to which the words were chanted. The tone for a particular occasion corresponded with that of the associated antiphon (a short text chanted before and after the canticle, and related to it in sense). Tallis's Magnificat, with a cantus firmus derived from the first tone, was suitable for a number of days during the year, including such major feasts as Christmas and Pentecost. The cantus firmus evidently began by descending a third (F–E–D), and returning to the repeated F that resulted from following the chant at a third below; but Tallis treated it with great freedom, generally acknowledging its presence with no more than a few notes, and sometimes placing it in a voice other than the customary tenor.

Tallis followed tradition again in writing some sections of his Magnificat for a reduced number and particular combination of voices, thus distinguishing passages by the intensity and quality of their sound. He omitted the second-highest part in

---

6 In the earliest layer of BL Additional MS 29996, at f.25^{v}, possibly copied in the late 1540s; printed in John Caldwell, ed., *Early Tudor organ music: I. Music for the Office* (Early English Church Music, 6: London, 1966), pp. 23–8. There are few surviving examples of Tallis's organ music for the Sarum rite, and it is difficult to know whether they belong to the reign of King Henry or to that of his daughter Mary. They are therefore considered together in Chapter 7.

7 The signs ⦶ and ₵ indicate the moods 'perfect of the less prolation' and 'imperfect of the less prolation' (Thomas Morley, *A plaine and easie introduction to practicall musicke* (London, 1597), pp. 18–19, where ⦶ is replaced by ○, and ₵ by ᴄ; ed. R. Alec Harman (London, 1952), pp. 30–31ff).

8 Faburden involved singing one part a fourth above the chant and another a third below it, resulting mainly in a series of $^{6}_{3}$ chords, though $^{8}_{5}$ chords were placed at the beginnings and ends of phrases. It was the lowest of the three parts that provided Tallis with his cantus firmus. Faburdens based on the first Magnificat tone could vary considerably, as is clear from sixteenth-century manuscripts. Examples are printed by Paul Doe in *Tallis*, 2nd edn (London, 1976), p. 27, from BL Additional MS 4911, f.98; and David Mateer, ed., *The Gyffard partbooks II* (Early English Church Music, 51: London, 2009), p. 128, from BL MS Royal Appendix 56, f.22^{v}. The latter manuscript, dating probably from *c.* 1525, includes a set of monophonic Magnificat settings, arranged in order by tone and ending: see Frank Ll. Harrison, 'Faburden in pratice', *Music Disciplina*, vol. 16 (1962), pp. 11–34, at 20–23. *The sight of faburden* is an anonymous treatise in BL Lansdowne MS 763 (f.116$^{\mathrm{r-v}}$), rescued by Tallis from Waltham Abbey (p. 7 above); see Brian Trowell, 'Faburden and fauxburden', *Musica Disciplina*, vol. 13 (1959), pp. 43–78, at 47–8.

verse 4, and the highest in most of verse 8. The first half of verse 12 is reduced as well, this time by the omission of the lowest part. In the second half of the verse all four voices come together to sing 'saeculorum. Amen'.

Some features of the Magnificat seem to betray Tallis's lack of experience. The melodic writing can appear aimless, and in spite of occasional fragments of imitation the lines often seem unconnected with one another. Yet, in order to be transmitted to the Gyffard scribe, the work must have been valued highly enough to achieve at least a limited circulation.

Votive Antiphons

Lying outside the observances of the Office, as an extra-liturgical act of devotion, was the singing of votive antiphons. A polyphonic antiphon might follow Compline, the final service of the day. Sometimes antiphons were addressed to saints, or Jesus, or the Trinity, but most commonly they honoured the Virgin Mary. The Mary antiphon was 'the universal and most characteristic expression of the devotional fervour of the later Middle Ages',[9] and created a need well met by Tallis's immediate predecessors. The Eton choirbook includes many antiphons among the 93 pieces listed in its index, and almost all of the 54 which survive in a complete or incomplete form are addressed to the Virgin Mary. Among the 72 pieces in the Peterhouse partbooks (copied *c.*1540) are 42 votive antiphons, of which 35 are addressed to the Virgin, in three instances together with another saint.[10]

The singing of Marian antiphons did not conflict with the 'Ten Articles' approved by Henry VIII in 1536 and backed up by Cromwell's parallel injunctions to the clergy, though both pronouncements made clear the role of saints only as intercessors.[11] A further set of injunctions, issued by Cromwell in 1538, condemned the singing in processions of 'Ora pro nobis' to so many saints that there was no

---

[9] Harrison, *Music in medieval Britain*, 4th edn (Buren, 1980), p. 219. For a concise account see David Skinner, 'The Marian anthem in late medieval England', in R.W. Swanson, ed., *The church and Mary* (Studies in Church History, 39: London, 2004), pp. 169–80. Several 'salve' ceremonies are described in Magnus Williamson, '*Pictura et scriptura*: the Eton Choirbook in its iconographical context', *Early Music*, 28 (2000), pp. 359–80.

[10] Cambridge, University Library, Peterhouse MSS 471–4 (formerly 40, 41, 31, 32). See Iain Fenlon, ed., *Cambridge music manuscripts, 900–1700* (Cambridge, 1982), pp. 132–5; Nicholas Sandon, 'The Henrician partbooks at Peterhouse, Cambridge', *Proceedings of the Royal Musical Association*, vol. 103 (1976–77), pp. 106–40; Nicholas Sandon, 'The Henrician Partbooks belonging to Peterhouse, Cambridge (Cambridge, University Library, Peterhouse Manuscripts 471–474): a study, with restorations of the incomplete compositions contained in them' (Doctoral thesis, University of Exeter, 1983).

[11] The articles recognized that it was 'very laudable to pray to saints … whose charity is ever permanent to be intercessors, and to pray for us and with us unto almighty God'; the injunctions emphasized that 'all goodness, health, and grace ought to be both asked and looked for only of God … and of none other'.

time to sing 'good suffrages' like 'Parce nobis Domine' and 'Libera nos Domine'. In future it was to be 'taught and preached' that it would be better to omit 'Ora pro nobis' and sing other suffrages. No doubt the injunctions were more effective in some places than in others, and more successful in limiting the singing of antiphons addressed to the Virgin; but it may have been after the injunctions were issued that Tallis's antiphon *Salve intemerata virgo Maria*, and a Mass based on it, were included in the Peterhouse books, possibly in the expectation that they would be sung in the reconstituted Canterbury Cathedral.

Salve intemerata seems to have been predated by two of Tallis's other Marian antiphons, *Ave Dei patris filia* and *Ave rosa sine spinis*, and must have been composed a decade or so before the Peterhouse books are thought to have been compiled. It is even possible that all three antiphons were written before the dissolution of Dover priory, where Tallis was the organist. Whether the resources needed to perform them were available there is an open question, and they may point to a connection with Canterbury Cathedral, where every day the choir of the Lady Chapel would have sung an antiphon before an image of the Virgin.[12]

Ave Dei patris filia has a verse text which was in print by about 1513.[13] No extant copy of Tallis's setting dates from before about 1591, and none is complete, though enough of the piece survives for reconstructions to have been made for the purpose of performance.[14]

In writing what may have been his first large-scale continuous work, Tallis rose splendidly to the occasion and provided music that was both celebratory and reflective. But he needed a plan to guide him, and turned to a setting of the words by Robert Fayrfax (1464–1521), whom he was eventually to follow

---

[12] For a study of *Salve intemerata* in this context see David Allinson, 'The rhetoric of devotion: some neglected elements in the context of the early Tudor votive antiphon' (Doctoral thesis, Exeter University, 1998), vol. 1, pp. 160–61.

[13] See Edgar Hoskins, *Horæ Beatæ Mariæ Virginis: or Sarum and York Primers, with kindred books, and Primers of the Reformed Roman Use* (London, 1901), pp. 16 (no. 42) and 128. Unlike the texts of Tallis's next two Mary antiphons, *Ave Dei patris filia* is from a source printed in London by Pynson, not in Paris for sale in London. For other composers whose antiphons set primer texts, see Hugh Benham, *Latin church music in England c.1460–1575* (London, 1977), p. 225.

[14] Sources are given by the EECM Primary Source Database, which builds on two printed supplements to the Early English Church Music series: Ralph T. Daniel and Peter le Huray, *The sources of English church music, 1549–1660*, parts I & II (Early English church music, supplementary volume 1, parts 1 and 2: London, 1972), and May Hofman and John Morehen, *Latin music in British sources, c.1485–c.1610* (Early English church music, supplementary volume 2: London, 1987). A table showing the state in which *Ave Dei patris filia* survives in different sources is included by David Allinson in Antico Edition RCM20 (Moretonhampstead, *c.*1996).

into the Chapel Royal. Fayrfax's piece appears to have been widely admired.[15] Tallis may have sung it and known it well. He adopted almost exactly its overall proportions, the division into two equal sections of the long text (seven rhymed four-line stanzas, followed by a prayer and Amen), and the combinations of voices which distinguish different passages. In modelling his work on Fayrfax's he was inevitably absorbing aspects of a long tradition, since the layout of Fayrfax's piece broadly resembles that of votive antiphons in the Eton choirbook, whose composers continued to incorporate features which had been used by men such as Leonel Power and John Dunstable.

Tallis adopted the familiar practice of writing perfect breves in the first main section and imperfect breves in the second main section (as he did in all his antiphons).[16] Like other English composers of the time he employed imitation sparingly. In some respects he nevertheless pursued a course of his own. His piece is less inclined than Fayrfax's to include stretches of near homophony, and more inclined to set syllables melismatically. Beyond some of the head-motifs at the beginnings of sections, there is little melodic resemblance between Tallis's setting and Fayrfax's. The younger composer's liking for arcs of melody, often combined into elongated spans, is much in evidence, although the spans may include passages of considerable melodic agility.

Tallis wrote in the same mode as Fayrfax, with D as the final – the 'Dorian' of Glarean's *Δωδεκαχορδον* (1547) – but he treated it differently. If we can assume that what is written in the sources is what the composers expected to hear, Fayrfax flattened B infrequently, while Tallis, from a younger generation, flattened it almost everywhere. He reserved B♮ for a few occasions when he needed a major chord on G, like the one which begins the striking 'Ave Jesu' that follows 'ancilla sincerissima'. The implication appears to be that the theoretical ideas composers subscribed to were undergoing change.

As far as it is possible to judge from his music, Tallis thought in terms of four traditional and rather loosely defined diatonic modes with finals on D, E, F and G; and he may have entertained the idea that each had two forms, the authentic or the plagal, determined by where the final lay in the octave covered by a melody written in the mode. There are difficulties in applying this idea of mode to polyphonic music, and it is certainly not altogether appropriate to sixteenth-century music, which increasingly adopted tonality as a major element in its organization, together

---

15 Davitt Moroney, 'Under fower sovereigns: Thomas Tallis and the transformation of English polyphony' (Doctoral thesis, University of California, Berkeley, 1980), pp. 20–22, acknowledging Robert Ford's communication of information apparently made public in an unpublished paper, 'Re-upholstery by a master craftsman: Tallis and Fayrfax', read at the eighth Annual Conference on Medieval and Renaissance Music, London, August 1980.

16 Mensural signatures in some sources of Tallis's *Ave Dei patris filia*, including the earliest, show the first half in triple time, although later sources mark both halves in duple time. While a number of antiphons were certainly written throughout in duple time (some are in the Peterhouse books), Tallis probably followed his model.

with a feeling for what eventually came to be termed 'key'. However, in the 1560s, for Matthew Parker's *The whole psalter*, Tallis wrote eight pieces which appear to be authentic and plagal settings with finals on the usual four notes (see p. 164). These settings were prefaced by a verse (not necessarily by Tallis), describing the natures of the 'eyght tunes'. What theorists called modes were often called 'tunes' or 'tones' by practising musicians, a terminology that came naturally to Morley when he was writing *A plaine and easie introduction to practicall musicke* (1597). Tallis's treatment of the D mode, while not new (it occurs several times in the Eton choirbook), turned it in effect into a transposition of the A mode (the 'Aeolian'), which Glarean saw himself as restoring after it had been lost. If Tallis can be said to have used the untransposed A mode in his Latin-texted music, it was in some sections of *Sancte Deus*. Its wider use in England had to wait for Byrd. Occasionally Tallis wrote in C (the 'Ionian'), which Glarean also claimed to have rediscovered, though its loss can have been only theoretical.

The settings of *Ave Dei patris filia* by Fayrfax and Tallis differ not only in their treatment of the D mode, but in their written indication of overall voice range. Each of them has a range of about three octaves between the lowest bass note and the highest treble note. This was not uncommon. But Tallis's range is written as *F-g''*, instead of Fayrfax's only slightly narrower *D-c''*. Although the two pieces could have been sung at approximately the same pitch to suit the needs of the choir, the pitch of the written ranges subtly influences the experience of singers and listeners. Because the voice parts in Tallis's piece, as notated, are higher than the comparable parts in Fayrfax's, they cover different portions of the mode, with a consequent influence on the positioning of whole tones and semitones within their ranges. The extreme high notes of the two pieces have different relationships with the final of the mode; and when, in the bass part, Fayrfax forms a cadence on the final, the voice is able to fall to the D below the staff, whereas in Tallis's piece it often has to rise to D on the middle line.[17]

Tallis's first independent antiphon, using the lessons learned from his study of Fayrfax, seems to have been ***Ave rosa sine spinis***. Its widely popular verse text of seven stanzas was printed in 1510.[18] The setting is in the same mode as *Ave Dei patris filia*, and the choice and placing of cadences is similar, but the piece conveys a greater sense of assurance and freedom. Tallis may have returned to it at some time, just as he evidently reworked pieces written during other periods of his life.

---

[17] At the end of the first main section of the piece, Essex Record Office MS D/DP Z6/1 gives *F* as the lowest note of what is evidently intended to be a major chord on *D*.

[18] Hoskins, *Horæ Beatæ Mariæ Virginis*, pp. 14 (no. 37) and 124; Eamon Duffy, *The stripping of the altars: traditional religion in England* c.*1400*-c.*1580* (New Haven, Ct, 1992), pp. 218, 223.

Example 2.1 *Ave rosa sine spinis*, the Amen

The Peterhouse partbooks are the earliest source, but a version preserved in later sources may have been 'lightly revised'.[19]

The two main sections have the usual mensural signs, though the second section is now shorter than the first, instead of being the same length, and the central stanza, which ends the first main section, is set at a slightly greater length than other stanzas. In both sections the choice and grouping of voices is linked in an uncomplicated manner to the pattern and meaning of the verses. These expand upon successive words of the *Ave Maria*, so that every verse except the

[19] Nicholas Sandon in Antico Edition RCM136 (Moretonhampstead, 1995), p. iii; he also suggests that Tallis's text should read 'Per pregustum hic internum', not 'Per pregustum hic in terra'. For a list of sources see the Antico edition and the EECM Primary Source Database.

last includes at least one of them. The highlighting of particular phrases is an important part of Tallis's method. 'Maria, stella dicta maris' (*Mary, called the star of the sea*) is distinguished by the lengths of the notes which begin it, while 'post mortem in aeternum' is emphasized by a cadence on C, two fifths removed around the circle of fifths from D, the modal final.

The clarity of the layout gives coherence to a piece where the voices display considerable independence of one another. In the first verse the mean and contratenor (the only voices singing) engage in snatches of imitation, but truly canonic writing is short-lived. The tenor and bass begin the second verse, and eventually exchange brief imitative phrases, but when the treble joins them, it adopts little of their material and floats freely above them. Only in the concluding Amen does imitation bind the voices tightly, in a series of exchanges that lead the treble to rise beyond its previous range to sing a climactic *a″* (Example 2.1).

Salve intemerata virgo Maria is almost certainly the third and last of Tallis's early Marian antiphons. It is included in a medius partbook (British Library MS Harley 1709), which is all that remains of a set of books of devotional polyphony composed in the reigns of Henry VII and Henry VIII, and is the oldest extant source containing music by Tallis.[20] Its scribe was clearly a professional, used to writing and decorating musical manuscripts. The note 'corrigitur' (*corrected*) written at the end of *Salve intemerata* indicates that at least one piece was checked for accuracy (Figure 2.1).[21] There is nothing to show whether the book was intended for a church or a private chapel, or for the library of a collector; but whatever its destination there are few signs of frequent use.

The date of Harley 1709 has been put at about 1530, or a little before: partly because the words of *Salve intemerata* are in a primer printed at Paris for sale in London, and dated 18 July 1527 (though Tallis could have set them earlier, if they were already circulating in manuscript, or later), and partly, one suspects, because of a belief that Tallis was born about 1505 and could not have written *Salve intemerata* until he was in his mid-twenties. Music composed considerably earlier is written on a single leaf in a hand closely similar to that of Harley 1709, but its identity has not been verified.[22] *Salve intemerata* occurs again, lacking only the tenor part, in the 'Peterhouse' partbooks; indeed, it occurs twice, in copies evidently made from different sources.

Whatever Tallis thought of the lengthy prose text facing him, he dealt with it as he dealt with other texts.[23] He may or may not have subscribed to Byrd's

[20] Sources of *Salve intemerata* are listed in Antico Edition RCM134, ed. Nicholas Sandon (Moretonhampstead, 1995), and the EECM Primary Source Database.

[21] Sandon has suggested that if 'corrigitur' applies to everything preceding it, the compiler may originally have intended it to end the book ('The manuscript London, British Library Harley 1709', in Susan Rankin and David Hiley, eds, *Music in the medieval English liturgy* (Oxford, 1993), pp. 355–79, at 357–8). This cannot be substantiated, however. Modern folio numbers pencilled in the book run 1*, 1–57; but without dismembering the book it is not clear how it was assembled or which leaves have been lost. *Salve intemerata* starts part of the way down f.46^{v}, and ends at the bottom of f.49^{r}.

[22] The single leaf is BL Additional MS 70516 (olim Loan 29/333), ff.79^{r}–81^{v}: see David Fallows, 'English song repertories of the mid-fifteenth century', *Proceedings of the Royal Musical Association*, vol. 103 (1976–77), pp. 61–79, at 71 (which refers to a former foliation), and Sandon, 'The manuscript London, British Library Harley 1709', at 368–70. At pp. 359–60 of the latter article Sandon writes: 'Were it not for the presence of Tallis's *Salve intemerata*, one would be happy to date Harley 1709 in the mid-1520s; none of the other compositions in it needs to be later than about 1525'; and he proposes a compromise date of the latter half of the 1520s.

[23] H.B. Collins thought the text of 'no conspicuous literary merit, being somewhat verbose, and the sentences too long and rather involved' ('Thomas Tallis', *Music & Letters*, 10 (1929), pp. 152–66, at 155). A quite different view is put forward by David Allinson in *The rhetoric of devotion*, vol. 1,. pp. 207–21, where the logic and content of the words are carefully examined. Peter Phillips has remarked more generally of the piece

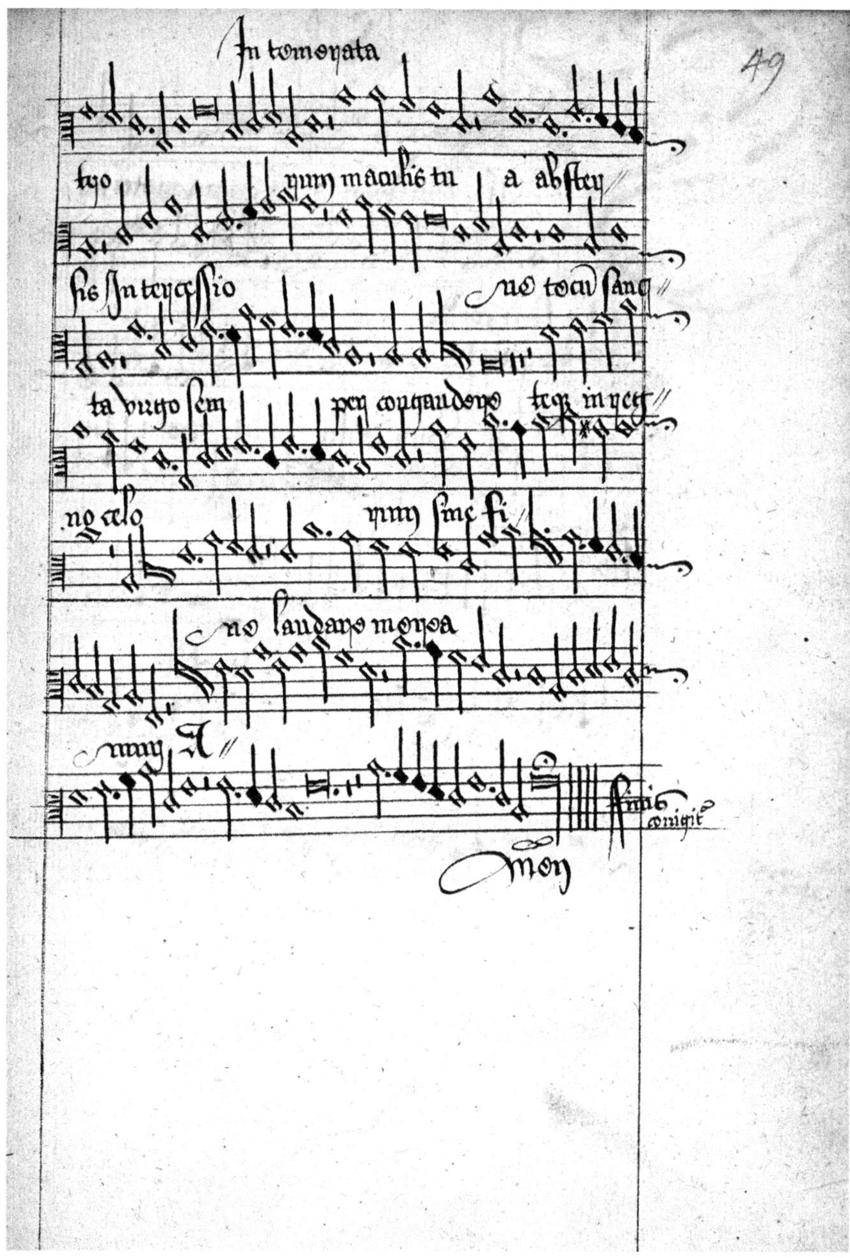

Figure 2.1 The end of *Salve intemerata*, from the earliest surviving manuscript containing music by Tallis. The note 'corrigitur' indicates that the copy was checked for accuracy (MS Harley 1709, f. 49r, by permission of the British Library Board)

belief, expressed in the first book of *Gradualia* (1605), that earnest contemplation of the ideas conveyed by religious texts leads unfailingly to musical inspiration, but there is little doubt that all his settings are based on careful readings of the words, and are intended to reinforce what they say. The concepts of contemporary education may be reflected here. Tallis's attention to the details of his texts was connected with rhetoric (the delivery of words in a way designed to impress the listener), a subject which was included in the trivium with grammar and logic. His concern with pattern and proportion in setting words to music shows at least an elementary interest in arithmetic, which was associated in the quadrivium with geometry, astronomy and music itself.[24]

Salve intemerata conveys a sense of its era, like Holbein's double portrait, painted in 1533, of Jean de Dinteville, the French ambassador to England, and Georges de Selve, Bishop of Lavaur. Holbein includes in his picture a music manuscript that is clearly of the same period as Harley 1709, though it is open to display two Lutheran hymns, reflecting the sympathy Selve felt for the Reformation in spite of his position among the French clergy. Holbein's subjects stand before a table bearing astronomical instruments and a book on arithmetic by Petrus Apianus. They are in a room with a patterned oriental carpet on the table, and a geometrical floor mosaic copied from the Cosmati pavement at Westminster Abbey.[25]

Tallis shared Holbein's concern with pattern. He perhaps shared some of his concern with symbolism as well, though symbolism is not an easy matter to deal with. The seven stanzas Tallis set in each of his earlier Mary antiphons may represent a number associated with the Virgin (her seven dolours, her seven joys), but going beyond that could be risky. Much the same is true of the numerical relationships underlying the structures of some Tudor compositions.[26] It is not

---

that 'Commentators have had trouble with *Salve intemerata'* (notes for the Tallis Scholars' recording *Lamentations of Jeremiah*, Gimell CDGIM 025: 1992). Tallis's setting has certainly attracted widely differing comments. For Collins, in spite of the words, it was 'the crown of Tallis's early work', showing 'a verve and animation which we seldom find in the composer's later work' (p. 156 of the article mentioned above). Frank Ll. Harrison thought 'the polyphony falls awkwardly between differentiation and integration, lacking the linear and rhythmic vitality of the earlier style and the logic and coherence of the later, while the rhythm sags at intermediate cadences through lack of overlapping phrases, and the themes are uneven in interest' (*Music in medieval Britain*, p. 335).

24 Roger Bray, *Music in Britain: the sixteenth century* (The Blackwell History of Music in Britain, 2: Oxford, 1995), pp. 3, 16; Roger Bray, 'Music and the quadrivium in early Tudor England', *Music & Letters*, vol. 76 (1995), pp. 1–18.

25 John North, *The ambassadors' secret*, revised edn (London, 2004).

26 A short and uncomplicated discussion can be found in Hugh Benham, *Latin church music in England*, pp. 43–7. More detailed consideration, relating to Taverner's works though with implications for those of Tallis, can be found in Benham, 'The formal design and construction of Taverner's works', *Musica Disciplina*, vol. 26 (1972), pp. 189–209. A different method of counting is described in Bray, 'Music and the quadrivium', pp. 15–18. Bray's method is further described in his article 'Editing and performing *musica*

always easy to penetrate a composer's intentions, since much depends on the way the lengths of sections are calculated, and it is not always clear what significance should be attached to the results. Counting for its own sake brings to mind the fate of the philarithmic Emberlin in Aldous Huxley's story *Eupompus gave splendour to art by numbers*. On the other hand, the proportions of *Salve intemerata* include at least one relationship which does not look entirely accidental.

Like Tallis's previous antiphons, *Salve intemerata* is in two main sections with different mensural signs. Its layout is sketched in Table 2.1 on p. 34, which shows the grouping of voices to create changing colours and gradations of sound.[27] Each of the three principal sections ends with a passage for all the voices, and the Amen forms either a separate section or a continuation of the third section. If the length of section I is calculated in units of three semibreves, and that of section IIA in units of four semibreves, the sections contain exactly the same number of units (93).[28] In order to realize the relationship between sections in performance, should four semibreves in section II have the same duration as three semibreves in section I? It is an open question.

If the numerical relationship between sections I and IIA was intentional, Tallis must deliberately have ignored the possibility, implicit in the text, that its words should be divided at a different place. Just over half the text, from the beginning to 'in finem mundi', praises the Virgin Mary; the rest, starting at 'Per haec nos praecellentissima gratie caelestis', prays for her intercession. Tallis did not divide the text where the prayer begins, but where 'tota vita permanseris' is followed by 'Tu nimirum universas', and the argument turns from Mary's purity of body to her purity of mind.

The many strengths of *Salve intemerata* – its rich and characteristic sound, and its ebb and flow of musical and emotional tension – depend to some extent on the support its composer derived from a model while he continued to gain experience and independence. *Salve intemerata* is not based on another work as closely as *Ave Dei patris filia* is based on Fayrfax's setting, but its plan gives strong hints that

---

speculativa', in John Morehen, ed., *English choral practice, 1400–1650* (Cambridge, 1995), pp. 48–73. In another essay Bray accounts for some slight discrepancies between actual and expected proportions by supposing that they result from inaccuracies in transmission (*Music in Britain: the sixteenth century*, p. 336, note 100).

27 The 'Per haec … singulariter infusa' section for three voices was often detached and appears in a number of sources as though a separate work. For this and other extracts from the antiphon see the EECM database; see also John Caldwell, ed., *The Mulliner book* (*Musica Britannica*, 1: London, 2011), p. 260.

28 The score is barred thus by Nicholas Sandon in Antico Edition RCM134 (Moretonhampstead, 1995). Three of his bars in section I are irregular: 46, 73 and 86, which all precede cadential notes, and must be regarded as containing four semibreves. Note that Sandon's edition is transposed upwards by a whole tone.

Table 2.1 Layout of *Salve intemerata*

Section I (ȸ)		
	'Salve intemerata ... mulieris sanctissime'	(a) C, B (b) Tr, T
	'sic a spiritu sancto ... Jesu Christi'	(c) Tr, C, T
	'et dum eum ... tota vita permanseris'	(d) Tr, M, C, T, B
Section II (¢)		
	A.	
	'Tu nimirum ... in finem mundi'	(a) M, T, B
	'Per hec nos ... singulariter infusa'	(b) Tr, C (c) Tr, M, C
	'te precamur ... secula genitum'	(d) Tr, M, C, T, B
	B.	
	'secundum humanitatem ... ex te natum'	(a) Tr, M (b) C, T, B
	'atque apud spiritum ... laudare mereamur'	(c) Tr, M, C, T, B
	'Amen'	Tr, M, C, T, B

Tr = treble, M = mean, C = contratenor, T= tenor, B = bass

Tallis was familiar with Taverner's *Gaude plurimum*. The division into sections and the scoring have distinct similarities.[29]

While the sectional division of *Salve intemerata* reflects the argument of the text, its words are tackled phrase by phrase. The vocal lines consist of a series of short phrases, each identified by its own point of imitation, and often with several notes allotted to a single syllable. Longer passages are characterized by the repetition of melodic or rhythmic motifs, and by the voices selected to sing them. The demands of the musical structure are more influential than logic and grammar, and there seems, for instance, to be no other reason why 'Annae mulieris sanctissime' should be linked more closely with the words that follow it than with 'matris' which precedes it. Yet Tallis's treatment of individual words and phrases is often highly successful, and attention is drawn to them in many different ways. The point which begins 'misericors patrona' (*merciful protectress*) is comprised uniformly of minims. The phrase 'castissima, incorruptissima' (*most chaste, most incorrupt*), is isolated and emphasized by cadences and rests. The first two phrases of section IIB, referring in turn to the divinity of Christ and to his humanity, are sung by one group of voices and repeated by another.

[29] Compare Table 6.1 in Hugh Benham, *John Taverner: his life and music* (Aldershot, 2003), p. 81. John Milsom notes that 'in the quasi-antiphonal exchanges at "secundum humanitatem" ... there even seems to be some actual modelling on Taverner's work', and refers to the corresponding passage, 'eundem igitur', in *Gaude plurimum* (see his 'English polyphonic style in transition: a study of the sacred music of Thomas Tallis' (Doctoral thesis, University of Oxford, 1983), vol. 1, p. 20).

Where the melodies of *Salve intemerata* are not extended by melismatic writing they are sensitive to the pitches, stresses, and contours of spoken Latin (though any general statement to this effect necessarily, and perhaps unwisely, assumes the accuracy and uniformity of manuscript copies). Melodic outlines formed by the highest and lowest voices are given particular attention. In the treble voice the highest note is normally *e''*, but it rises to *f''* to emphasize 'illuminata' in the first part of section I, and again to emphasize 'condonandis' (*forgiveness*) in the prayer of section IIA.[30] An *f''* is sung again in the middle of the Amen, where Tallis prepares for it a few notes earlier by flattening B in the sequential phrase running through the bass (p. 36, Example 2.2).

B♭ occurs only once before in the piece, in the tenor part at 'ipso mundi primordio'. Intentionally or not, Tallis had hampered himself by setting *Salve intemerata* in the E mode (Glarean's 'Phrygian'). The choice was unusual, perhaps because contemporary practice limited the cadences available in the Phrygian. Most of the cadences or cadence-like formations in *Salve intemerata* are built on E or A. Tallis rarely returned to the mode, and by the time he used it in his first set of Lamentations he had learned how to traverse a range of tonalities in one piece. To find *Salve intemerata* short of tonal variety is of course to listen to it with modern ears. (The tonality of even Tallis's largest antiphon, *Gaude gloriosa Dei mater*, written more than 20 years later, is not particularly adventurous.) But perhaps Tallis sensed something slightly monochromatic about what he had already written, and as he approached the melodic climax in the Amen he manipulated the mode to extend his palette.

The words of ***Sancte Deus, Sancte fortis*** link parts of texts which were sung separately as antiphons.[31] The use of the resulting text was specified in the statutes for Wolsey's Cardinal College, first drawn up in 1525. It was set by John Taverner, who was *informator choristarum* at the College from 1526 to 1530, and by William Whytbroke, who was a chaplain in Taverner's choir before moving to St Paul's Cathedral in 1531.[32] Whytbroke's setting seems to have been inspired by Taverner's.[33]

30 The fact that *Salve intemerata* appears to have a voice range a semitone lower than *Ave Dei patris filia* and *Ave rosa sine spinis* is due to the piece being in a different mode, making it impossible to notate it at the same pitch.

31 The text combines parts of the Improperia for Good Friday and the ninth response at Matins for the Dead. See Harrison, *Music in medieval Britain*, pp. 60, 83–4, 174. 'Sancte Deus . immortalis, miserere nobis', was printed in *Enchiridion, preclare ecclesie Sarum devotissimis praecationibus ac venustissimus et imaginibus* (Paris, widow of Thielman Kerver for Alard Plomier, 2 September 1528); see Hoskins, *Horæ Beatæ Mariæ Virginis*, p. 135.

32 The statutes of Cardinal College were revised in 1527, and further revised in 1532 when the college was refounded by Henry VIII. *Sancte Deus* is mentioned in each version (*Statutes of the colleges of Oxford* [ed. E.A. Bond] (London, 1853), vol. 2, 'Cardinal College', pp. 58, 165, 188).

33 Benham, *John Taverner*, pp. 135, 299.

Example 2.2 *Salve intemerata*, the Amen

Tallis's setting of the text appears to be related to one by Philip van Wilder, with which it occurs in the Gyffard partbooks, the only source of both pieces.[34] The structures and musical material of the two settings are very much alike. Both are in four parts, and the ranges of the voices are similar. At the written pitch, the highest part of each is for a boy's voice, while the lowest has the tenor range. Perhaps they were composed in a spirit of what Peacham was later to call 'friendly aemulation'. It is evident that they were regarded as a pair by the compiler of

[34] BL Additional MSS 17802–5.

continued

the partbooks, where Tallis's setting appears immediately after Wilder's. It may be that they were written after Tallis arrived at court, where Wilder had been employed as a musician from the 1520s, and since the 1530s had been attached to the King's privy chamber. Wilder's piece may have been composed for the group of singers, including boys, which he led at court. Although both he and Tallis went on to serve Edward VI, their settings of *Sancte Deus, Sancte fortis* seem likely to have been written before the death of Henry VIII, with whose views, as expressed in Cromwell's injunctions, the words would have conformed. It may not be too much to think of the two pieces as sacred songs for the solace of a

Example 2.2 *concluded*

monarch with religious tastes.[35] It is natural to suppose that they may have been made after Tallis's arrival at court (by 1543) and before the death of King Henry (January 1546/7).

The influence of Wilder may explain why *Sancte Deus, Sancte fortis* does not seem entirely typical of Tallis's work, but there are other reasons too. Whereas Tallis's Marian antiphons are essentially works of glorification and conceived on a suitably large scale, *Sancte Deus* is a personal meditation in the form of a petition addressed to Christ. It is short, and its organization is simple. It has the signature ¢ throughout, but it is divided into clearly separated short sections, in each of which the final chord is marked with a fermata sign. So, for emphasis, are the chords setting 'Nunc' (in 'Nunc, Christe, te petimus', *Now, Christ, we beseech you*) and the syllables of 'noli' (in 'noli damnare redemptos', *do not condemn the redeemed*).[36] Each section terminates with a cadence on A (the final of the mode), or its fifth (E), or more distantly on B in the setting of 'noli damnare redemptos', so as to lend weight to the plea. A few notes of imitation introduce nearly every verbal phrase, though imitation is no more a structural element than it is in the lengthy Marian antiphons. In proportion to its size, the piece relies less on melismatic writing than Tallis's larger works; yet homophony is almost

---

[35] The nine 'men and children' Wilder directed at the time of Henry VIII's funeral included four (or five) singers, evidently boys, who received less than an adult's allocation of cloth (TNA LC2/3/1, f.188 (also numbered f.64v), and LC2/3/2, f.50; Andrew Ashbee, *Records of English court music* (Snodland, *later* Aldershot, 1986–96), vol. 7, pp. 107–8, 110.

[36] Benham suggests, apropos of Taverner's piece, that pauses after the phrases 'Sancte Deus', 'Sancte fortis' and 'Sancte immortalis' may have marked acts of reverence to the crucifix (*John Taverner*, p. 134). Tallis does not pause after 'immortalis'.

entirely absent, and only the words 'Nunc' and 'noli' are quite unobscured by the counterpoint. The simplicity of 'Nunc' is especially striking after the preceding 'English' cadence, with its clash of G and G♯. It is where the second part of the text begins.

Masses

Tallis's ***Salve intemerata*** Mass was added to the Peterhouse partbooks at a late stage in their assembly, and so must have been composed in the decade or so following completion of the antiphon on which it was based. No earlier source has survived, and indeed the tenor book of the Peterhouse set has been lost, though this does not obscure the way that music from the antiphon is reused and redistributed in the Mass, which is for the same voices and in the same mode. Masses based on existing material ('parody' or 'imitation' or, better, 'derived' Masses) were familiar on the Continent by the time Josquin des Prez died in 1521, and composers like Jacobus Clemens (roughly contemporary with Tallis) and Nicolas Gombert (about 10 years older) based most of their Masses on existing compositions. The practice was not entirely new in England.[37] Fayrfax had reused material from his antiphon *O bone Jesu* in both a Mass and a Magnificat. Taverner had made more considerable use of common material in his antiphon *Mater Christi* and the Mass of the same name. But it was Taverner's *Mean* Mass which Tallis had very much in mind when he wrote the *Salve intemerata* Mass.

In transferring material from his antiphon to the Mass based on it, Tallis lifted sections of varying length from the earlier work and placed them non-consecutively throughout the later, with the addition of linking or longer passages of new material. Table 2.2 (p. 40) illustrates the use in the Mass of material from the antiphon. Bar numbers are given as an indication of areas where transfers have taken place, but it is not always possible to be exact. New material is sometimes similar to old material, and similar fragments of melody often occur without a genuine transfer having occurred. Some sections of the antiphon are more radically adapted than others, and the reuse of material seldom takes place in a completely straightforward way. Transferred material may be contracted or expanded, and adjustments affecting the length and repetition of notes are made to accommodate new words. A transferred passage may overlap with other material, old or new, sometimes to a considerable extent. A connecting passage may be constructed from antiphon material, but without resembling anything in the antiphon very closely.

The music joining reused passages, and filling in gaps, shows how well Tallis was able to recapture his earlier inspiration. But some of the new material acknowledges the inspiration of Taverner's *Mean* Mass. Tallis was not alone in adopting the *Mean* Mass as a model. Tye did so in his five-part Mass, as did

[37] See Nicholas Sandon, 'Paired and grouped works for the Latin rite by Tudor composers', *Music Review*, vol. 44 (1983), pp. 8–12.

Table 2.2 Sources of music in the Mass *Salve intemerata*

Bar numbers in the outside columns assume that ⏀ is barred every three semibreves and ¢ every four semibreves.[a] Sections marked * contain one bar with an extra semibreve.

Mass		**Antiphon**	
Gloria[b]			
	Gloria in excelsis Deo. [Plainchant]		
⏀		⏀	
1–6	Et in terra pax ... voluntantis	Salve intemerata virgo Maria	1–6
6–12	Laudamus te ... adoramus te	Anne mulieris sanctissime	19–23
12–42	Glorificamus te ... filius Patris		
¢		¢	
43–53	Qui tollis ... deprecationem nostram	secundum luminatatem ... ex te natum	187–197
57–61*	miserere nobis	maculis tua abstersis	207–211
61–65	Quoniam tu solus sanctus ... solus latissimus	atque apud spiritum sanctum	198–203
66–75	Jesu Christe. Amen.	sine fine ... Amen	231–237
Credo			
	Credo in unum Deum [Plainchant]		
⏀		⏀	
1–6	Patrem omnipotentem ... caeli et terrae	Salve intemerata virgo Maria	1–6
6–20	visibilium et invisibilium. Et in unum Dominum ... unigenitum.	Anne mulieris ... illuminata fuisti	18–30
20–30	Et ex Patre natum ante omnia saecula.Deum de Deo, lumen de lumine, Deum verum de Deo vero	et dum eum conciperes ... et dum eum pareres	47–52
32–52*	Genitum non factum ... descendit de caelis	semperque post partem ... et immaculatissima	59–74*
¢		¢	
53–77*	Et incarnatus est ... secundum scripturas [compare the same passage in Taverner's *Mean* Mass]		
77–81	Et ascendit in caelum: sedet ad dexteram Patris [compare the same passage in Taverner's *Mean* Mass]	teque in regno caelorum	219–222
	[Et iterum venturus est ... remissionem peccatorum.][c]		
⏀			
82–94	Et expecto ... venturi saeculi. Amen		

Mass		**Antiphon**	
Sanctus			
ɸ		ɸ	
1–6	Sanctus	Salve intemerata virgo Maria	1–6
6–9	Sanctus	Anne mulieris sanctissime	18–23
10–20	Sanctus Dominus Deus sabaoth.	misericors patrona es ... nobis condonandis	147–158
21–36	Pleni sunt caeli et terra gloria tua		
36–51	Hosanna in excelsis	et corpore ... tota vita	79–89*
¢			
52–69	Benedictus qui venit ... in nomine Domini. [compare the same passage in Taverner's *Mean* Mass]		
69–80	Hosanna in excelsis	eiusque filium ... secundum divinitatem	168–177
Agnus Dei			
ɸ		ɸ	
1–6	Agnus Dei	Salve intemerata	1–6
6–9	Agnus Dei	Anne mulieris sanctissime	18–25
9–38*	qui tollis ... miserere nobis		
¢		¢	
39–54	Agnus Dei qui tollis ... dona nobis pacem	sine fine ... Amen	221–237*

[a] Both works are barred in this way in Antico Edition RCM134, ed Nick Sandon (Moretonhampstead, 1995).
[b] Like many other Mass settings in pre-Reformation England, the *Salve intemerata* Mass starts with the Gloria. In the Sarum rite it was usual to chant the Kyrie, with textual interpolations (tropes) suited to the day.
[c] These words are omitted, as they are from some other English Mass settings of the time (Hugh Benham, *Latin church music in England* c.*1460–1575* (London, 1977), p. 13). The whole Credo text would however have been said quietly, or mouthed silently, by the officiating priest.

Sheppard in his *Frences* Mass. Byrd took it as his model when he turned to writing Masses.[38] Tallis's reference to Taverner is clearest in his Benedictus (part of the Sanctus) (Examples 2.3a and 2.3b, pp. 42 and 45).

Most of the 'movements' present in the Mass are divided, like the antiphon, into two parts with the signs ɸ and ¢. The Credo returns to ɸ in a third section.

[38] Nigel Davison, 'Structure and unity in four free-composed Tudor Masses', *Music Review*, 34 (1973), pp. 328–38; Philip Brett, 'Homage to Taverner in Byrd's Masses', *Early Music*, 9 (1981), pp. 169–76 (reprinted in Brett, *William Byrd and his contemporaries* (Berkeley, 2007), pp. 8–21).

Example 2.3a The beginning of the *Benedictus* from Taverner's *Mean* Mass

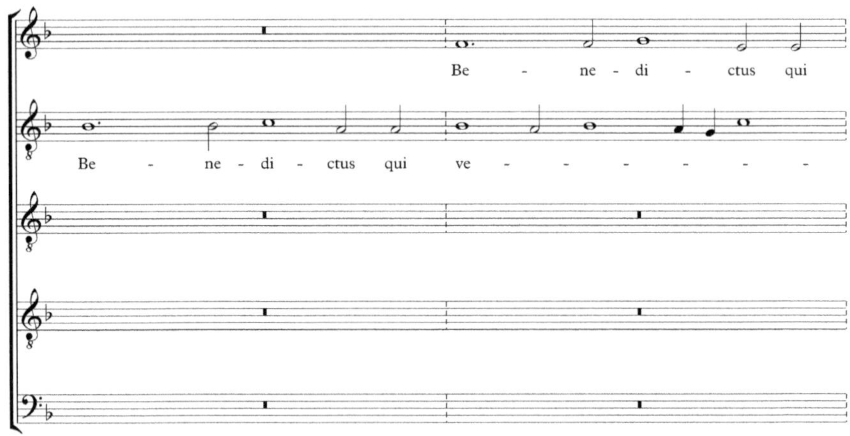

Any passage of the antiphon which is transferred to the Mass is moved to a section of the Mass having the same sign.

Two short passages near the beginning of the antiphon, 'Salve intemerata virgo Maria' and 'Annae mulieris sanctissime', are combined to form an extended head-motif which appears at the start of each Mass movement (in the Gloria and Credo they follow the initial chanted word). The music lying between these passages in the antiphon is not transferred to the Mass. Other passages not added to the new work include the setting of 'castissima, incorruptissima', which originally received special treatment (see p. 34). Two passages for three voices, 'sic a spiritu sancto … Jesu Christi' and 'Tu nimirum universas … a Deo singulariter infusa',

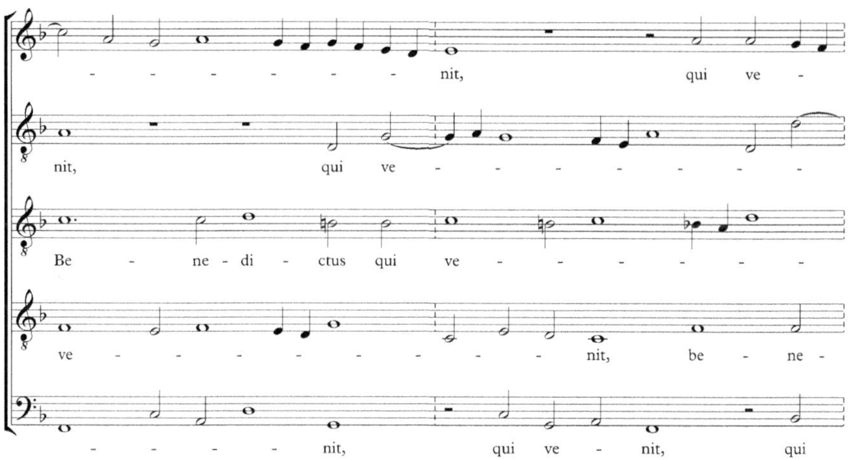

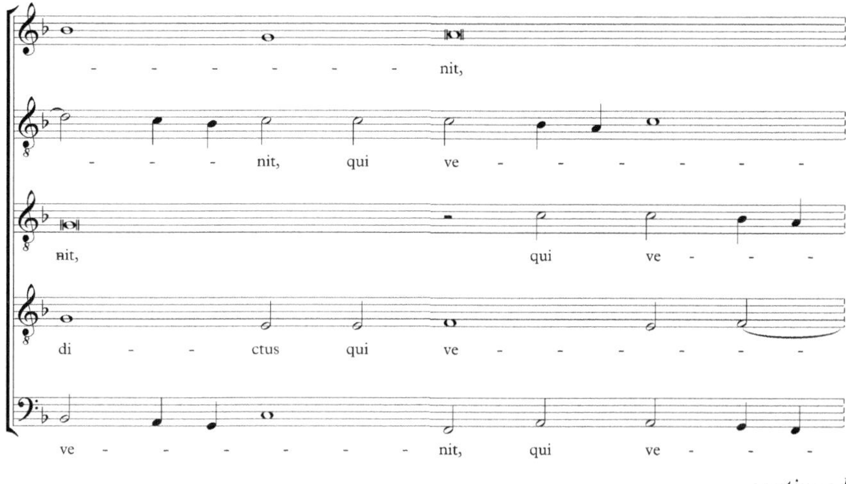

continued

are also omitted, together with the long passage 'te precamur … saecula genitum' for five voices.

Apart from the passages forming the head-motif, there is one instance of material from the antiphon being used twice in the Mass. The antiphon's music for 'sine fine … Amen' reappears at the end of the Gloria ('Jesu Christe. Amen') and more extensively at the end of the Agnus Dei ('qui tollis … dona nobis pacem'). There seem to be reminiscences of this music also at the ends of the Credo and Gloria, though the similarities are not so great as to suggest the presence of a tail-motif of the kind used by Taverner in his *Mean* Mass.

Example 2.3a *concluded*

There is a greater repetition of words in the Mass than in the antiphon, and their setting is more syllabic. This marks a development in Tallis's style. A lack of tonal adventurousness in both the antiphon and Mass no doubt eased the task of transferring music, but sometimes material is used more appropriately after transferral: the rising notes of 'teque in regno caelorum' at the end of the antiphon are given to 'Et ascendit in caelum' in the Credo of the Mass. Elsewhere similar ideas call forth similar music without any transfer taking place: there are resemblances between the antiphon's 'laudare mereamur' and the 'Hosanna' of the Mass's Sanctus.

A few years after the completion of the *Salve intemerata* Mass, something radically different appeared, to the later puzzlement of the Tudor Church Music editors. When they came to publish an unnamed **Mass for four voices**, attributed to Tallis in the Gyffard partbooks, they had this to say:

> This Mass exhibits peculiarities of part-writing which make it especially regrettable that no other text has been found either to corroborate or to emend them. The Editors would, however, point out that instances of rather similar diatonic clashes occur in the works of Taverner, notably in the Mass *O Michael*.[39]

But the *O Michael* Mass itself presents problems which have led to Taverner's authorship being questioned.[40] No one seems so far to have questioned the authenticity of the 'Tallis' Mass (not in print, anyway), and the Gyffard scribe, who

39 Thomas Tallis, *Tudor church music ... Volume VI: Thomas Tallis c.1505–1585* (London, 1928), p. xxv.

40 Benham, *John Taverner*, pp. 50, 58, 160–61.

Example 2.3b The beginning of the *Benedictus* from Tallis's *Salve intemerata* Mass

continued

wrote the name 'talles' firmly at the beginning and end of each movement of the piece, was in no doubt about who composed it. Nevertheless, a fresh examination of the work must now take account of Stefan Scot's discovery that its Credo is – language apart – almost identical to the Creed of Sheppard's First Service, which like the Mass is found only in a single source (though its attribution to Sheppard

Example 2.3b *concluded*

appears to be secure).[41] The chief differences are that Sheppard's Creed is designed to be sung antiphonally by the two sides of the choir, and has no passage parallel to the Mass's setting of the words 'Et incarnatus … sepultus est'. Some minor

[41] The source is York Minster MS M 13 (S), where the First Service follows Sheppard's Second Service. See David Griffiths, *A catalogue of the music manuscripts in York Minster Library* ([York], 1981).

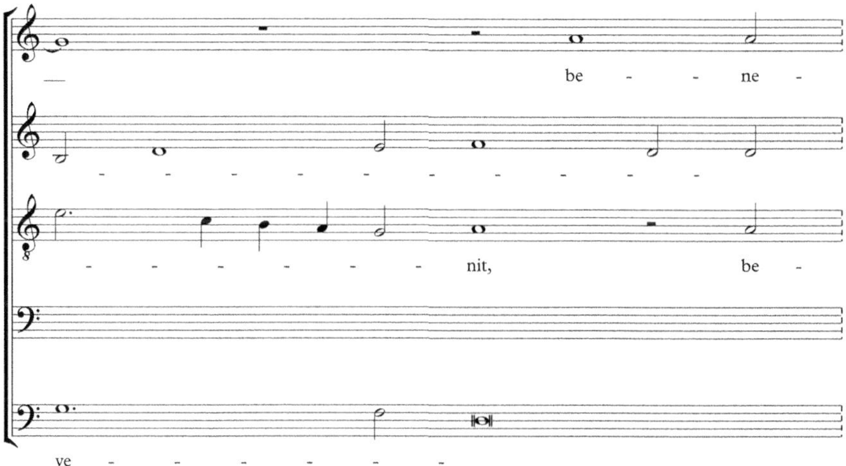

rhythmic differences between the two pieces arise from the need to fit different words to the music.[42]

The words provide one of the strongest clues to the original composer of the shared movement. For example, scalar phrases falling more than an octave, which in the Creed set the words 'and descended into hell', are less appropriately applied to the words 'Genitum non factum' (*Begotten, not made*) in the Credo, while the rising notes setting 'He ascended into heaven' are used for 'Qui propter nos homines' (*Who for us men*). The conclusion must be that Tallis was the borrower. This is quite in keeping with his known habits. His inclusion in the *Salve intemerata* Mass of material lifted from Taverner's *Mean* Mass was mentioned above (see p. 39–41). Roger Bray has drawn attention to 'a network of cross-quotation, allusion and therefore presumably emulation' in works by Sheppard, Tye and Tallis, with the last 'apparently the emulator in each case', though extending and developing the newly absorbed material in his own work.[43]

Here it is necessary to look forward to the next chapter, and glance at matters covered more fully there. The words of most of the movements of Sheppard's First Service seem to come from the 1549 *Book of Common Prayer*; but that contains no words for the Creed, directing simply that 'the minister shal say the Crede, and the Lordes praier in englishe, with a loude voice, &c'. Although variations may exist between different editions and even copies of almost any book from

[42] See the notes to *The church music of John Sheppard ... The collected vernacular works – Volume I*, recorded by the Academia Musica Choir (PRCD 1081: 2013). The notes are by Stefan Scot, whose edition of the First Service will appear in volume 4 of Sheppard's works in the Early English Church Music series. His generosity in providing a pre-publication copy of his edition, and in discussing his discovery, is reflected in the present pages.

[43] Bray, *Music in Britain: the sixteenth century*, p. 22.

a Tudor press, there seems little doubt that the words of Sheppard's Creed are from *The primer* of 1545.[44] The versions of the Creed published in *A necessary doctrine and erudition* (1543)[45] and the second Edwardian Prayer Book (1552) are distinguished by small but significant differences which suggest that they were not used by Sheppard. How widely, and from what date, the text published in 1545 may have been in circulation is uncertain; but Sheppard's Creed, and the rest of the First Service, must have been completed before mid-1553, when Queen Mary ascended the throne and Catholic services were resumed. It is unlikely that the Creed was inserted into Sheppard's Service by another hand at a later date, because it is too clearly of a piece with the rest of the work.

It may be possible to narrow the date of Sheppard's Creed still further, since the Mass into which Tallis incorporated it was probably written before 1547, when King Edward came to the throne and the open performance of a Mass would not have been permitted. This would help to explain why the style of Tallis's Mass has a good deal in common with that of his English-texted four-voice Benedictus, another piece which sets words from the *The primer* (see p. 77). While it is conceivable that in Edward's reign a Mass might have been sung secretly at the house of some Catholic patron, there is no evidence that Tallis was involved in performances of this kind, as Byrd was to be in the reign of Queen Elizabeth. A later date for the Mass may be regarded at best as doubtful, because it does not seem to be in keeping with the kind of music Tallis is thought to have written when Catholic services began again in Queen Mary's reign (though it would be wrong to pretend that his Marian pieces can be identified with anything like complete certainty).

If we accept that Tallis was the borrower, we must ask why that was so. It could have been because he wanted to write something in conformity with reformers' demands for church music to avoid excessive elaboration. These gathered force during the earliest years of his employment in the Chapel Royal. Unless we doubt the authenticity of the Mass for four voices, or assume that the Gyffard scribe had an exceptionally poor copy before him, an attempt by Tallis to write in a new and unfamiliar manner might explain at least some of the features which the Tudor Church Music editors found perplexing.[46] He may have needed a model to get him

44 *The primer, set foorth by the Kynges Maiestie and his clergie* (London, 1545), called 'The King's primer'.

45 *A necessary doctrine and erudition for any Christen man, sette furthe by the kynges maiestie of Englande* (London, 1543), known as 'The King's Book'. Its words were used in some early settings of the Creed in the Wanley partbooks (see the critical notes in James Wrightson, ed., *The Wanley manuscripts* (Recent researches in the music of the Renaissance, 99–101: Madison, Wisc., 1995), vol. 1, pp. xxiii–l), and recur in a few later settings.

46 The editors were not alone. A review by H.B. Collins referred to the Mass's probably early date, 'judging from its largely homophonic character, the frequent full closes, the rather infantile stops, and the somewhat clumsy workmanship of the more polyphonic passages' ('Thomas Tallis', p. 157). Almost 50 years later Paul Doe did not fault its technique, but found 'the combined effect of melodic, harmonic, and rhythmic restraint'

started, and Sheppard's Creed may have provided it. Although Sheppard was at Magdalen College, Oxford, until 1548, and his name is not found in the incomplete records of the Chapel Royal until the end of Edward's reign, it is conceivable that he and Tallis were in touch – though so little is known about communication between composers, or the circulation of manuscripts, that it is useless to guess how Tallis came by a copy of Sheppard's Creed. It was not his only model, for his Mass has some of the characteristics of the *Plainsong* Mass by Taverner (*d.*1545), to whose music he looked for inspiration on other occasions.[47] Tallis's setting of 'Et in terra pax' at the very beginning of the Mass for four voices may be more than a casual reminiscence of Taverner's work (Examples 2.4a and b, pp. 50 and 51).

It is difficult to decide whether Tallis had the whole of Sheppard's Service before him when he embarked on the Mass, or whether parts of the Service are Edwardian, but his reliance on the Creed is clear. There are, however, some differences. Although he wrote in the same key as Sheppard, and like Sheppard regarded *E* as the lowest note of the bass voice's range,[48] the Service is written for a full choir and its overall voice range extends up to *a″*. At the written pitch, the top voice of Tallis's Mass goes no higher than *a′*. The total range of the voices barely exceeds that of parts normally sung by men, and is only a shade wider than that of Tallis's four-voice Benedictus. One wonders whether both the Mass and Benedictus were written for the conducts of a church where boy singers were not regularly available.

It was only in the Gloria and Credo of the Mass that Tallis used without change the head-motif which occurs in each movement of Sheppard's Service.[49] But if we approached the Mass unaware of its connection with Sheppard's work, we might easily be persuaded that Tallis started with the Gloria and drew material from it for the subsequent movements. Although not all of them begin with the head-motif, they at least begin with a phrase that bears some relationship to it. Among further examples of derivation or association within the Mass, the Credo's 'Et incarnatus est … passus et sepultus' (not derived from Sheppard's Creed) resembles the Gloria's 'Domine Deus, Agnus Dei … Qui sedes ad dexteram'. In the Sanctus, the notes of 'Gloria tua' and 'in nomine Domini' are taken from the

was 'inevitably one of dullness' (*Tallis* (1968), p. 20; repeated in the 2nd edn of 1976). Nearly 30 years further on, Nicholas Sandon thought that 'working with only four voices and writing in a very restrained style, Tallis creates a remarkably strong sense of variety', and mentioned the composer's 'polished craftsmanship' (notes to the recording by Chapelle du Roi: Signum SIGCD002, 1997).

47 For the *Plainsong* Mass see Benham, *John Taverner*, pp. 199–203, where it is suggested that the title 'must refer to the simple rhythmic notation'. Paul Doe wondered whether Taverner's Mass and several other Masses in the Gyffard partbooks, with similar characteristics, might form a group written in the early 1540s (Doe, 'Latin polyphony under Henry VIII', *Proceedings of the Royal Musical Association*, vol. 95 (1968/69), pp. 81–96, at 90–92). On the *Plainsong* Mass see also Benham, *John Taverner*, pp. 199–203.

48 The copyist of York Minster MS M 13 (S) sometimes writes an octave *C–c* for the bass at a cadence, but this appears to be a scribal flourish.

49 In the Venite it is in the tenor part, not the mean.

Example 2.4a The beginning of the Gloria from Taverner's *Plainsong* Mass

Gloria's 'Quoniam tu solus' and 'Domine Fili unigenite'. The Agnus Dei takes its whole second section from the Gloria's 'propter magnam gloriam tuam … Deus Pater omnipotens', while 'dona nobis pacem' is from 'cum Sancto Spiritu'. Within movements, too, material is repeated.[50]

[50] Davison discusses how this process works in the Benedictus ('Structure and unity in four free-composed Tudor masses', at 338).

Example 2.4b The beginning of the Gloria from Tallis's Mass for four voices

The Mass is modest in scale, and the absence of a cantus firmus contributes to its compact nature. The tonal scope of the piece is restricted. Word setting is mostly syllabic. Melismatic writing is reserved mainly for the Sanctus and Agnus Dei. Verbal phrases are repeated with fresh or varied music. The text is set in short sections, accorded differing treatments. Homophony is balanced by polyphony that is often imitative. The Mass in fact displays an exuberance of invention. John Milsom has written of its 'hybrid quality', and observed that 'it is as though Tallis has chosen to bring together and contrast the entire spectrum of his textural resources'.[51] He has also pointed to the continuity between aspects of the Mass and Tallis's early Elizabethan motets (non-liturgical settings of Latin religious texts). The second 'Hosanna' of the Sanctus, containing 'by far the longest and most sophisticatedly "Continental" set of entries in all of Tallis' surviving pre-Elizabethan music', lacks any climactic statement, but contains a counter-exposition as 'a means of consolidating and adding bulk'. In pieces 'such as *O sacrum convivium*, *Absterge Domine* and *O salutaris hostia*, Tallis extends

[51] Milsom, 'English polyphonic style in transition', vol. 1, p. 140.

the principle to cover not merely a single exposition within the work but several or even all' expositions.[52]

Short Pieces for the Lady Mass

An *Alleluia* and a setting of *Euge caeli porta* by Tallis are both based on Lady Mass chants. In the early sixteenth century a Mass in honour of the Virgin Mary, using texts and chants dictated by the calendar, would have been a daily celebration in Canterbury Cathedral's Lady Chapel and in the chapels of other monastic communities.

The ***Alleluia*** was sung before the verse *Ora pro nobis*.[53] It may have been composed before the singing of 'Ora pro nobis' was discouraged by Cromwell in 1538, and before Canterbury's Benedictine priory surrendered to the King in 1539. The chant is set out, almost entirely in breves, in the second highest part. Above and beneath it other voices sing largely independent lines. There are a few suggestions of imitation, and in the last third of the piece one brief phrase is passed repeatedly from voice to voice, but Tallis's main interest was in the sound of treble voices soaring, as though pictorially, above the voices beneath.

Euge caeli porta is the only verse Tallis is known to have set from the sequence *Ave praeclara Maris Stella*, though he may well have composed more, leaving just the odd-numbered verses to be chanted or played on the organ.[54] His setting is for four voices, which at the written pitch make an unusual combination (a treble, two altos, and a tenor), though the pitch could well have been changed for performance. The chant, in a decorated form, occupies the part lying second from the bottom. Imitation is non-existent, and the piece depends for its tranquil mood entirely on the quiet interplay of separate lines.

Solo Responds

A respond (or responsory) consists of responses and versicles (marked ℟ and ℣ in the breviary) which follow a reading. Sections are sung alternately by a soloist

---

52 Ibid., vol. 1, pp. 140–41; vol. 2, Appendix 5.6.

53 The *Alleluia* is in Gyffard partbooks, BL Additional MSS 17802–5. It is for Tuesdays from Purification to Advent, except from Septuagesima to Easter (F.H. Dickinson, ed., *Missale ad usum insignis et praeclarae Ecclesiae Sarum* (Burntisland, 1861–83), col. 781*).

54 *Euge caeli porta* is in Bodleian Library MSS Tenbury 354–8 (*c.*1600 or after), and BL Additional MS 34049 (of roughly the same date). A sequence is an extra-liturgical text in verse. Tallis's sequence is for Lady Mass on Sundays from Purification to Advent, and on the octave of the Assumption (Dickinson, *Missale ad usum insignis et praeclarae Ecclesiae Sarum*, col. 879). The words, from Hermannus Contractus's *Ave praeclara* are often given as 'Euge Dei porta'.

(or a group of singers performing the solo passages) and the choir.[55] The simplest form of plainsong respond starts with a response begun by the soloist(s) and continued by the choir; this is followed by a versicle sung by the soloist(s), before the choir repeats a part of the response it has already sung. The addition of more responses and versicles creates more complex patterns. Plainsong was at first replaced by polyphony in the solo sections. Pieces of this sort are called 'solo responds'. In 'choral responds', a type developed somewhat later, the passages sung by the choir are replaced by polyphony.

Responds were evidently popular with collectors of music over a long period. In the fifteenth century the owner of one manuscript gathered a number of pre-Tudor settings, apparently for his own interest. They included several of *Audivi vocem*, *In pace in idipsum* and *In manus tuas*, all with texts that Tallis was to set in due course.[56] The greater part of Tallis's extant music for the Office consists of respond settings with a liturgical form. (In his later years he made some non-liturgical settings of respond texts.) His solo responds, all for four voices, are *Audivi* (for All Saints' Day), *Hodie nobis caelorum Rex* (for Christmas Day), and *In pace* (for Lent). The Gyffard partbooks are the only source of these pieces, but they also contain four-part settings of *Audivi* by John Taverner (*c.*1490–1545) and John Sheppard (*c.*1515–58); *Hodie* by Taverner, Sheppard and Robert Cowper (*c.*1474–after *c.*1535); and *In pace* by Sheppard, Christopher Tye (*c.*1505–73?) and John Blitheman (*c.*1525–91). Other Gyffard responds include three settings by Sheppard of *In manus tuas*, which Tallis is not known to have tackled before the 1560s or early 1570s, when he set it non-liturgically.

The composers' dates illustrate the difficulty of placing Tallis's solo responds within a narrow time-frame. As he was capable of writing on a grand scale early in his career, the relative brevity and simplicity of his solo responds may not indicate the period when they were written. The genre afforded little scope for extended polyphony, and tradition may have dictated composition for four voices. They are usually assumed to be fairly early, because the solo respond is thought to have been superseded by the choral respond in King Henry's reign. Taverner's two settings of *Dum transisset sabbatum* appear to have begun the change from one type of respond to the other.

---

55 Harper, *The forms and orders of western liturgy*, pp. 71–2, 82–3.

56 Cambridge, Magdalene College, Pepys 1236, of Kentish origin, is dated *c.*1460–*c.*1465 by Sydney Robinson Charles, and 1465–75 by Bowers (see Charles, 'The provenance and date of the Pepys MS 1236', *Musica Disciplina*, vol. 16 (1962), pp. 57–71; Charles, ed., *The music of the Pepys MS 1236* (Corpus mensurabilis musicae, 40: Dallas, Tex., 1967); and Roger Bowers's description of the manuscript in Ian Fenlon, ed., *Cambridge music manuscripts, 900–1700* (Cambridge, 1982), pp. 111–14). Pepys 1236 contains three anonymous settings (two now incomplete) of *In pace* for two voices, two settings by John Tuder of *Audivi* for two voices, two settings by William Corbrand of *In manus tuas* for three voices, and a setting of the verse ('Gloria') of *Hodie nobis* for three voices.

Audivi vocem, a respond for All Saints' Day, has an elementary pattern:

℟ (soloists) Audivi (choir) vocem de caelo venientem: venite omnes virgines sapientissimae. Oleum recondite in vasis vestris dum sponsus advenerit.
℣ (soloists) Media nocte clamor factus est, ecce Sponsus venit
℟ (choir) Oleum recondite in vasis vestris dum sponsus advenerit.

(℟ *I heard a voice from heaven: come, all the wisest virgins. Fill your vessels with oil, for the bridegroom approaches.* ℣ *In the middle of the night there was a cry: behold, the bridegroom approaches.*)

Directions for performing responds illustrate the theatrical nature of church services. In some places *Audivi vocem* was begun after a boy chorister had read the eighth lesson, from the parable of the wise and foolish virgins. The solo sections were then sung by five boys representing the wise virgins. The boys stood at the choir step, wearing surplices, holding lighted candles and facing the altar, and at the word 'ecce' (*Behold*) they turned towards the choir.[57] It is difficult to see how the drama involving five boys might have been enacted when a four-part setting for different voices was sung, and perhaps it was possible only when the respond was chanted throughout.

In Tallis's setting the 'solo' passages take the form of imitative polyphony. The sections are short, but their confident technique suggests that the piece may not be much, if any, earlier than the Mass for four voices. The word 'Audivi' and the phrases of the verse are drawn out melismatically, although the ghost of the chant is more or less discernible in all the sections. At 'clamor factus est' it manifests itself most clearly in the highest part. Here, as in some other pieces, Tallis seems to use long notes for emphasis. At 'ecce' (*behold*) he avoids a dramatic gesture like the one in Taverner's *Audivi*, where each syllable of the word is set as a chord. Instead, the outer voices begin with one point, while the inner voices begin with another, and all the voices continue with imitative lines independent of the chant.

The pattern of ***Hodie nobis caelorum Rex*** is much like that of *Audivi vocem*:

℟ (soloists, *polyphony*) Hodie (choir, *plainsong*) nobis caelorum rex de virgine nasci dignatus est: ut hominem perditum ad caelestia regna revocaret: gaudet exercitus angelorum. Quia salus aeterna humano generi apparuit.
℣ (soloists, *polyphony*) Gloria in excelsis Deo: et in terra pax hominibus bonae voluntatis.
℟ (choir, *plainsong*) Quia salus aeterna humano generi apparuit.

(℟ *Today the king of heaven has condescended to be born of a virgin for us, so that he might call lost men back to the kingdom of heaven: the host of angels*

57 Frere, *The Use of Sarum*, vol. 1, p. 121.

rejoices, because eternal salvation has appeared to mankind. ℣ *Glory to God in the highest, and on earth peace to men of goodwill.*)

One method of singing the respond required two clerks of the second form, in surplices, to begin it on the choir step, and then withdraw to their stall while the choir continued. The verse was sung by five boys wearing surplices, and with white amices on their heads. They stood facing the choir in a high place above the altar, holding lighted candles, and representing the angels who, in the Biblical account, proclaimed Christ's birth to the shepherds.[58] As in the case of *Audivi*, it is not clear how this piece of theatre could have been acted out when a four-part setting was used.

Tallis's setting is anyway unsuitable for boys alone, and at the written pitch might be slightly on the low side for a choir of the usual make-up. This must be because the piece is in the E mode, and if it had been written a fourth higher (the first of the upward transpositions easily possible in sixteenth-century notation), a key signature of one flat would have had to be added to a piece now in A. Although Byrd was prepared to publish two pieces in A(♭) as late as 1589,[59] Tallis probably felt it unnecessary to introduce an unusual key signature when the pitches of his setting and the chant could both be adjusted by the singers.

Tallis's other solo responds refer more or less clearly to the notes of the chant, but in *Hodie* the plainsong melody is hardly recognizable beyond its first three notes, which contain a falling minor third, and then not in every part. Even in setting the words 'et in terra pax', where it was customary to introduce the chant melody, Tallis did not follow the examples of Cowper, Taverner and Sheppard. For the most part the voices choose their own independent paths throughout the piece, avoiding homophony but clearly outlining a series of underlying chords. The style is close to that of Tallis's four-part Mass. It would be too much to suggest that the whole group of Tallis's solo responds dates from the mid-1540s, but it must be a distinct possibility.

In pace in idipsum has a second verse with a chant adapted from that of the first verse, so it is longer and a little more complex than Tallis's other solo responds:

[58] Frere, ibid., vol. 2, p. 30; Gregorian Institute of Canada, *The Sarum Rite*, tome B, fasc. 6, pp. 293–4 (online at http://www.sarum-chant.ca). See also Roger Bowers, 'To chorus from quartet: the performing resource for English church polyphony, *c.*1390–1559', in John Morehen, ed., *English choral practice, 1400–1650* (Cambridge, 1995), pp. 38–9; reprinted in Bowers, *English church polyphony: singers and sources from the 14th to the 17th century* (Variorum Collected Studies: Aldershot, 1999).

[59] *Memento Domine* and *In resurrectione tua*, both in Byrd's *Liber primus sacrarum cantionum* (1589). The second ends in A(♭), but spends a good deal of time in D(♭); so does Byrd's unpublished *Benigne fac Domine*.

℟ (soloists, *polyphony*) In pace (choir, *plainsong*) in idipsum: dormiam et requiescam.
℣ (soloists, *polyphony*) Si dedero somnum oculis meis: et palpebris meis dormitationem,
℟ (choir, *plainsong*) Dormiam et requiescam.
℣ (soloists, *polyphony*) Gloria Patri et Filio: et Spiritui Sancto.
℟ (choir, *plainsong*) In pace in idipsum: dormiam et requiescam.[60]

(℟ *In peace itself I shall sleep and rest.* ℣ *If I surrender my eyes to slumber, and my eyelids to drowsiness,* ℟ *I shall sleep and rest.* ℣ *Glory to the Father, Son, and the Holy Ghost.*)

While the polyphonic passages add a good deal of ornamentation they often follow the plainsong quite closely, though since the setting is consistently high some adjustment is needed to bring chant and polyphony to the same pitch.[61]

The polyphonic sections of *In pace* are distinguished from those of Tallis's other solo responds in two more ways: single vowels are often sung to many notes, and imitation between the voices is a marked feature. The other solo responds show a tendency to stretch vowels, but the vocal lines of *In pace* at times resemble those in Tallis's votive antiphons, and they include some word-painting. Doe notes that the music is sometimes 'deliberately protracted to suggest somnolence', and that 'dormitationem' has a 'nodding dotted rhythm'. Dependence on imitation is a new development in Tallis's music. It is not yet used fully as a structural element, but it links the piece more closely than his other solo responds with the choral responds which were to follow (see p. 98).

How Tallis gained his knowledge of the imitative style is not fully apparent. No doubt he had access to manuscript copies, now unknown, of music by Continental composers, and quite possibly he had access to printed music, such as Petrucci's editions of Josquin's works (some of these found their way into the library founded by Henry VIII's godson, Henry Fitzalan).[62] Possibly, too, it was easier for Tallis to learn about European developments after he had joined the Chapel Royal than it was before. *In pace* conveys the feeling that he was experimenting with a style he had mastered, but had not long absorbed. There is little tonal variety, and the long 'Si dedero' section is anchored to a C tonality. It is really only in the last polyphonic section, when the two lower voices enter with 'Gloria' for the second time, that a B♭ chord gives sustained emphasis to a new colour.

---

[60] The Sarum breviary directs that when the respond is repeated after the Gloria Patri, 'In pace' should be sung by the chorus.

[61] See Doe, *Tallis*, 2nd edn, pp. 30–31 (where note values are halved).

[62] Henry Fitzalan, 12th Earl of Arundel (1511?–1580). See John Milsom, 'The Nonsuch music library', in Chris Banks and others, eds, *Sundry sorts of music books* (London, 1993), pp. 146–82, at 159–60.

Chapter 3
The Later Years of Henry VIII and the Reign of Edward VI: Biographical and Historical Background

On 12 July 1543 Henry VIII married the twice-widowed Catherine Parr, the sixth and last of his queens.[1] The plague was then rife in London, and the marriage took place at Hampton Court. Stephen Gardiner, the Bishop of Winchester, conducted the ceremony before only a score of people. The new Queen Catherine was a woman of good sense, and during her marriage to the King she behaved kindly towards his children Mary (the daughter of Catherine of Aragon), Elizabeth (the daughter of Anne Boleyn), and Edward (the son of Jane Seymour).

Shortly before the marriage, in February 1542/3, Henry had concluded an agreement with the Emperor Charles V for an attack on France. In July 1544, leaving Queen Catherine as Regent, and Cranmer as head of the Council (which included Thirlby), the King crossed to Calais, and remained in France until Boulogne capitulated in September of the same year. After a continued campaign with no convincing outcome, peace was concluded on 7 June 1546.

In the late summer of 1546 Henry made a progress to palaces within easy reach of London, returned to Whitehall on 3 January, and died there on 28 January. For three days Henry's death was kept from general knowledge, while agreement was reached about the provisions for government under his nine-year-old heir. For the next three years power was to be exercised by the Privy Council, with the newly created Duke of Somerset (Edward Seymour, the young King's uncle) at its head.

Edward's accession was proclaimed on 31 January 1546/7, and preparations were made for the late King's funeral. The Gentlemen and children of the Chapel were among the royal servants and many others for whom cloth was provided to make mourning liveries.[2] On 14 February a procession four miles long set off with Henry's body. The Gentlemen of the Chapel 'hadd allowance of Rydinge Gownes & Cooates in Considerac*i*on they Roode all to wyndesore [with] the Coorse'.[3]

[1] Anne Boleyn (whom Henry married before the annulment of his marriage to Catherine of Aragon) was executed in 1536. He afterwards married Jane Seymour (died in childbed 1537), Anne of Cleves (marriage annulled 1540), and Catherine Howard (executed 1542).

[2] TNA LC2/2; Andrew Ashbee, *Records of English court music* (Snodland, *later* Aldershot, 1986–96), vol. 7, pp. 108–9.

[3] TNA E101/427/6, f.17^{r}; Ashbee, *Records of English court music*, vol. 7, p. 125.

Having remained overnight at Syon, the body was carried to St George's Chapel. There, after Gardiner had celebrated the funeral Mass, it was buried in a grave occupied by the remains of Henry's third queen, Jane, whose son was now King Edward VI.[4]

Scarlet cloth for liveries was issued in preparation for the King's coronation.[5] On 20 February, Edward went in procession from the Tower to Westminster, and 'the bisshops in their pontificalibus & the deane of westm*inste*r w*ith* all the Cannons & singing men of the same / & the subdeane of the king*es* chappell / w*ith* all the nowmbre of the singing [men] of the same … receavid the king*es* ma*ies*tie' at Westminster Hall; and 'all the said singing men from the said halle doore at westm*inste*r / as they wente before in their place & order continualli sange certaine Respondes & Antephons'. The Gentlemen of the Chapel were led by the Subdean, John Donne,[6] because Dean Thirlby was now at the imperial court of Charles V, to which he had been appointed the resident English ambassador in 1545.

When the crowning had taken place, 'The singing men in the quire sange and the orgaines was playde owt very armoniously'. (One account says that 'the quere with the organs dyd syng Te Deum'.) The service continued with 'oblacion made w*ith* breade & wyne', and then 'his grace was hadde againe into his traverse whereat he reaposed hymselfe unto thende of masse / notwithstanding in this meane season / that the pr*e*face and the reste of the masse was solemnie songe'.[7] The subsequent festivities appear to have included a theatrical performance of some kind, in which the new king may have taken part.[8] It was presented by the Gentlemen and children of the Chapel Royal, the latter under their master Richard Bower.

There are signs in the new reign that Tallis had become a well-established figure among the Gentlemen of the Chapel Royal. On 24 August 1549 Richard Pygott, who before entering the Chapel Royal had been master of the choristers in Cardinal Wolsey's chapel, appointed Tallis to be an overseer of his will, together with Thomas Bury and Thomas Byrd.[9] In lists of Gentlemen some newcomers were now listed below Tallis, while subsidy rolls of 1549 and 1551 suggest that, although not among the wealthiest members of the Chapel, he was modestly better

---

4 Charles Wriothesley, *A chronicle of England during the reigns of the Tudors, from A.D. 1485 to 1559* (Camden Society, new series, 11, 20: London, 1875–77), vol. 1, p. 181; TNA, SP10/1/17, ff.71–86; Ashbee, *Records of English court music*, vol. 7, p. 104.

5 TNA LC2/3/1, LC2/3/2; Ashbee, *Records of English court music*, vol. 7, pp. 105–8.

6 For a note on Donne's career, see Andrew Ashbee and David Lasocki, *A biographical dictionary of English court musicians* (Aldershot, 1998), vol. 1, pp. 349–50.

7 BL Additional MS 71009, ff.52^{v}, with a few cropped letters restored; the interpolation in parentheses is from John Gough Nichols, ed., *Literary remains of King Edward the Sixth* (Roxburghe Club: London, 1857), p. ccxcv.

8 Albert Feuillerat, ed., *Documents relating to the revels at court in the time of King Edward VI and Queen Mary (the Loseley manuscripts)* (W. Bang, Materialien zur Kunde des älteren englischen Dramas, 44: Louvain, 1914), p. 256.

9 TNA PROB 11/32, q.42; Ashbee and Lasocki, *A biographical dictionary*, vol. 2, p. 934.

off than several other Gentlemen.[10] His level of responsibility is not clearly stated. His name occurs some way down the list of Gentlemen who received scarlet cloth for the coronation, but some of those named further up the list may have had little or no role in the Chapel's day-to-day affairs. John Fisher died in the coronation year. Henry Stephenson was nearing the end of his life; so, probably, was Robert Okeland. Two others, Pygott and Robert Phillips, did not outlive Edward's reign, and it is uncertain whether Richard Stephens did so. Bury was to die early in Queen Mary's reign, perhaps to be followed by William Barbour. John Allen may have moved to Westminster Abbey.

Neither the experience we may presume Tallis to have had in handling a choir, nor his proficiency as composer and organist, seem to have been shared by Gentlemen such as Thomas Byrd, Robert Perry, William Hutchins, Robert Richmond and Thomas Waite, who lived into the reign of Queen Elizabeth.[11] It looks as if, until the recruitment of John Sheppard late in King Edward's reign, Tallis must have had unique responsibilities, working alongside Richard Bower. John Immyns may have been right when he wrote of Tallis as 'gentleman & Master of the Chappell to K. Henry ye 8th, K. Edward ye 6th, Q. Mary & Q. Elizabeth', though no court document is known to describe him in those terms.[12] What scope there was for Tallis to play the organ in Edward's reign is difficult to say, though its use may have continued at least as long in the Chapel Royal as at St Paul's, where the organ was not silenced until late in 1552.[13]

If Tallis was indeed in charge of the Chapel's music, his task must have been made onerous by a new religious dispensation and consequent changes in the Chapel's work. Archbishop Cranmer, the sole ecclesiastic on the Council, had worked quietly for reform under Henry VIII, but at Edward's coronation he delivered a speech in place of a sermon, pressing him to ensure that idolatry was destroyed and images were removed.[14] A series of directives afterwards conveyed decisions about the manner of worship.[15] In July 1547 the Council banned candles and shrines. Another indication of intent was given when, at Westminster Abbey

---

[10] TNA E179/69/58; E179/69/60; Ashbee, *Records of English court music*, vol. 7, pp. 419, 421.

[11] For all these musicians, see Ashbee and Lasocki, *A biographical dictionary*.

[12] Immyns (1724–64) was appointed lutenist of the Chapel Royal in 1752. He had studied with Pepusch and been his copyist. He founded the Madrigal Society, for which in 1751 he transcribed *Spem in alium* from Egerton MS 3512, adding the above note (Bertram Schofield, 'The manuscripts of Tallis's forty-part motet', *The Musical Quarterly*, vol. 37 (1951), pp. 176–83).

[13] *Chronicle of the Grey Friars of London*, ed. John Gough Nichols (Camden Society, 1st series, 53: London, 1852), p. 75.

[14] John Strype, *Memorials of the most reverend father in God, Thomas Cranmer* (London, 1694), book 2, pp. 144–5.

[15] Walter Howard Frere and William Waugh McClure Kennedy, eds, *Visitation articles and injunctions of the period of the Reformation* (Alcuin Club Collections, 14–16: London, 1910), vol. 2.

on 4 November, the state opening of Parliament and Convocation was marked by the singing in English of the Ordinary of the Mass, excluding the Kyrie.[16] In the following January the familiar ceremonies for Candlemas, Ash Wednesday, Palm Sunday and Good Friday were dispensed with, and in February images in stained-glass, wood and stone were banned. Within a year of Edward's accession royal injunctions imposed the reading in English of the Epistle and Gospel at High Mass, while Compline, 'being a Part of the Evening Prayer, was sang in *English* in the King's Chappel, before any Act of Parliament enjoined it'.[17] An English form of Communion was introduced into the Latin Mass at Easter 1548.[18] Wriothesley recorded that 'in Maye [1548] Poules quire with diuers other parishes in London song all the service in English, both mattens, masse, and even-songe', and 'The xiith daie of Maie, 1548, King Henrie the seauenth aniversarie was kept at Westminster, the masse song all in English, with the consecration of the sacrament also spoken in English', besides other changes.[19]

These events underline the facts that the Reformation had been taking place in England throughout Tallis's adult life, and that an English liturgy had grown up piecemeal.[20] *The primer* of 1545 was not the first primer to contain English forms of Matins, Evensong, the Litany, and other texts which were absorbed into the Books of Common Prayer, but it was issued with the approval of Henry VIII.[21] It was in English, he explained, 'for that our people and subjectes which have no understa*n*dyng in the Latin tong and yet have the knowledge of readyng, may praye in their vulgare tong, which is to them best knowen: that by the meane therof they shuld be the more provoked to true devotion, and the better set their heartes upon those thinges that they pray for'. The King's injunction introducing *The primer* said that children should 'customably & ordinarily use the same untyl they be of co*m*petent understa*n*dyng and knowledge to perceyve it in Latin. At what tyme they may at their libertie either use this Prymer in Englishe, or that whiche is by oure authorytie likewyse made in the Latyn tong, in all poinctes correspondent unto this in Englishe'. It was ordered that no other primer, English or Latin, should afterwards be used.

There was no corresponding guidance about the provision of music. Royal injunctions issued generally in the first year of King Edward's reign said no more than that, before High Mass, the priests and choir should 'kneel in the midst of

16 Wriothesley, *A chronicle of England*, vol. 1, p. 187.

17 John Strype, *Historical memorials, chiefly ecclesiastical ... under King Henry VIII, King Edward VI and Queen Mary the First* (London, 1721), vol. 2, part 1, p. 25.

18 *The order of the Communion, 1548. A facsimile of the British Museum copy C.25, f.15*, ed. H. A. Wilson (Henry Bradshaw Society, 34: London, 1908).

19 Wriothesley, *A chronicle of England*, vol. 2, p. 2.

20 See Walter Howard Frere, 'Edwardine vernacular services before the first Prayer Book', *The Journal of Theological Studies*, vol. 1 (1899–1900), pp. 229–46.

21 A concise account of its history is given by Diarmaid MacCulloch in *Thomas Cranmer: a life* (New Haven, 1996), pp. 334–6.

the church, and sing or say plainly and distinctly the Litany which is set forth in English, with all the suffrages following'. Advice for particular institutions added little or nothing. Royal injunctions prepared for Lincoln Cathedral were more explicit only in requiring anthems to be sung 'with a plain and distinct note for every syllable one'.[22] Somerset, the Lord Protector, who had been empowered to act with or without the advice of the Privy Council, was led to write to the vice-chancellors and heads of colleges of the universities about religious observances. His letter to Cambridge, dated 4 September 1548, said that 'untill suche time as an ordre bee taken and prescribed by his highnes ... to be univ*er*sallie kept through out the hole roialme or by visitours of his highnes', services should 'use one uniforme ordre, ryte and ceremonyes in the masse / matens / and Evensonge and all dyvine service in the same to be saide or songe such as is presentlie used in the king*es* ma*ie*s*t*ies Chappell and none other'.[23]

Temporary arrangements were superseded by the English services set out in *The Booke of the Common Prayer and administracion of the sacramentes*. In 1548/9 the first Edwardian Act of Uniformity required the new form of worship to be used everywhere by the following Whitsunday (9 June).[24] Not everything had gone smoothly during the Act's passage through Parliament. At the third reading of the Uniformity Bill in January, Thirlby – recalled from his post of ambassador in 1548 – had voted against it, and before the Act came into force his name was sent to a heresy commission. In February 1549/50 the Privy Council decided to abolish his Westminster diocese, though he remained the Dean of the Chapel Royal. He also continued to be engaged in government business, and in April was made Bishop of Norwich (a diocese he visited infrequently). He was not sent back to Brussels until April 1553.

Another statute of 1549 banned a range of books, including those which, at King Henry's death, had been in the vestry of the Chapel Royal (see p. 16). It did away with antiphoners, missals, grails, processionals, manuals (setting out forms to be observed in adminstering the sacraments), legends (saints' lives), pies (rules for dealing with more than one office on a single day), porteouses (portable breviaries), primers in Latin or English, couchers (desktop breviaries), journals (diurnals) and ordinals (setting out the ritual order of the liturgy).[25]

---

22 Frere and Kennedy, *Visitation articles*, vol. 2, pp. 124, 168.

23 Corpus Christi College, Cambridge, MS 106, p. 493c–d (available at http://www.parkerweb.stanford.edu).

24 2 & 3 Edward VI, c. 1. The Act permitted 'anye man that understandeth the Greke Latten and Hebrewe tongue, or other straunge tongue, to saye and have saide' the prayers of Matins and Evensong 'in Latten or anye suche other tongue, sayinge the same privatelie as they doe understande'. The use of those languages was also permitted in the chapels of Oxford and Cambridge Universities, 'The holie Co*mm*unyon commonly called the Mass excepted'.

25 3 & 4 Edward VI, c. 10. The original, in the Parliamentary Archives, reveals that in *Statutes of the realm* (London, 1810), 'scrayles' is a misreading of 'Grayles'.

John Merbecke's *The Booke of Common Praier noted* (that is, set to music) was published in 1550 by Richard Grafton, the King's printer. It may have had some official backing, since the committee which completed the first Prayer Book met at Windsor Castle, where Merbecke was a lay clerk and organist of St George's Chapel. The book contained simple plainchant for 'so muche of the order of Common prayer as is to be song in Churches', while omitting the Litany which had been printed with music in 1544. Merbecke's book contained adaptations of Sarum chants, and freshly composed chants influenced by traditional models, but parts of it soon became obsolete. The Prayer Book of 1549 had been a compromise, and Cranmer was not alone among the reformers in feeling dissatisfied with it. A new Prayer Book was prepared and was ready in the spring of 1552, though publication was delayed almost until its exclusive use became mandatory on All Saints' Day (1 November), as required by a second Act of Uniformity.[26]

Apart from differences of theological significance, the two Edwardian Prayer Books appear superficially to have differed in the attention they gave to music, though this may be the result of accidental variations of little real importance. The first Prayer Book envisaged the clerks singing at several points during Communion, while the second specifically mentioned only 'Glorye bee to God on hyghe' as words to be 'sayd or song'. Before the Te Deum at Matins (1549) or Morning Prayer (1552) both permitted the singing of lessons 'in such places where they doe syng', though to a plain tune 'after the manner of distinct reading'.

The second Prayer Book did not last long on its first introduction. King Edward died on 6 July 1553, after an illness lasting for several months. Mourning liveries were provided for more than 20 adult singers and 12 children of the Chapel Royal – which, regardless of the religious and musical changes that had taken place during Edward's short reign, was still as large as it had been at the death of Henry VIII. Mourning was supplied as well for the singing men and boys of Westminster Abbey, where Cranmer presided over the King's burial on 8 August.[27]

---

26 5 & 6 Edw VI, c 1.

27 TNA LC2/4/1, f.17$^{r–v}$; E101/427/6, ff.18^{r}, 28^{r}; Ashbee, *Records of English court music*, vol. 7, pp. 127–9.

Chapter 4
The Later Years of Henry VIII and the Reign of Edward VI: Music with English Words

The letter Somerset sent to the universities in 1548 (see p. 61) assumed a knowledge of what went on in the Chapel Royal. Whether there was any justification for the assumption is far from sure. Guesses about the music sung by the members of King Edward's Chapel must be based on very general descriptions, or on what is known to have been available. That includes Cranmer's Litany, and the chants published by Merbecke, the latter representing the kind of adaptation which have been necessary more often than surviving sources reveal. Use was no doubt made also of existing or freshly composed choral music, with words drawn from the new services or supplementing them in an acceptable way. Three sources in particular illustrate mid-sixteenth-century English-texted music for groups of singers, and Tallis makes appearances in each of them.

The 'Lumley' partbooks, a collection of music from King Edward's reign and before, were compiled by a number of scribes over the period *c.*1547–*c.*1552.[1] They belonged to Henry Fitzalan, Earl of Arundel, whose library was merged after 1552 with that of his son-in-law John, Baron Lumley. The first pieces copied into them were simple and largely anonymous, and included numerous settings of psalms. The books contain two pieces by Tallis: *Remember not* and a Benedictus.

The largest body of Edwardian sacred pieces is contained in the 'Wanley' partbooks, a set in which, after it had passed through the hands of several previous owners, the Earl of Oxford's librarian, Humfrey Wanley, wrote his name in 1715.[2] They are thought to have been compiled *c.*1548–50, but seem to have been little used. The contents range from the simple to the complex, and display a wide array of influences, styles and techniques, old and new. They also include some adaptations: two Communion settings in English, for example, are based on Masses by Taverner. Their modern editor has noted that in many cases composers

---

1 BL MSS Royal Appendix 74–6 (bass book missing); Judith Blezzard, ed., *The Tudor church music of the Lumley books* (Recent Researches in the Music of the Renaissance, 65: Madison, Wis., 1985).

2 Oxford, Bodleian Library, Mus. Sch. e.420–22 (tenor book missing); James Wrightson, ed., *The Wanley manuscripts* (Recent researches in the music of the Renaissance, 99–101: Madison, Wisc., 1995); contents listed in Peter le Huray, *Music and the Reformation in England 1549–1660* (London, 1967; rev. Cambridge, 1978), pp. 173–5.

'clearly made textual audibility a priority'.[3] Tallis is represented by two pieces: *Hear the voice and prayer*, and *If ye love me*.

Another set of partbooks, which John Day started printing in 1560 as *Certaine notes set forth in foure and three parts*, was completed in 1565 with the new title *Mornyng and euenyng prayer and communion*. (The earlier title was attached only to the bassus book, and abandoned before printing was finished. The revised title will be used in what follows.) Although the set was printed in the 1560s it contains much music that is plainly Edwardian.[4] Chapel Royal composers such as Robert Okeland and Thomas Causton (or Caustun, an Edwardian yeoman of the vestry, who became a Gentleman of the Chapel in Queen Mary's reign) were responsible for a number of the pieces in Day's collection. It contains four of Tallis's pieces: the two which are in the 'Wanley' books, plus *Lord in thee is all my trust* and *Remember not*. Yet, while Day included a good many settings of English liturgical texts, none was by Tallis. Can it really be that he wrote nothing of this kind in King Edward's reign? That is a question which will arise again in connection with his Short Service (see p. 82).

The handful of Tallis's pieces in the three sources mentioned seems a very small output for a leading composer, even allowing for the occurrence of other pieces elsewhere; but his full contribution to the Chapel's Edwardian repertoire may not be readily apparent. It is notable that, of the composers named by Day, only Tallis is given the title 'M[aster]', probably in recognition of his senior post in the Chapel Royal.[5] If he was obliged by supervisory duties in the Chapel to ensure that new music was written, and that existing music was adapted to satisfy new needs, he would have exerted a considerable and widespread influence on the creation of an Anglican style and body of works without his part in the task being fully evident from pieces bearing his name. On the other hand, although he may have owed his position partly to a capacity for organization and leadership,

---

3 Wrightson, *The Wanley manuscripts*, vol. 1, introduction. See also James Wrightson, *The 'Wanley' manuscripts: a critical commentary* (Outstanding Dissertations in Music from British Universities: New York, 1989).

4 Howard M. Nixon, 'Day's *Service Book*, 1560–1565', *British Library Journal*, vol. 10 (1984), pp. 1–31; John Aplin, 'The origins of John Day's "Certaine notes"', *Music & Letters*, vol. 62 (1981), pp. 295–9.

5 Byrd is similarly singled out by Morley, in his list of composers who would not have dreamed of writing 'two perfect cordes of one kind together' (Thomas Morley, *A plaine and easie introduction to practicall musicke* (London, 1597), p. 151). Morley's usage elsewhere in his book is variable, however. The titles bestowed upon composers in sixteenth-century sources are mentioned in Roger Bray, 'Music and the quadrivium in early Tudor England', *Music & Letters*, vol. 76 (1995), pp. 1–18, at 11: in the Gyffard partbooks, 'in addition to those with degrees, *informatores choristarum* and Gentlemen of the Chapel Royal appear to qualify for the title "master"'. (Note, however, that the date proposed for the compilation of the Gyffard partbooks is now 'the second decade of Elizabeth's reign' (David Mateer, 'The Gyffard partbooks: composers, owners, date and provenance', [*Royal Musical Association*] *Research Chronicle*, vol. 28 (1995), pp. 21–50, at 40).

his reputation sprang from his response as a composer to the musical demands of the time. There is much to ponder in Davitt Moroney's perceptive remark that 'He rose to pre-eminence in English musical life with the introduction of the new Protestant liturgy'.[6]

The loss of the breviary, missal, and other books banned by the statute of 1549 (see p. 61), was paralleled by the loss of familiar chants, liturgical texts and practices, even though many continued to exist in new guises. These things had not only provided a context and material for the composition and performance of music for the Sarum rite, but had imposed form on much of it. The need for a fresh start stimulated new developments, and in searching for a way forward Tallis must often have felt, like Haydn in a later century, that he was forced by circumstances to become original.

Composers writing for the late Henrician and the Edwardian church could not, of course, ignore what had been written before. What they produced was bound to reflect their experience of composing and performing music for the Sarum rite and its related ceremonies. It also included elements of the English song tradition, both religious and secular. The grouping of voices was still a valid way of building structures and distinguishing one section of a work from another. So was the contrast of counterpoint and homophony, though the latter might be used more often than in the past. Passages might still be repeated for musical reasons, and the loss of texts which demanded repetition may have encouraged the use of repetitive patterns borrowed from secular sources.[7] Such means remained a necessity in the formation of musical structures until composers hit on new ways of integrating long stretches of counterpoint, and introduced an imaginative use of tonal logic into the shaping of their works.

On the whole, many of the compositional problems Tallis encountered were not radically different from those he had faced in setting Latin texts, and he could use methods which had already proved successful. It was their application to different texts which produced different patterns. The continuity is clear in a piece such as *Blessed are those* (see p. 73). At first glance it is surprising – even astonishing – for a work like the Short Service to have issued from the pen of a composer who, earlier in his career, found in the text of *Salve intemerata* the inspiration for a piece of such a different kind. Yet the emphasis sometimes placed on apparent changes in Tallis's style during his long career is not altogether justified. His style evolved rather than altering course, and the quality of his output was maintained. Each of his pieces for the new church, no matter how simple, is well constructed and imbued with an individual character. All possess musical form and musical interest. As a group they exhibit a remarkable variety, and show how much

---

6 Davitt Moroney, 'Under fower sovereigns: Thomas Tallis and the transformation of English polyphony' (Doctoral thesis, University of California, Berkeley, 1980), p. 22.

7 See John Milsom, 'Songs, carols and *contrafacta* in the early history of the Tudor anthem', *Proceedings of the Royal Musical Association*, vol. 107 (1980–81), pp. 34–45.

freedom could be exercised in interpreting the injunction to write music allowing words to be 'understanded and perceived'.

In compiling *Mornyng and euenyng prayer and communion* Day attempted – perhaps with the assistance of an anonymous editor (possibly Causton), but without complete success – to separate settings of words for the English liturgy from pieces that can loosely be described as devotional songs. Manuscript sources, which could be supplemented as new music came to hand, are naturally less likely to make these distinctions. It is in any case often hard to see where the difference lies between liturgical and non-liturgical compositions, except in the origins and natures of their texts, and sometimes in the forces needed to perform them. The fine – or non-existent – distinction between the music of a devotional song and that of a secular song is evident in the case of *Fond youth is a bubble*, which may easily have had religious words before it acquired others known only from Mulliner's title (see p. 87). In the following paragraphs the headings 'Anthems' and 'Music for the English liturgy' are used, but it is simply to bring order to what could otherwise be a rambling discussion.

Anthems

'Anthem' had no precisely limited meaning in Tallis's time.[8] As the cognate of 'antiphon' the word was in common use long before the middle of the sixteenth century. Chaucer referred to the antiphon *Alma redemptoris mater* as an anthem, a word he did not use elsewhere.[9] At St Mary-at-Hill the custom in the fifteenth century was for an 'Antempne of owre ladye' to be sung at evensong on Christmas Day when all those wearing surplices entered the choir of the church in procession, carrying candles; and in 1529–30 the church paid for five 'prykked song bok*es*' (presumably partbooks) containing Masses and five containing 'Antemys'.[10] For the most part the Prayer Books avoided the word (but see p. 75), and it was scarcely used in royal injunctions other than to indicate what was or was not forbidden.[11] It is not clear whether this was a deliberate attempt to avoid a term suggesting 'antiphon', though the once popular singing of antiphons in praise of the saints,

[8] Most of the pieces treated here as anthems were edited by Leonard Ellinwood in Thomas Tallis, *English sacred music: I. Anthems* (Early English Church Music, 12: London, 1971, rev. Paul Doe 1973), but he included *Christ rising again* in *English sacred music: II. Service music* (Early English Church Music, 13: London, 1971, rev. Paul Doe 1974).

[9] *Prioress's Tale*, lines 641, 655, 660.

[10] Henry Littlehales, ed., *The medieval records of a London city church (St Mary at Hill) A.D. 1420–1559* (Early English Text Society, original series, 125, 128: London, 1904–05), pp. 16, 351.

[11] Walter Howard Frere and William Waugh McClure Kennedy, eds, *Visitation articles and injunctions of the period of the Reformation* (Alcuin Club Collections, 14–16: London, 1910), vol. 2, pp. 151, 154.

usually in Latin, was now strongly discouraged. English songs in praise of Christ, or settings of biblical texts, were a different matter.

The singing of 'an hymn, or such-like song', at the beginning or end of common prayers, was recognized as acceptable by royal injunctions issued in 1559 (see p. 155), and is assumed to have been permitted in King Edward's reign. 'Hymn' was used in the general sense of 'a song in praise of God', but other terms were employed as well, and seldom with much exactness. In *Mornyng and euenyng prayer and communion*, settings of texts for the services named are followed by pieces labelled 'Prayer' or 'Anthem', though the distinction seems arbitrary. Tallis's *Hear the voice and prayer*, called 'A prayer' in *Mornyng and euenyng prayer*, is called 'Antem' in the Wanley partbooks. His *Remember not, O Lord God* is 'The Anthem' in *Mornyng and euenyng prayer*, but it is 'A prayer' in *The whole psalmes in foure partes*, printed by Day in 1563.

Remember not, O Lord God has a psalm text which, as 'The antheme', follows the seven penitential psalms in *The primer* of 1545. *The primer*'s translation accounts for the phrases 'World without end' and 'So be it' tacked on to the end. 'So be it' often appears in primer texts, but was replaced by 'Amen' in later versions of *Remember not*. The piece was the first by Tallis to be entered, anonymously, in the Lumley partbooks, where it is mistitled 'Ne reminiscaris'. ('Ne reminiscaris' is the incipit of the antiphon traditionally recited alongside the Penitential Psalms. The words of *Remember not* are adapted from Psalm 79 (Vulgate 78), verses 8–10 and 14. In Latin, verse 8 begins 'Ne memineris'.) A longer version of *Remember not* – presumably, though not provably, the result of a subsequent expansion – also exists, as a sizeable work requiring a divided choir. The Anglican church may have given up the use of Latin in its services, but it did not entirely dismiss theatricality.[12]

The first setting has affinities with Tudor English-language hymns. Although it has a prose text, the opening words, 'Remember not, O Lord God, our old iniquities', enabled Tallis to set them (with 'Lord' prolonged in three of the voices) as though they are in common metre (alternate lines of four and three iambic feet), and the rest of the text is often set with groups of syllables sung rapidly, so that in spite of inevitable cross-rhythms the music preserves suggestions of an underlying iambic metre. Tallis's intentions can be obscured by the insertion of modern bar lines. In its earliest form *Remember not* also has affinities with Henrician part songs. Short repeated passages ending the three main sections may be relics of a part song ancestry, and the piece could well have been copied as a devotional piece for domestic performance.

---

[12] The word 'anthem' continued to be associated with the idea, if not necessarily the practice, of antiphonal singing, cf. Johannes Boemus, *The fardle of facions*, trans. William Waterman (London, 1555), 'Of Asia', XII: 'The Anthemes (which Ambrose, Bysshoppe of Millayne wrate, and endited) Damasus put ordre that the quiere should sing side aftre side'; Henry Cockeram, *The English dictionarie: or interpreter of hard English words* (London, 1623): '*Anthemne*, a Song which Church-men sing by course one after another'.

The piece is a four-part harmonization, very largely homophonic, of a tune placed in the highest part but below the treble range.[13] Though simple, the tune has some characteristics of Tallis's more fully developed melodies, rising and falling and with carefully placed peaks. Awareness of the words' meaning is evident in the exclamations 'Help us, help us God' and 'Where is their God?', both made prominent by starting on the high C otherwise reserved for the penultimate phrase 'world without end'. Sensitivity to the drama of the words he set was hardly likely to fail Tallis in the atmosphere of the Reformation, when the authority of church tradition was replaced by the authority of the scriptures.

Remember not is generally in the transposed A mode. The harmonies are uncomplicated, often with the root note doubled, and the tonal range is limited, but a distinct character is imparted by harmonic procedures involving the customary sharpening of certain notes, and by frequent minor chords on G. Strict modality was probably not in Tallis's mind any more than it was in the minds of contemporaries who wrote (or improvised) keyboard music built on sequences of chords, but the sound of *Remember not* conjures up a world which in some respects was still mediaeval.

The expanded version of *Remember not* appears in three different guises in Elizabethan sources.[14] It is without words in the Mulliner Book, a keyboard anthology compiled round about 1560.[15] On the cover, in the compiler's hand, is the inscription 'Sum liber thomae mullineri iohanne heywoode teste'. Since Heywood lived in London, where he held posts at court and St Paul's Cathedral, it is unlikely that the inscription was made until after 1557–58, a period when Mulliner was probably a clerk at Magdalen College, Oxford; but it must have been made before Heywood went abroad in 1564, the year in which Mulliner was appointed 'modulator organum' at Corpus Christi College, Oxford.[16] Heywood's connections may have enabled Mulliner to collect many pieces by composers who worked, or had worked, at the Chapel Royal and St Paul's.

Another expanded version of *Remember not* was first printed in Day's *Mornyng and euenyng* prayer, begun in 1560.[17] A shorter expanded version was printed by Day in *The whole psalmes in foure partes* (1563). The essential sound quality of

---

13 John Aplin connects it with a type of faburden: see ' "The fourth kind of faburden": the identity of an English four-part style', *Music & Letters*, vol. 61 (1980), pp. 245–65, at 248, 261.

14 It is of course possible that the Lumley version is an abridgement of a longer original, as John Milson says in 'Tallis's first and second thoughts', *Journal of the Royal Musical Association*, vol. 113 (1988), pp. 203–22, at 218; but it seems improbable.

15 BL Additional MS 30513, ff.49^{v}–50^{v}; John Caldwell, ed., *The Mulliner Book, newly transcribed and edited* (*Musica Britannica*, 1: London, 2011), pp. 65–6.

16 See Jane Flynn, 'Thomas Mulliner: an apprentice of John Heywood?', in Susan Boynton and Eric Rice, eds, *Young choristers 650–1700* (Woodbridge, 2008), pp. 173–94.

17 A version of *Remember not* which appears to relate to the version in *Mornyng and euenyng prayer*, but which includes features perhaps acquired in transmission or performance, is in BL Additional MS 29289, ff.92^{v}–93^{r} (pencil numbering; originally

the Wanley original is unchanged in these versions, though the voice ranges are slightly increased, and some passages appear to have been allocated to one side of the choir or the other. Tallis's polyphonic skill is held severely in check, apart from the decoration of cadences. There is no hint of the tonal adventurousness exhibited in his later works with Latin texts.

The three expansions are clearly related. The one in *Mornyng and euenyng prayer* is the longest, and contains passages omitted by the Mulliner Book and *The whole psalmes*. John Caldwell has noted that the omitted passages are those which, in *Mornyng and euenyng prayer*, seem to be intended for either the decani or cantoris side of the choir alone. Mulliner omits passages for one side, and *The whole psalmes* omits passages for the other side.[18] Both Mulliner and *The whole psalmes* omit two more phrases of Day's version (bars 80–85 of no. 43a in Caldwell's edition of the Mulliner Book). It is odd that in *The whole psalmes* Day should have included an evidently incomplete version of something he had printed in full three years earlier, but he may have thought the long version unsuitable for his intended market.

There can be no certain explanation of why there were different expanded versions, but it is conceivable that Tallis first extended *Remember not* for the Edwardian Chapel Royal. If so, there were probably different sets of partbooks for the cantoris and decani sides of the choir. It may be that the two sets of books were disposed of during Queen Mary's reign, were separated, and became the sources of subsequent incomplete copies. The longest version of the anthem, printed by Day, could represent a final revision made for the Elizabethan Chapel Royal or for printed publication, though the possibility that it is pre-Elizabethan cannot be ruled out.

The Wanley partbooks (*c.*1548–50) contain two of Tallis's pieces which were printed by Day. ***Hear the voice and prayer*** has words apparently adapted from the Great Bible of 1539,[19] and set – like those of a Benedictus by Tallis in the Lumley partbooks (see p. 77) – for four adult voices. Although the anthem is of more modest proportions, it is written in an imitative counterpoint which also links it with the Benedictus. In the second section this reaches a carefully contrived climax that gains strength from being repeated. The repetition adds a certain weight and creates a musical form. It also suggests that a search for the parentage of the piece might lead 'by way of the part song to mid-Tudor taste for foreign music in general and the chanson in particular'.[20] But it recalls besides (or, rather, looks forward to)

101^{v}–102^{r}). The manuscript is an altus partbook dated and signed '1629: A[drian] Batten' on f.110^{r} (pencil numbering).

[18] Caldwell, *The Mulliner Book*, p. 246. The passages which are repeated in the Lumley books are not lost in later versions, but are no longer repeated.

[19] I Kings 8:28–30 in the Authorized Version (where the translation is markedly different).

[20] John Milsom, 'English polyphonic style in transition: a study of the sacred music of Thomas Tallis' (Doctoral thesis, Oxford University, 1983), vol. 1, p. 13. See also John Milsom, 'Songs, carols and *contrafacta*', pp. 34–45.

the repetitions in some of Tallis's choral responds – pieces from which, in terms of polyphonic style, *Hear the voice and prayer* is no distance at all.

If ye love me is again for four adult voices, and its words are again from the Great Bible.[21] The translation became the Whit Sunday gospel reading in the 1549 *Book of Common Prayer*, but Tallis's setting was quite possibly earlier, and may have been intended simply for recreational singing. It begins homophonically, but soon continues contrapuntally. Although shorter and less ambitious than *Hear the voice and prayer*, it has a repeated second section reminiscent of many part songs.[22] There is in fact an anonymous part song with words beginning 'If ye love me', probably dating from the reign of Henry VIII.[23]

O Lord, in thee is all my trust is among several of Tallis's anthems not preserved in Edwardian sources, but it was included in *Mornyng and euenyng prayer* and may belong to the same period as the anthems already discussed.[24] The three eight-line verses of the anonymous text all have the same music. Day also printed the first stanza, with Tallis's harmonization, in *The whole psalmes in four partes* (1562). Earlier that year, in *The whole booke of psalmes*, he had printed the unharmonized tune with no attribution. But there is no evidence that Tallis harmonized an existing tune, and its quality argues that it is his.[25] The title-page of *The whole booke of psalmes* makes clear that Day expected the contents to be sung in domestic music-making, since they were 'Very mete to be vsed of all sortes of people priuately for their solace & comfort, laying apart all vngodly songes and ballades, which tende only to the norishing of vyce, and corrupting of youth'.

Tallis's tune remained popular over a long period, and was printed with other harmonizations. Unusually among Tallis's anthems, it is in triple time, and the tune suggests a rather elegant dance. Simple as it is, it is a work of more than ordinary competence. It starts with a series of peaks rising successively from *e′* to *g′* before it descends to *d′*. A second series rising from *a′* to *c″* is followed by another descent to *d′*. Tallis includes chords on every note of the scale, and adds rhythmic variety by making sure that the lower voices are not always in step with the tune (Example 4.1).

21 John 14:15–17.

22 On the repeats in Tallis's anthems in ABB form, see John Morehen, 'The "Burden of proof": the editor as detective, in John Morehen, ed., *English choral practice, 1400–1650* (Cambridge, 1995), pp. 200–20, at 201–2.

23 The source is a bass partbook: TNA, SP1/246, ff.18^{r}–32^{v} (printed numbers). See also *Letters and papers, foreign and domestic of the reign of Henry VIII ... Addenda. Vol. I. Part II* (London, 1932), p. 614, no.1880.

24 *Mornyng and Euenyng Prayer* does not indicate the repetition of the final bars shown in other sources.

25 Nicholas Temperley has written that *O Lord in thee is all my trust* 'is striking in its emotional intensity by comparison with the almost uniform dullness of the average English psalm tune of the time', and 'may well have been composed by Tallis' (Grove Music Online, art. 'Hymn', 2).

Example 4.1 *O Lord, in thee is all my trust*

continued

Example 4.1 *concluded*

Some anthems by Tallis do not appear in the either the Wanley or Lumley partbooks, and were not printed by Day. Two have survived without all their parts. Only the treble of ***Teach me thy way*** is extant, in a partbook of *c.*1570.[26] Other pieces in the partbook are Tallis's *O Lord, give thy holy spirit*, with a text not published until 1566, and his *Verily, verily*, which looks like an Elizabethan work,[27] but *Teach me thy way* might arguably be Edwardian. The text (part of Psalm 86) is derived from the Great Bible and, judging from the music we have, the setting may have included both homophonic and contrapuntal passages, and a repeated second section.

The single source of *Teach me thy way* also contains the treble of ***A new commandment give I unto you***.[28] The second alto and tenor are supplied by seventeenth-century sources, but the bass is missing. Like *Teach me thy way* it may be as early, or almost as early, as Tallis's pieces in the Wanley books. It is apparently intended for adult voices;[29] and its words (from John 13) were probably taken from the Great Bible (which in this passage hardly differs from Tyndale's prior translation). Most syllables are sung to one note, though there is little attempt to align the words of different voices or to avoid word repetition.

[26] BL Additional MS 15166.

[27] See p. 161 for these pieces.

[28] A setting of *I give you a new commandment*, which Mulliner attributed to Tallis, is by Sheppard.

[29] Its low written pitch caused Ellinwood to transpose it a fourth upwards (Tallis, *English sacred music: I*, pp. 19–24).

Homophony is confined to very short passages at the beginning and end. The extant voices show that after the first eight semibreves the piece embarks on continuous and highly imitative polyphony, the first half of which is repeated with different words (beginning 'By this shall ev'ry man know'). Tallis's concern for proportion is evident even in a short span, since he divides each half of the polyphonic section into three shorter sections (identified by their own points), roughly 1:1:2 in length. The last point includes a high B♭, heard before but now used to emphasize the word 'love', sung and repeated by the two alto voices.

Blessed are those that be undefiled is unusual among Tallis's anthems. It is set for five voices, although four was the number most common in early Anglican music, and the number for which John Day, who must have had a sense of what would sell, printed many pieces. That may be why *Blessed are those*, which has claims to be Edwardian, seems at first not to have been widely copied. The earliest sources – where it appears in the company of five- and six-part pieces of the mid-sixteenth-century or before – are Elizabethan, and probably none was started before the 1570s.[30]

Blessed are those has words taken from Psalm 119. In the 1549 Prayer Book, but not subsequent Prayer Books, verses 1–8 of the psalm were prescribed as the Introit at Communion on the first Sunday after Trinity. Tallis's setting omits verses 7–8, while including the doxology. The Prayer Book translation, which is more or less the one set by Tallis, was drawn with minor adaptations from the Great Bible. Both the Great Bible and the Prayer Book preserved the Latin title 'Beati immaculati', familiar from the Vulgate ('Beati inmaculati'). A treble partbook from Ludlow similarly heads the piece 'beati in maculati in via', but there is no need to suppose that it was adapted from a setting of the Latin text.[31] Nine years into Queen Elizabeth's reign, a table at the end of Matthew Parker's *The whole psalter* would give Latin incipits for all the psalms.

In length *Blessed are those* compares with the expanded version of *Remember not*, though the way in which its voices are grouped suggests that it was planned from the outset as a long piece. The grouping seems to owe something to Taverner's antiphons *O Christe Jesu* (perhaps written by 1530) and *Mater Christi* (which was circulating by about 1540). *Blessed are those* and *Mater Christi* occur together in one source,[32] almost as if to exemplify the connection between pieces labelled 'anthem' and 'antiphon'. Sometimes the continuity is very clear. Like Taverner,

---

30 Listed in Tallis, ibid., p. 123.

31 Shropshire Archives, LB15/1/226, formerly 356 Mus. MS 2, dated *c.*1570–*c.*1610 in Alan Smith, 'Elizabethan church music at Ludlow', *Music & Letters*, vol. 49 (1968), pp. 108–21, at 118. A Latin incipit makes adaptation from a previous Latin setting no more likely than in the case of *Remember not*, and there is nothing to support the suggestion in le Huray, *Music and the Reformation*, pp. 194–5, that *Blessed are those* was adapted from a setting of the Latin text.

32 Bodleian Library MSS Tenbury 354–8.

Tallis recalls an older antiphon style by beginning with a passage for two voices, as he had in *Salve intemerata*, a work which occurs immediately before *Mater Christi* in the Peterhouse books. Yet, while Tallis follows Taverner in contrasting the voices of boys and men, he also reverts to his own practice in the first two verses of *Ave dei patris filia*, where the contratenor often sings with the two upper voices or the two lower voices. Although there were occasions when Tallis left a large vertical space between a high and a low voice, when they were the only ones singing (for instance, in the 'Benedicta tu in mulieribus' passage of *Ave rosa sine spinis*), he frequently preferred to write for adjacent voices. Characteristic melodic shapes discernible in *Blessed are those* are another recollection of Tallis's early antiphons, although in the later piece most syllables are sung to only one note.

Almost all of *Blessed are those* is written in a loosely imitative counterpoint free from much elaboration, though Tallis is careful about the placing of short homophonic passages: one serves, for instance, to introduce the doxology before imitation creates a climactic ending. Tonality plays little part in the structure, and most of the prominent cadences are formed on C. The fundamental element is the grouping of voices, and it relates closely to the sense of the words. This was how Tallis dealt with long texts in his early antiphons, and it serves as a reminder that dealing with his Latin-texted music and English-texted music in separate chapters is not a musical necessity, but only an authorial convenience.

The sections sometimes overlap, but they form a well-defined pattern (Table 4.1). The first four use all the voice combinations found elsewhere in the piece. Nine similar sections make up the rest of the anthem. In eight of them, the combinations

Table 4.1 Voice combinations in *Blessed are those*

Combination		Voices (highest to lowest)
A	'Blessed are those'	1, 2
B	'Blessed are they'	1, 2, 3
C	'Blessed are they'	3, 4, 5
D	'For they who do no wickedness'	1, 2, 3, 4, 5
B	'Thou hast charged'	1, 2, 3
C	'Thou hast charged'	3, 4, 5
A	'O that our ways'	1, 2
C	'O that our ways'	3, 4, 5
A	'That we might keep'	1, 2
C	'That we might keep'	3, 4, 5
B	'So shall we not'	1, 2, 3
D	'Glory to the Father'	1, 2, 3, 4, 5

form a reversible sequence. They are followed, like the three sections which begin the piece, by a section for all five voices.

A five-part setting of ***Christ rising again–Christ is risen again*** is attributed in separate sources to both Tallis and Byrd. The composite text[33] is one which the 1548 Prayer Book included among the 'proper Psalmes and Lesssons' as an 'anthem' (in this instance the word *was* used) to be 'solemnly sung or said' before the morning service on Easter Day. The Prayer Books of 1552 and 1559 turned it into an anthem which replaced Psalm 95 during the morning service on Easter Day. Probably there is no significance to the omission of 'Alleluia' after each section of the text in the later Prayer Books.

The text was set by several Tudor and later composers. A setting for consort and two voices, sometimes expanding to chorus, was printed by Byrd in his *Songs of sundrie natures* (1589), and there are variant manuscript versions of this setting.[34] The setting attributed to both Byrd and Tallis is quite different. In one set of partbooks books it is anonymous.[35] It is attributed to Tallis in the index of a late seventeenth-century organ book at Berkeley,[36] but to Byrd in the 'Chirk' partbooks.[37] The attribution in the latter might well be due to the entry of the piece immediately after the setting which is certainly Byrd's. Many of the ascriptions in the partbooks are accurate, but a number are questionable.[38] Those in the organ book appear on the whole to be more accurate, which lends support to the idea that *Christ rising* may in fact be by Tallis. At any rate, it seems most improbable that the piece is by Byrd. In his edition of Byrd's anthems Craig Monson rejected its ascription to him on account of its 'strict imitative symmetries', and the 'clear separation of imitative paragraphs and the static tonality'.[39] It would be hard to disagree with that judgement, and the organ book may be right.[40]

---

33 From Romans vi.9–11 and I Corinthians xv.20–22.

34 William Byrd, *The English anthems*, ed. Craig Monson (The Byrd edition, 11: London, 1983), pp. 219–21.

35 New York Public Library, Drexel 4180–85, compiled by John Merro (*c*.1615–30), a singing man at Gloucester Cathedral. The piece is reported by the EECM Primary Source Database also to appear in a bass partbook at Gloucester Cathedral, but information kindly supplied by Christopher Jeens, the cathedral library's archivist, indicates that at the moment it is not easy to relate references made to the music collection with what is actually in it.

36 University of California Library, Berkeley, MS 751 [formerly M2.C645].

37 New York Public Library, MS Mus. Res. *MNZ. See Peter le Huray, 'The Chirk Castle partbooks', *Early Music History*, vol. 2 (1982), pp. 17–42. Contents listed in the EECM Database.

38 See le Huray, 'The Chirk Castle partbooks', pp. 17–42, Appendix A.

39 Byrd, *English anthems*, p. xiii.

40 In his *William Byrd: a research and information guide. Third edition* (New York, 2012), p. 94, Richard Turbet suggested we should 'compare the phrase at "For seeing that by man" with an identical set of entries at bars [31]ff. in Tallis's keyboard *Fantasy*'. This

There is little doubt that the composer of *Christ rising* thought carefully about the work, but – deliberately or not – confined himself within very narrow limits, barely departing from the D tonality in which the piece begins (it is not until halfway through the Amen that there is a cadence on C), and restricting almost every syllable to one note (though the extent to which different voices sing the same syllable of the text at the same time is also restricted). He treated each of the two main parts of the text as a series of short sections. Each section is constructed from an individual point, sometimes with a brevity that demands repetition. (The exchange of material between the two alto voices when 'but in that he liveth unto God' is repeated is a device occurring in pieces certainly by Tallis.) The composer's invention is quite up to producing a fresh point for each group of words, but very often there are similarities between points and fragments of melody which create a sense of unity. Any temptation to rely on obvious word-painting is avoided, even if each main section begins with a slight nod towards the idea of rising. Reliance on strict imitation is fitful, and when it does occur it is often short-lived, and may be between groups of voices rather than single voices.

If Tallis did indeed set the words, when could he have done so? The contents of the organ book cover a long period – from Tye, van Wilder and Tallis, to Benjamin Rogers, Christopher Gibbons and Albertus Bryne. Besides *Christ rising* they include *With all our hearts* and *I call and cry*, contrafacta of two works by Tallis which were printed in the *Cantiones* of 1575. *Christ rising* does not seem to be a contrafactum: it would, for one thing, have been difficult to have fitted the words to pre-existent music, mainly with one word to a syllable. There is in fact no reason why Tallis could not have made a setting in King Edward's reign. The 'one note to a syllable' style is in keeping with what he was then writing. At least one other setting of the words must be Edwardian, since it was made by John Sheppard, who is unlikely to have made it in Queen Mary's reign, and lived only a month into the reign of Elizabeth.

A further anthem ascribed to Tallis needs to be mentioned here, simply for completeness. It is ***The simple sheep that went astray***, of which the words only are given in two seventeenth-century compilations associated with the Chapel Royal.[41] There is nothing to show whether the piece was a contrafactum or not. Among the contents of the manuscripts are the words of *I call and cry, With all our heart and mouth* and *Blessed be thy name*, which are contrafacta, and *Blessed are those who are undefiled* and *O Lord in Thee is all my trust*, which are not contrafacta.

---

refers to the version of *Alleluia. Per te genetrix* printed in Tallis's *Complete keyboard works*, ed D. Stevens (London, 1953).

41 Bodleian Library MS Rawl. Poet. 23, and BL MS Harley 6346. Among the contents of the manuscripts are the words of *Blessed are those who are undefiled* and *O Lord in Thee is all my trust*, which are not contrafacta, and *I call and cry, With all our heart and mouth* and *Blessed be thy name*, which are contrafacta.

Music for the English Liturgy

Tallis's **Benedictus** for four voices occurs only in the Lumley partbooks, among the last pieces to have been entered. He could have made his setting either before or after 1549. The words he set differ a little from the usual sixteenth-century translation, but are those of an Office text which primers made available in English before its inclusion in the Prayer Books.[42] The growth of texts for the services of the English church was by no means systematic. Variants occur in different editions and printings of each Prayer Book, phrases remained in use after they had ostensibly been replaced, and texts were no doubt circulating in unreliable manuscript copies.[43]

The low overall range of the Benedictus (*F-g'*) implies that, like Tallis's Mass for four voices (see p. 49), it was for adult voices. At least one church – St Mary-at-Hill, where Tallis worked a decade earlier – retained a group of conducts in King Edward's reign, but apparently no regular boy choristers.[44] Other pieces for the same combination of voices are *Hear the voice and prayer*, *A new commandment give I unto you* and *If ye love me.*

The Benedictus illustrates at some length the generalities of a style Tallis adopted in writing several shorter pieces. Imitative counterpoint, with the uppermost two voices frequently exchanging places, is interspersed with short homophonic passages providing contrast and distinguishing parts of the text. The word-setting of even the polyphonic sections is largely syllabic, with verbal phrases ending simultaneously in all voices. This description does little justice to Tallis's resourcefulness, however, or to the arresting effects he achieves by simple means. One such is the cadential false relationship at 'prepare his ways'. The succeeding passage is followed by something still more striking. At the words 'for the remission of their sins' the tonality, which has previously clung closely to D or A, moves to C, before a sudden return to A, with a sharpened C, vividly illuminates the beginning of the phrase 'To give light to them that sit in darkness' (p. 78, Example 4.2). The end of the phrase calls for C to be unsharpened again, conjuring up darkness and the shadow of death.

---

42 Tallis's setting has 'the prophet of the most high'. John Hilsey's *Manual of prayers, or the prymer in Englishe* (London, 1539), the King's Primer, and the Prayer Books, like Bibles from Tyndale onwards, have 'the prophet of the highest'.

43 Walter Howard Frere, 'Edwardine vernacular services before the first Prayer Book', *The Journal of Theological Studies*, vol. 1 (1899–1900), pp. 229–246; Stefan Scot, 'The Prayer Book in practice: textual anomalies and their implications in Tudor musical settings of the first Book of Common Prayer', *Brio*, vol. 34 (1997), pp. 81–9; Stefan Scot, 'Text and context: the provision of music and ceremonial in the services of the first Book of Common Prayer (1549)' (Doctoral thesis, University of Surrey, 1999).

44 Littlehales, ed., *The medieval records of a London city church*, p. 390.

Example 4.2 From Tallis's Benedictus for four voices

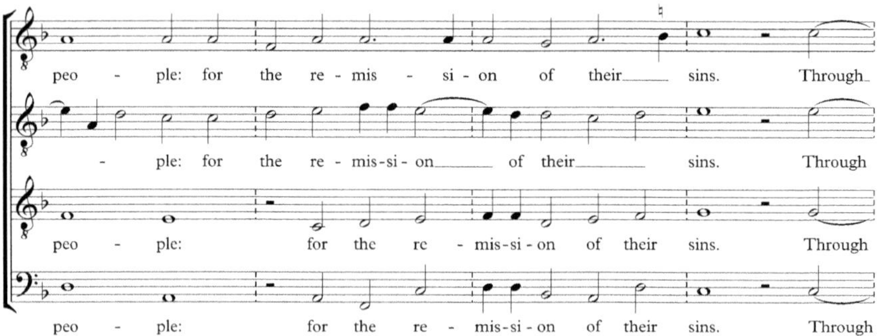

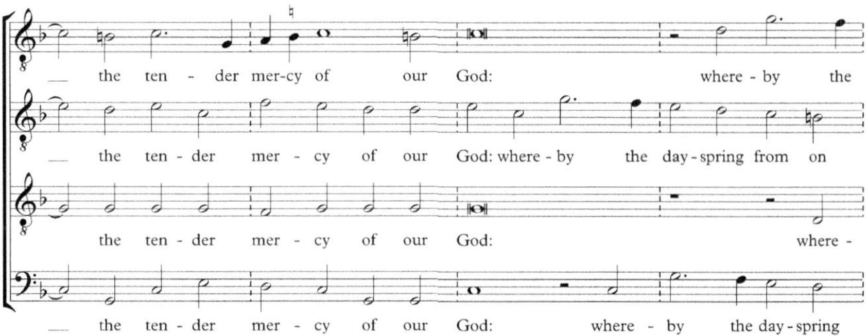

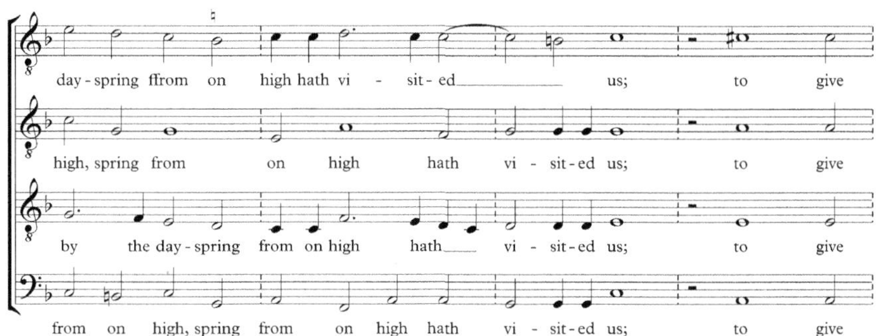

An English-texted five-part Te Deum by Tallis, 'for meanes' (without trebles), survives in an incomplete set of partbooks dated 1625 by the copyist, John Barnard, and in an organ book of *c.*1640.[45] Where the words, as we have them, differ from those of either the 1545 *Primer* or the 1552 Prayer Book, they follow those of the

45 Royal College of Music, London, five books from MSS 1045–51 (Barnard); Christ Church, Oxford, MS 1001.

1549 Prayer Book. The style of the Te Deum is recognizably similar to that of the Benedictus, though the Te Deum is on a larger scale and is for five voices (mean, two contratenors, tenor and bass). And in some respects it is not far removed from the style of *Christ rising*.

The long and repetitive text is divided after verse 14 (ending 'Thou art the King of Glory, O Christ'). Tallis apparently made the same division in another English Te Deum, found in a partbook from Ludlow (see below).[46] The two sections of the setting copied by Barnard are broken into smaller units, sometimes for different sides of the choir, sometimes differentiated by homophonic or contrapuntal writing. Since the two halves of the piece both end on A, and B is usually flattened throughout, Tallis may have thought of it as written vaguely in the transposed E mode, but tonality plays only a small part in the structure. It is instead through his motivic inventiveness and his sense of pacing that Tallis overcomes the problems posed by a text which could easily have encouraged fragmentation.

The Te Deum seems to acknowledge both the Anglican preference for clarity and moderation, and a new need to get through a long text without undue delay. Compared with Tallis's early Latin antiphons, polyphonic passages tend to be more compact, with one voice often following hard on the heels of another, and there is a more frequent resort to homophony. The piece reveals a remarkable ability to maintain momentum while contrasting adjacent sections, and while using a seemingly endless and varied supply of points distributed between the voices in a frequently changing order. Yet in the passages for the full choir, at the ends of the main sections of the work, the repetition of a point creates a cumulative effect of great power. The ending of the whole work (from 'O lord in thee have I trusted') so impressed Causton that he transferred it into his own Service 'for children' (which sets the 1552 Prayer Book text).[47]

To break the Te Deum into sections, and to vary its texture, Tallis appears to have used a further device. According to the organ book copy, the phrase 'Thou didst not abhor the Virgin's womb' is to be sung as a gymel for four means, which should probably be divided so that two sing on each side of the choir.[48] Quite possibly, as conjectured by Ellinwood,[49] the means were also divided elsewhere to form six parts, with the basses additionally divided to form seven parts in the final passage for the full choir. The first generation of Anglican composers sometimes

---

46 So did Byrd in both his Short Service and his Great Service. For the influence of the Latin chant on vernacular settings, including Tallis's, see John Aplin, 'The survival of plainsong in Anglican music: some early English Te-Deum settings', *Journal of the American Musicological Society*, vol. 32 (1979), pp. 247–75, at 274–5.

47 Peter Phillips, *English sacred music 1549–1649* (Oxford, 1991), pp. 392–6; John Milsom, 'Caustun's contrafacta', *Journal of the Royal Musical Association*, vol. 132 (2007), pp. 1–31, at 19–21.

48 Gymel, from Latin *cantus gemellus*: 'twin song'.

49 Tallis, *English sacred music: I*, p. 204.

clung to the aesthetic ideals of its predecessors, who were fond of lavish six-part scorings with divided parts.[50]

The bass part of another Te Deum is preserved incompletely in a book from St Laurence's church at Ludlow.[51] The book has several leaves missing, but it now begins with portions of two English-texted four-part pieces by Tye and Sheppard. They are followed by much of the Te Deum, which lacks its beginning and starts at 'powres therin To the thus cryethe cherubin & seraphin contynuallie'. (Some passages are absent because they were not sung by the bass voice.) It has an attribution to 'Mr Talis' at the end. The Te Deum is followed by an anonymous 'Benedictus .v. partis' (another setting for the Morning Service), and a 'Patrem of .v. p*artes*' (the Creed). No number of singers is given for a subsequent Sanctus, or for untitled passages from the Gloria, a Magnificat (lacking its ending), and a Nunc dimittis (lacking its beginning). Three following pieces are by, or possibly by, William Parsons; two of these are described as in five parts. The manuscript ends with a four-part piece by Sheppard.

The phrase 'To the thus cryethe cherubin & seraphin contynuallie' is not in either Edwardian Prayer Book or in The King's primer. The manuscript may nevertheless be Edwardian, as suggested by its inclusion of English-texted pieces by Tye, Sheppard and William Parsons. There seems no good reason to suppose that Tallis was responsible for anything but the Te Deum, or to think that the Te Deum and unascribed sections of the Morning Service were originally parts of one work. Although the beginning of the Sanctus ('Holy, holy, holy' set as six breves with coronas) recalls the central 'Ave Jesu' in Tallis's *Ave Dei patris filia*, and (more distantly) the 'Sanctus' and 'Hosanna' in his four-part Mass, the Ludlow pieces seem generally too disparate in style to be the work of any single composer. The Sanctus and Gloria alone have a time signature (¢), and were perhaps copied from a single source. They both end on C. Other sections end on A (Te Deum), F (Benedictus) and C (Patrem), and the endings of the Magnificat and Nunc dimittis are missing. The key signatures of the pieces differ as well. The Te Deum and Benedictus have one flat (written additionally above the staff when the voice goes high enough); the other sections are without a flat.

Although we have only the bass, it appears that the Ludlow Te Deum was in a mixture of the simultaneous and polyphonic styles. There are long stretches with few rests in the bass voice, which rules out thorough point-by-point imitation. Like Tallis's Te Deum 'for meanes', it has passages marked 'Gimmell' (at the phrase 'We therefore pray thee help thy servants, whom thou hast redeemed with thy precious blood' and its repetition), though it is not clear how far the gymel extends.

50 See, for example, the Mass *O Michael*, attributed with some uncertainty to Taverner (Hugh Benham, *John Taverner: his life and music* (Aldershot, 2003), pp. 160–68). The division of voices yields different seven-part combinations in the Credo and Agnus Dei.

51 Shropshire Archives LB/15/1/225, formerly 356 Mus. MS 1, dated *c.*1570 (on unknown grounds): see Smith, 'Elizabethan church music at Ludlow', pp. 108–21, at 116–17.

Services

Tallis is known to have made two settings embracing all those parts of Prayer Book services usually sung at Matins (or Morning Prayer), Communion, and Evensong (or Evening Prayer).[52] One is generally referred to as the 'Short' (or 'Dorian') Service; the other is described as 'Five Parts Two in One'. Only the first is complete, and both are difficult to date.

No copy of the **Short Service** is earlier than the 1620s.[53] A few pre-Elizabethan pieces appear alongside the Service in some manuscripts, but these sources also contain a good deal of later music.[54] The work was first printed by John Barnard in *The first book of selected church musick* (1641).

The work survives with a text that is essentially that of the 1552 and 1559 Prayer Books. Although words from the 1549 Prayer Book occur here and there, Tallis's setting of the responses to the Commandments (sung in the Communion Service) must have been composed after the first Prayer Book was printed, because that does not include them. In the Creed of Holy Communion, too, we can be sure that Tallis was setting the words of either the 1552 or 1559 Prayer Book, since it includes the words 'whose kingdom shall have none end' which were not in the 1549 Prayer Book. In neither case is there any sign of music for the later words having been inserted into an earlier setting. It therefore looks as if the *Short Service* was written late in the reign of King Edward (Mary was proclaimed Queen in July 1553, after Jane's brief reign), or in the reign of Queen Elizabeth. One possibility is that it was composed for the Edwardian Chapel Royal, either to increase the small number of 'complete' services available,[55] or expressly to provide a setting of the 1552 text. (It may of course have been composed before the 1552 text was settled, though that is no more than a possibility.) Although it is difficult to believe that Tallis wrote no service for the Edwardian Chapel, the Short Service could alternatively be Elizabethan, or partly Elizabethan, and perhaps composed to give the 1559 Prayer Book musical as well as legal authority. Canonic writing in two of the movements may hint at this; but if so the work was completed early enough

[52] Morning Prayer: *Venite* (Psalm 95), *Te Deum, Benedictus*. Communion: *Responses to the Commandments* (not in the 1549 Prayer Book), *Creed, Sanctus*. Evening Prayer: *Magnificat, Nunc dimittis*.

[53] It is necessary to scotch the idea that in 1560 John Day declined to print the Service, having originally agreed to do so. This has been put forward by Elizabeth Evenden, (*Patents, pictures and patronage: John Day and the Tudor book trade* (Aldershot, 2008), pp. 72–3 and 77), but it is based on a misreading of Peter Phillips's *English sacred music*, p. 400, where he makes only the unobjectionable observation: 'It may well be that the music was not ready for publication in 1560, that is, in time for Day.'

[54] For example, Lambeth Palace Ms 764, *c.*1635–42, and the Chirk Castle MSS, *c.*1620–35 (New York Public Library MS Mus. Res. *MNZ and Christ Church, Oxford, MS Mus. 6).

[55] See the table in le Huray, *Music and the Reformation in England*, pp. 183–5.

to influence Byrd's Short Service.[56] That seems to belong to the decade (from February 1562/3) when Byrd was employed at Lincoln Cathedral, and probably nearer the beginning of that period than the end. It will be obvious that a decision to consider the Short Service in this chapter is subjective, but there is no strong reason for delaying consideration until a later chapter.

The sections of a 'complete' Anglican service are not for consecutive performance, yet like the sections of many a Latin Mass those of Tallis's Short Service have a considerable unity.[57] They maintain an individual style and manner of expression, clear and without excess. They are restrained, but by no means austere or unemotional. Tallis's methods here are not those found in his more sensational Latin pieces, but they are still those of a thoughtful and meticulous craftsman, who has chosen to restrict his materials. The tonality is limited to what can be achieved in the D mode (with no flat).[58] The treble voice is not used: hence Barnard's concluding note, 'Here endeth the First Service of 4 parts, for meanes'. Save in the Creed and Nunc dimittis, homophony or near homophony is used throughout. The upper voices are seldom widely spaced, and more often than not chords are complete and in what is now called root position, so that the harmonization conveys a sense of fullness and security. Burney was moved to say of Tallis's work that 'the harmony in which he has clothed it is admirable; and the modulation being so antique, chiefly in the common chords or fundamental harmony to each note of the diatonic scale, often where the moderns have sixths, sevenths and their inversions, produces a solemn and very different effect from any Music that has been composed during the present century'.[59]

Part of the work's character is due also to the way the music mirrors the structure of the text. Sung portions of the Anglican service consist largely of sentences combining balanced statements: 'The sea is his, and he made it: and his hands prepared the dry land.' Most of the Short Service consists of matching musical phrases, each statement being answered by a varied repetition, usually of a different length. As words are rarely repeated and few syllables are sung to more than one note, the whole work is concisely constructed.

It is plain from the sources that a good deal of the Short Service was sung antiphonally, though this may sometimes have been the result of local practices (antiphonal performance of the Magnificat is indicated only by some Restoration manuscripts from Ely Cathedral). Local practice may also be mirrored in a setting

---

56 Craig Monson, ' "Throughout all generations": intimations of influence in the Short Service styles of Tallis, Byrd and Morley', in Alan Brown and Richard Turbet, eds, *Byrd studies* (Cambridge, 1992), pp. 83–111.

57 John Aplin, 'Cyclic techniques in the earliest Anglican services', *Journal of the American Musicological Society*, vol. 35 (1982), pp. 409–35, at 429–34.

58 There are just a few passages where B♭ occurs, e.g. in the Magnificat at 'hath sent empty away', though it is not in all sources.

59 Charles Burney, *A general history of music from the earliest ages to the present time* (London, 1776–89), vol. 3, p. 72.

of the offertory sentence 'Not everyone that sayeth unto me'. Since it is present only in the Chirk manuscripts,[60] there is some doubt about its authenticity. On the other hand, it convinced David Evans, who edited the manuscripts.[61]

A structure which, in other hands, might have become rigidly repetitious is handled by Tallis with flexibility and imagination. Phrases are allowed to find their own lengths, without being forced; melodic shapes often have the grace of those in his earlier Latin-texted music. Note lengths are varied to suit the natural pace of the words and their syllables, and always the music is appropriate to the emotional content of the text. Occasionally there is some word-painting of a rather obvious kind: for instance in the Creed, at 'Came down from heaven, and was incarnate'. The setting of these words does not differ greatly from several other passages with a descending treble (such as 'The glorious company of the Apostles praise thee', in the Te Deum), but it expresses a seemly joy before the sobriety of 'And was crucified also for us under Pontius Pilate'. The whole passage, from 'Being of one substance' to 'of the Virgin Mary', is unusually contrapuntal, and the outer voices are canonic. Canon is employed as well in much of the *Nunc dimittis*, where starting with 'For mine eyes have seen thy salvation' lower voices take it in turn to echo phrases sung by the highest voice.[62]

Canon seems to have been used more extensively in another Service. The inclusion of the work in this chapter is due to the kind of arbitrary decision already made in the case of the Short Service. The title of Tallis's **Service 'of fyve parts Too in one'** indicates clearly enough that it was for five voices, and probably that it contained a notable amount of canonic writing for two voices.[63] But it is known only from a bass partbook of *c.*1633–36. Tallis and Christopher Tye are easily the oldest

---

60 New York Public Library, Chirk Castle manuscripts, and the associated organ book, Christ Church, Oxford Mus. MS. 6.

61 David Evans, ed., *Three Chirk Castle miniatures* (Bangor, 2012): 'the suave harmony is characteristic of Tallis'. In his notes to the Brabant Ensemble's recording, conducted by Stephen Rice (Hyperion CDA 67695), Evans says the piece 'bears the distinctive stamp of Tallis's chordal progressions'.

62 Milsom, 'English polyphonic style in transition', vol. 1, p. 146; vol. 2, Appendix 5.8B. Milsom notes that in the *Creed* the canon, in the outer voices, 'varies in interval from octave to fifth and back to octave as the setting progresses, and answers not at two or four minims but at three, displacing the accent in the comes' (i.e. in the 'companion' or answering voice).

63 The likely nature of the work is explored by Andrew Johnstone in 'Tallis's service "of Five Parts Two in One" re-evaluated', in Katelijne Schiltz and Bonnie J. Blackburn, eds., *Canons and canonic techniques, 14th-16th centuries: theory, practice, and reception history. Proceedings of the International Conference, Leuven, 4–6 October 2005* (Analysis in Context, Leuven Studies in Musicology, 1: Leuven, 2007), pp. 381–405. Johnstone has also made a reconstruction of the service's Magnificat and Nunc dimittis (see the review by Honey Meconi in *Renaissance Quarterly*, vol. 61 (2008), pp. 984–6). A performance at Waltham Abbey on 26 October 2005 was broadcast on BBC Radio 3.

composers whose music is included in the manuscript, which appears to contain pieces still in use (possibly in the Chapel Royal) during the later years of Charles I. A companion manuscript contains the bass of Tallis's Short Service.[64]

If it could be proved that the 'two in one' Service was an Edwardian work, it would show that insistence on the clarity of the words did not preclude the use of canon. Alternatively, the use of canon – a technique that found an increasingly frequent and important place in Tallis's work – might mean that it was an Elizabethan piece. The words apparently set by Tallis underscore the unreliability of textual evidence as a means of dating his music. We do not know where or how Tallis obtained or received the texts he set, whether the surviving text of 'Five Parts Two in One' reflects a long piecemeal process of composition, or whether the work remains as Tallis left it. Where the Prayer Books of 1549 and 1552 differ, the words transmitted are for the most part those of 1552 (which the Elizabethan Prayer Book of 1559 followed closely), though some sections draw on both the 1549 and 1552 Prayer Books. At best, this suggests no great concern about the purity of the verbal text.[65] Yet the copy has some authority, even though it was made some 50 years after Tallis's death: it is in the hand of John Stephens, the Chapel Royal's copyist, and may therefore derive from an older copy used in the Chapel.

---

64 The canonic piece is in St John's College, Oxford, MS Mus. 181; the other manuscript is Mus. 180.

65 The texts consulted are: *The Booke of the Common Prayer and administracion of the sacramentes* (London, Whitchurch, 1549), and *The Boke of Common Prayer and administracion of the sacramentes* (London, Whitchurch, 1552), both as reprinted in *The first and second Prayer Books of Edward VI* (Everyman's Library, 448: London, 1968); and *The Book of Common Prayer 1559*, ed. John E. Booty (Washington, DC, 1976). The following comparison is based on the assumption that these are accurate, and represent all the sixteenth-century printings of each Prayer Book. It is assumed, too, that Ellinwood's edition accurately reproduces the text of MS Mus. 181.

Matins/Morning Prayer. Venite (Psalm 95): follows 1552, which has 'show ourselves glad' (1549 and 1559 have 'show ourself'); Te Deum: Tallis has 'Heaven and earth are replenished with the majesty of thy glory' (1549), and 'the Holy Ghost the comforter' (1552/1559, but also in Merbecke's The Boke of Common Praier noted, 1550); Benedictus: Tallis generally follows 1552/1559, but has 'fathers' and 'father' (from 1549) instead of 'forefathers' and 'forefather' (1552/1559), and omits 'their' from 'the remission of their sins' (present in 1549 and 1552/1559).

Communion. Responses to the Commandments: Tallis follows 1552/1559; Creed: Tallis follows 1549 and 1559 at 'God of God' (1552 has 'God of Gods'), but 1552/1559 by including 'whose kingdom shall have none end' (Ellinwood has 'no end'); Sanctus: follows 1552/1559; Gloria: follows 1552/1559.

Evensong/Evening Prayer. Magnificat: 'empty away' is the 1552/1559 text, 'promised to our father Abraham and his seed' is closer to 1549 than to 1552/1559 (which have 'forefathers'); Nunc dimittis: follows 1552/1559.

Secular Songs

No more than four songs by Tallis have survived with secular words, or titles suggesting them: *When shall my sorrowful sighing slack*, *Fond youth is a bubble* (which may not originally have been a secular song), *Like as the doleful dove*, and *O ye tender babes*.[66] All occur, without words, in Thomas Mulliner's keyboard anthology, probably compiled between 1558 and 1564 (see p. 68). As they were entered at different times, it is likely that they were collected individually (only *O ye tender babes* and *When shall my sorrowful sighing slack* occur close to each other, separated by another piece). It is impossible to date them precisely, and they are considered here as much for convenience as any other reason. They obviously cannot be later than the period when Mulliner was making copies in his book, but – as the following notes will show – they could individually have been written at various times in the 1540s and 1550s. Mulliner copied the songs as keyboard pieces in four parts, although they may all have been composed as part songs, and it is of course possible that some, at least, were at times adapted and performed in other ways. Of those he preserved, only *When shall my sorrowful sighing slack* is known also from other sources, some of which are incomplete and some of which present differing versions. The fact that several of the sources are of Scottish origin seems to illustrate the vagaries of survival.[67]

When shall my sorrowful sighing slack? is a setting of words by the Earl of Surrey, conceivably dating from Tallis's first years at court.[68] Mulliner must have copied it at around the time when the words were printed in 'Tottel's Miscellany'.[69] An independent keyboard version of the song was 'very likely copied in the 1560s'

66 A further song, *As Caesar wept*, is attributed to Tallis in one set of partbooks, where it appears without words, but to Byrd in other sources. Tallis is named as the composer in BL Additional MSS 18936–7, whose attributions are 'untrustworthy'; Byrd is named in Bodleian Library MS Mus. Sch. e.423 and Additional MS 31992 (a lute book), whose attributions are 'very reliable' (William Byrd, *Consort songs for voice and viols*, ed. Philip Brett (The Byrd Edition, 15: London, 1970), p. xxx). Harvard College Library MS Mus. 30 names no composer. Brett accepts that the song is Byrd's.

67 Sources are listed in Caldwell, *The Mulliner book*, p. 254, and Thomas Tallis, *English sacred music: I*, p. 132. Ellinwood's list omits York Minster Library MS M 91 (S), 'very likely copied in the 1560s': see Iain Fenlon and John Milsom, '"Ruled paper imprinted": music paper and patents in sixteenth-century England', *Journal of the American Musicological Society*, vol. 37 (1984), pp. 139–63, at 147. For the York versions of *When shall my sorrowful sighing*, including one for keyboard which is more idiomatic than Mulliner's, see John Caldwell, ed., *Tudor keyboard music* c.*1520–1580* (*Musica Britannica*, 66: London, 1995), pp. 146–7, 196.

68 Henry Howard, Earl of Surrey (*b.* 1516 or 1517) was executed on 19 January 1546/7.

69 *Songes and sonettes, written by the ryght honorable Lorde Henry Haward late Earle of Surrey, and other* (London, 1557).

into another manuscript.[70] The Lumley partbooks may transmit an early version of the song, but as well as being incomplete the copy they offer is in some respects defective.[71] The extent to which the song depends on imitative contrapuntal writing reveals its relationship to a piece like *Hear the voice and prayer*, which occurs in the Wanley partbooks. In the song, however, only the last line of the words is repeated instead of the longer passage which ends the anthem.

The music Mulliner heads ***Fond youth is a bubble*** is simple but skilfully made, uncomplicated but moving. It is similar in style to several sacred pieces in the Wanley partbooks, including Tallis's *If ye love me* (see p. 70), and like that it is connected with Henrician part songs by features such as its ABB form. 'Fond youth is a bubble' was probably the incipit of a verse Mulliner associated with Tallis's music, though no recorded poem of the period seems to begin in that way. Different words, beginning 'Purge me O Lord, from all my sin', are attached to the music in a manuscript dated 1615 but made earlier.[72] They fit the beginning of the piece much better than 'Fond youth is a bubble', and may therefore be those originally set by Tallis. Words rather awkwardly imposed on the music in a copy made by E.T. Warren about 1760 are (except for the first two) from Spenser's *Shepheardes calendar*.[73] But if Mulliner's collection is correctly dated above, the words he knew cannot have been by Spenser (*b.*1552?), even if his verses were circulating before their publication in 1579.

As copied by Mulliner, ***Like as the doleful dove*** is written at a pitch low enough to suggest that it was transposed downwards for the keyboard, or that it may originally have been a solo song with an instrumental accompaniment.[74] It consists almost entirely of consecutive four-part chords, each setting a single

70 York Minster Library MS M 91 (S): see Caldwell, *Tudor keyboard music c.1520–1580*, pp. 146–7, 196.

71 BL MSS Royal Appendix 74–6 (bass book missing), *c.*1547-*c.*1552; see Caldwell, *The Mulliner book*, p. 254. The edition printed by Ellinwood (*English sacred music: I*, pp. 106–10) takes its alto and tenor from the Lumley books, and its treble and bass from Mulliner. The differences between versions in different sources are discussed by John Milsom in 'Tallis's first and second thoughts', pp. 203–22, at 214–17.

72 BL Additional MSS 30480–84 (the 'Hamond' partbooks); for the date see Iain Fenlon and John Milsom, '"Ruled paper imprinted"', pp. 139–63, at 161. See also: Caldwell, *The Mulliner book*, pp. 38–41, 243; Thomas Tallis, *English sacred music: I*, pp. 40–42, 95–7, 126, 131.

73 Mulliner's words are not listed in William A. Ringler's *Bibliography and index of English verse in manuscript 1501–1550 ... prepared and completed by Michael Rudick and Susan J. Ringler* (New York, 1992). Christopher Goodwin has spotted a simile comparing life to a bubble in the works of Thomas Howell, whose *Arbor of Amitie* appeared in 1568. Lines beginning 'For Youngth is a bubble blown up with breath' occur in Spenser's *The shepheardes calendar*, published in 1579.

74 The *C* in Mulliner's keyboard transcription of *Like as the doleful dove* is unlikely to derive directly from a vocal part, but is absorbed into Ellinwood's vocal reconstruction in Tallis, *English sacred music: I*.

syllable. The words are attributed to William Hunnis, who began publishing his verses in 1550 with *Certayne psalmes chosen out of the psalter of David.* Those set by Tallis were not printed until they were added in 1578 to *The paradyse of dainty devises*, the most popular of Elizabethan poetic anthologies, which from 1576 to 1606 went through 10 editions. It derived from a compilation made by Richard Edwards, who joined the Chapel Royal before the end of Queen Mary's reign, and in 1561 succeeded Richard Bower as Master of the Children. On Bower's death in 1566 Edwards was succeeded in turn by Hunnis, who had become a Gentleman of the Chapel by 1552. Possibly he wrote *Like as the doleful dove* at some time in the next few years, but there is nothing to show whether either the poem or Tallis's setting is connected with one of the plays presented from time to time by the children of the Chapel.[75]

O ye tender babes could well have been written as a *jeu d'esprit* for the boys of a choir with which Tallis was associated. Considering the date of the words, it may have been that of the Chapel Royal, though Mulliner's connection with Heywood may have given him access to a copy belonging to the choir of St Paul's.[76] The title Mulliner gave to his textless copy almost certainly indicates its origin as a setting of words from, or suggested by, the prefatory address in *An introduction of the eyght partes of speche*, published in 1542.[77] Since the prose text fits the music poorly, Tallis may have set an adaptation – possibly, as Milsom has suggested, a metrical version.[78] It would not have been out of place in a play acted by the children of the Chapel. But such a performance need not have been entirely vocal, as is made clear by the stage directions for John Redford's play *Wit and Science* likely to have been acted by the children of St Paul's. When the song called 'Remembrance' is to be performed they say 'Heere cu*me*th in fowre wyth violes & syng'.[79]

[75] The poem *Like as the doleful dove* is no. 107 in [Richard Edwards], *The paradise of dainty devices (1576–1606)* ed. Hyder Edward Rollins (Cambridge, Mass., 1927). The addition of Hunnis's verses to the anthology is shown in Rollins's table between pp. xiv and xv. The words and the music were first printed together in John Hawkins, *A general history of the science and practice of music* (London, 1776), vol. 5, pp. 450–51.

[76] Caldwell, *The Mulliner book*, p. 253.

[77] *An introduction of the eyght partes of speche* (London, 1542). See Denis Stevens, 'A musical admonition for Tudor schoolboys', *Music & Letters*, vol. 39 (1957), pp. 49–52, which includes a transcription, a fourth higher than Mulliner's version, to which the words have been added; another transcription, at Mulliner's pitch, is in Tallis, *English sacred music: I*, pp. 102–5.

[78] John Milsom, 'English polyphonic style in transition, vol. 1, p. 24.

[79] Harley, *The world of William Byrd: musicians, merchants and magnates* (Farnham, 2010), p. 16.

Chapter 5

The Reign of Mary I: Biographical and Historical Background

King Edward's death was at first kept secret, just as his father's had been. After a few days Lady Jane Grey, to whom he had been persuaded to will the crown, was proclaimed Queen. She was almost as quickly deposed. Political manoeuvring and military posturing by the supporters of the late King's sister Mary led to her proclamation as Queen on 19 July 1553. On 3 August she entered the City, where she was greeted by her sister Elizabeth. Although Mary would have liked Edward's burial in Westminster Abbey to be conducted with Catholic rites, she wisely settled for a Protestant funeral. A requiem Mass was held in the Chapel Royal three days later.

The restoration of the Latin rite, and especially the Mass, was one of Mary's objectives. Shortly before the end of August 'the olde service in the Lattin tongue with the masse was begun and sunge in Powles in the Shrowdes, now St. Faythes parishe. And lykewise it was begun in 4 or 5 other parishes within the Cittie of London, not by commaundement but of the peoples devotion.'[1] Mass was resumed at Canterbury Cathedral by Richard Thornden, Cranmer's suffragan, thereby starting rumours that the Archbishop had yielded on a principal issue of the Edwardian Reformation. At Tallis's old church in London, St Mary-at-Hill, new antiphonaries, grails (graduals), hymnals and processionals were quickly purchased, and on Martinmas (11 November) the Gentlemen of the Chapel Royal, who seem to have had close connections with the church, sang a Mass there.[2]

Among the many other matters pursued simultaneously in the early months of Mary's rule were the removal of priests who had married, and action against men who were seen to have committed treason. It was in the midst of them that the crowning of the new Queen took place. Her coronation procession from the Tower to Westminster Abbey on 1 October 1553, and the ceremony which followed, were events of great splendour. The Gentlemen of the Chapel Royal were as usual

---

1 Charles Wriothesley, *A chronicle of England during the reigns of the Tudors, from A. D. 1485 to 1559* (Camden Society, new series, 11, 20: London, 1875–77), vol. 2, p. 101. St Faith's church had been demolished, and the parishioners worshipped in the crypt, or shrouds, of the cathedral.

2 LMA P69/MRY4/B/005/MS01239/001/003 (former Guildhall Library MS 1239/1, part 3), f.759^r–760^r; Henry Littlehales, *The medieval records of a London city church (St Mary at Hill) A.D. 1420–1559* (Early English Text Society, original series, 125, 128: London, 1904–05), pp. 395–6.

among the many given new scarlet liveries. At the coronation feast members of the Chapel performed an interlude 'as in tymes past hathe ben accustomed to be don'.[3] For the first Christmastide of the new reign the Chapel presented another play, which included parts for 'the bad angell' and 'the good angell'. We are left to wonder whether Tallis was among the actors and what his role might have been. Exactly which play was performed is also uncertain, but it clearly belonged to the same tradition as the fifteenth-century *Castle of Perseverance* and scenes which would later appear in Marlowe's *History of Doctor Faustus*.[4]

Members of the Chapel Royal must at some stage have sworn their allegiance to the new Queen. Their number remained steady during Mary's reign, and so did the pay of a Gentleman (the basic daily rate was still 7½d).[5] The impression that Tallis was the Chapel's *de facto* musical head is reinforced by the Queen's grant of a valuable lease, which in 1557 he would receive jointly with Richard Bower, the master of the children of the Chapel (see p. 96). Tallis's association with Bower reveals something of his connections in the world beyond the Chapel. When Bower came to make his will in 1561, the overseers he appointed were Tallis and the lawyer William Roper. Among Roper's properties was the family estate at Well Hall, not far from Greenwich. His second son, Anthony, is mentioned in the will of Tallis's wife Joan. Anthony inherited from William an estate at Farningham in Kent, where he lived and is buried, and the manor of Harlington in Middlesex, where Tallis's colleague William Byrd was living by the end of 1577.[6]

There is evidence to suggest that Byrd became Tallis's pupil in the late 1550s.[7] He was almost certainly a chorister at St Paul's Cathedral, and his exceptional talent may have led Sebastian Westcote, who had charge of the choristers there, to seek Tallis's help in providing him with instruction in composition. When Byrd was himself a Gentleman of the Chapel Royal, Westcote may have sent Peter Philips

[3] TNA E101/417/5, ff.9r, 27r; Andrew Ashbee, *Records of English court music* (Snodland, *later* Aldershot, 1986–96), vol. 7, pp. 130–32; Albert Feuillerat, ed., *Documents relating to the revels ... in the time of King Edward VI and Queen Mary (the Loseley manuscripts)* (W. Bang, Materialien zur Kunde des älteren englischen Dramas, 44: Louvain, 1914), p. 149.

[4] Ibid., pp. 152, 290; Andrew Ashbee, *Records of English court music*, vol. 7, pp. 131–2. See also *Respublica. An interlude for Christmas 1553. Attributed to Nicholas Udall*, ed. W.W. Greg (Early English Text Society, original series, 226: London, 1952), pp. viii–x; and David Loewenstein and Janet Mueller, eds, *The Cambridge history of early modern English literature* (The new Cambridge history of English literature: Cambridge, 2002), p. 245.

[5] Society of Antiquaries, MS 125, f.36r; BL MS Stowe 571, f.36v; Ashbee, *Records of English court music*, vol. 7, p. 127, and vol. 8, p. 11.

[6] John Bennett, 'A Tallis patron?', [*Royal Musical Association*] *Research Chronicle*, 21 (1988), pp. 41–4; Malcolm Rose, 'The history and significance of the Lodewijk Theewes claviorgan', *Early Music*, 32 (2004), pp. 577–93; John Harley, *The world of William Byrd: musicians, merchants and magnates* (Farnham, 2010), pp. 202–4.

[7] Harley, *The world of William Byrd*, pp. 46–50.

and Thomas Morley to him for the same purpose. It is hard to think of anyone but Tallis who could have provided the kind of help needed by as gifted a pupil as Byrd undoubtedly was. The only contemporary reference to Byrd's studies with Tallis is however in a Latin poem by Ferdinando Heybourne, prefacing *Cantiones, quae ab argumento sacrae vocantur*, published by Tallis and Byrd in 1575.[8] Heybourne's verses seemingly claim that he himself studied with Tallis, though nothing else is known of this and his few surviving keyboard compositions show Byrd's influence. It was claimed by Hawkins that Elway Bevin (not born until *c.* 1554) was another pupil of Tallis, but this is uncorroborated elsewhere. The statement was repeated by the author of a note in British Library Additional manuscript 31403, who may simply have copied what Hawkins wrote.[9] There appears to be no other reference to pupils of Tallis who became professional musicians, though it is difficult to believe there were none.

Assuming that Byrd was studying with Tallis, he saw see something of life in the Chapel Royal at an eventful time. In the absence of the Dean of the Chapel in Brussels (see p. 58), the Gentlemen presumably received clerical guidance in performing their duties from Emery Tuckfield, who had become Subdean in 1548 and seemingly adapted himself without undue difficulty to a new religious climate. He remained in post until 1557, when he was succeeded by Edmund Daniel. What, as a group or as individuals, the Gentlemen made of events unfolding bewilderingly around them can only be guessed, but they had a grandstand view.

---

8 Heybourne was probably the source of Anthony à Wood's statement that Byrd was 'bred up to musick under Tho. Tallis' (Bodleian Library MS Wood D.19(4), ff.19^v–20^v, transcribed with other notes about Tallis and Byrd in Richard Turbet, *William Byrd: a guide to research* (New York, 1987), pp. 329–33). Two further notes by Wood about Tallis (the first clearly confusing him with Byrd) seem never to have been printed, and are therefore given here. Folio numbers are those added to the manuscript in pencil.

f.123^r: 'Mr. Tallis, was scholar to Mr Bird & organist to K. Jam. I. Known all over England Wales & Ireland, in all Cath. & Collegiat chur[ch]es there for his extraordinary abilities in composing services & Anthems for such churches – He was a very able mathematician & learnt & [improved?] yt facultie purposely yt he might compose things ye better – sc Dr Rogers [i.e. Benjamin Rogers]'.

f. 124^r: 'Tallis (or Tallisius) Thomas The first noted musitian in Q. Elizab. reigne

Divine services & Anthems – the words of nine or more, ye may see in James Cliffords collection [In margin: '[Cat. ?] 5.79']

wee have some of his compositions for instrumentall musick in several parts in our publ. musick school [i.e. at Oxford]'.

9 The note, on f.2^r of the manuscript is in a hand which looks late enough for the writer to have seen Hawkins's words (John Hawkins, *A general history of the science and practice of music* (London, 1776), vol. 3, p. 373). Hawkins made an error about the date of Bevin's appointment as a Gentleman Extraordinary of the Chapel Royal, giving it as 3 June 1589, whereas the year was 1605. He also said Bevin was expelled from the Chapel as a Catholic in 1637, but this is unconfirmed by any other source.

Thirlby was temporarily recalled for Mary's first Parliament, which assembled in October 1553; he returned to Brussels late in December, after religious legislation passed under Edward VI had been nullified and public worship had been restored to the form it enjoyed in the last year of Henry VIII.[10] When Mary's third Parliament had completed its business, just over a year later, all religious legislation passed against the papacy from 1529 had been repealed (while allowing Mary to keep the title of Supreme Head of the English Church), and measures against heresy which had been repealed under Henry VIII and Edward VI had been reinstated (including an Act of 1401 for the burning of heretics).

Thrust into the crowded later months of 1553 were two more matters of the greatest significance. One was the trial of Thomas Cranmer, still the Archbishop of Canterbury, who was charged with treason and imprisoned in the Tower on account of his role in setting Jane Grey on the throne. The other was discussion of whom the Queen should marry. International as much as domestic politics decreed that he should be Prince Philip of Spain, son of the Emperor Charles – perhaps not too difficult a choice for the daughter of Catherine of Aragon to accept. Thirlby was again recalled, this time to assist at the wedding. Philip arrived in England in July 1554, accompanied by 42 of his own musicians: 21 singers, two organists and a group of instrumentalists.[11] He met his bride at Winchester, three days before they were married at the cathedral on 25 July by the Bishop of Winchester, Stephen Gardiner. There, 'duryng hie masse tyme the Quenes Chappell matched with the quire' of the cathedral, and the organs played.[12]

Cranmer was by then in Oxford, where he had been sent in March 1554 after the failure in February of the younger Thomas Wyatt's rebellion, inspired by the prospect of the Queen's marriage to a Spaniard. It was not until June 1555 that a mandate was issued in Rome for Cranmer's trial on charges of heresy. His fellow prisoners, the former bishops Nicholas Ridley and Hugh Latimer, were tried separately. There was little doubt about the outcome to be expected of proceedings in the University church. In October Cranmer was obliged to watch from his prison while Ridley and Latimer were burned. He was formally deprived of his archbishopric in December, and was himself burned before Balliol College in March 1555/6. How much the determined imposition of Mary's religious policies had affected Tallis and most of his colleagues, there is no knowing. For the most part there is no record of their personal beliefs. The only known example of dissent among the Gentlemen of the Chapel Royal involved William Hunnis and John Benbowe, who in 1555 were implicated in the Dudley plot, intended to place the then Princess Elizabeth on the throne and marry her to Edward Courtenay, the Earl

---

10 1 Mary st. 2, c. 2, published separately as *An acte for the repeale of certayne actes made in the tyme of King Edwarde the sixte* (London, 1553).

11 John M. Ward, 'Spanish musicians in sixteenth-century England', in Gustave Reese and Robert J. Snow, eds, *Essays in musicology in honor of Dragon Plamenac on his 70th birthday* (Pittsburgh, Pa, 1969), pp. 353–64.

12 John Elder, *The copie of a letter sent in to Scotlande* (London, 1555).

of Devonshire. Hunnis was arrested in March 1555/6, and sent to the Tower. It is assumed that he lost his place in the Chapel, though he was in favour early in the next reign.[13] Benbowe is thought to have kept his place.

On the day after Cranmer's death, he was succeeded as Archbishop by Cardinal Reginald Pole. Pole had left England in 1532, but returned as papal legate on 20 November 1554 with the object of reconciling England to the papacy. Thirlby, whom Pole had previously met in Brussels, was one of those who greeted him at Dover. At Westminster, on 30 November, the nation was absolved from schism and received back into the Roman Catholic church. On the following Sunday (the first in Advent) Pole visited St Paul's, where the Lord Mayor, aldermen and livery companies turned out with Gardiner (now Lord Chancellor) and all the bishops to welcome him. At ten o'clock 'ye kyng grace cam to powlles', accompanied by an enormous retinue of several nationalities. Mass was celebrated, and 'both ye quen chapell & ye kyng*es* and powll*es* quer sang'.[14] Afterwards, at Paul's Cross, Gardiner preached on a text which had been read in the cathedral: 'Now is the time for us to awaken'. A chronicler noted that 'ye kynge & ye cardenall were present stondynge above ovar the lord mayres hedd', and afterwards 'ye bells in pawles began to rynge & in othar churchis whiche made souche noyse that I coulde not vndarstond iij wordes togethar'.[15]

The period of Queen Mary's marriage to Philip of Spain saw a change in Tallis's personal life. He was a witness of the will of Thomas Bury, who died at some time in 1554.[16] The will mentions Bury's wife 'Jane' (Joan), and it was evidently she whom in 1546 he had been given permission to marry while retaining a prebend from the collegiate church at Penkridge in Staffordshire.[17] In an age when illness and disease might strike at any time, remarriage was common among both women and men, and often took place soon after the death of a partner. Bury's widow chose to marry Thomas Tallis, who was a friend of her late husband, and with whose person, profession and circumstances she was familiar. Bury must have been a widower when he had been permitted to marry Joan in 1546, since his will refers to his daughter 'Johan' (Joan), who was old enough to have married 'James

---

13 The story of the conspiracy is summarized in Andrew Ashbee and David Lasocki, *A biographical dictionary of English court musicians* (Aldershot, 1998), vol. 1, pp. 144, 610; the documents are described in Ashbee, *Records of English court music*, vol. 7, pp. 422–3.

14 BL MS Cotton Vitellius F. V; Henry Machyn, *The diary*, ed. John Gough Nichols (Camden Society, old series, 42: London, 1848), p. 78.

15 BL MS Harley 540, ff.19^{v}–20^{r}; Charles Lethbridge Kingsford, ed., 'Two London chronicles from the collection of John Stow', in *Camden miscellany*, 12 (Camden, 3rd series, 18: London, 1910), p. 56.

16 Bury's will is dated 7 February 1553/4 (Kent History and Library Centre, DRb/Pwr 11, f.254); no probate is recorded (Ashbee and Lasocki, *A biographical dictionary of English court musicians*, vol. 1, pp. 220–21).

17 *Letters and papers, foreign and domestic of the reign of Henry VIII* (London, 1864–1932), vol. 21 pt 2, p. 86 (no.199/78); Ashbee, *Records of English court music*, vol. 7, p. 101.

Acoor'. Bury's will also mentions an apparently young son Thomas, for whose schooling he made provision. Other relations of the new Joan Tallis included a third Joan, whose surname is variously spelled 'Payre', 'Payer', 'Paire' or 'Peare'. In Thomas Tallis's will she is described as his wife's sister's daughter. The will of Tallis's wife refers to Joan Payre as her 'cousin' (which often meant 'niece'), who had a son named Francis and a daughter named Elizabeth.

The difference Tallis's marriage made to his life cannot be judged, since so little of his previous existence is documented. No record has come to light of his having been married before or having any children. The wedding was presumably conducted according to the Sarum rite,[18] and the most likely place for it to have taken place is the church of St Alfege in Greenwich (more precisely in 'East Greenwich'), a stone's throw from Joan's home and from Greenwich Palace. The date of the marriage is uncertain, as the parish register has not survived, but the first memorial erected to Tallis (see p. 213) cannot have been quite correct in saying he and Joan had lived together for 'full thre and thirty Yeres', since that would place their marriage no later than 1552, while Bury was still alive.

From Tallis's point of view the union offered a satisfactory prospect. Joan, who may have been younger than he, was left reasonably well off by the terms of Bury's will, with a house and a neighbouring tenement in Greenwich. But she remained proud of her domestic skills, and mentioned in her own will her 'sheet*es* of myne owne spyninge'. The lawyer, antiquarian and topographical historian William Lambarde, who founded Queen Elizabeth's College, a group of almshouses in Greenwich, refers to Joan's property as consisting of '2 mess[uages], 2 yards, 1 barn, and 1 garden, holden of ye manor of Westcombe by fealtie and 2s. yearly rent'. He says that on the death of Thomas Bury the ownership reverted to him;[19] but that Joan Tallis held the property by Bury's will, until in 1580 Tallis and his wife 'disclosed their right therein'. Lambarde then sold the property to Joan for 100 marks, 'she paying 2s. yearly to my manor as before, and granting 10s. yearly to ye poor of ye College for ever'. One of the houses became 'the Old Greyhound Inn, on which site the house, in the occupation of Mr. Richard Best, hath since been erected'.[20] The site, on the east side of modern Stockwell Street, just south of the junction with Church Street and Greenwich High Road, is shown on an anonymous map from the collection of A. R. Martin (Figure 5.1).[21] The library of the University of Greenwich now stands on the side of Stockwell Street shown on the map.

---

[18] William Maskell, ed., *Monumenta ritualia ecclesiae Anglicanae* (London, 1846–7), vol. 1, p. 41ff.

[19] His father, John Lambarde, had bought the property in 1553 (Henry H. Drake, ed., *Hasted's history of Kent, corrected, enlarged and continued … The hundred of Blackheath* (London, 1886), p. 51).

[20] For Lambarde's account of the ownership of the property, and the site of Best's house see ibid., pp. 89–90. See also note 22 below.

[21] The map can be dated *c.*1825, since it shows St Mary's church (consecrated 1825) but does not show Nelson Road (constructed 1826–29).

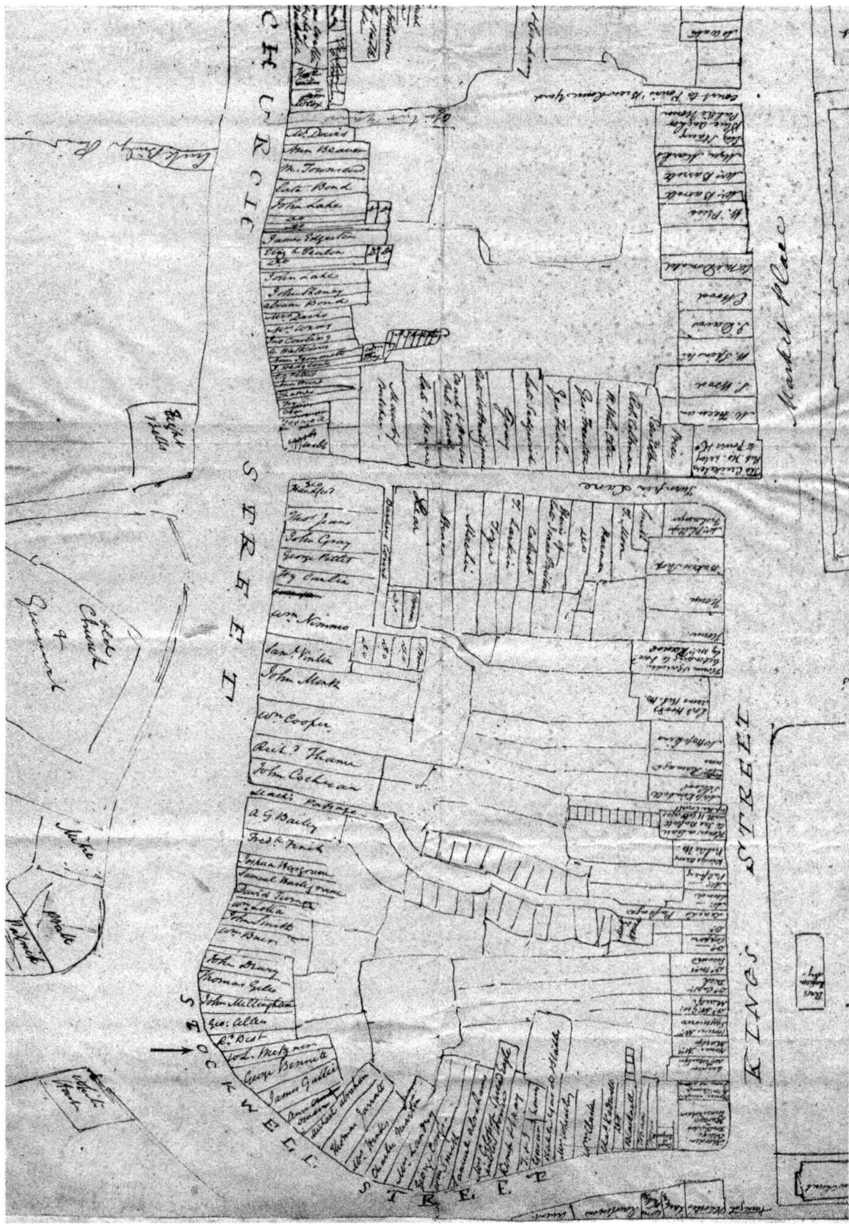

Figure 5.1 A map of *c.*1825, showing the site of Tallis's house in Greenwich, later belonging to Richard Best and here marked by an added arrow. (Greenwich Heritage Centre, document M.C. 652, by permission of the Centre)

The kind of home occupied by Thomas and Joan Tallis is brought vividly to life by Joan's will (Appendix A), which contains a long description of the contents. The property owned by Joan was the subject of a decree made by the Commissioners of Charitable Uses on 18 January 1622, some 35 years after her death. It tells us that the property was acquired by Humphrey Kelleck, but in doing so it seems to mistake Joan Tallis's relationship to Joan Payre.[22]

The Queen's marriage was overshadowed by matters of public concern. As early as September 1554 rumours had already started to circulate of her pregnancy, for which she so much hoped,[23] but they proved to be false. Philip left for Flanders in September 1555, and though he returned briefly in March 1556/7, he left again in July, after England had entered into a European war in his support. One of its results was the loss of the Continental foothold established by Edward III in 1347: Calais, the home of the wool staple, fell on 7 January 1557/8.

It was on the previous 27 November, as this disaster approached, that Mary granted Tallis, jointly with Richard Bower, a lease of 21 years on the manor of Minster, in the Isle of Thanet, which had once belonged to the monastery of St Augustine, Canterbury. Like many Tudor leases, the one granted to Tallis and Bower had a complicated history. Part of it was quickly transferred (on 25 December), to Sir Edward Waldegrave.[24] In the next reign a document of 23 June 1567 stated that, at its termination, it was to be awarded to Edward Cary, a Groom of the Privy Chamber who was a cousin of Lord Hunsdon.[25]

In 1557 Mary again thought herself pregnant, but she was again disappointed. It became plain that she was severely ill, and she died at St James's Palace on 17 November 1558. A few hours later, a short distance away at Lambeth Palace, Archbishop Pole died too.

---

22 John Kimbell, *An account of the legacies, gifts, rents, fees &c ... of the parish of St. Alphege Greenwich* (Greenwich, 1816), p. 57ff. According to the decree, 'Joan Tallis, widow, deceased, in her life time (Scil*icet*) the 12th day of June, 1587, was seized in her Demesne, as of fee, of and in one messuage or tenement, with the appurtenances, in East Greenwich, now in the tenure of Ralph Messingham, and of and in one other messuage in East Greenwich aforesaid, with the appurtenances, now in the tenure of Christopher Peake, and before in the possession of Thomas Palmer, deceased … .' It also says: 'Christopher Peake bought and acquired the said messuage, now in his possession, of one Humphrey Kelleck … [who] took to wife the daughter of John Pare, the which said John Pare took to wife Joan Tallis, daughter and heir of the aforesaid Joan Tallis, deceased … .'

23 On 27 October 1554 Cardinal Pole wrote to the Queen about 'the grace of conceiving fruit, in her corporeal womb' (*Calendar of state papers and manuscripts, relating to English affairs, existing in the archives and collections of Venice, and in other libraries of northern Italy*, ed. Rawdon Brown (London, 1864–1947), vol. 5, p. 587 (no. 958).

24 BL MS Harley 239, ff.74^{r} and 75^{v}; TNA C66/929, mm. 6–7; *Calendar of the patent rolls ... Philip and Mary, vol. IV, A. D. 1566–1569* (London, 1939), p. 256.

25 TNA C66/1037, m.17; *Calendar of the patent rolls ... Elizabeth I, volume IV, 1566–1569* (London, 1964), p. 91 (no. 574), where 'Parye' is an error for 'Carye'.

Chapter 6
The Reign of Mary I: Music with Latin Words

It seems that, in terms of the amount of music he was required to write, little was asked of Tallis during the few years he spent in Henry VIII's Chapel Royal, and not much more was demanded when he served in the Chapel of Edward VI. Well, perhaps. It would be nice to think that we have most of the music Tallis composed before 1553 and that it can be confidently assigned to one reign or another. The fact is that we cannot be entirely sure what was in the books of the Chapel Royal, or most other institutions, at any period of Tallis's life. Nor can we be sure how much was destroyed when one monarch was followed by another of a different religious persuasion, though we can guess that changes of regime are among the reasons why so few manuscripts have come down to us.

Furthermore, whatever part of the Chapel's Henrician repertoire survived the reign of Edward VI, it could easily have been deemed out of date or inappropriate for the next reign, so that fresh music was probably needed for the Catholic services reintroduced by Queen Mary. If it is true that Tallis had risen to pre-eminence with the introduction of the Protestant liturgy in King Edward's time (see p. 65), it seems to be equally true that his musical imagination was stirred by new demands when Queen Mary came to the throne. It is conceivable, as well, that he was stimulated by working in harness with a composer of Sheppard's stature and by teaching a pupil as able as Byrd. In Thomas Whythorne's opinion, Tallis, Sheppard and Byrd were 'The most famous musicians in this time'.[1]

It has been suggested that Tallis and Sheppard (who had joined the Chapel Royal late in King Edward's reign) may have been creating what amounted to an annual cycle for the Office.[2] There is no doubt that they especially among the Chapel's composers wrote many pieces that formed a repertoire of Office

1 Thomas Whythorne, *The autobiography of Thomas Whythorne*, ed James M. Osborn (Oxford, 1961), p. 302, note written after July 1592, spelling normalized.

2 Paul Doe, *Tallis* (London, 1968). 2nd edn (London, 1976), p. 34; Doe, 'Latin polyphony under Henry VIII', *Proceedings of the Royal Musical Association*, vol. 95 (1968/69), pp. 81–95, at 93–4 (where Doe's change of mind about date is apparent); Joseph Kerman, *The masses and motets of William Byrd* (London, 1981), p 25; John Milsom, review of Joseph Kerman, *The masses and motets of William Byrd*, in [*Royal Musical Association*] *Research Chronicle*, no. 19 (1983–85), pp. 85–95, at 92; Daniel Bennett Page, 'Uniform and Catholic: church music in the reign of Mary Tudor (1553–1558)' (Doctoral thesis, Brandeis University, 1996), pp. 211–13.

polyphony, though some duplication in their output casts doubt on any notion that they were working to a fixed plan. It is more certain, if Tallis's music which appears to date from the mid-century really represents what he composed before and after Queen Mary's accession, that it was a period in which he wrote some kinds of music he had not tackled before. He wrote no more solo responds, but turned his hand to writing choral responds. He seems for the first time to have made vocal settings of hymns, unless it is simply that earlier examples are not extant. And there is one short processional refrain, which appears to be something quite new in his output (though it would be rather surprising if he had never previously composed anything of the sort). Even in genres he had worked in before, the antiphon and the Mass, he now produced more imposing pieces.

Choral Responds

While maintaining the contrast between soloists and choir that exists in solo responds (p. 52), choral responds reverse the pattern, so that polyphony replaces passages of plainsong allocated to the choir instead of replacing passages of plainsong allocated to the soloists. Tallis's Office music includes several examples.

The procedure may be due to the growth, in secular foundations, of choirs able to tackle polyphony which had formerly been left to soloists.[3] This is not to suggest that solo responds suddenly became old-fashioned (the dates of the few composers listed earlier (see p. 53) makes it apparent that this was not so), but the new method of composing responds apparently began with, and was almost certainly given impetus by, Taverner's two settings of *Dum transisset sabbatum*.[4] Since Taverner died in 1545, his pieces could have formed models for Tallis during a part of Henry VIII's reign. Indeed the choral responds to be considered here were suitable for days which were celebrated at court throughout most of King Henry's reign, and at least in his later years were observed publicly by Henry himself.[5] When Tallis joined the Chapel Royal the King was receiving communion on five feast days, including Easter Day, Whitsunday and Corpus Christi. He took part in processions to celebrate the Purification of the Virgin Mary, Easter Day, Whit Sunday, Corpus Christi and Trinity Sunday (incidentally the Chapel Royal's

[3] Frank Ll. Harrison, *Music in medieval Britain*, 4th edn (Buren, 1980), p. 369.

[4] The settings attributed to Taverner are conventionally numbered I or II according to their positions in Christ Church, Oxford, MSS 979–83. The authenticity of the 'second' setting 'should at least be questioned' (Hugh Benham, *John Taverner: his life and music* (Aldershot, 2003), p. 238).

[5] Fiona Kisby, 'The royal household chapel in early-Tudor London, 1485–1547' (Doctoral thesis, University of London, 1996), pp. 144, 167; Fiona Kisby, ' "When the King goeth a procession": chapel ceremonies and services, the ritual year, and religious reforms at the early Tudor court, 1485–1547', *Journal of British Studies*, vol. 40 (2001), pp. 44–75 (especially Table 1 on pp. 54–5, and Table 3 on pp. 72–3).

dedication day).[6] Easter Day and Whit Sunday were marked by the Wearing of the Purple or 'crown wearing'. (So was Christmas Day, for which Tallis is not known to have written a choral respond.)

It is, however, quite likely that Mary revived her father's practices, and that Tallis's earliest choral settings of respond texts belong to the group of pieces which, it is conjectured, he and Sheppard composed when they were colleagues in the Chapel Royal. Tallis's *Dum transisset sabbatum*, *Candidi facti sunt Nazarei eius* and *Honor virtus et potestas* are for five voices; *Homo quidam fecit cenam magnam* and *Videte miraculum matris Domini* are for six voices; and *Loquebantur variis linguis apostoli* is for seven voices. They are discussed below. The treatment of the words in two further settings of respond texts (*In ieiunio et fletu* and *In manus tuas*) means that they are probably Elizabethan, and they will be discussed in Chapter 10.

A list of Tallis's choral responds, with the days to which they are appropriate, is given in Table 6.1. Apart from *Dum transisset*, they are known only from sources much later than the probable date of composition, which – not least because of Tallis's habit of revising his works – means that we cannot be quite sure of their original form.[7]

Table 6.1 Tallis's Marian choral responds

For five voices
[*Dum transisset*] *sabbatum* (the third response at Matins on Easter Day; afterwards sung during Easter week and on the five following Sundays)
[*Candidi*] *facti sunt* (for first Vespers and Matins on the feast day of an evangelist or apostle, or more than one apostle, during the Easter period)
[*Honor*] *virtus et potestas* (the sixth respond, second nocturn, for Matins on Trinity Sunday)
For six voices
[*Homo*] *quidam fecit cenam* (for first Vespers on the Feast of Corpus Christi)
[*Videte*] *miraculum* (for first Vespers on the Feast of the Purification of the Virgin Mary)
For seven voices
[*Loquebantur*] *variis linguis* (for Sext on Whit Sunday)

Note: Bracketed words are either omitted or delayed in surviving copies.

6 Kisby, 'The royal household chapel in early-Tudor London', p. 144.

7 John Milsom, 'Tallis's first and second thoughts', *Journal of the Royal Musical Association*, vol. 113 (1988), pp. 203–22, at 219–20.

A choral respond is normally begun by soloists singing the first word(s) of the response to the plainsong melody, after which the choir follows with a polyphonic setting of the remaining words. (In Table 6.1, square brackets enclose the words sung as plainsong.) The verse is next sung as plainsong by the soloists, and then a part of the response is repeated and sung polyphonically by the choir. There may be an additional verse, after which the repeated part of the response is again sung polyphonically. Most of Tallis's settings appear to have been adapted for non-liturgical performance, however, and this will be considered in a moment.

In the polyphonic passages of each of Tallis's choral responds, one voice sings the plainsong melody throughout as a cantus firmus written almost entirely in semibreves – a treatment possibly derived from Taverner – and to a large extent it dictates harmonic progress. The presence of a cantus firmus may be connected with the greater number of voices employed in the choral responds than in the solo responds; Sheppard, too, incorporated the chant as a cantus firmus into responds for five or six voices, but not usually into those for fewer voices. Tallis generally gives the chant to a voice in the middle or lower range, where the tenor still retained something of the importance accorded to it by Tinctoris, and even by Zarlino, who continued to call it the voice which 'rules and governs'.[8] (Tallis's *Dum transisset* is unusual in having the cantus firmus in the highest voice.) The slow speed of the cantus firmus means that the free voices are often well ahead of it in setting the text, and they have to rest or repeat words in order to stay more or less in step. It is not a complication which would have been welcome to Henrician reformers, but it supports the idea that Tallis's choral responds were, mostly at least, written in Mary's reign. If any was written earlier, it is likely to have been *Dum transisset*, stimulated by Taverner's setting.

In each respond, in accordance with the plan described above, the choral setting omits from the part which has the cantus firmus the initial word(s) sung by the soloists. Tallis's settings of *Homo quidam fecit cenam* and *Loquebantur variis linguis* have been preserved in copies where the omission occurs also in the other parts, making the original liturgical form clear. Some manuscript sources of *Dum transisset*, too, omit the initial words from the choral setting.[9] The other three responds have been preserved only in copies where the choral passages have

---

[8] Johannes Tinctoris, Liber de natura et proprietate tonorum [1476], ch. XXXIV, in Charles-Edmund-Henri Coussemaker, ed., *Scriptorum de musica medii aevi* (Paris, 1864–76), vol. 4, pp. 16b–41a; Gioseffo Zarlino, *Le istitutioni harmoniche* (Venice, 1558), p. 239.

[9] Most of the pre-publication sources are incomplete: 'single partbooks from otherwise lost sources'. The 'one intact reading, in Lbl [BL Additional MS] 31390, does seem to represent Tallis's earlier thoughts', but is without the words (Milsom, 'Tallis's first and second thoughts', p. 218). The reading in Additional MS 31390 (completed by 1578?) differs 'in many small and several significant respects' from the printed version (John Milsom, 'English polyphonic style in transition: a study of the sacred music of Thomas Tallis' (Doctoral thesis, University of Oxford, 1983), vol. 1, p. 38). Differences are sometimes (not always) supported by readings in King's College, Cambridge, Rowe MS 316; Bodleian Library, Oxford, Tenbury MS 389; and Shropshire Record Office MS LB/15/1/226.

been adjusted to incorporate the initial words. The supposition must be that these copies spring from non-liturgical versions made after Queen Mary's reign, and probably for private or domestic performance since it is highly unlikely that they were sung later in any church or chapel, even at the universities. Besides *In ieiunio et fletu* and *In manus tuas*, mentioned above, three non-liturgical versions of choral responds by Tallis were printed in *Cantiones, quae ab argumento sacrae vocantur*, which he and Byrd published in 1575: *Dum transisset sabbatum*, *Candidi facti sunt*, and *Honor virtus et potestas*.[10]

In spite of their adaptation for post-Catholic times, copies of Tallis' choral responds reveal their origins. Frequent ligatures in the cantus firmi, even in the printed copies, are reminders of the original chant, and repeat signs in all the parts indicate the intended liturgical repetitions.

Tallis's three five-part choral responds make a varied group. ***Dum transisset sabbatum*** includes a 'Gloria Patri' as a second verse, and a repeated 'Alleluia', so that the shape of the whole piece, in its liturgical form, is:

> ℟ (soloists, *plainsong*) Dum transisset (choir, *polyphony*) sabbatum: Maria Magdalene et Maria Jacobi et Salome emerunt aromata. Ut venientes ungerent Jesum. Alleluia alleluia.
> ℣ (soloists, *plainsong*) Et valde mane una sabbatorum veniunt ad monumentum: orto iam sole.
> ℟ (choir, *polyphony*) Ut venientes ungerent Jesum. Alleluia alleluia.
> ℣ (soloists, *plainsong*) Gloria Patri et Filio: et Spiritui Sancto.
> ℟ (choir, *polyphony*) Alleluia alleluia.
>
> (℟ *When the sabbath was over, Mary Magdalene, and Mary the mother of James, and Salome bought sweet spices, that they might come and anoint Jesus. Alleluia.* ℣ *And very early in the morning on the first day of the week, they came to the sepulchre at sunrise.*)

In the *Cantiones* of 1575 its origin was lightly disguised by amendments to the initial words. Among other changes made was the introduction of a very brief quotation, in the discantus part of the Alleluia, from Taverner's *Dum transisset* [I].[11] It is absent from the version, evidently not copied from the *Cantiones*, in British

[10] The repetition of the initial words of respond texts was taken up by younger composers, such as Robert Parsons. He also made other innovations in setting respond texts, but with non-liturgical results. In *Peccantem me quotidie* he incorporated the incipit into the polyphony from the outset, but did not set the verse; while in *Libera me Domine de morte eterna* the entire response and verse are set polyphonically.

[11] Milsom, 'Tallis's first and second thoughts', pp. 218–19. For a more detailed account of the versions, see Thomas Tallis and William Byrd, *Cantiones sacrae 1575*, ed. John Milsom (Early English Church Music, 56: London, 2014), pp. 222–41.

Library Additional manuscript 31390, and may have been added as a tribute to Taverner's pioneering setting, or perhaps more generally to a composer whom Tallis admired. The original version is shown above the later version in Example 6.1, p. 103. The piece was further disguised by its listing as 'Sabbatum' in the index of the collection. Other responds were listed in a similar way. Perhaps this is evidence of extra caution, or at least a display of tact, in publishing a book which included music with a Catholic origin but which was dedicated to a Queen who was the head of the English church, and who had been excommunicated by Pope Pius V in 1570.[12] Superficially the piece was simply a setting of a Biblical text (Mark 16:1), suitable for recreational performance in the home. Without the plainsong incipit and verses, which Catholics could easily have supplied from a surviving chant book, it was – like all the pieces in the *Cantiones* – an entirely 'lawful' song, just as Henry Edyall implied when he was questioned in 1586 about the music sung in Lord Paget's house.[13]

By the time Tallis wrote his choral responds, imitation had become for him a means of integration and development. This may have been encouraged by Taverner's settings of *Dum transisset*,[14] and it is skilfully combined with the harmonies determined in each piece by the cantus firmus. But on close inspection, what seems at first glance to be imitation often turns out to be illusory. It is seldom carried on for long, because the cantus firmus drives the music in a different direction. The free voices rarely make more than a cursory acknowledgement of the cantus firmus melody. In *Dum transisset* they condense the first six notes of the cantus firmus into four.

Despite its similarities to Tallis's other choral responds, *Dum transisset* has some singular features. It is alone in the neatly ordered entries of its free voices, beginning alternately on C and F, from top to bottom, both at the beginning and a little later at the words 'Maria Magdalene'. Tallis must have thought the pattern was too neat to bear repetition elsewhere. The piece is unique too in placing the cantus firmus in the treble part. At the written pitch, *c''–b♭''*, this results in such a high range for the whole piece that it must be sung perhaps a fifth lower than the notes suggest to modern performers. It is nevertheless the cantus firmus which stimulates an interesting tonal plan. Tallis begins as though he is writing in the D(♭) mode, and – prompted by the chant – inserts a cadence on D at the word 'aromata'. He continues to follow the chant, but the section of the chant preceding the Alleluia ends at 'Jesum' with the notes *f''–e''*, suggesting a plagal cadence on A. His handling of the Alleluia is adroit and imaginative. Below the notes included in the chant, the polyphony traces an ingenious path, and embraces chords with

12 The papal bull had also sought to release the Queen's subjects from their allegiance.

13 He said he 'did use himself to singe in his lordships howse songs of m^r^ byrdes and m^r^ Tallys. and no other unlawfull songe' (TNA SP12/193/63, 24 September 1586; John Harley, *William Byrd: Gentleman of the Chapel Royal* (Aldershot, 1997, rev. 1999), p. 49); Jeremy L. Smith, '"Unlawful song": Byrd, the Babington plot and the Paget choir', *Early Music*, vol. 38 (2010), pp. 497–508.

14 Milsom, *English polyphonic style in transition*, vol. 1, p. 135.

roots at six different pitches as the entries of a repeated figure become gradually lower. Finally, and rather unexpectedly (since it follows a passage containing B♭ chords), the Alleluia settles into E, the key suggested by the last note of the chant, which Tallis prolongs (Example 6.1). There is an anticipation here of the tonal tours Tallis would make in some of his later Latin-texted works.

Example 6.1 The Alleluia from *Dum transisset sabbatum*

continued

Example 6.1 *concluded*

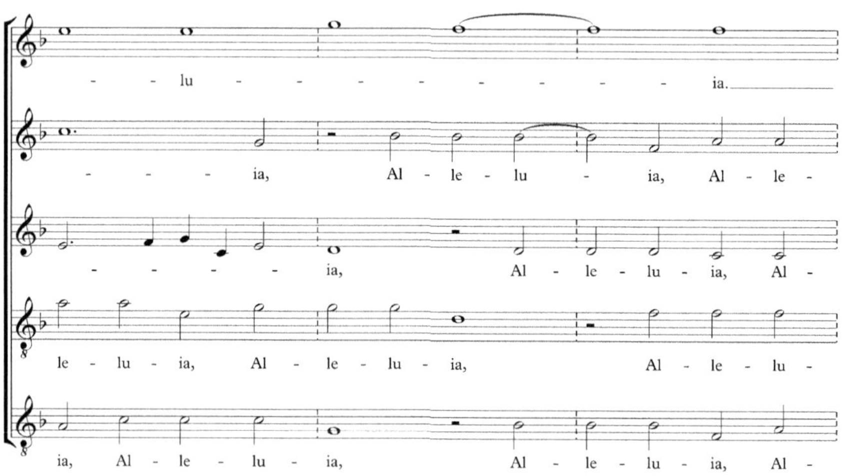

Candidi facti sunt and ***Honor virtus et potestas*** are not known to have circulated before their publication in the *Cantiones*, but repeat signs in the printed partbooks show that they originally conformed to the patterns laid down in the Sarum breviary.[15]

> ℟ (soloists, *plainsong*) Candidi (choir, *polyphony*) facti sunt Nazarei eius, alleluia: splendorem Deo dederunt, alleluia. Et sicut lac coagulati sunt. Alleluia, alleluia.
> ℣ (soloists, *plainsong*) In omnem terram exivit sonus eorum: et in fines orbis terrae verba eorum.
> ℟ (choir, *polyphony*) Et sicut lac coagulati sunt, alleluia.
> ℣ (soloists, *plainsong*) Gloria Patri et Filio: et Spiritui Sancto.
> ℟ (choir, *polyphony*) Alleluia.
>
> (℟ *His Nazarenes were made radiantly white, alleluia; they gave splendour to God, alleluia. And they were changed like milk turning to curds, alleluia.* ℣ *Their sound has gone through all lands; and their words to the ends of the earth.*)
>
> ℟ (soloists, *plainsong*) Honor (choir, *polyphony*) virtus et potestas et imperium sit Trinitati in Unitate, Unitati in Trinitate. In perenni saeculorum tempore.
> ℣ (solists, *plainsong*) Trinitati laus perennis, Unitati sit decus perpetim.
> ℟ (choir, *polyphony*) In perenni saeculorum tempore.

continued

[15] The Tudor Church Music edition misinterprets the sign in *Honor virtus et potestas*, assuming that the piece ends with an integrated repeat. One wonders whether this and similar errors were made by sixteenth-century singers who, by the time the *Cantiones* appeared, would in many cases have known little of what the Sarum rite had once prescribed.

℣ (soloists, *plainsong*) Gloria Patri et Filio: et Spiritui Sancto.
℟ (choir, *polyphony*) In perenni saeculorum tempore.

(℟ *Honour, power, might and dominion be to the Three Persons in One, the One in Three, throughout time everlasting.* ℣ *Everlasting praise be to the Trinity, to the One be unceasing glory.*)

These pieces may have been selected for publication because they were unfamiliar, in contrast to *Dum transisset*, which seems already to have achieved some popularity.[16]

The cantus firmi of *Candidi facti sunt* and *Honor virtus et potestas* are given to the tenor voice.[17] This causes *Candidi* to be written at a low pitch, with the bass descending to written *D* instead of the written *E* or *F* usual in Tallis's music. *Honor virtus et potestas*, on the other hand, is written somewhat higher than might be expected. No doubt the pitch of both pieces was adjusted in performance to suit the original singers, and needs adjustment by their modern counterparts, while recognizing that in *Candidi* Tallis presumably wanted the sound of a choir without trebles.

The entries of the voices in each piece are less regular than in *Dum transisset*. The cantus firmus of *Candidi facti sunt* enters on D, while the free voices all enter on F, though their order and distance of entry is irregular. They make no effort to anticipate or echo the cantus firmus, but concentrate on their own loosely imitative progress and, to good effect, on the interspersed Alleluias. In *Honor virtus et potestas* the voices are paired, entering on G or C, with the lower voice preceding the higher. Only the first three notes of each free voice anticipate the cantus firmus, and in the bass they are strangely separated. Any further reference to the cantus firmus seems no more than accidental until the beginning of the 'In perenni saeculorum' section. Then the chant not only provides a few notes for the free voices, but initiates an unusual feature. The first 11 motes of the chant to which the words 'In perenni' are sung are repeated when 'saeculorum' is reached. Tallis accordingly repeats and varies the polyphonic structure (Example 6.2, p. 107).

Neither of the two choral responds for six voices, ***Homo quidam fecit cenam*** and ***Videte miraculum***, appears in a source earlier than about 1580,[18] but both seem to

[16] For further possible reasons, and for variant versions, see Thomas Tallis and William Byrd, *Cantiones sacrae 1575*, ed John Milsom, pp. 242–9, 321–8.

[17] Tallis may have known a version of the *Honor virtus et potestas* chant in which B was not regularly flattened, or he may have adapted it for his own purposes (compare the version published at http://www.sarum-chant.ca by the Gregorian Institute of Canada). In the *Cantiones* B♭ is introduced only towards the end of the tenor and contratenor parts of the piece.

[18] Both are in Christ Church, Oxford, MSS 979–83 (five partbooks from a set of six; tenor missing). The missing part of *Homo quidam fecit* is supplied by New York Public Library MSS Drexel 4180–85. The tenor part of *Videte miraculum* in the Tudor Church Music edition is presumably the work of an editor, based on the chant.

Example 6.2 The ending of *Honor virtus et potestas*, containing the varied repeat

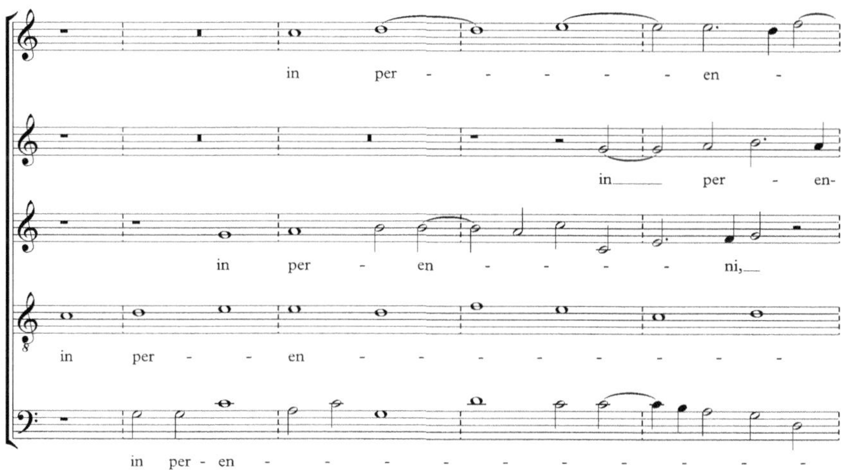

continued

belong with other six-part works written in Queen Mary's time. They are unlikely to be earlier, and – unless they were written for private performances sponsored by some unknown patron – unlikely to be later. (They are discussed on pp. 110–11.)

Example 6.2 *concluded*

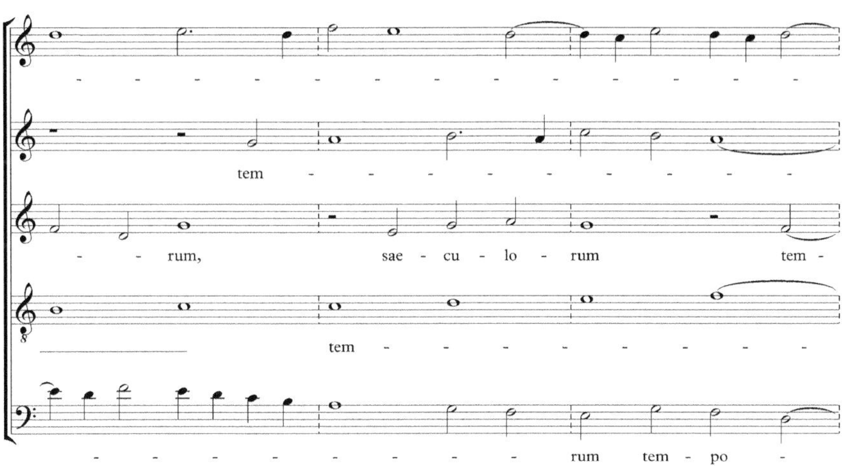
tem
- rum, sae - cu - lo - rum tem -
tem
rum tem - po -

po - re.
po - re, tem - po - re.
po - re.
po - re.
re, tem - po - re.

℟ (soloists, plainsong) Homo (choir, *polyphony*) quidam fecit cenam magnam, et misit servum suum hora cene dicere invitatis ut venirent, Quia parata sunt omnia.
℣ (soloists, plainsong) Venite, comedite panem meum: et bibite vinum quod miscui vobis.
℟ (choir, *polyphony*) Quia parata sunt omnia.
℣ (soloists, plainsong) Gloria Patri et Filio: et Spiritui Sancto.
℟ (choir, *polyphony*) Quia parata sunt omnia.

(*A certain man made a great supper, and sent his servant at supper time to tell those who were invited to come, for all things are ready. Come and eat my bread, and drink the wine that I have blended for you.*)

℟ (soloists, plainsong) Videte (choir, *polyphony*) miraculum matris Domini, concepit virgo virilis ignara consortii. Stans onerata nobili onere Maria. Et matrem se laetam cognoscit: quae se nescit uxorem.
℣(soloists, plainsong) Haec speciosum forma prae filiis hominum castis concepit visceribus: et benedicta in aeternum Deum nobis protulit et hominem.
℟ (choir, *polyphony*) Stans onerata nobili onere Maria. Et matrem se laetam cognoscit, quae se nescit uxorem.
℣ (soloists, plainsong) Gloria Patri et Filio: et Spiritui Sancto.
℟ (choir, *polyphony*) Et matrem se laetam cognoscit: quae se nescit uxorem.

(℟ *Behold the miracle of the Lord's mother, the virgin who has conceived without knowing a man. Mary who stands laden with her noble burden. Not knowing that she is a wife, she rejoices to be a mother.* ℣ *She has conceived in her chaste womb one who is beautiful beyond the sons of men, and blessed for ever; she has brought forth God and man for us.*)

The cantus firmus of *Homo quidam fecit cenam* has a wider range (a ninth) than any other in Tallis's choral responds. This is perhaps why it is transposed up a fourth and placed in the contratenor part, with the result that Tallis finds himself writing a piece with a signature of two flats, and terminating on B♭ instead of the G on which his pieces with a two-flat signature usually end. In clothing chant with polyphony he was led into slightly unfamiliar territory, just as he had been in setting *Jesu salvator* and *Dum transisset sabbatum*.

In the second, repeated, section of the antiphon, the cantus firmus includes a group of three low notes (F G F), sandwiched between identical groups of seven notes (B♭ C B♭ C E♭ D B♭) which permit the repetition of a short canon between the highest and lowest voices – importantly those defining the outlines of the piece. The three low notes do not appear in the version of the chant occurring in the Sarum antiphonaries printed at Paris in 1519–20 for the English market. As Tallis generally uses the notes of a chant quite accurately, they may indicate that the destruction of liturgical books in the wake of the Edwardian statute of 1549 (see p. 61) made it necessary for Queen Mary's chapel to obtain new ones containing a variant form of the chant, though the variation was nowhere near as extreme as in some versions in Continental antiphonaries.

Videte miraculum shows Tallis concerned as always to fashion an appropriate setting for the words presented to him. Here he creates an atmosphere of calm. He is more interested in the sounds yielded by different musical textures than in a display of musical ingenuity. The chant and the text are lengthy, but haste would be out of place in conveying a sense of stillness and the miracle the words describe: 'a virgin has conceived'. There is little attempt to manipulate the tonality, even to the limited extent allowed by the E-mode chant, and the music derives a good deal of its effect from repeated cadences on A.

Imitation is largely impressionistic in the first section of the work. The next section, repeated after the versicle, falls into two parts, of which the second is repeated alone after the doxology. The words 'Stans onerata nobili onere Maria', at the beginning of the second section, are suitably introduced by homophony that lingers into the counterpoint following it. At the beginning of the next part, 'Et matrem se laetam cognoscit: quae se nescit uxorem', the chant provides material for some canonic development.[19] But the writing is not sustained, and soon dissolves back into the kind of impressionistic imitation with which the piece began.

Tallis's sole respond for seven voices, ***Loquebantur variis linguis***, is another work found only in late sources.[20] The number of voices may represent the seven gifts of the Holy Spirit which descended upon the apostles – though it may equally well indicate no more than an intention to compose something especially impressive.

> ℟ (soloists, plainsong) Loquebantur (choir, *polyphony*) variis linguis apostoli, Alleluia. Magnalia Dei, Alleluia.
> ℣ (soloists, plainsong) Repleti sunt omnes Spiritu Sancto: et coeperunt loqui.
> ℟ (choir, *polyphony*) Magnalia Dei, Alleluia.
> ℣ (soloists, plainsong) Gloria Patri et Filio: et Spiritui Sancto.
> ℟ (choir, *polyphony*) Alleluia.
>
> (℟ *The apostles were speaking in various languages, alleluia, about the great works of God. Alleluia.* ℣ *They were all filled with the Holy Spirit, and began to speak.*)

The cantus firmus of *Loquebantur variis linguis* inspired no wide-ranging tonal explorations, but its presence is manifested in other ways. This is obvious at the beginning of the piece, where each of the free voices starts with the four opening notes of the cantus firmus, or a transposition of them. Later, where the contratenor sings 'apostoli alleluia', and again in the 'Magnalia Dei' section, the narrow range

19 See Milsom, *English polyphonic style in transition*, vol. 1, p. 135.

20 Christ Church, Oxford, MSS 979–83, and BL MS R. M. 24.d.2.

of the cantus firmus and its repetition of notes and small groups of notes provide a foundation for a structure more suggestive of imitation than dependent on it.

Hymns

When a hymn was chanted throughout as plainsong, its verses (including the doxology) were all sung to the same melody. The initial line was sung by a soloist (or soloists, depending on the importance of the day), and the first verse was completed by the soloist's side of the choir. Thereafter, the verses were sung alternately by the two sides of the choir, which joined to sing the concluding doxology. This practice is reflected in Tallis's polyphonic settings of hymns. The even-numbered verses are set polyphonically, incorporating the chant into one of the vocal parts as a cantus firmus. The doxology, when there is one, is always set polyphonically, regardless of whether it is the equivalent of an even-numbered or odd-numbered verse. Harrison remarked that the overall result is akin to contrapuntal variations on a theme.[21] In references to hymns in the following paragraphs, the incipits of the first (chanted) and second (polyphonic) verse are both given.

Tallis included four Latin hymns in the 1575 *Cantiones*. Two are almost certainly Elizabethan, and will be discussed in chapter 14. So will two settings of *Te lucis ante terminum–Procul recedant somnia.* The setting of only the second verse may indicate that they were originally composed for liturgical use; but it seems more than possible that they are Elizabethan pieces. Postponing consideration of them will in any case provide an opportunity for discussing the way they are fitted into the plan of the *Cantiones*. One hymn setting, *Sermone blando angelus–Illae dum pergunt*, appears very likely to be a Marian piece although it was included in the *Cantiones*, and it will be considered shortly.[22] A number of other hymns are also placed in this chapter, for reasons similar to those which caused most of Tallis's choral responds to be treated as works belonging to Queen Mary's reign. They occur in sources a good deal later than their putative date (and so may have undergone some alteration in transmission), but they have underlying liturgical forms, and may well have resulted from a burst of Marian composition in which Tallis and Sheppard were the principal participants.[23] (The question of whether any were written in the reign of Henry VIII has been argued both ways, with

[21] Harrison, *Music in medieval Britain*, p. 382.

[22] Because John Baldwin owned the printed copy of *Sermone blando* he probably thought there was no need to enter it into his manuscript partbooks when he entered the four other hymns dealt with here. The partbooks, now Christ Church, Oxford, Mus 979–83, are in fact bound up with a set of *Cantiones* partbooks. The occurrence of pieces together in a collector's retrospective manuscript does not of course mean that Tallis composed them as a group.

[23] For sources see the EECM Primary Source Database.

no certain conclusion.)[24] Table 6.2 lists the hymns dealt with here. They are all for five voices, and the highest voice is always a cantus firmus derived from the Sarum chant.

Table 6.2 Tallis's probably Marian hymns

For days which may have been specially celebrated at court

Quod chorus vatum–Haec Deum caeli (for first Vespers of the feast of the Purification of the Virgin Mary)

*Salvator mundi Domine–Adesto nunc propitius** (for Compline at the Christmas vigil)

*Iam Christus astra ascenderat–Solemnis urgebat dies** (for first Vespers on Whit Sunday)

For other days

Sermone blando angelus–Illae dum pergunt (Lauds, first Sunday after Easter until Ascension)

*Jesu salvator saeculi verbum–Tu fabricator omnium** (Compline, first Sunday after Easter until Ascension)

* Set by Sheppard as well

Note: Dashes separate the incipits of first (chanted) verses from the incipits of second (polyphonic) verses.

Too few hymns by English composers survive to suggest what home-grown examples Tallis might have known, and it is impossible to say what access he had to settings by Continental composers. His hymns have parallels with some of those published abroad – for example in Adrian Willaert's *Hymnorum musica* (1542), with even-numbered verses set polyphonically and the chant as a cantus firmus, often in an upper part – but it would be difficult to identify particular models.

Sarum hymn chants usually set each syllable to just one or two short notes, and only occasionally to three or four, so that those with a number of verses are despatched rapidly. But when the chant is used as a cantus firmus, with each note transformed (in Tallis's notation) into a minim or a semibreve, or more, a hymn with all its chanted and polyphonic verses becomes a substantial work. For the most part Tallis's cantus firmi follow the chants fairly closely, as far as the pitch of notes is concerned. The surviving sources suggest that he made his own decisions when it came to matching words to notes derived from the chant, though this impression may be exaggerated by changes made in the course of repeated copying, especially when the word underlay in a copy-text was imprecise or virtually non-existent.

The initial polyphonic verse, or pair of polyphonic verses, always has the signature C, but the last polyphonic verse or the doxology has the signature ₵. (In *Sermone blando angelus–Illae dum pergunt*, the one case where there is a third polyphonic verse as well as a doxology, both have the ₵ signature.) The first sign

24 Paul Doe, 'Latin polyphony under Henry VIII', p. 92; Doe, *Tallis*, p. 34.

means that a breve has the value of two semibreves, each worth three minims.[25] (It is unclear whether Tallis regarded the breve, rather than the minim, as having a constant length.) The second sign has the meaning it has elsewhere in Tallis's music, so that a breve has the value of two semibreves, each worth two minims. The similarity imparted to the hymns by these attributes is more apparent than real; their diversity and Tallis's inventiveness are evident when we look at them one by one.

During the reigns of Henry VIII and Queen Mary the words of ***Salvator mundi Domine–Adesto nunc propitius*** had a dual purpose. As well as being those of a hymn for Compline at the Christmas vigil, they had a daily place in religious observance. King Henry's statutes for new foundation cathedrals are exemplified by those issued to Carlisle on 6 June 1545: 'Let those about to go to bed say the hymn, Salvator Mundi, Domine, &c.' This was repeated in statutes delivered to Durham Cathedral by Philip and Mary, under the great seal: 'before they go to bed let them say the hymn O Saviour of the world [*Salvator mundi*], with the psalm Out of the depths [*De profundis*]'.[26]

The hymn has four verses, plus a doxology and Amen. Verses 2 and 4 are set polyphonically, with the ͼ signature. They have similar though not identical cantus firmi constructed from the chant, but as far as the other voices are concerned the two verses are set independently. This extends to the harmonization of the chant as well as the counterpoint. The hymn is the most freely composed of all those in the group under discussion, and it is perhaps for this reason that Tallis sticks closely to the G tonality, with F rarely sharpened, and never forms an intermediate cadence on a note more distant than D or A. The doxology and Amen, set polyphonically with the signature ¢, follow immediately after verse 4. Here the chant is decorated more than in the previous verses, and the lower voices often move together in minims, adding a special quality to their pseudo-imitation.

Jesu salvator saeculi verbum–Tu fabricator omnium has five verses plus a doxology and an Amen; but instead of setting verses 2 and 4 differently, Tallis sets them to the same music. The chant of *Jesu salvator* is transposed to form the cantus firmus, with the result that each verse ends in the unusual key of C

[25] The 'mood imperfect of the more prolation': see Thomas Morley, *A plaine and easie introduction to practicall musicke* (London, 1597), p. 21; ed. R. Alec Harman (London, 1952), p. 36. It is unclear how this sign came to be used in hymns. Paul Doe has suggested a relationship with some German hymn settings ('Latin polyphony under Henry VIII', p. 92). In his short organ setting of *Natus est nobis* Tallis imposed the same metre on the chant.

[26] Carlisle Cathedral, *The Statutes of the cathedral church of Carlisle. Translated ... by J.E. Prescott* (London, 1903), p. 89; Durham Cathedral, *The statutes of the cathedral church of Durham. With other documents relating to its foundation and endowment by King Henry the Eighth and Queen Mary* [ed A. Hamilton Thompson from a text prepared by J. Meade Falkner] (Surtees Society: Durham and London, 1929), pp. 180–81.

with one flat. A good deal of the setting is homophonic, or nearly so, as if the ideas of reformers in previous reigns had entered into Tallis's writing. Yet this is not so everywhere. While the voices may begin in complete rhythmic unanimity, the lower voices are apt to become increasingly independent, so that the scoring evolves from simple block contrast to subtly changing colours. The setting ends with an extended and beautifully balanced Amen.

The result is interesting to compare with some of Tallis's English-texted music written in the reign of Edward VI, or shortly before it. There was more continuity in musical ideas than in the politics of religion. Allowing for the fact that *If ye love me* has a prose text and that the words of *Jesu salvator–Tu fabricator* are in verse, the English anthem and the Latin hymn have several things in common (Examples 6.3a and b, pp. 116–17). The first two verbal phrases of *If ye love me* are set homophonically; the next two phrases are polyphonic. In *Jesu salvator–Tu fabricator* the first three short lines of verses 2 and 4 are more or less homophonic, but for the fourth line the entries of two voices are delayed, creating a feeling of polyphony. Without seriously inhibiting the voices' independence, the second (repeated) section of the English anthem and the doxology of the Latin hymn both rely to a large extent on the notes of different voices sounding simultaneously.

Quod chorus vatum–Haec Deum caeli has five verses and an Amen, but verse 5 is not a doxology. Tallis therefore sets verses 2 and 4, with each mensural signature applied to just a single verse. The first polyphonic verse, 'Haec Deum caeli', is the only one in all Tallis's hymns where the cantus firmus is written almost entirely in alternate semibreves and minims. Any resemblance to a dance tune or popular song is masked by the irregular and overlapping phrases of the four lower voices. These observe the harmonies the chant suggests, but make no melodic reference to it. It is the bass which generates patterns that are carried into the other voices.

In the second polyphonic verse the chant is set out mainly in semibreves. A cadence divides the verse at 'Regis eterni', throwing emphasis on those words and on the following word, 'Genetrix'. Before the division the bass repeats a phrase (once with a slight variation) which has the character of an ostinato. After the division the phrase is repeated in an extended form, and echoed by other voices.

Although ***Iam Christus astra ascenderat–Solemnis urgebat dies*** runs to six verses. It follows the general plan of Tallis's shorter hymns. Odd-numbered verses are chanted, and verses 2 and 4 are set polyphonically in triple time, to the same music. In the polyphonic verses the contratenor follows the superius in strict canon at an octave below. The other voices are less tightly organized, but from time to time they share ideas with the canonic voices or with one another. The original chant of verse 6 is identical to the chant of the other verses, but because it is the last even-numbered verse the polyphonic setting is in duple time, with the cantus firmus mostly in semibreves while the other voices create an independent imitative texture.

The greater length of ***Sermone blando angelus–Illae dum pergunt*** (seven verses followed by a doxology and Amen) brings about a slight modification of the usual layout. Verses 2 and 4 have the signature ☾ and are set to the same music.

Example 6.3a The first section of *If ye love me*

The signature's influence on the cantus firmus is plain in these verses, though it is less regular than in *Quod chorus vatum*. The sixth verse and the doxology have the signature ¢ and the same music. The repetition of music for different words necessarily involves minor adjustments, and in each set of verses it provides an opportunity for an exchange of the discantus and contratenor parts, which are both for the full-range tenor voice, and which sometimes cross.

Example 6.3b *Jesu salvator saeculi*, second verse, 'Tu fabricator omnium' (*You, the maker of all things and shaper of the seasons, restore our toil-worn bodies with the peace of night.*)

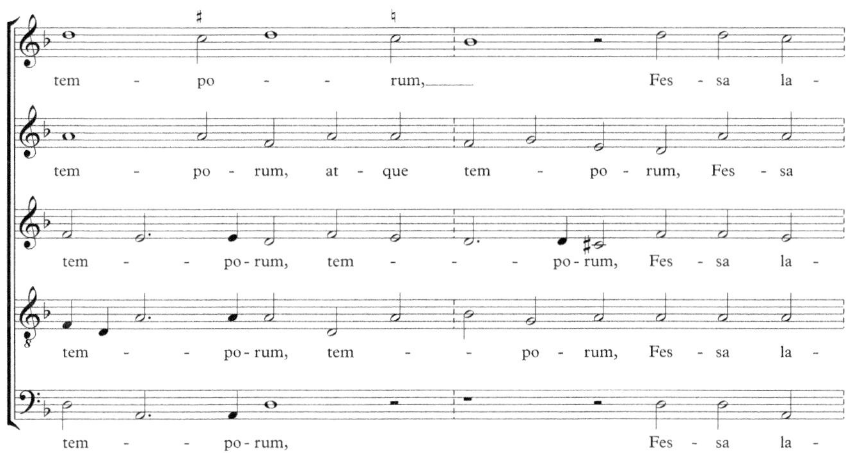

continued

Tallis evidently thought well of the verses he set polyphonically, and as noted above he included them (indexed as 'Illae dum pergunt') in the 1575 *Cantiones*. In the first two polyphonic verses a group of lower voices begins every line of the text, so that when the chant enters in the superius part it seems to be imitating a phrase which has already been heard.

Example 6.3b *concluded*

Things are organized differently in the third polyphonic verse and the doxology. The chant is now written in semibreves and begins each verse, and real imitation occurs more frequently between the four lower parts. The tonality is altered, too. In verses 2 and 4 the cadences occur on F, D, G and F. In verse 6 and the doxology they occur on F, B♭, C and F.

Short Pieces Surviving without Words

Rex sanctorum occurs, with the title and Tallis's name attached but without words, only in a set of partbooks compiled about the beginning of the seventeenth century.[27] It is for three voices, and appears to be connected with the singing of the litany *Rex sanctorum angelorum* in procession after the blessing of the font on Holy Saturday (the day after Good Friday). The traditional mode of performance required three senior members of the choir to begin, with the choir repeating the 'Rex sanctorum' refrain after each verse.[28]

Three-part settings of *Rex sanctorum* appear in English manuscripts dating from as far back as the fifteenth century. They incorporate the chant into the top voice, but decorate it freely, with next to no imitation.[29] The music attributed to Tallis seems to be a good deal later. It is not based even loosely on the chant, and much of it is imitative in all parts – more so than in most of Tallis's early pieces. It could very well have been written in Queen Mary's time, since processional music for the Easter season was being composed right up to her death. *Similes illis fiant*, a collaborative piece by Sheppard, Mundy and Byrd, was for the daily procession to the fonts, and would have been preceded by a setting of the words 'Alleluia. Laudate pueri', customarily sung before the font by three boys.[30] Byrd's setting of those words (conflated with *Alleluia. Confitemini Domino*), though not suitable for boys at the written pitch, appears in the partbooks containing Tallis's *Rex sanctorum*.

An Elizabethan source credits to Tallis a single textless part from a setting of the Easter gradual ***Haec dies quam fecit Dominus***, but it is evidently a fragment of a Marian piece.[31] None of Tallis's Elizabethan pieces is so closely connected

---

[27] BL Additional MSS 18936–9 (omitting 18938, since *Rex sanctorum* has no tenor part), on f.11^{v} of each manuscript. A fifth partbook is missing, but is unlikely to have contained any part of *Rex sanctorum*.

[28] *Processionale ad vsus insignis eccl[es]i.e. Sar[um]* (Antwerp, 1545), ff.cj^{r}–cij^{r}; F.H. Dickinson, ed., *Missale ad usum insignis et praeclarae Ecclesiae Sarum* (Burntisland, 1861–83), col. 347; *The Sarum Missal*, ed. J. Wickham Legg (Oxford, 1916), pp. 159, 132. See Walter Howard Frere, ed., *The Use of Sarum* (Cambridge, 1898–1901), vol. 2, p. 167; Harrison, *Music in medieval Britain*, pp. 93, 409.

[29] BL MS Egerton 3307, ff.33^{r}–36^{r}, and Cambridge, Magdalene College, Pepys MS 1236, f.63^{v}, printed side by side in Manfred F. Bukofzer, *Studies in medieval and Renaissance music* (London, 1961), p. 144. See also Andrew Hughes, ed., *Fifteenth-century liturgical music* (Early English Church Music, 8: London, 1968), no. 27, pp. 108–14; Gwynn S. McPeek, ed., *The British Library manuscript Egerton 3307* (London, 1963), no. 10, pp. 29–30; Sydney Robinson Charles, ed., *The music of the Pepys MS 1236*, ed. (Corpus Mensurabilis Musicae, 40: Dallas, Tex., 1967), no. 70, p. 98. The first two editions show the manner of performance, the chant, and the words of the refrain and first six verses.

[30] Frere, *The Use of Sarum*, vol. 2, p. 72.

[31] BL Additional MS 32377 contains dates from 1584 to 1588, and also motets published by Byrd in 1589 and 1591, though apparently not copied from the print: see

with the Mass; and fitting the fragment together with the appropriate chant suggests that the contrapuntal setting began with the second word, leaving the first to be chanted.[32] It is marked '5 Part*es*', and may have been copied for instrumental performance, since it follows a large group of five-part consort pieces.

Large-scale Works

Two works conceived on a grand scale are generally assumed to belong to Queen Mary's short reign. This depends to some extent on the slightly shaky assumption that the pieces are connected with her as a person. But, although both pieces draw on forms and techniques used by English composers before King Henry's break with Rome, it would be difficult to suggest any occasion early in Tallis's career for which he might have written either the antiphon *Gaude gloriosa Dei mater* or the Mass *Puer natus est*, even if it were conceded that he was capable of doing so. If they are indeed Marian works, the point of them may be in part that they contain features of music Tallis knew when the Catholic church in England occupied a position to which the Queen intended it should return.

No manuscript of ***Gaude gloriosa Dei mater*** survives from before about 1580,[33] although music related to it occurs in a fragment of uncertain but apparently earlier date. This is a single voice-part equipped with English words.[34] There is too little evidence to indicate firmly whether the English version preceded or followed the surviving Latin version; but we can feel some confidence that the Latin-texted work we have took shape after Mary's accession, and resulted from the court's return to Catholic practices. The advances in conception and technique it shows in comparison with Tallis's previous antiphons make this a reasonable assumption.

Warwick Edwards, 'The sources of Elizabethan consort music' (Doctoral thesis, University of Cambridge, 1974, vol. 1, p. 136).

32 John Milsom, *English polyphonic style in transition*, vol. 2, appendix 2.2.

33 The earliest sources are Bodleian Library MSS Mus. Sch. e.423, and Christ Church, Oxford, MSS 979–83.

34 The discovery of Corpus Christi College, Oxford, MS 566 is described by T. H. Aston in the college's *Annual report and The Pelican* for 1978–79, pp. 10–11, where the words are described as 'faintly reminscent of Psalms 9 and 10'. Two paper fragments were found 'behind the secondary plaster in the Fraenkel Room, used simply as stuffing in a crack by a post in the timber-framed east wall'. One was 'part of the quarto volume of Pius II's *Epistole varie* published in Lyons in 1518'; the other, bearing the musical text in question, has a watermark which cannot be dated exactly. See also John Milsom, 'Songs, carols and *contrafacta* in the early history of the Tudor anthem', *Proceedings of the Royal Musical Association*, vol. 107 (1980–81), pp. 34–45, at 35; Milsom, 'A new Tallis contrafactum', *The Musical Times*, vol. 123 (1982), pp. 429–31; Milsom, 'Tallis's first and second thoughts', pp. 203–22, at 205–7.

Tallis's *Gaude gloriosa* marks a return to favour of the votive antiphon after the greater attention paid by composers to responds and hymns in the 1530s and 1540s. It is the culmination of a series of Tudor Marian antiphons beginning with the word 'Gaude', many of which were entered in the Eton choirbook at the end of the fifteenth century. Like a number of others, it is for six voices (which are sometimes divided). Tallis used the combination of voices adopted by Sheppard for his *Gaude Virgo Christipera*,[35] but otherwise the pieces have little in common. *Gaude gloriosa* has a clearer family resemblance – but is it as parent or child? – to William Mundy's two Marian antiphons for the same voices, *Vox patris caelestis* and the less effective *Maria Virgo Sanctissima*. These probably date from the reign of Queen Mary, since Mundy was almost certainly too young to have written them before the reign of Edward VI, during which they could not have been performed. They would not have been needed after Elizabeth came to the throne.

Two occasions which may have given rise to Mundy's *Vox patris caelestis* have been identified: the annual celebration on 15 August of the feast of the Assumption of the Virgin, who was the patron saint of St Mary-at-Hill where Mundy was the parish clerk; and 30 September 1553, the day before Queen Mary's coronation, when she witnessed a pageant in the yard of St Paul's Cathedral, heard an oration by John Heywood, and listened to music sung in the Cathedral's schoolhouse.[36] Whatever the background to either of Mundy's pieces, the similarities between them and Tallis's *Gaude gloriosa* suggest that one composer sat down to write with the work of the other in mind.

The question of priority cannot be decided conclusively, though as Tallis was the senior composer, and as Mundy was the parish clerk of St Mary-at-Hill and did not become a Gentleman of the Chapel Royal until 1564, it may be thought that Tallis is the more likely to have composed a work for the eve of the coronation, while Mundy is the more likely to have written works celebrating his church's patron saint. Indeed, his two antiphons could have been sung in different years. The unverifiable notion that Tallis's antiphon is connected with the coronation seems to spring from a passage in its anonymous text. The first verse, praising the Virgin for having reached the heavenly throne, could be interpreted as a flattering allusion to the Queen. This is not as preposterous as it seems, for it was believed (albeit by an English Protestant exile) that, when Cardinal Pole met the Queen on

---

35 Treble, alto, two full-range tenors (contratenors, in the sixteenth-century sense), tenor and bass. A date as early as 1540 has been thought possible for *Gaude Virgo Christipera*, though this seems to be based on the idea that the main period of votive antiphon composition had ended by that time (David Chadd's article on Sheppard in Grove Music Online, accessed 2 October 2013). The earliest sources are the same as those of *Gaude gloriosa Dei mater*.

36 Kerry McCarthy, 'William Mundy's "Vox patris caelestis" and the assumption of the Virgin Mary', *Music & Letters*, vol. 85 (2004), pp. 353–67; John Milsom, 'William Mundy's "Vox patris caelestis" and the accession of Mary Tudor', *Music & Letters*, vol. 91 (2010), pp. 1–38.

his return to England he had uttered the words 'Hail, Mary, full of grace, &c'.[37] Whatever the date of *Gaude gloriosa*, there is little doubt that it was intended for an important event. More than 20 years after he composed his previous Marian antiphons, Tallis wrote one that was both bolder and bigger. Although he reverted to long melodies and the protracted melismatic treatment of vowels, his writing now had more character and purpose.

The text is made up of nine verses (perhaps because nine is one of several numbers symbolically associated with the Virgin Mary), and each begins with the exclamation 'Gaude'. The words pass gradually from the Virgin's virtues to her role as an intercessor on behalf of those who are to be damned, and to a prayer seeking her help. It was natural for Tallis to take account of the broad structure of the text, but his setting has its own musical plan (Table 6.3, p. 123).

Tallis's innate sense of architecture is manifest in a work that closely links text and music.[38] Inventiveness is in evidence throughout. The beginnings of verses are treated in diverse ways, even though the initial syllable of 'Gaude' is always long. The two voices which open the first verse start with a unison that quickly expands to become a tenth. (This seems to have been in Byrd's mind when he set 'Gaude Maria Virgo' in his first book of *Gradualia*, published in 1605.)[39] The second verse starts with two voices singing a few notes in imitation. The openings of the next two verses are both densely textured, with all six voices in action. It takes a few moments for imitation to appear in verse 3, and then it is confined to only three parts. In verse 4, by contrast, it is present in all the voices from the outset. The beginnings of the verses which follow are no less varied, and no less strikingly individual.

Overall, *Gaude gloriosa* is in the D(♭) mode. But even in so large a piece, Tallis avoids any conspicuous use of tonal development until halfway through section II; then it becomes a substantial constituent of the structure. The opening verse, sung by only three voices, is tonally fairly static, and at the end of the first phrase a cadence on D lends prominence to 'honorificanda' (*honoured*). In the second verse the whole invocation is sung by two voices, until they are joined by a third singing high above, and then by a fourth to illustrate the sweet praises of angels resounding in the heavens. The phrase which follows, 'iam enim laeteris visione

---

37 William Salkyn ('Servant of Master Richard Hilles') writing from Strasbourg to Heinrich Bullinger, 29 December 1554 (Hastings Robinson, ed., *Original letters relative to the English Reformation* (Parker Society, 37–38: Cambridge, 1846–47), vol. 1, letter CLXIX, pp. 346–8).

38 Bray states the proportions which he believes underlie *Gaude gloriosa* as 99 78 27 171 / 102 96 66 90 176 (Roger Bray, ed., *Music in Britain: the sixteenth century* (Blackwell history of music in Britain, 2: Oxford, 1995), p. 85). It is clear that some of these figures relate closely to the number of semibreves in verses, but others appear to be more recondite. Bray also draws attention to the ratios he discovers between some of the figures or combinations of figures.

39 Joseph Kerman, *The Masses and motets of William Byrd*, p. 257.

Table 6.3 Layout of *Gaude gloriosa Dei mater*

Section I (ϕ)		
Verse 1	Bars 1–34	M, C1, B 'Gaude gloriosa Dei mater ... exaltata adepta es thronum'
Verse 2	Bars 34–69	C2, T (from bar 34) 'Gaude Virgo Maria' Tr, C2, T (from bar 40) 'cui angelicae turmae ...' Tr, C1, C2, T (from bar 46) 'resonant laudes ...' Tr, M, C1, C2, T, B (from bar 60) 'omnia serviunt'
Verse 3	Bars 70–98	Tr, M, C1, C2, T, B 'Gaude concivis ...'
Verse 4	Bars 96–127	Tr, M, C1, C2, T, B 'Gaude flos florum ... Matrem glorificat'
Section II (¢)		
Verse 5	Bars 128–180	Divided Tr and M; B added from bar 144 'Gaude Virgo Maria quam dignam ... te Matrem glorificat'
Verse 6	Bars 181–228	C1, C2, T 'Gaude Virgo Maria quae corpore ... supplicamus'
Verse 7	Bars 228–262	Tr, M, C1, C2, T, B 'Gaude Maria intercessorum ... salvatrix celebranda'
Verse 8	Bars 261–307	M, C2, divided B 'Gaude sancta Virgo Maria ... a potestate diabolica liberati'
Verse 9	Bars 308–395 (Amen from 366)	T, M, C1, C2, T, B 'Gaude Virgo Maria Christi benedicta Mater ... caelorum regnum. Amen'

Notes: Bar numbers are calculated by counting 3 semibreves to a bar in section I, and 4 semibreves to a bar in section II. For the purposes of this Table bars 228 and 304 have been regarded as containing three semibreves. Verses may overlap.

Voices: Tr = treble, M = mean, C1 and C2 = contratenors, T= tenor, B = bass

Regis cui omnia serviunt' (*now indeed you rejoice at the sight of the King whom all things serve*), is sung by all six voices and ends with an extended cadence on A. Here some of the voices are given the long notes which occur in Tallis's music when he wants to make the listener particularly aware of the words he is setting, as if uttering them slowly commands greater attention (Example 6.4, p. 124).

The third and fourth verses are treated as a single unit praising the Virgin, and are sung by the full choir. Cadence-like formations on A and D respectively provide punctuation after 'sanctorum' and 'portasti', although some tonal variety is introduced by chords on C where the mean and bass voices end 'Mater' and begin 'digne'. In the fourth verse emphasis is placed on G by chords built on the breves ending important words or phrases sung by the bass voice – 'speciosissima' (*most beautiful*), 'virga iuris' (*rod of the law*), 'pes labentis' (*support of the fallen*), 'mundi lux' (*light of the world*), the last marked by a dotted breve – before the verse moves back through A to end on D.

Example 6.4 From the second verse of *Gaude gloriosa*

The way in which Tallis combines technical skill with sensitivity to the words of the text, and with a high degree of aural imagination, is well illustrated by the fourth verse. It begins with 'Gaude flos florum speciosissima' (*Rejoice, flower of flowers, supremely beautiful*) sung to arching phrases rising through the voices. Initially they include between them all the notes of the D(♭) mode; but when the

bass voice ends its first phrase the mode has been transformed by the alteration of the flat to a natural, the bass is supporting a major chord on G, and F♮ is about to become F♯. It is an easy step to major chords on D and A at the words 'virga iuris' (*rod of justice*), before there is a return to G, and the original notes of the mode are then restored for the words 'forma morum' (*model of morals*). In the process the bass has moved through a series of intervals of a fourth, supporting what are in effect three plagal cadences. All this has been accomplished with only the alterations to the pitch of notes which contemporary practice customarily permitted or required.

The fifth verse deals with the church's celebration of Mary, for which the two highest voices are divided in a 'double gymel'. They are supported by the bass's repetitions of significant parts of the text, ending in turn on A, G, and finally D (through several repetitions of 'glorificat'). D remains the predominant tonality throughout the sixth verse, where the contratenor part is divided, and is supported by the tenor.

In the seventh verse, where Mary is addressed as an intercessor and saviour, Tallis sets 'intercessorum adiutrix et damnandorum salvator celebranda' (*renowned helper of those who seek aid, and saviour of the damned*) in long notes for the tenor and bass voices, and briefly for the contratenor. He is trying to impress the ideas of damnation and salvation upon the listener as strongly as he did in *Sancte Deus*. There is no certainty that this exposes Tallis's personal beliefs, but if it does not he makes a remarkably good job of communicating those of his employer. The singing of the lower voices in this passage is eerie, while the voices singing sweetly above them represent Mary's intercession. There is drama here, just as there was in the representation of the good and bad angels in the play performed by the Chapel Royal soon after Queen Mary's coronation (see p. 90), and Tallis no doubt made sure it was brought out in performance. The eighth verse proceeds more serenely, but the division of the bass part lends weight to the idea of Christ saving the dead from eternal punishment, with 'salvamur' emphasized by a major chord on C.

The C major chord, with a root two fifths distant from the key note, recurs in the long last verse, ending the phrases 'Gaude Virgo Maria' and 'Christi benedicta mater'. The succeeding prayer leads again to a chord on C to end the bass's first utterance of 'caelorum regnum' (*the kingdom of heaven*), a phrase that is repeated with final chords on G, then A, and at last on D as the verse moves seamlessly into a long and splendid Amen – a vision revealed after a long journey. It is for the Amen that Tallis has saved both the highest note in the piece (*a''*), and changes of tonal colouring created by movement through D, A, C, F, D, F, and A, before the music settles finally and firmly on D.

Gaude gloriosa is an admirable showcase for Tallis's style in the middle of the century. His fondness for arcs of melody is well in evidence. Some are broken into phrases forming shorter arcs. Some describe an almost unbroken trajectory. In other cases short arcs are joined to form longer lines, or a long arc may pursue an irregular path. In still others, the rising part of the arc is truncated (or dispensed with altogether), to leave a long, often irregular descent.

The vocal lines are governed by what can be sung, and how it may be heard by listeners. Leaps of a fourth or fifth, upwards or downwards, are common, but larger leaps are divided into smaller intervals or broken by a rest. Successive large leaps in the same direction are avoided unless a rest is interposed. Successive leaps of a third, tending to form a triadic shape, are rare; but if they do occur, it is usual for at least two adjacent notes to belong to different chords. The repetition of a note at the same pitch without an intervening rest is also rare, unless the second note begins a new syllable. Everything reveals a constant alertness to the practicalities of performance and perception.

The Mass ***Puer natus est*** has survived, although not completely, because in the early seventeenth century sections of it were copied into a group of manuscripts compiled for Edward Paston, a Catholic amateur musician and collector of music. The Mass is a large and complex work, with some of the characteristics of 'speculative' music, but not obviously intended for any academic purpose, and not – at least in its surviving state – set down in some recondite notation.[40]

[40] For a discussion of *musica speculativa* in sixteenth-century England, see Roger Bray, 'Music and the quadrivium in early Tudor England', *Music & Letters*, vol. 76 (1995), pp. 1–18, and Roger Bray, 'Editing and performing *musica speculativa*', in John Morehen, ed., *English choral practice, 1400–1650* (Cambridge, 1995), pp. 48–73. Note, however, that Thomas Morley's definition of speculative music is more narrowly framed than Bray's article appears to suggest. It is 'that kinde of musicke which by Mathematicall helpes, seeketh out the causes, properties, and natures of soundes by themselves, and compared with others proceeding no further, but content with the onlie [*sic*] contemplation of the Art'

Its size and complexity lead to the suppositions that the Mass must have been composed over a protracted period, and that it must have been written for some special (but not necessarily public) occasion, although there is nothing to confirm either. Ideas which have been advanced regarding the second are that Tallis's choice of cantus firmus – a chant sung to the words 'Puer natus est nobis' (*Unto us a child is born*) – was connected with the Queen's supposed pregnancy in 1554, and that it may have been designed for a combined performance by the Queen's singers and those brought to England by her husband, Philip of Spain.[41] It is true that William Chedsey preached at St Paul's Cathedral on an Annunciation text before the end of November 1554, and that before the Lord Mayor and aldermen and 10 bishops he spoke of the Queen as 'quick with childe'; and we know from Henry Machyn's report that when Mass was celebrated before an even more distinguished gathering at St Paul's on 2 December 'ye quen chapell & ye kyng*es* and powll*es* quer sang' (though he does not say whether they sang together or separately).[42] But while these events suggest the atmosphere which may have surrounded a time when the Mass was first performed, they do not explain why it is based on a cantus firmus taken from an introit sung on Christmas morning. No liturgical requirement was imposed by the presence of a Christmas cantus firmus, and the Mass might have been seen as a piece for the whole of any Christmas season, beginning on the evening of 24 December. That would rule out a suggestion, sometimes put forward, that it was connected with Cardinal Pole's absolution of the nation in November 1554. The first Christmas following Mary's marriage is as good a guess as any regarding the occasion of its first performance.[43] If planning started early enough, it would have allowed Tallis time to write and rehearse the Mass. There is no real evidence that the scoring was chosen (as has been supposed) to suit the

(*A plaine and easie introduction to practicall musicke* (London, 1597), Annotations to p. 2, vers. 26; ed. R. Alec Harman (London, 1952), p. 101).

41 Joseph Kerman, 'The *Missa Puer natus est*' (in Chris Banks and others, eds, *Sundry sorts of music books* (1993), pp. 40–53, at 40–41, in Kerman, *Write all these down* (Berkeley,1994), pp. 125–38, at 126); David Wulstan, *Tudor music* (London, 1985), pp. 295–6. David Humphreys (letter in *Early Music*, vol. 28 (2000), pp. 508–9) rightly expressed scepticism about the suggestion sometimes made regarding a connection of the *Puer natus* Mass with Queen Mary's supposed pregnancy. It is, however, possible to doubt his remark that the Mass 'has at least some of the characteristics of a university degree exercise – which suggests that both Mass and *Suscipe* could have been submitted together as degree exercises'. There is no reason to suppose that the Mass and *Susicipe quaeso Domine* are connected, or that Tallis ever sought a degree.

42 For Chedsey, see Charles Wriothesley, *A chronicle of England during the reigns of the Tudors, from A. D. 1485 to 1559* (Camden Society, new series, 11, 20: London, 1875–77), vol. 2, p. 124. For the choirs: BL MS Cotton, Vitellius F.V, f.40^r^; Henry Machyn, *The diary*, ed. John Gough Nichols (Camden Society, first series, 42: London, 1848), p. 78.

43 This seems first to have been suggested by Jeremy Noble: see Paul Doe, *Tallis*, 2nd edn, p. 21.

Spanish singers,[44] or that the choice of cantus firmus was inspired by the Queen's supposed condition, although that would have been a happy coincidence.

Joseph Kerman described the Mass's progressive rediscovery, in which he played a leading part, and elucidated the principles on which it is constructed.[45] The Gloria, Sanctus and Benedictus, and the Agnus Dei are complete enough for a reconstruction to have been made by Sally Dunkley and David Wulstan.[46] Bar numbers used below refer to their edition. Of the Credo, only the end has been found, from the words 'Et expecto resurrectionem' onwards. Since the Credo in each of Tallis's other Masses omits the words 'Et iterum venturus est' to 'in remissionem peccatorum', it is assumed that this was also the case with the *Puer natus est* Mass. (Similar, if not identical, omissions were made by composers at least as far back as Dunstable and as late as Tye.) The major loss from the *Puer natus* est Mass therefore extends from the beginning of the Credo as far as 'sedet ad dexteram Patris'.

The composition of large festal Masses had dried up in England by about 1540, and Tallis may have acknowledged a return to past Catholic practices by including in his great Mass elements of music written while he was young – though he incorporated more recent elements as well. He could have borrowed the idea of using his cantus firmus twice over from an earlier Mass with a cantus firmus based on the Corpus Christi antiphon *O quam suavis est*. This has been attributed to John Lloyd, who was with Thomas Bury, Joan Tallis's first husband, at the Field of the Cloth of Gold.[47] Both the *O quam suavis est* Mass, and the antiphon *Ave regina* (also attributed to Lloyd), are written in complex notations intended to demonstrate their composer's learning and ingenuity. There is nothing out of the ordinary about Tallis's notation, as we have it, but in deriving his own cantus firmus from the chant of the introit *Puer natus est* he used a code similar to one found in Lloyd's antiphon, where the lengths of notes in one voice depend on the vowels in the words. Tallis may have been aware of a literary parallel, too. The poet John Skelton – who tutored Henry VIII when he was a prince, and celebrated

44 Wulstan, *Tudor music*, p. 296.

45 Kerman, 'The *Missa Puer natus est* by Thomas Tallis' (in Banks and others, eds, *Sundry sorts of music books*, pp.40–53; revised in Kerman, *Write all these down*, pp. 126–7).

46 Thomas Tallis, *Mass Puer natus est nobis*, ed. Sally Dunkley and David Wulstan (Oxford, 1977, rev. 1980, 2009).

47 The attribution has been both contested and restated. Lloyd's authorship of the Mass *O quam suavis* and the antiphon *Ave regina celorum* is dismissed by Roger Bowers in Iain Fenlon, ed., *Cambridge music manuscripts, 900–1700* (Cambridge, 1982), pp. 118–19, as based on a misreading of a cryptic clue in Cambridge University Library MS Nn.vi.46. It is dismissed again in Bowers's article on Lloyd in *The Oxford dictionary of national biography* (online edition, January 2008, accessed 13 April 2013); in this article George Newton is suggested as a possible composer ('dokter Newton' is mentioned in *The autobiography of Thomas Whythorne*, ed. James M. Osborne (Oxford, 1961), p. 300). Lloyd is 'almost certainly' accepted as the composer of the *O quam* suavis Mass in an article about him by John Caldwell and Roger Bray in *Grove Music Online* (accessed 11 April 2013).

his accession with *A lawde and prayse* in 1509 – used a code in which the vowels were numbered from 1 to 5. It occurs in *Ware the hawk,* dating from 1503–12 (and, perhaps significantly, reprinted *c.*1554), and in *The garlande or chapelet of laurell*, which seems to have been assembled from 1495 onwards and was printed in 1523.[48]

At the written pitch, the seven voices used by Tallis cover a span from *d''* down to *F* (about the bottom of his usual bass range: only occasionally does he write *E* or *D*). The reason for the scoring has been the subject of speculation,[49] but it is not unique, and it is similar to the one that Tallis used earlier in his five-part Te Deum 'for meanes' whenever the voices are divided (see p. 80), as well as in other Latin-texted pieces.[50]

The cantus firmus is given to a tenor voice. It is formed by first dividing the chant into sections: (1) 'Puer natus est nobis', (2) 'et filius datus est nobis', (3) 'cuius imperium super humerum eius', (4) 'et vocabitur nomen eius', (5) 'magni consilii', (6) 'angelus'. The occurrence of these sections in the movements of the Mass is shown in Table 6.4 on pp. 130–31. If, as seems likely, the whole of the chant was used twice, the missing portion of the Credo must have been based on sections 4 and 5.

Each note of the chant is transcribed according to a predetermined unit of length, multiplied by a number derived from the vowel originally sung to the note in the introit. In the Gloria the unit of length is at first a semibreve, and the vowel code is: a = 1, e = 2, i = 3, o = 4, u = 5. Once the length of a cantus firmus note has been calculated, it may be divided into shorter notes, or joined with an adjacent note of the same pitch. A vowel originally sung to more than one note has its code number applied to each note concerned. Rests inserted in the cantus firmus are independent of the code, and may be very long. The code can have the disadvantage of being too rigid, and can cause the cantus firmus to be stuck on one note for a considerable time. In one section of the Gloria, it remains on *F* for 19 breves (bars 142–160). The practices of scribes usually make it difficult to know whether the code is applied to the final notes of movements.

Example 6.5a on p. 132 illustrates the application of the vowel code at the start of the Sanctus, where the cantus firmus is derived from the first section of the chant: (i) shows that section of the chant, with figures representing the number of units (in this case minim units) obtained from each vowel; (ii) shows how the notes and

---

48 Skelton further numbered the consonants according to their positions in the alphabet (I and J being regarded as one letter), so that 2 represented both B and E. See John Skelton, *The complete English poems...*, rev. edn, ed John Scattergood (Liverpool, 2015), notes on pp. 363–4 to *Ware the hauke* (lines 239–45), and on p. 486 to *The garlande or chapelet of laurell* (lines 741ff).

49 See Wulstan, *Tudor music*, pp. 295–6; Kerman, 'The *Missa Puer natus est*' (in Banks and others, eds, *Sundry sorts of music books*, at 40–41, in Kerman, *Write all these down*, p. 126).

50 For a more recent and well-informed discussion see Roger Bowers, 'Sounding pitch in Thomas Tallis, Mass "Puer natus est nobis"', *Early Music Review*, 197 (2014), pp. 11–14.

Table 6.4 Layout of the Mass *Puer natus est*

	(Editorial bars)	Section of chant	Vowel code and unit	Mensuration sign	Section of Mass
Gloria	(1–65) (66–188)	1 and 2 3	a = 1, e = 2, etc. Semibreve Breve	¢ ¢	'et in terra pax ... Filius Patris' 'Qui tollis ... in gloria Dei Patris. Amen'
Credo	[The missing section of the Credo probably used sections 4 and 5 of the chant]				
			a = 1, e = 2, etc.		
	(1–6) (7–20)	——— 6 modified	 Dotted semibreve	⦶ ϲ3[a]	'Et expecto resurrectionem mortuorum' 'et vitam venturi saeculi. Amen'
[a] A dotted breve has the value previously given to a breve					
			a = 1, e = 2, etc.		
Sanctus	(1–17)[b]	1	Minim	¢	'Sanctus ... Dominus Deus Sabaoth'
[b] Midpoint of bars 1–34					
	(18–34) (35–87)	1 reversed 2[c]	Minim Minim	¢ ¢	'Dominus Deus Sabaoth' 'Pleni sunt coeli ... Hosanna in excelsis'
[c] Groups of notes written as ligatures in the chant are immediately repeated in reverse in the cantus firmus					

			e = 4, i = 3, u = 1 (no ‘a’ or ‘o’)		
Benedictus	(88–150)	3	Semibreve	¢	‘Benedictus qui venit ... Hosanna in excelsis
			a = 1, e = 2, etc.		
Agnus Dei	(1–37)d	4 (part 1)	Dotted breve	¢	‘Agnus Dei ... miserere nobis’
[d] Midpoint of bars 1–74					
	(38–74)	4 (part 2)	Dotted semibreve	¢[e]	
[e] The only source has ¢ in the tenor part at bar 62					
	(75–125)	5 and 6[f]	Minim	¢	‘Agnus Dei ... dona nobis pacem’
[f] Notes are transferred to the cantus firmus in the order 1, 2, 1, 2, 3, 2, 3, 4, 3, etc.					

Note: Bar numbers are from the edition by Sally Dunkley and David Wulstan (Oxenford Imprint, 1977, rev. 1980, 2009). This edition halves note values, and raises the pitch by a minor third.

Example 6.5a The cantus firmus in the Sanctus of the Mass *Puer natus est nobis*

i) The chant, with figures showing the number of units obtained from vowels

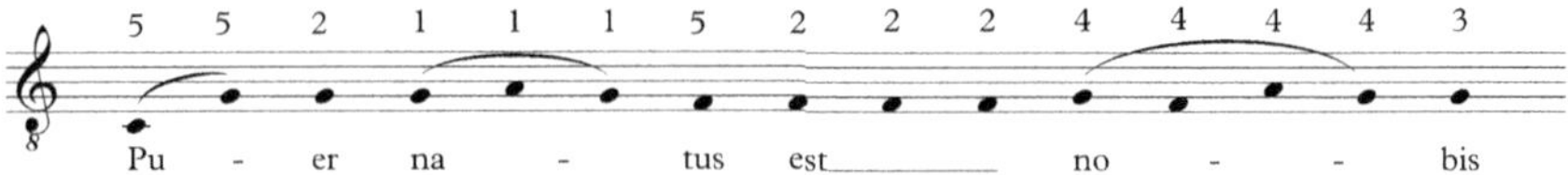

ii) Derivation of a cantus firmus from the notes and units

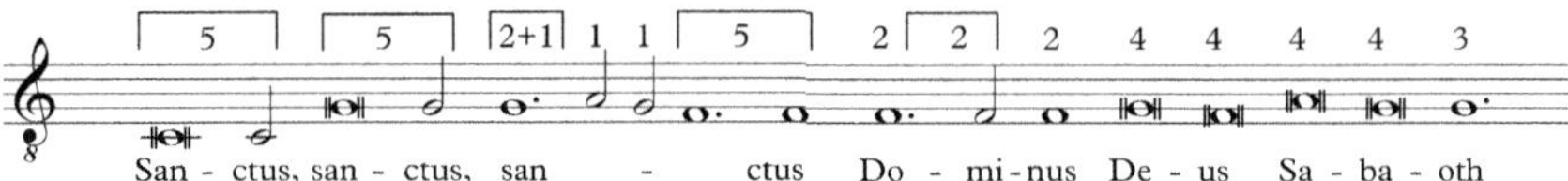

units are applied to produce a cantus firmus.[51] Example 6.5b sets out the first part of the movement in score.[52]

In the Benedictus the vowel code is reversed (a = 5, and so on to u = 1). Other variations occur elsewhere in the Mass. The Sanctus repeats a section of the cantus firmus in reverse. In the second half of the Agnus Dei, the notes of sections 5 and 6 of the chant are transferred into the cantus firmus in the following way. The vowel code is applied as before, but if notes are numbered according to their order of occurrence in the chant (1, 2, 3, 4, 5, etc.), they now appear in the order 1, 2, 1, 2, 3, 2, 3, 4, 3, 4, 5, 4, etc. (Tallis did not follow this method strictly in transferring the beginnings of sections 5 and 6, probably because it would have resulted in cantus firmus notes that were too short.) When the new series is separated into groups of three numbers (1 2 1, 2 3 2, 3 4 3, 4 5 4, etc.) the sums of numbers in each group form the arithmetical progression 4, 7, 10, 13, etc. Tallis may have arrived at this accidentally, though it looks very much as if he had some knowledge of arithmetic, and in his own way was applying it as Dunstable had applied it in his compositions.

Table 6.4 shows how the vowel code is combined with other predetermined features. But the nature of the sources from which the Mass has necessarily had to be reconstructed means that their reliability is sometimes difficult to assess. The whole Mass could, for example, originally have been in perfect time, indicated by ⦶, which, as Kerman recognized, may have become changed to ¢ in the hands

[51] The example is indebted to John Caldwell's illustration of the procedure at the beginning of the Gloria (*The Oxford history of English music* (Oxford, 1991–98), vol. 1, p. 299).

[52] The reconstruction of the missing part, printed in small notes, is from the edition by Sally Dunkley and David Wulstan.

Example 6.5b The beginning of the Sanctus of the Mass *Puer natus est nobis*

continued

Example 6.5b *concluded*

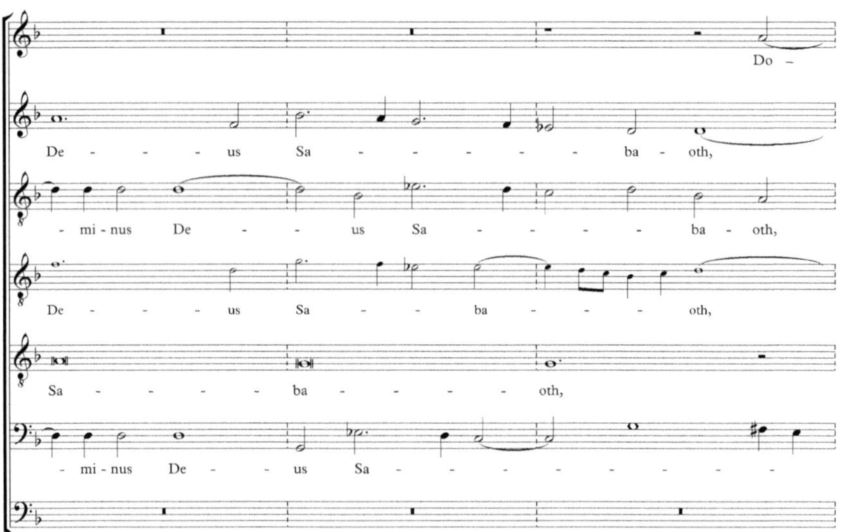

of later scribes.[53] This is related to the questions, discussed by Kerman, of how breves are to be understood, and the way in which Tallis calculated the lengths

[53] Kerman, 'The *Missa Puer natus est* by Thomas Tallis' (in Banks and others, eds, *Sundry sorts of music books*, pp. 45–7, in Kerman, *Write all these down*, pp. 129–32).

of portions of his Mass.[54] It is connected in turn to the lengthening of the cantus firmus by the insertion of rests. Without more certainty than the sources afford, it is hard to take the matter much further. It would be all too easy to invent things Tallis never thought of.

Fascinating as may be the calculations underlying the structure of the *Puer natus est* Mass, and the insight they allow into aspects of Tallis's way of thinking, they were only the beginning of his work in setting and illuminating the text. A long cantus firmus and six free voices provided him with a wide range of resources. The three more or less complete principal movements all start impressively with a largely chordal head theme, incorporating a rising fourth in the highest part (as in Example 6.5b). This fourth (G–C) is a tonal reflection of the rising fifth (C–G) which begins the chant, and may have been introduced when Tallis penned the first few notes of the Mass. (If the missing portion of the Credo turns up it will probably be found to start in much the same way.) The head theme keeps its character at the start of the Agnus Dei, even though the cantus firmus is not present.

By and large the division of movements into sections employing the full or a reduced number of voices, which was a feature of Tallis's early works, no longer obtains. Voices are, however, rested often enough to define individual passages and to vary the colouration and the density of sound. The partial homophony found in some of Tallis's English anthems has now found its way into the more complex texture of a spacious Latin work. In places as many as five voices sing homophonically, while the others have different phrasings. In the Gloria, for example, at 'qui sedes ad dexteram Patris', only the highest voice and the tenor (whose notes are determined by the cantus firmus) are not perfectly in step.

Very long phrases and highly melismatic writing have given way to shorter spans with greater directional purpose. The cantus firmus's melodic influence on other voices is generally small, except where melody is dictated by harmonic considerations. Melodies often contain a fifth or fourth which may derive from those intervals in the head theme, or which may simply have become a feature of Tallis's style. (Larger melodic intervals generally include at least one intervening note.)

Imitation defines short phrases of the text. The impression is less of a fully integrated imitative structure than of a narrative gradually unfolding, always lively, never tedious. Motifs are not only short-lived, but are often repeated imprecisely. Sometimes no more than two or three voices may be involved in imitation; and sometimes more than one imitative motif may be in play (see the setting of 'Gratias agimus tibi' in the Gloria). On occasion a motif already introduced may swiftly reappear in its original form; at other times it may differ in detail while retaining a recognizable shape. There is a notable exception to this, for in the last section of

[54] An analysis of the Sanctus is offered in Roger Bray, ed., *Music in Britain: the sixteenth century* (Blackwell history of music in Britain, 2: Oxford, 1995), p. 81.

the Agnus Dei (bar 80) the two highest voices launch into a canon at the unison which lasts almost to the end of the movement.[55]

Tallis set the text with his usual attention to the meaning of the words. A hint of homophony sometimes draws attention to the ideas expressed, as it does at 'Laudamus te' in the Gloria. Elsewhere in the Gloria 'Qui sedes ad dexteram Patris' (*who sit at the Father's right hand*) seems to have inspired repeated notes. A change of imitative texture marks out 'miserere nobis'. Repetition by a different group of voices emphasizes 'Quoniam tu solus Sanctus, tu solus Dominus, tu solus Altissimus' (*Because you alone are the Holy One, the Lord, the Most High*).

There are no unusually striking changes of tonality in the Mass, though the tonality is by no means severely limited. The sources are written with a key signature of one flat in some parts, and Tallis probably thought of the whole work as in F or D(♭), though sections of it do not always end on either F or D. Although there is a repeated emphasis on F or a closely related tonality in the Gloria, especially where several voices pause together or where a phrase in the bass voice is followed by a rest, the movement ends with a chord on G which is dictated, at least in part, by the cantus firmus. The extant final section of the Credo ends with a chord on C. The two main sections of the Sanctus end on C and D, and those of the Agnus on G and C.

Never again would Tallis write so large a work. For one thing, it marked the end of the Tudor Mass until Byrd composed three examples in the early 1590s, undoubtedly for secret celebrations in Catholic households. And then, just as Tallis had often done, it was Taverner to whom Byrd turned for a model (in the Sanctus of his Mass for four voices).[56]

---

[55] Richard Turbet has suggested that the notes which begin this canon seem to be recalled in Byrd's second four-part In Nomine (cf. William Byrd, *Consort music*, ed. Kenneth Elliott (The Collected Works of William Byrd [later redesignated The Byrd Edition], 17: London, 1971), p. 84, bar 23ff). Although the resemblance is brief it is not impossible, for the In Nomine must have been written when the Mass was not very old – conceivably some years before Byrd went to Lincoln in 1563 – and a phrase may have lodged in his mind.

[56] Philip Brett, 'Homage to Taverner in Byrd's Masses', *Early Music*, vol. 9 (1981), pp. 169–76 (reprinted in Philip Brett, *William Byrd and his contemporaries* (2007), pp. 8–21).

Chapter 7
Instrumental Music of the Mid-Century

The sum of Tallis's extant works written for instruments is very small. Nearly all are keyboard pieces based on plainsong, and are assumed to have been written for performance on the organ during Sarum services, either in the reign of King Henry or in the reign of Queen Mary. They are considered together in this chapter because there is no unchallengeable argument for assigning any of them to one reign rather than the other. Two more keyboard pieces, the purpose of which is unknown, will also be discussed here, as will a handful of pieces for consort or vocalized performance. A pair of *Felix namque* settings for keyboard, dated 1562 and 1564, will be considered in Chapter 10, together with a piece known as *Two parts in one*.

Keyboard Music

It is thought that when an organ was substituted for the vocal performance of chant, the organist's duties often demanded little more than the spontaneous decoration of the melody.[1] But there must have been occasions when improvisation would not do, and something had to be written down in advance. No doubt, too, composers found satisfaction in working out on paper ideas which could not be developed fully on the spur of the moment, and passed the results round among colleagues. Some music may have been preserved because it had multiple functions. Simple pieces were no doubt useful for teaching purposes. Others piece may have been circulating as material for amateurs to play, or for professionals to play to them. Sixteenth-century English keyboard sources convey a mixed repertoire, and are few in number. Considering that Tallis played the organ throughout a long life, he must have committed to paper considerably more music for the instrument than has survived.

The earliest of his extant keyboard settings may be that of ***Alleluia. Per te Dei genetrix***, which until the chant was identified was described as a fantasy.[2] It is one of three pieces written on four leaves of paper dated to *c.*1530 or after

---

1 Frank Ll. Harrison, *Music in medieval Britain*, 4th edn (Buren, 1980), pp. 214–18; John Caldwell, ed., *Early Tudor organ music: I. Music for the Office* (Early English Church Music, 6: London, 1966), pp. vii–xiii; Denis Stevens, ed., *Early Tudor organ music II. Music for the Mass* (Early English Church Music: London, [1969]), pp. ix–xii.

2 The chant was identified by Jason Smart (John Caldwell, ed., *Tudor keyboard music* c.*1520–1580* (*Musica Britannica*, 66: London, 1995), p. xxiv). The piece is entitled 'Fantasy' in *Thomas Tallis, Complete keyboard works*, ed. Denis Stevens (London, 1953).

from the identity of their printed staves with those in a songbook published during that year.[3] The other two pieces are by John Ambrose (*fl. c.*1520–45) and John Redford (*d.*1547). The block from which the staves were printed could have been in use before or after 1530 (though it does not seem to have become worn), and the scribe could have written on sheets which had been preserved for some years after printing. So what are we to think about the date? Although it is by no means incontestable, it is possible that all three pieces were copied at the same time from a single manuscript, and that like the others Tallis's was composed before the mid-1540s.[4]

Alleleuia. Per te Dei genetrix is based on a chant for Mass in honour of the Virgin Mary, and sets the passages sung by the soloist(s).[5] The setting is in two sections, one based on the first 14 notes of the Alleluia, the other based on the first 80 notes of the main portion of the chant. As in many organ settings, the notes of the cantus firmus can be hard to disentangle from their surroundings – not only because the chant is decorated and 'broken in division',[6] but because, in this case, Tallis begins the second section of his setting with an introductory passage in two parts based on the first seven notes of the chant. These notes are repeated when a third part is added and the chant is continued to the end of the section.

The setting inevitably has characteristics found in the organ works of Redford and his contemporaries, but it also exhibits Tallis's keen sense of direction and development. In the second and longer section, lines of melody, not unlike those in the composer's vocal music, combine to form varied textures as the music makes its way to a climax where undulating rows of crotchets move in parallel.

The bulk of Tallis's surviving keyboard music is found in Thomas Mulliner's book. Apart from *Alleluia. Per te Dei genetrix*, there are only four pre-Elizabethan keyboard works attributed to Tallis which Mulliner did not collect. Ten of the twelve pieces he copied are entered consecutively, and so may have come from a common source. (This does not count the 'Per haec nos' section of *Salve intemerata*, apparently included as suitable for keyboard performance.)

Mulliner's book seems to have been compiled in the period 1558–64 (see p. 68), but the contents cover a long period and include more music by

---

3 See the entry for MS Mus. 1034(A) in the online catalogue of music at Christ Church, Oxford. The staves are also used in a volume of music printed by double impression, which includes a list of contents headed 'In this boke ar co*n*teynyd. xx. so*n*ges' (BL K.1.e.1). Another copy of Tallis's piece, omitting the first section, is in Christ Church, Oxford, MS Mus. 371, which may have been copied in the 1560s. For differences between the copies see Caldwell, *Tudor keyboard music*, pp. 2–3, 183. Both manuscripts attribute the music to Tallis, but neither gives it a title.

4 See p. 75 above for the possibility that a passage of *Alleleuia. Per te genetrix* recurs in Tallis's *Christ rising*, which sets a text from the 1548 Prayer Book.

5 For the manner of performance, see Caldwell, *Tudor keyboard music*, pp. 2–3, 172, 183.

6 Thomas Morley, *A plaine and easie introduction to practicall musicke* (London, 1597), pp. 96–7; ed. R. Alec Harman (London, 1952), pp. 177–9.

Redford (*d.*1547) than by any later composer. They are therefore of little help in dating Tallis's pieces. There are other difficulties, too. For example, none of Tallis's organ settings of hymns relates to any of his vocal hymn settings; and they are incomplete since, as copied by Mulliner, none of them provides the music for more than one verse. They are probably drawn from sets of odd-numbered verses for organ, which were alternated with the even-numbered verses sung by a choir (see p. 112). Where Mulliner includes two settings by Tallis of one hymn tune they are separated by other pieces, and may not belong together.

The first of Tallis's pieces entered by Mulliner, separately from the others, is a short and simple setting of the Christmas antiphon ***Natus est nobis***, akin to some of the organ music of Redford's generation. While the left hand plays a continuous stream of quavers, the right hand plays the chant in alternate minims and crotchets, recalling Tallis's treatment of the chant in his vocal setting of the hymn *Quod chorus vatum–Haec Deum caeli* (see p. 115). *Natus est nobis* might have made a useful piece in teaching a pupil to play keyboard instruments.[7] There are several other pieces in the early pages of Mulliner's collection which could also have been employed in teaching, even if that was not their original purpose.

Tallis's setting of the hymn ***Iam lucis orto sidere*** is entered separately from the rest of his hymn settings, but is one of a group of pieces made up largely of songs presented in keyboard score, including Tallis's *O ye tender* babes and *When shall my sorrowful sighing slack*. Its keyboard origin is nevertheless clear in the way a part may vanish and be replaced by a new part at a different pitch. Another characteristic of Tallis's keyboard music, also present in *Iam lucis*, is his repetition throughout a piece of a single unifying subject. Both are illustrated in Example 7.1 (p. 140). So is Tallis's taste for a slightly ornate ending, common to many of his organ pieces.

Mulliner's main group of Tallis's chant-based pieces begins with the first of his two settings of the hymn ***Veni redemptor gentium***. The second setting occurs later in the group. Other multiple settings by Tallis, entered as separate pieces by Mulliner, are *Ecce tempus idoneum* (two versions) and *Clarifica me Pater* (three versions). A reason for thinking that these are in fact separate is that Mulliner treated Blitheman's six settings of *Gloria tibi Trinitas* differently, copying them consecutively as though they belong together.

The first setting of *Veni redemptor gentium* makes even clearer than *Iam lucis* that the part-writing is for the organ, not voices. In the middle of the piece four parts turn for a moment into five. It is true keyboard music, not simply vocal music written out for keyboard performance. The same thing happens in the hymn ***Ex more docti mistico***, though in one way it differs from *Iam lucis* and *Veni redemptor*. It does not display Tallis's habit, mentioned above and apparent in both those settings, of concluding with a bar or two of more elaborate writing.

7 See Jane Flynn, 'The education of choristers in England during the sixteenth century', in John Morehen, ed., *English choral practice* (Cambridge, 1995), pp. 180–99 (especially Table 8:1 at p. 182).

Example 7.1 *Iam lucis orto sidere*

a) The beginning

b) The ending

This appears again in two settings of the hymn ***Ecce tempus idoneum***, though their styles are otherwise different. The second of them (not attributed by Mulliner to any composer, though it is surely a part of the Tallis group) explores the possibilities of keyboard counterpoint more fully than the first.

A verse of ***Iste confessor*** is a little different from Tallis's other keyboard hymn settings collected by Mulliner. It is his only organ verse in three parts, like Redford's two settings of the *Iste confessor* chant which Mulliner also copied, though the stepped motif introduced by Tallis makes his piece more obviously instrumental than either of Redford's.

Mulliner gives no title to any of Tallis's settings of the antiphon ***Clarifica me Pater***. These works do not form a clearly designed group like Byrd's three treatments of the chant, and it is doubtful whether they can have been conceived as one. The first is based on the chant of the Magnificat antiphon for Vespers on Palm Sunday. The

Example 7.2 The beginning of *Clarifica me Pater* (II)

second and third appear to be built on a version of the chant used as a Benedictus antiphon for Lauds on the Vigil of the Ascension, and they include the Alleluia.[8]

All the *Clarifica me* settings (conventionally numbered I, II and III) illustrate two features that are often present in Tallis's liturgical organ pieces. One is his concentration on the logic of his melodic line at the expense of smooth harmonies. Tallis seems to revel in the occasionally harsh chords and the clashes this brings about (Example 7.2).

The other feature, previously mentioned in connection with *Iam lucis orto sidere*, is the use of a single subject, generally repeated without striking changes. The first setting incorporates a figure that starts in the bass and rises through the other parts, is repeated throughout the piece, and is eventually taken up by pairs of

[8] John Caldwell, *English keyboard music before the nineteenth century* (Oxford, 1973), p. 72; John Caldwell, 'Keyboard plainsong settings in England, 1500–1660', *Musica Disciplina*, vol. 19 (1965), pp. 129–53, at 142–4; John Caldwell, ed, *The Mulliner book, newly transcribed and edited* (*Musica Britannica*, 1: London, 2011), p. 257.

voices in parallel. A reiterated figure in the second *Clarifica me* is similar to one running through the second *Veni redemptor* setting.

A dozen or so bars of imitative writing ascribed to Tallis in Mulliner's collection is usually known as ***A point***, the title the compiler gave to six short pieces. Two come from Tye's anthem *Praise ye the Lord*, and Sheppard is named by Mulliner as the composer of another. The origin of Tallis's fragment has not been discovered, but its ending is elaborated like the endings of several of his organ settings.

Tallis's ***Gloria tibi Trinitas*** for keyboard, a piece not collected by Mulliner, is found in a manuscript probably compiled in the 1560s.[9] This does little to narrow down the date of the piece, as the composers represented in the manuscript range from Redford to Byrd. The setting is based on the passage of chant which, extracted from the Benedictus of Taverner's Mass *Gloria tibi Trinitas,* became the basis of the consort In Nomine. Composers were no doubt attracted to it because the four-part In Nomine section is the only place in his Mass where Taverner wrote out a complete unit of the chant in even breves.[10]

Tallis's setting has the added subtitle 'ij parts on a rownd tyme'. The piece is indeed in two parts, in canon at the octave, but it is hard to account for the title unless the canon suggested a round to the copyist, and 'tyme' is an error for 'tune'. The two-part nature of the piece (though not its canonic structure) links it to another setting of the chant in the same manuscript, this time by Nicholas Strogers and entitled 'Innomine'. The pieces are also linked by the unusual difficulty of tracing the progress of the chant in each of them. Although its path is made somewhat clearer by a comparison of the two settings, and of both with other settings, it is a presence rather than a distinctly audible melody.[11] Nowhere else did Tallis allow himself the same degree of licence in handling a cantus firmus.

Consort Music and a Wordless Song

Two four-part **In Nomines** by Tallis are usually assumed, like other works of the kind, to have been written for a consort of viols. They are conventionally numbered I and II, the first beginning with a rising scale and the second with a leaping figure. Their sources include none that appears to have been copied before the later years of Tallis's life, but both works may well have been composed in the 1550s.[12]

---

9 Christ Church MS Mus 371. See Iain Fenlon and John Milsom, '"Ruled Paper Imprinted": music paper and patents in sixteenth-century England', *Journal of the American Musicological Society*, vol. 37 (1984), pp. 139–63, at 147, 162. The manuscript also contains a copy of *Alleluia. Per te Dei genetrix*.

10 The Mass is based on an antiphon sung at first Vespers on Trinity Sunday.

11 Compare numbers 6–14 in Caldwell, *Tudor keyboard music*.

12 Oliver Neighbour, *The consort and keyboard music of William Byrd* (London, 1978), p. 27, and the subsequent discussion of In Nomines by younger composers.

Tye, the other important early composer of In Nomines, seems to have begun writing his more numerous pieces of the sort at about the same time. Almost all of Tye's In Nomines are in five parts, which became the norm, but Tallis's are for only four instruments, leading an unknown hand – with no great musical benefit – to insert an extra part above the bass of the second.[13] It does not prove that Tallis's pieces are early examples of the genre, but it suggests the possibility.

Tallis may or may not have played the viol, but he obviously appreciated the capabilities of an instrumental consort. Writing for a group of instruments encouraged the melodic agility which finds its way into his music both for voices (see p. 26) and for keyboard, but imposed fewer limitations than either. This does not, however, detract from the air of slightly wistful reflection conveyed by both In Nomines. They are instrumental music for private performance and thoughtful appreciation of their different characters. Both have the cantus firmus in the alto part, but the structures built around it are distinct. In the first In Nomine all the added voices begin with the same rising figure, though the tenor and bass soon embark on a rather loose canon at the octave. The material of the canon is sometimes borrowed or refashioned by the treble, which elsewhere introduces and at times repeats phrases of its own. The second In Nomine develops from a point which starts with three notes at the same pitch, but afterwards takes on a different guise in each of the composed parts. In the alto the first three notes (semibreve, minim, minim) become three minims, while a descending phrase which follows them gradually assumes greater importance, only to be replaced by another phrase consisting of thirds and a fifth. The tenor grows along similar lines. In the bass the figure with repeated notes becomes a series of elementary motifs with little more than a supporting role, but eventually takes up the 'thirds and a fifth' figure initiated by the treble.[14]

The manuscript which confers a fifth part on Tallis's second In Nomine also contains an anonymous, untitled, wordless piece in five parts, which in another source[15] is attributed to Tallis and given the title ***A solfinge songe***. Alternative methods of performance are made clear by the title-page of the first manuscript: 'A booke of In nomines and other solfainge songs of v: vj vij: and viij: pts for

[13] Tallis's 'first' In Nomine is in BL Additional MS 33933 and Edinburgh University Library MSS La.III.483, together comprising four partbooks copied by Thomas Wode in 1575–78. The 'second' In Nomine, with a fifth part added, is in BL Additional MS 31390, perhaps completed by 1578. For other sources see Paul Doe, ed., *Elizabethan consort music: I* (*Musica Britannica*, 44: London, 1979). Wode's admiring remarks about both In Nomines are printed by Doe, who also includes a facsimile of one set (pp. xxx, 184); see also Neighbour, *The consort and keyboard music of William Byrd*, p. 30.

[14] For a recurrence of this figure in works by Parsons and Byrd, see Richard Turbet, 'The consort music of William Byrd', *The Viol*, vol.1 (2005–6), pp. 18–19.

[15] BL Additional MS 32377, where Tallis's piece follows three pieces by Mundy which are also entitled 'solfing song'.

voyces or instrumentes'. Comparable title-pages can be found among books that flowed from the Italian music presses. In England, into the seventeenth century, alternative modes of performance continued to be offered in books describing their contents as 'apt for voices or viols', or 'apt both for viols and voices'.

The title of Tallis's song associates it on one hand with the practice of learning music by singing solmization syllables, and on the other with the more advanced practice described by Morley, when he referred to music 'sung as most men doe commonlie sing it: that is, leauing out the dittie and singing onely the bare note, as it were a musicke made onelie for instruments'.[16] It is impossible to be sure about the original nature of the piece. Its rhythm is more pronounced and more dance-like than Tallis's In Nomines. At the same time, as John Milsom has pointed out, its imitative texture and ABA form are strongly reminiscent of the work of Tallis's colleague Philip van Wilder, who until the end of Henry VIII's reign directed a group of singers at court. Many of his works are chansons, in a style linking them to Wilder's native Netherlands as well as his adopted country.[17]

Milsom has also drawn attention to the two surviving parts of what appears to have been a fantasia-like piece for consort, some of which Tallis used in *Absterge Domine* and *O sacrum convivium* (and which is therefore present in *I call and cry*).[18] This is dealt with more fully on p. 191.

[16] Thomas Morley, *A plaine and easie introduction to practicall musicke* (London, 1597), p. 179; ed. R. Alec Harman (London, 1952), p. 293.

[17] The words 'Je nilli croyss' are written in a corner of the page on which the piece appears without a title or the name of the composer. Doe, *Elizabethan consort music: I* notes that they apparently have no connection with Pierre Sandrin's chanson 'Je ne le croy'.

[18] John Milsom, 'A Tallis fantasia', *The Musical Times*, vol. 126 (1985), pp. 658–62.

Chapter 8
The Reign of Elizabeth I: Biographical and Historical Background

Mary's only possible successor was her half-sister Elizabeth, as even Philip acknowledged. She was duly proclaimed Queen, and entered London on 23 November 1558. Mary was buried in Henry VII's Chapel at Westminster Abbey on 14 December. A month later the new Queen was carried in an open litter through pageants and cheering crowds from the Tower to Whitehall. Her coronation service at the Abbey on 15 January was the last to be performed in Latin. For the funeral and coronation the members of the Chapel Royal again had new liveries, black for the first and scarlet for the second.[1] The Gentlemen of the Chapel seem not to have performed a play this Christmastide; instead entertainments at Greenwich and Richmond during the Christmas season and Shrovetide were presented by the children of St Paul's, the first with the gentlemen of Gray's Inn, and the second with the Admiral's Men.[2]

Changes were made circumspectly among the Queen's ministers and household officers. Tallis's own position was probably of little political consequence, and appears to have been secure. He had in any case been a loyal, obedient and gifted servant of three monarchs, and there was no reason to suppose that he might not serve their successor just as faithfully. But among the Chapel's clergy there were swift dismissals. Queen Mary's Subdean, Edmund Daniel, appointed as recently as 1557, was speedily removed for opposing the reintroduction of Protestantism, and was succeeded by John Angell, who had been a member of the Chapel since the reign of Edward VI. The Dean himself, Thomas Thirlby, lost his post during the first week of the new reign. A new Dean, George Carew, was appointed before the end of 1558, and remained in place until his death in 1583. It took longer to fill the vacant Archbishopric of Canterbury: Matthew Parker was nominated for the appointment in July 1559, but was not consecrated until mid-December.

Much of the religious legislation enacted under Mary was repealed. New Acts of Supremacy and Uniformity were passed into law in April 1559.[3] The oath of loyalty to the Queen, which must have been sworn by Tallis and the other Gentlemen and the vestry officer, is preserved in the Chapel's cheque book in

---

[1] TNA LC2/4/2, f.29$^{r–v}$; LC2/4/3, pp. 97–8; Andrew Ashbee, *Records of English court music* (Snodland, *later* Aldershot, 1986–96), vol. 6, pp. 1–4.

[2] Albert Feuillerat, ed., *Documents relating to the Office of the Revels in the time of Queen Elizabeth* (W. Bang, Materialien zur Kunde des älteren englischen Dramas, 21: Louvain, 1908), p. 388.

[3] 1 Elizabeth, cc. 1 and 2.

a form suggesting it was entered after the passage of the Act of Supremacy.[4] An amended Prayer Book, the use of which became compulsory everywhere on 24 June 1559, was adopted in the Chapel on 9 May. Until then the Prayer Book of 1549, favoured by the Queen, was probably used for Chapel services.[5]

The reintroduction of the Prayer Book must have imposed moderation on the way services were conducted, but there was no limit to the display made in the Chapel buildings on special occasions. At Whitehall on 30 September 1565, when Queen Elizabeth stood as godmother at the christening of 'the child of Lady Cicile, Wife to John[,] Erle of Este Friesland, called the Marques of Bawden, and Sister to Eryke King of Sweden':

> The back Part of the Stalles in the Royal Chappell wherein the Gentlemen of the Chappell doe sing, was hanged with rich Tapestry representing the 12 Monthes, and the Front of the said Stalles was also covered with rich Arras. The upper Part of the Chappell, from the Table of Administration to the Stalles, was hanged with Cloathe of Gold, and on the South Side was a rich Travers for the Queene. The Communion Table was richely furnished with Plate and Jewells, viz. a Fountayne and Basen of Mother of Pearl; a Basen and Fountayne gylte, rayled with Gould; a rich Basen, garnished with Stones and Peerles; a Shipe or Arke garnished with Stones; Two great Leires,[6] garneshed with Stones, and Two lesser Leires, garnished with Stones and Pearles; a Bird of Agath, furnished with Stones; a Cupp of Agath, furnished with Stones and Perles; a Bole of Corall, garnished with Pearles; a Bole of Christall, with a Cover; Two Candlestickes of Christall; Two Shippes of Mother of Pearle; One Tablet of Gold, set with Diamonds; another Shipe of Mother of Pearle; Two Payre of Candlestickes of Gould; Two great Candlestickes, double gilt, with Lights of Virgin Waxe; and a Crosse. Over the sayd Table, on the Wall, upon the Cloath of Gold, was fastened a Frount[7] of rich Cloath of Gould sett with Pelicannes; before the sayd Table hung reaching to the Ground, another Frount of the sayd Suit. Also there was lett downe from the Rooff of the sayd Chappel Ten Candlestickes in Maner of Lampes of Silver and gilte, with greate Chaines, every One having Three great Waxe Lights. Over the aforesayd Table was sett on a Shelfe as high as the Windowe, Twenty-one Candlestickes of Gold and Silver double gylte, with xxiiii. Lights. On the North Side of the Quire between the Organes and the upper Windowe, stood XVII Candlesticks double gilt, with XVII Lights; and on the Toppes of the Stalles were fastened certaine

4 Andrew Ashbee and John Harley, *The cheque books of the Chapel Royal* (Aldershot, 2000), vol. 1, pp. 57–8. The recorded oath echoes the Act in referring to the Queen as 'supreme governor … in all spiritual or ecclesiastical things'.

5 Roger Bowers, 'The Chapel Royal, the first Edwardian Prayer Book, and Elizabeth's settlement of religion, 1559', *The Historical Journal*, 43 (2000), pp. 317–44.

6 Ewers.

7 Facing.

> Candlestickes with 12 Lights, soe that the whole Lights sett there were Eighty-three. There was made at the upper Endes of the Stalles, athwart the Chappell, a Rayle which was covered with Cloath of Gold ... In the upper Part of the said Chappell, afore the Table of Administration, and against the Traverse, there was sett uppon a great Mount, the which was Eight Square[8] and Three Stepes high, a Fount of Silver and gilte, the inside covered with Lynnen Cloath, and the Outside hanged with rich Tapestry. The Steppes of the Fount, and all the upper Part of the sayd Chappell under Foote, was layd with Carpetts ... .[9]

Of particular musical interest is a further statement that the 'Service was began by the gentlemen of the Chappell and the Cornets', making clear that wind instruments were used in the Elizabethan Chapel to strengthen the choir or to add spice to the proceedings.

The manner of the Queen's attendance at chapel no doubt changed over the years, but Paul Hentzner, a German visitor who saw her going to the chapel at Greenwich in 1598, wrote that:

> wherever she turned her face, as she was going along, everybody fell down on their knees. The ladies of the court followed next to her, very handsome and well-shaped, and for the most part dressed in white; she was guarded on each side by the gentlemen pensioners, fifty in number, with gilt battle-axes. In the antichapel next the hall where we were, petitions were presented to her, and she received them most graciously, which occasioned the acclamation of LONG LIVE QUEEN ELIZABETH! she answered it with, I THANK YOU, MY GOOD PEOPLE. In the chapel was excellent music; as soon as it and the service were over, which scarce exceeded half an hour, the Queen returned in the same state and order, and prepared to go to dinner.[10]

Routine records confirm Tallis's continuing membership of the Chapel Royal. There are four surviving certificates of his assessment for tax purposes, covering a period from 1563 to 1585. The first two value him at £24 'in fee'; the third values him at £20 'in wages and ffee', and mentions his home address: 'Thomas Tallis in p*ar*ochia de Grenew*i*ch infra hundred de Blackheathe'. The fourth, written shortly before he died, values him at only £11 in fee, so perhaps he had by then retired

---

8 A regular octagon.

9 John Leland, *De rebus Britannicis collectanea*, ed. T. Hearne (London, 1774), vol. 2 ('Tomi Primi Pars Secunda' on an inner leaf), pp. 691–4: 'From a Manuscript late in the Possession of John Anstis, Esq; Garter, and now of Jo. Edmondson, Esq; Mowbray Herald'. The manuscript may have been sold by Willcock on 27 June 1786 (the second day of the sale), as part of Edmondson's library. The sale included Anstis's 'MS of Ceremonials of the Christenings of Princes' (a copy of the catalogue is BL 11900.bb.35).

10 *Paul Hentzner's travels in England* (London, 1797), pp. 35–6.

on a reduced income.[11] There are several lay subsidy lists, as well. One of them, prepared in connection with a levy in the first year of Elizabeth's reign, looks as if it mentions only the five wealthiest Gentlemen. Tallis and three others, including Richard Bower, are each valued at £40 in goods; Robert Bassock is valued at £60 in goods.[12] It is not always easy to interpret the subsidy lists: sometimes the position of names in them seems to be arbitrary, and it is not evident how valuations were made. Bower's £40 appears not to represent 'goods', but the annual salary awarded to him when he was appointed Master of the Children in 1545, which took account of the cost of feeding, clothing, teaching and caring for twelve boys. It was confirmed in 1553.[13] Another list, from 1563/4, places Tallis at the head of the Gentlemen (though it appears that the order in which Gentlemen are listed often signifies little), and values him at £24 – more than twice the sum of £11 at which most of the Gentlemen were valued. Robert Morecock was valued, without explanation, at £30. William Hunnis was valued at £40 in 'lands and fees', though he did not formally become the Master of the Children until 1566, after the death of Bower's successor, Richard Edwards, who like Bower had received £40 for the education and maintenance of the boys.[14] A few other Gentlemen were (or appear to have been) valued 'in goods' above the general amount, and such exceptions continued to be shown in later lists. In 1566/7 Tallis was well down the list, but he was still valued at £24, and Hunnis was still valued at £40. This state of affairs was repeated in 1570/1, with Hunnis first and Tallis second in the list, and in 1576 when, apart from Hunnis, those valued at more than the general rate were gathered together near the end.[15]

Whatever the relationship between Tallis's fee and his valuation in the subsidy rolls, there is nothing to show that the fee took account of any special responsibilities which may have fallen to him as an organist. Indeed, it is not always clear who the Chapel's organists were, or whether they were formally appointed as such (see p. 17). Nothing is heard about it until 1575, when in their *Cantiones* Tallis and Byrd described themselves as Gentlemen and Organists of the Queen's private Chapel. The picture is clouded by the practice of making dual appointments. John Blitheman, an outstanding performer on the organ, became a Gentleman of the Chapel Royal before the end of 1558 and held the post until he died in 1591; but

---

11 TNA E115/368/132 (23 May 1563), E115/368/133 (8 March 1567/8), E115/369/146 (29 September 1571), E115/371/121 (1 June 1585).

12 BL Lansdowne MS 3, f.200^r; Ashbee, *Records of English court music*, vol. 8, pp. 13–14. One of those valued at £40 is Robert Perry (in lands and fees). If just one person is concerned, he is also listed with musicians of the Queen's chamber, where he is valued at £27 in fees.

13 Reign of Henry VIII: TNA C166/785, m. 44; C82/84; *Letters and papers, foreign and domestic of the reign of Henry VIII* (London, 1864–1932), vol. 20, part 2, p. 447 (no. 910/11). Reign of Mary: TNA C82/976; C66/874; *Calendar of the patent rolls ... Philip and Mary vol. I, A. D. 1553–1554* (London, 1937), p. 279.

14 TNA E403/2452, f.67^r; C66/968, m. 12.

15 TNA, E179, nos. 69/81, 69/82, 70/117, 69/93; Ashbee, *Records of Englsih court music*, vol. 6, pp. 12, 17, 24, 34.

for at least some of the time he retained an existing association with Christ Church, Oxford, where from 1569 to 1578 he was evidently the head of the lay clerks. This was not exceptional. Another holder of two posts was Richard Farrant, who left the Chapel in 1564 to become Master of the Children at St George's, Windsor. He returned in 1570, apparently without relinquishing his ties with Windsor, and seems to have taken over some of William Hunnis's duties relating to the children of the Chapel. The holding of dual positions continued in later years.[16]

Next to nothing is known of Tallis's musical activities outside the Chapel Royal, but a little light is cast on the external patronage he may have enjoyed by the circumstances under which one of his works was composed and first performed in the late 1560s. The piece is *Spem in alium*, and knowledge of its origin comes from the commonplace book of Thomas Wateridge (Figure 8.1, p. 150). He recounts a story he heard from 'Ellis Swayne at my chamber ye 27 Novr. 1611, Mr. Gulson and Richard Grovesey beinge present'. Its anecdotal nature may justify some mild scepticism about its complete reliability, but it is the only account we have:

> In Queene Elizabeths time y^{ere} was à songe sen*t* into England of 30 p*ar*ts (whence ye Italians obteyned ye name to be called ye Apices of ye world) wch beeinge Songe mad*e* a heavenly Harmony. The Duke of [blank] bearinge à great love to Musicke asked whether none of our English men could sett as good à songe, and Tallice beeinge very skillfull was felt to try whether he would under take ye Matter wch he did & made one of 40 p*ar*tes wch was songe in ye longe gallery at Arundell house wch so farre surpassed ye other y^{t} the Duke hearinge of y^{t} songe tooke his chayne of gold fro*m* of his necke & putt y^{t} about Tallice his necke & gave yt him ./–./ wch songe was againe songe at ye Princes coronation./[17]

There are reasons for thinking that the 'songe sent into England' was in fact in 40 parts, and was a Mass by Alessandro Striggio. He visited England in 1567 and met Queen Elizabeth, whom he praised in his madrigal *D'ogni gratia et d'amor*. During his visit he may well have shown his Mass to English musicians, even if a performance was not arranged.[18]

16 Thomas Tomkins, Edmund Hooper and Nathaniel Giles were among the Chapel Royal musicians who simultaneously held appointments elsewhere: see Andrew Ashbee and David Lasocki, *A biographical dictionary of English court musicians* (Aldershot, 1998).

17 Cambridge University Library, MS Dd.5.14, f.73^{v}. The anecdote was first transcribed by H. Fleetwood Sheppard, and published under the heading 'Tallis and his song of forty parts', in *The Musical Times and Singing Class Circular*, vol. 19 (1878), pp. 97–8. The performance 'at ye Princes coronation' will be discussed below (see p. 183).

18 Davitt Moroney, 'Alessandro Striggio's Mass in forty and sixty parts', *Journal of the American Musicological Society*, vol. 60 (2007), pp. 1–69, which at pp. 28–33 conveniently summarizes discussion up to the date of publication.

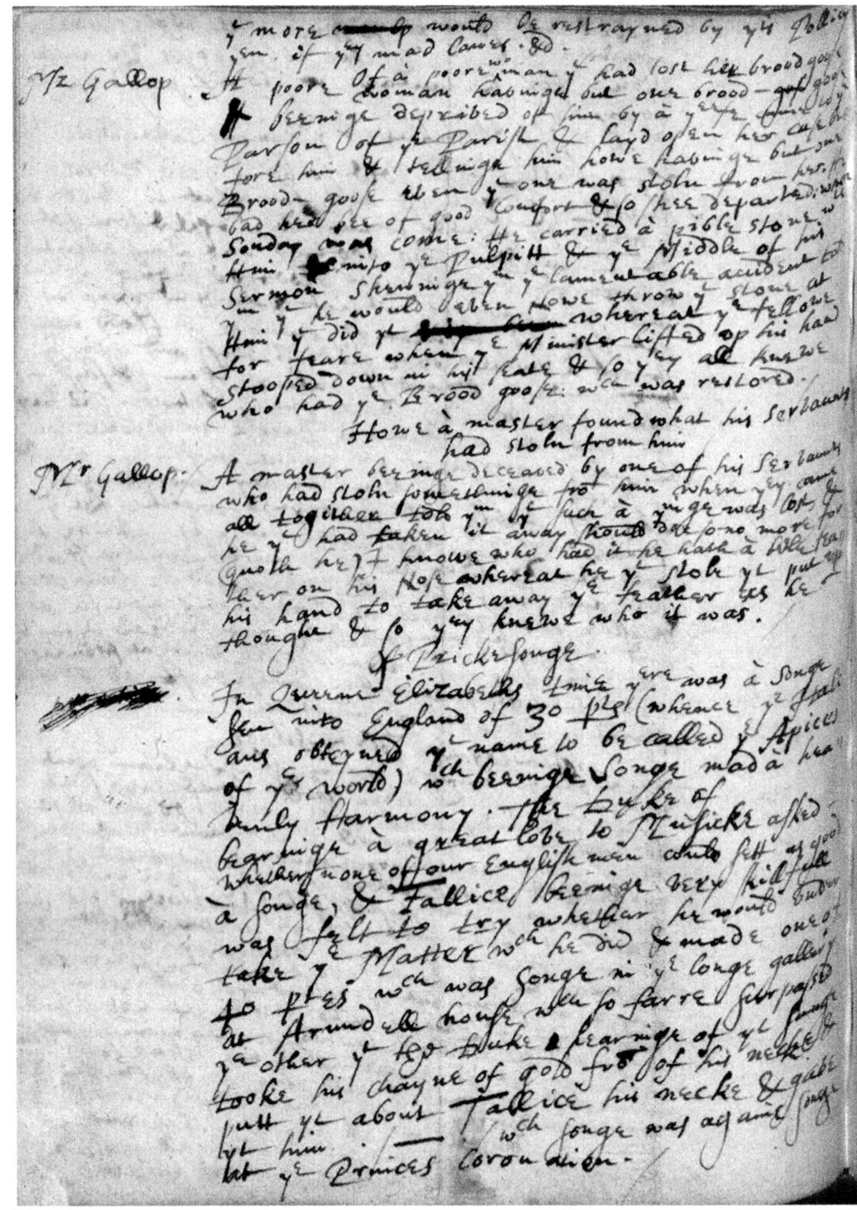

Figure 8.1 Thomas Wateridge's account of the origin of Tallis's *Spem in alium* (Cambridge University Library, MS Dd.5.14, f.73v, by permission of the Syndics of Cambridge University Library)

Arundel House was the London home of Henry Fitzalan, the twelfth Earl of Arundel.[19] He had served as Lord Chamberlain under Henry VIII and Edward VI. Under Mary he was the Lord High Steward, a position he continued to hold in Elizabeth's reign. From Mary he had received Henry VIII's Nonsuch Palace in Surrey, and the gift was confirmed by Elizabeth. Evidence of the musical establishment he maintained there suggests that it was large by the standards of his own or any other time.[20] It would be surprising if Arundel House were not the scene of parallel musical activity, and equally surprising if Tallis were not among the musicians Arundel knew well.[21] The duke who removed a gold chain from his own neck and placed it round Tallis's was probably one of Arundel's sons-in-law, Thomas Howard, the fourth Duke of Norfolk.[22] If so, the event must have taken place after Striggio's visit in mid-1567, but before October 1569, when Norfolk was arrested and committed to the Tower on the grounds of plotting against the Queen. He was tried for high treason on 16 January 1571/2 and executed in June 1572.

Shortly after Norfolk's trial Byrd returned to the Chapel Royal, after spending nine years as organist and master of the choristers at Lincoln Cathedral. He was sworn in as a Gentleman on 22 February 1571/2. Tallis, who was at least 30 years older than Byrd, formed a firm friendship with his young colleague, prompting the unanswerable question of whether Tallis found in Byrd a surrogate son. Tallis's will shows that he stood as godfather to Byrd's second son, Thomas, who was probably born in 1576, and whose baptismal name could honour either Byrd's own father or Tallis, or both. The words of the will express Tallis's wish that, after Joan Tallis's death, his godson should receive 'my moyety for the printinge of musicall books, songs and ruled paper duringe the terme of the yeares yet to come, the which the Queenes Ma*ies*tie gave joyntly betwene Mr Will*ia*m Birde … & mee'. It went on to say that if Thomas Byrd died before the printing patent had expired, all the profit should go to William Byrd.

19 Charles Lethbridge Kingsford, 'Bath Inn or Arundel House', *Archaeologia*, 2nd series, vol. 72 (1922), pp. 243–77.

20 Charles W. Warren, 'Music at Nonesuch', *Musical Quarterly*, vol. 54 (1968), pp. 47–57.

21 Sebastian Westcote was at Nonsuch in 1559 when Queen Elizabeth saw 'a play of ye chylderyn of powles' in 1559; so were 'phelypes' (probably Robert Philips), and John Heywood (BL MS Cotton, Vitellius F.V, f.10b^v^; Henry Machyn, *The diary*, ed. John Gough Nichols (Camden Society, first series, 42: London, 1848), p. 206). The speculative suggestion that *Spem* might have been performed at Nonsuch was made by John Milsom, in 'English polyphonic style in transition: a study of the sacred music of Thomas Tallis' (Doctoral thesis, University of Oxford, 1983), vol. 1, pp. 191–2, and repeated in 'The Nonsuch music library', in Chris Banks and others, eds, *Sundry sorts of music books* (London, 1993), pp. 146–82, at 168–9.

22 Denis Stevens, 'A songe of fortie partes, made by Mr. Tallys', *Early Music*, vol. 10 (1982), pp. 171–81.

The patent was granted by the Queen on 22 January 1574/5.[23] The recipients' *Cantiones, quae ab argumento sacrae vocantur* ('Songs, which by reason of their subject matter are called sacred') was the first work to appear under it, in the form of partbooks containing a collection of their own compositions with Latin texts.[24] They chose as the printer Thomas Vautrollier, who in 1570 had already printed a London edition of music by Orlande de Lassus, dedicated to the Earl of Arundel. This drew on *Mellange d'Orlande de Lassus*, which LeRoy and Ballard had published in Paris earlier in the same year. It is not impossible that Tallis and Byrd had determined to seek a patent for the printing of music after learning that, about 1571, Lassus had received one from Charles IX of France.

There is no exact record of when the two composers' *Cantiones* appeared. Since it was printed under a specific privilege it may not have been entered in the Stationers' register.[25] Even if it was, there is now a gap at the point where we should expect an entry to occur, and the register is not resumed until 17 July 1576.[26] The work of setting up the type, correcting the proofs, printing the sheets, and assembling them as partbooks must have taken some time. The fact that errors (which may differ from copy to copy) are very few suggests that the composers chose their printer with care, and probably too that Byrd, if not Tallis, went through the proofs as scrupulously as he went through his own later publications.[27]

The collection was dedicated to the Queen, and may perhaps have been presented to her on Accession Day (17 November) 1575. At court Accession Day was an occasion for tilts supervised by the Office of Revels, and elsewhere for the ringing of church bells and other acts of celebration. In 1575 the day marked the 17th anniversary of the Queen's coming to the throne. The *Cantiones* appropriately contained 17 pieces by each composer, and Tallis concluded it with a demonstration of his canonic skills. His *Miserere nostri*, apparently written specially for the occasion, was the 17th of his works in the collection (allowing for some creative arithmetic), and was for seven voices, with the first bass singing a melody of 17 notes (see p. 205). Not all Tallis's contributions to the publication were new, and for some of them he drew on works written as much as 20 years earlier.

---

23 TNA C66/1129, m. 2; *Calendar of the patent rolls ... Elizabeth I, volume VI, 1572–1575* (London, 1973), p. 471 (no. 2898); text in Richard Turbet, *William Byrd: a guide to research* (New York, 1987), pp. 325–7. 'The extract and effect' of the patent, printed in *Cantiones sacrae*, could well have been drafted by Byrd, who was in the habit of writing some of his own legal documents.

24 The printing and publication of the collection is examined in Thomas Tallis and William Byrd. *Cantiones sacrae 1575*, ed. John Milsom (Early English Church Music, 56: London, 2014), pp. xxii–xxvii.

25 W.W. Greg, *Some aspects and problems of London publishing between 1550 and 1650* (Oxford, 1956), p. 93.

26 Stationers' Company, *A transcript of the registers of the Company of Stationers*, ed. Edward Arber (London, 1875-94), vol. 2, p. 301 (number at foot of page).

27 John Milsom, 'Tallis, Byrd and the "incorrected copy": some cautionary notes for editors of early music printed from movable type', *Music & Letters*, vol. 77 (1996), pp. 348–67.

The introductory material, like the words of the songs, was in Latin – which the Queen read and wrote easily – and expressed the patriotic intention of promoting the reputation of English music. This purpose was bolstered by anonymous verses 'De Anglorum musica', printed on the verso of each partbook's title-page. Further verses by Ferdinando Richardson (Heybourne) and Richard Mulcaster emphasized the merit of the composers and the innovative nature of their publication.

It seems a convincing guess that the enterprising young Byrd, from a commercially successful family, was the moving spirit behind the *Cantiones*, edited the music and liaised with the printer, Thomas Vautrollier. But it is convincing mainly because we know so much more of Byrd's background and character than of Tallis's. It is quite possible that Tallis recognized the potential of music printing as early as 1560, when some of his pieces were included in John Day's *Mornyng and euenyng prayer and communion*. It is also possible that the older partner was as fully involved as the younger in the patriotic purpose expressed by the prefatory material, in the selection of material for inclusion in their joint venture, and in its careful organization.

In 1577 Tallis and Byrd stated that they had lost at least 200 marks over the *Cantiones* (a little above £66 apiece), and petitioned the Queen for a lease, to last 21 years, of land bringing in £40 a year. The loss for each composer amounted to more than two years' salary, though by this time the annual stipend of a Gentleman of the Chapel Royal was £30. The petitioners laid it on thick. They said that Byrd had been called to the royal service from a post 'where he was well settled', and that:

> the saide Thomas Tallys is now verie aged, and hath served yo*ur* Ma*ies*tie and yo*ur* Royal ancestor*s* these ffortie yeres, and hadd as yet never anie manner of preferment (Except onely one lease w*hi*ch yo*ur* M*aiest*ies late deare syster quene Marie gave him, which lease beinge now the best p*ar*te of his lyvinge, is w*i*thin one yere of expira*ci*on, and the rev*er*c*i*on thereof by yo*ur* Ma*ies*tie graunted on unto another …'.[28]

They did not get quite as much as they asked for. Although the Queen approved the granting of a lease of not more than £30, what they received was made up of six leases valued in total at slightly less.[29] Since it was Byrd who submitted

28 John Harley, *William Byrd: Gentleman of the Chapel Royal* (Aldershot, 1997, rev. 1999), pp. 65–6 (for the complete petition); Harley, *The world of William Byrd: musicians, merchants and magnates* (Farnham, 2010), pp. 143–4. 'Forty years' is an exaggeration, but may have been used in the sense of 'a long time'.

29 Hatfield House, Cecil papers, vol. 160, ff.213^{r}-214^{v}; TNA C66/1169, mm.40–42. See also Historical Manuscripts Commission, *Calendar of the manuscripts of … the Marquis of Salisbury* (London, 1899–1970), vol. 2, p. 155; *Calendar of the patent rolls … Elizabeth I, volume VII, 1575–1578* (London, 1982), p. 117; Harley, *William Byrd Gentleman of the Chapel Royal*, pp. 66–7.

a declaration about this to the Lord Treasurer, it is a fair assumption that he had handled the petition in the first place.[30]

Both composers must have been pleased when the *Cantiones* was offered for sale at the Frankfurt Fair in 1578.[31] There is however no record of resulting purchases, and copies now in Continental libraries have a later provenance.[32] When the London printer Henry Bynneman died in 1583 he had unsold 'bookes' in his possession, 'of Birdes and Tallis musicke in number seaven hundred and seaventeene', the meaning of which is open to doubt.[33] Nevertheless, even if the *Cantiones* did not sell rapidly, Tallis's bequest of his share of the patent must mean that he thought it worth having, possibly because the printing of ruled paper was profitable.[34] On the face of things the patent seems to have brought in little until after Tallis's death, when with a new printer Byrd embarked in earnest on the publication of his own and others' music.

In their petition of 1577, Byrd and Tallis said that the latter was 'verie aged', and indeed after the publication of the *Cantiones* Tallis seems to have written nothing more. Thomas Whythorne, reflecting on the ages of man, thought 'the first part of the old man's age' began at forty, and Byrd was later surprised to find himself still alive in his sixties – though, like his brother John, he went on to live into his eighties.[35] Tallis must have been in his seventies when the petition was submitted. He evidently maintained some sort of connection with the Chapel, since he is mentioned with other Gentleman in a letter addressed to Byrd in 1580 (see p. 211), but it may be that he retired, leaving Byrd in charge of the Chapel's music. Added to the £11 in fee he was receiving at the time of his death (see p. 147), and his wife's property, his share of the leases granted by the Queen in answer to the petition probably enabled him to live comfortably during his remaining years.

---

30 David Skinner has kindly drawn attention to BL Lansdowne MS 25, ff.201^r-202^v (document 97, 'A certificate unto the right honorable the Lord Burghley'). The unsigned declaration attached to it is in Byrd's hand (compare the word 'Certficat' with the same word in TNA E407/72, reproduced in Edmund H. Fellowes, *William Byrd*, 2nd edn (London, 1948), opposite p. 42).

31 John Harley, 'New light on William Byrd', *Music & Letters*, vol. 79 (1998), pp. 475–88, at 478–9.

32 Richard Turbet, 'Music by Byrd and his British contemporaries in European libraries', *The Musical Times*, vol. 154 (2013), pp. 33–42.

33 Mark Eccles, 'Bynneman's books', *The Library*, 5th series, vol. 12 (1957), pp. 81–92. The question of the publication's success or failure is re-examined in Thomas Tallis and William Byrd, *Cantiones sacrae 1575*,ed John Milsom, pp. xxvii–xxx.

34 BL Lansdowne MS 48, ff.190^r and 192^r (Christopher Barker's report to Burghley, 1582).

35 Thomas Whythorne, *The autobiography of Thomas Whythorne*, ed. James M. Osborn (Oxford, 1961), p. 135; William Byrd, dedication of *Gradualia ... Liber secundus* (1607).

Chapter 9
The Reign of Elizabeth I: Music with English Words

When Queen Elizabeth came to the throne in 1558, Tallis was probably in his fifties. His pupil William Byrd, about whom there is a total absence of information at this time, could conceivably have remained with him and acted as his assistant in the Chapel Royal. Richard Bower, the Master of the Children, seems to have been assisted by another young Chapel musician, Robert Parsons.[1] It may have been Parsons, rather than Byrd, who was being groomed for a senior post in the Chapel, for it was he who stayed there, while in the spring of 1563 Byrd took up a post at Lincoln Cathedral. Byrd was not recalled to the Chapel until Parsons died in 1571/2. Byrd's formal recruitment, after nine years of experience as organist, master of choristers and composer in a provincial cathedral, conveys the sense of Tallis's successor being put in place.

It is possible that, even before Byrd's return, Tallis was not overworked as a composer for the Elizabethan Chapel Royal. The small number of his Elizabethan pieces with sacred English texts gives the impression that there was no great demand for a constant stream of works, and that such need as there was for new music setting and supplementing Prayer Book services could largely be satisfied by a handful of other composers. Many of Tallis's pieces conceivably written for the Chapel were psalm settings, and two-thirds of those set groups of verses from Psalm 119. But as at least one group of verses appears to have been composed in the 1570s (see p. 160), it is likely that he continued to provide some music for the Chapel even after Byrd had established himself there. Byrd, too, appears to have written little music for the Chapel Royal. Considering that he did not enter upon semi-retirement until almost 20 years after his appointment as a Gentleman of the Chapel, during which time he became the most famous and admired musician in England, his substantial body of works includes a disproportionately small number likely to have been written for the institution he graced.

Royal injunctions issued by Queen Elizabeth in 1559 repeated and somewhat clarified what those issued in the reign of Edward VI had to say about music. They began by stating that 'in divers collegiate and also some parish churches heretofore there hath been livings appointed for the maintenance of men and children to use singing in the church'. They added that the Queen wished to maintain the science of music, without its being 'in any part so abused in the Church that thereby

[1] Parsons twice signed receipts on Bower's behalf (TNA E405/126; Andrew Ashbee, *Records of English court music* (Snodland, *later* Aldershot, 1986–96), vol. 6, p. 174).

the Common Prayer should be the worse understanded of the hearers', and that there should be 'a modest and distinct song, so used in all parts of the Common Prayer in the Church, that the same may be plainly understanded, as if it were read without singing'.[2] Tallis's Elizabethan music for Prayer Book services follows this instruction to the letter.

The Litany

The church music written in King Edward's reign had included some 'complete' settings of Prayer Book services, consisting of the Te Deum, Benedictus, Magnificat and Nunc dimittis (all sometimes regarded as canticles) and other texts (Venite, Creed, Sanctus and Gloria). Individual sections of the Prayer Book services were set more often, though the *Litany* received very few early multi-voice settings.

Cranmer had reduced the number of invocations to saints contained in the Sarum Litany, and the Prayer Books had reduced it still further. What remained in the 1552 Prayer Book was a series of petitions and responses sung alternately by the precentor and choir, 'upon Sundayes, Wednesdayes, and Fridayes, and at other times, when it shalbe commanded by the ordinary'. A couple of early settings, confined to the choir's responses, were entered in the Wanley and Lumley partbooks; and John Day's *Mornyng and euenyng prayer and communion* contains an anonymous four-part setting of the Litany with Cranmer's chant as its tenor part. But the general lack of Edwardian settings leads to the supposition that a setting made by Tallis, and absent from Day's collection, is Elizabethan. As it was the model for a setting Byrd undoubtedly made early in his career, maybe before he went to Lincoln, it is probable that Tallis's setting was composed in the first few years of Elizabeth's reign.

Cranmer's chant, published in 1544, is the basis of Tallis's Litany, where – transposed and adapted to fit the revised words – it provides the treble part. As far as 'Son of God, we beseech thee to hear us' it is followed closely. Except for the cadences at the ends of the responses, the choral passages are entirely in one-note-to-a-syllable root-position homophony. From 'O Lamb of God' onwards Tallis replaced Cranmer's chant with one of his own devising. This may be because he wished to provide a more expansive ending. It appears to have caused a scribe at Durham Cathedral to call the setting 'The new Lettanye'.[3] Intentionally or not, the title emphasizes the shortage of other settings.

---

2 Walter Howard Frere and William Waugh McClure Kennedy, eds, *Visitation articles and injunctions of the period of the Reformation* (Alcuin Club Collections, 14–16: London, 1910), vol. 3, p. 23. See also Peter le Huray, *Music and the Reformation in England 1549–1660* (London, 1967; rev. Cambridge, 1978); John Harper, *The forms and orders of western liturgy from the tenth to the eighteenth century* (Oxford, 1991), pp. 186–7.

3 Thomas Tallis, *English sacred music: II. Service music*, ed. Leonard Ellinwood (Early English Church Music, 13: London, 1971, rev. Paul Doe 1974), p. 207.

Preces and Responses

Not much Elizabethan service music is to be found in sources of the sixteenth or early seventeenth centuries. This could be due in part to its unsuitability for domestic use.[4] What is included suggests that, besides showing little interest in the Litany, composers of Elizabeth's reign were not intent on making choral settings of the preces and responses (groups of versicles occurring during Morning and Evening Prayer). The need for them may have been limited, since settings of the preces and responses 'are almost invariably found in conjunction with settings of Proper Psalms for use on principal church festivals'.[5]

Tallis may have been the first to make settings of these texts. Although their earliest extant sources are from the second quarter of the seventeenth century, their approximate date is apparent in their influence on Byrd, who took them as the starting point for his own early pieces of the same kind.[6] This could well have been when he was at Lincoln, or even before he went there.

The music of Tallis's preces and responses is self-effacing in its simplicity. Careful attention is paid to the lengths of syllables, but emotion is severely restrained. What Craig Monson says about Byrd's Anglican music applies equally well to his models: 'for the music to call attention to itself by an overtly dramatic, "expressive" approach to word-setting ... would violate the essential aesthetic of the style'.[7] We can only guess how much of this aesthetic was Tallis's invention, and how much the Queen's leading church musician was responding to the guidance of senior clerics.

In Prayer Book services the preces follow the Lord's Prayer, said after the Absolution at Morning Prayer and at the beginning of Evening Prayer. The responses follow the Creed at each service. Tallis made two settings of the preces and two of the responses.[8] The labels 'first' and 'second' have become attached to the preces and responses, though this may be of no significance. Manuscripts in the hand of John Barnard contain the first preces and the first responses;[9] but Barnard's printed collection of 1641, *The first book of selected church music*, contains the first preces and the second responses.

---

4 William Byrd, *The English services*, ed. Craig Monson (The Byrd Edition, 10a: London, 1980), p. v. Monson's observations about the reliability of the sources should also be noted.

5 John Morehen, 'English church music', in Roger Bray, ed., *Music in Britain: the sixteenth century* (Blackwell history of music in Britain, 2: Oxford, 1995), pp. 94–146, at 135.

6 Craig Monson, 'The preces, psalms and litanies of Byrd and Tallis: another "virtuous contention in love"' *Music Review* vol. 40 (1979), 257–71.

7 Byrd, *The English services*, p. vi.

8 If the surviving copies represent what Tallis set, small differences between the words in the 1549 Prayer Book and those in the Prayer Books of 1552 and 1559 suggest that he used the later text.

9 Royal College of Music, London, MSS 1045–51.

Tallis's preces and responses resemble his Litany in style, though it is not evident that they are based on any pre-existing chant.[10] The preces are introduced and broken by the precentor's intonations, and at the end they are relieved by the more clearly contrapuntal setting of 'Praise ye the Lord'. It is not plain why settings in different keys were needed, and why (as written) the second is a fourth higher than the first. Nor is it easy to see why the first phrase of the first set of preces should be in four parts instead of the five parts in which the piece continues. The second setting has four voices throughout.

Like the preces, Tallis's two settings of the responses are harmonizations of melodies resembling Merbecke's, but this time they are in the same key and each is for five voices. There is sometimes little difference between them; but without knowing their compositional history it is once again impossible to say why two settings were needed, and what the relationship between them may be.

Remarks about the responses, published by the composer and organist Samuel Sebastian Wesley in 1849, illustrate the fate of Tallis's music in the centuries that followed his death. By Wesley's time the greater part was little known, and much of what was remembered was not representative of the whole. In praising the music of Josquin for its 'largeness of conception and breadth of effect', Wesley added that it was:

> quite annihilative of the claims to peculiar merit ostentatiously put forth in behalf of our Tallis, – a portion of whose writings, when performed at the present day, tends to bring anything but good will to the musical offices; being destitute, it really should be said, of almost every kind of merit, and constituting one interminable monotony which no one can, or ought to, put up with.

But in a footnote he added: 'This does not apply to his fine Responses.'[11]

---

[10] In John Barnard's *The first book of selected church musick, consisting of services and anthems, such as are now used in the cathedrall, and collegiat churches of this kingdome* (London, 1641) the intonations are sung on C, the note on which the tenor sings the first section (though it sings the second and third sections on G). Ellinwood's edition of the first preces transposes the precentor's intonations to G, perhaps assuming that if any part is to be regarded as singing a chant it is the treble; but Ellinwood likewise transposes the intonations of the second preces.

[11] Samuel Sebastian Wesley, *A few words on cathedral music and the musical system of the Church, with a plan of reform* (London, 1849), pp. 45–6; facsimile edn, with introduction and notes by W. Francis Westbrook and Gerald W. Spink (London, 1961). In chapter 4 of *Thomas Tallis and his music in Victorian England* (Woodbridge, 2008), Suzanne Cole traces the disproportionate Victorian enthusiasm for Tallis's preces and responses, together with the Litany, and examines the routes by which these pieces were transmitted to the nineteenth century. See also Suzanne Cole, 'Who is the father? Changing perceptions of Tallis and Byrd in late nineteenth-century England', *Music & Letters*, vol. 89 (2008), pp. 212–26, at 216–17.

Psalms

Tallis made at least 11 English psalm settings in Elizabeth's reign, including eight settings of groups of verses from Psalm 119 (Table 9.1). *The Book of Common Prayer* described Psalm 119 as 'overlong to be read at one time', and it was consequently divided into 22 sections in accordance with a table set out in the Great Bible and 'The table and calendar, expressing the order of the psalms and lessons' at the beginning of each edition of the Prayer Book. Three settings of verses from Psalm 119 are in Barnard's manuscript and printed partbooks. They are for five voices and their style relates them to the preces and responses. Barnard's printed collection appears to associate them with the first preces, but the title 'Mr. *Tho. Tallis* first Preces and Psalmes' may be misleading, and the authority of his source is unknown.[12] The groups of verses set by Tallis (9–16, 17–24, 25–32) are those for use at Evening Prayer on the 24th day of each month.[13] The bass of Tallis's setting of verses 1–8, for the same day, has survived without the other parts.[14] In view of the number of Tallis's psalms associated with the Christmas season, it may be that the verses from Psalm 119 were intended for Christmas Eve.

Table 9.1 Tallis's Elizabethan psalm settings

Ps. 86.11–12	*Teach me thy way**
Ps. 110	*The Lord upon thy right hand**
Ps. 119.1–8	*O that my ways**
Ps. 119.9–16	*Wherewith shall a young man*
Ps. 119.17–24	*O do well unto thy servant*
Ps. 119.25–32	*My soul cleaveth to the dust*
Ps. 119.145–152	*Be thou nigh at hand**
Ps. 119.153–160	*O consider mine adversity**
Ps. 119.161–168	*Princes have persecuted me**
Ps. 119.169–176	*I have gone astray**
Ps. 132	*How he sware unto the Lord**
Ps. 136	*O give thanks unto the Lord**

This list excludes pieces for Parker's Psalter. Settings marked with an asterisk are incomplete.

12 John Barnard, *The first book of selected church musick*.

13 In *The first book of selected church music* the three settings follow consecutively after the first preces, with the instruction 'These *Psa.* are to be sung the 24. day of the moneth at Evening Prayer'. Presumably this is meant to indicate a choice between them rather than consecutive performance.

14 Oxford, St John's College, MS 180 contains the bass of all four groups of verses. The bass of verses 1–8 is also in Lambeth Palace MS 764.

It is possible that Tallis assembled psalms suitable for the Christmas season over an extended period, since single parts survive from a number of other settings. Two are for Psalms 110 and 132, prescribed for Evening Prayer on Christmas Day. As they are the second and third proper psalms for the occasion, a setting of the first proper psalm for the Christmas evening service (Psalm 89) may have been lost. Four incomplete settings have texts from Psalm 119 (verses 145–52, 153–60, 161–8, 169–76), for Evening Prayer on St Stephen's Day, which follows Christmas Day.[15] There is also a textless organ part which, on account of its length, Ellinwood has suggested may represent a setting of Psalm 136, prescribed for Evening Prayer on the 28th day of each month. The festival of the Holy Innocents falls on this day in December. In manuscript 180 at St John's College, Oxford, Psalm 110 is described as belonging to Tallis's 'second Psalms', and Psalm 119 as belonging to his 'third Psalms', and it is instructed that both should be sung with his second preces.[16] Several sources contain annotations to other such pieces – those by Byrd for example – but they are too late and insufficiently detailed to resolve the question of what went on during Queen Elizabeth's reign.[17]

The three complete settings of verses from Psalm 119 are each based on a tenor part related, more or less closely, to one of the traditional psalm tones. The tenor of verses 9–16 and 17–24 has resemblances to tone 1, and that of verses 25–32 resembles tone 7. All the verses of one setting are based on the same sequence of notes, divided into two shorter sequences. Chords are mostly in root position. The lengths of the notes are dictated by the syllables of the text. Verses are sung alternately by the decani and cantoris sides of the choir, although the doxology of the third setting ends with a passage for the full choir.

The settings of verses 9–16 and 17–24 are not as severe as Tallis's settings of the preces and responses, but they belong to the same world. Since both are based on tone 1 and are in the same key (though harmonized differently), they may have been written as a pair for some purpose. The setting of verses 25–32, based on a different tone and in a different key, is often harmonized more boldly, and is akin to a few of Tallis's late settings of Latin texts. It comes from the same region of his imagination as *In manus tuas* and one or two other pieces in the 1575 *Cantiones*.[18]

[15] Tallis, *English sacred music: II, service music*, p. 209. See also John Aplin, '"The fourth kind of faburden": the identity of an English four-part style', *Music & Letters*, vol. 61 (1980), pp. 245–65, at 251–2.

[16] It appears that when Barnard copied verses 9–16 into Royal College of Music MSS 1045–51 he did not have access to Tallis's setting of verses 1–8, since he recorded verse 9 as a phrase for the precentor alone.

[17] Byrd, *The English services*, pp. 170–73.

[18] John Milsom observes that it 'approaches the sound-world of *O nata lux* and *In manus tuas*', included in the *Cantiones* of 1575 ('English polyphonic style in transition: a study of the sacred music of Thomas Tallis' (Doctoral thesis, University of Oxford, 1983), vol. 1, p. 51).

Anthems

The royal injunctions of 1559 (see p. 155) say that:

> for the comforting of such that delight in music, it may be permitted, that in the beginning, or in the end of Common Prayers, either at morning or evening, there may be sung an hymn, or such-like song, to the praise of Almighty God, in the best sort of melody and music that may be conveniently devised, having respect that the sentence [meaning] of the hymn may be understanded and perceived.[19]

The inexactness of the term 'hymn' has already been mentioned (see p. 67). Only two pieces of 'such-like song' by Tallis can in any case be assigned with some certainty to the Elizabethan years, and these can be regarded as anthems.

Verily, verily, I say unto you has words from the Great Bible's translation of 1539 (John 6:53–6). The earliest source of Tallis's setting is a treble partbook of *c.*1570.[20] This also contains *A new commandment give I unto you*, which may be Edwardian (see p. 72), but *Verily, verily* has every appearance of being a later work. While it resembles Tallis's earlier anthems in its mixture of homophony and polyphony, with homophony tending to predominate, it lacks the repeated section they often include, and its observance of speech rhythms and accentuation is more dramatic. The varied tonality of *Verily, verily* calls to mind some of Tallis's Latin-texted pieces of the 1570s .[21]

O Lord, give thy holy spirit may not have been written long before its entry in the first source to include *Verily, verily*, which it follows. It is in turn followed by Tallis's *A new commandment*, but although sandwiched between two pieces undoubtedly by Tallis it is subscribed 'M[r] Tallis, otherwyse Charles'.[22] Later sources suggest no doubt about its attribution to Tallis.

While *O Lord, give thy holy spirit* seems superficially to have some Edwardian features – its repeated ending, for instance, and its restricted tonality – its text is adapted from one in Henry Bull's popular collection *Christian prayers*, published

---

19 Frere and Kennedy, *Visitation articles and injunctions*, vol. 3, p. 23. See also le Huray, *Music and the Reformation*, p. 31ff; Harper, *The forms and orders of western liturgy*, pp. 186–7.

20 BL Additional MS 15166.

21 The considerations noted here seem to outweigh the one put forward by John Aplin, which he bases on Tallis's four-part writing ("The fourth kind of faburden", pp. 245–65, at 261–2). John Milsom notes, in connection with Tallis's Short Service, that 'there is a good possibility that this style of writing continued to find a place in early Elizabethan music' (*English polyphonic style in transition*, vol. 1, p. 29).

22 BL Additional MS 15166, f.80^{r-v}. This is dated to the late 1560s by Iain Fenlon and John Milsom in '"Ruled paper imprinted": music paper and patents in sixteenth-century England', *Journal of the American Musicological Society*, vol. 37 (1984), pp. 139–63, at p. 166.

Example 9.1 The repeated ending of *O Lord, give thy holy spirit*

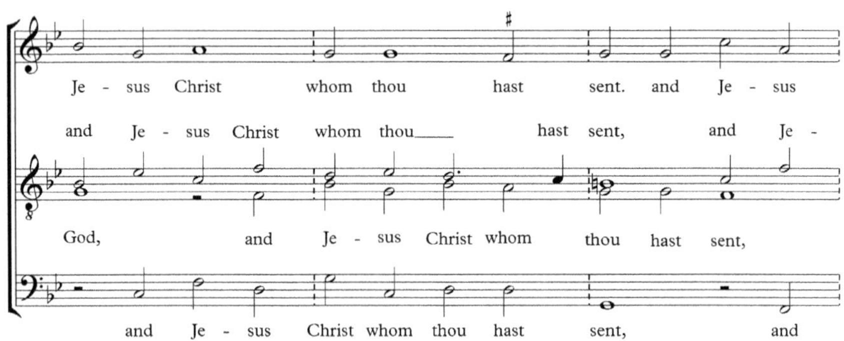

in 1566 and in several editions thereafter.[23] It differs in several ways from earlier English-texted pieces by Tallis. Sections overlap, there are no passages of genuine homophony, and although two or three of the voices sometimes proceed briefly in parallel, all of them as often as not lead independent lives (Example 9.1). Just as tellingly, the highest voice ends with a repeated G not matched in Tallis's anthems but comparable to the sustained notes in the final bars of *O sacrum convivium* and both settings of *Salvator mundi*.

Parker's Psalter

In a note dated 6 August 1557, Matthew Parker wrote that he had completed an English metrical translation of the Psalms at some indefinite time in the past.[24] The records of the Stationers' Company show that Parker's translation was registered by John Day during the year beginning 22 July 1567. Day published it, undated and without the author's name, as *The whole psalter translated into English metre, which contayneth an hundreth and fifty psalmes*. Parker's severely limited abilities as a poet would have justified his anonymity, but he no doubt felt that it was unbecoming for an Archbishop of Canterbury to appear in print as a versifier. His name is revealed only as an acrostic in his preface to Psalm 119.[25]

---

23 Henry Bull, ed., *Christian prayers and holy meditations* (London, 1566); reprinted in The Parker Society, Publications, 38 (Cambridge, 1842), with 'the praiers commonly called Lidleys praiers'.

24 Matthew Parker, *Correspondence of Matthew Parker ... from A.D. 1535 to his death A.D. 1575*, ed. John Bruce and Thomas Thomason Perowne (Parker Society: Cambridge, 1853), pp. ix, 483.

25 In a paper read in 1984, Ann E. Faulkner referred to a draft confirming Parker's authorship. This appears to be Middle Temple Library misc. MS 36, though it is not identified in 'The Parker–Tallis psalter collaboration: the untold story', in *Abstracts of papers read at the fifteenth annual meeting of the American Musicological Society meeting*

Four-part musical settings of verses from eight psalms were appended, together with a setting of *Come Holy Ghost*, Parker's version of *Veni Creator Spiritus*, one of the extra translations which follow his psalter. The psalm settings are numbered ('The first Tune', and so on), and all are subscribed 'p*er* Talys'.[26] It seems possible that Day worked from Tallis's original manuscript, without the intervention of a copyist, but it is less likely that what he printed reflects the composer's notation exactly. (Whythorne remarked on the limitations of Day's music font in his *Songes, for three, fower, and five voyces* of 1571.)[27] The earliest manuscript source of any of Tallis's settings is British Library Additional MS 15166, a treble partbook containing psalms by various composers. It includes pieces from the Parker–Tallis publication, but there seems no reason to suppose that it predates the printed edition or to accord its variants any special authority.

Tallis's musical settings are prefaced by a verse describing 'The nature of the eyght tunes', and a note stating: 'The Tenor of these partes be for the people when they will syng alone, the other parts, put for greater queers [choirs], or to suche as will syng or play them privatelye.' Here 'tunes' does not to refer to the melodies composed by Tallis, but to the modes in which they are written. Rather than describing the nature of the settings, the verse derives from traditional ideas about the qualities of the eight 'tones' or 'tunes', as the modes of mediaeval and Renaissance theory were often called in England. The verse is in fact a translation of part of a table on signature Ei^{v} of the main text, setting out 'Octo tonorum distinctiones & proprietates' (see p. 241).

Judging from the tenors, the settings are arranged to represent alternately the authentic and plagal forms of the modes with finals on D, E, F and G. This agrees with Parker's table of 'Octo tonorum', and the cycle is the only one of English origin to be ordered modally. If there ever were others, they have disappeared. The supplementary setting of 'Come Holy Ghost' is in C, possibly representing the Ionian mode which in his *Δοδεκαχορδον* (1547) Glarean claimed to have rediscovered. The note explaining that the tenor parts are 'for the people when

jointly with the with the Society for Music Theory, Philadelphia, Pennsylvania, October 25–28, 1984, edited by Anne Dhu Shapiro and Peter Breslauer (Philadelphia: American Musicological Society, 1984), p. 68.

26 Parker later asked Thomas Whythorne, who in 1571 or soon after became the master of the music in his chapel, to make additional settings of some psalms (Thomas Whythorne, *The autobiography of Thomas Whythorne*, ed. James M. Osborn (Oxford, 1961), pp. xlviii–xlix, 255, 272). The incipits of the psalms set by Tallis are: (1) *Man blest no doubt*, (2) *Let God arise*, (3) *Why fumeth in sight*, (4) *O come in one*, (5) *Even like the hunted hind*, (6) *Expend, O Lord*, (7) *Why bragst in malice high* (8) *God grant with grace*. The tune of *Come Holy Ghost* has become known as the 'Ordinal', because of the liturgical use of the original Latin hymn. In the notes to his edition Ellinwood remarks on the resemblance of Tallis's setting to the carol 'This endris night', but the similarity is slight.

27 Tenor partbook, note to the reader. On the other hand Day was adventurous in other directions, and in *A testimonie of antiquitie* [1566?] was the first printer in England to use a font containing Old English characters.

they will syng alone' reflects the long-established importance of the tenor part in composition, though it is in some cases the melody of the mean part which later generations have remembered.[28]

Tallis's settings are of different metrical types, so contrived that, between them, they fit many of Parker's translations, not just those whose words are printed with the music. Most of them have also been used in later hymnals.[29] They are a considerable advance on *The Psalter of Dauid* printed in 1549 with a four-part musical score 'which agreth wyth the metre of this Psalter in suche sorte, that it serueth for all the Psalmes therof'.[30] In a table following Tallis's settings, three signs (\ , / , ~) are used to indicate which psalms can be sung to each setting – though the words do not always fit the tunes as straightforwardly as the table implies.[31] The signs also show that, besides being ordered by mode, the eight settings are ordered symmetrically according to their suitability for Parker's translations: (1) ~ , (2, 3) \ , (4, 5) / , (6, 7) \ , (8) ~. It is no wonder that the contents of Tallis and Byrd's *Cantiones* were so carefully ordered, and that Byrd's later publications followed suit.[32]

Most of Tallis's eight settings have simple musical forms, as does the additional *Come Holy Ghost* (p. 166, Table 9.2). But the eighth, *God grant with grace*, caps the principal group with a canon – inevitably known as 'Tallis's canon' – which sets as a continuous text the first two verses of Parker's translation of Psalm 67.[33] Not the least of the canon's several surprises is that so much ingenuity could be expended

---

28 In Tallis, *English sacred music: II, service music*, p. xi, Ellinwood notes that modern hymnals have sometimes exchanged the tenor and mean parts. In 'Tallis' tunes and Tudor psalmody', *Musica Disciplina*, vol. 2 (1948), pp. 189–203, at 194, he says: 'Several ... settings, notably the second, fourth, and sixth, have better melodies in the Meane than in the Tenor'. Vaughan Williams used both the mean and the tenor of the third tune in his *Fantasia on a theme of Thomas Tallis*. He also included several of the tunes in *The English hymnal* (Oxford, 1906), of which he was the music editor.

29 In 'Tallis' tunes and Tudor psalmody' Ellinwood identifies the types as Common Metre Double: 86.86.86.86 (settings 1, 2, 3, 6), Long Metre Double: 88.88.88.88 (settings 4, 8), Short Metre Double: 66.86.66.86 (setting 5), undesignated: 66.66.66.66 (setting 7). See also Tallis, *English sacred music: II, service music*, pp. 207–8.

30 Robert Crowley, *The Psalter of Dauid newely translated into Englysh metre* (London, 1549), 'To the Christian Reader'.

31 And the table is not free from error. Parker provided two translations of Psalm 52 in different metres, 'Why boast thyself' and 'Why bragst in malice high', but both are indexed as suitable for the same music.

32 John Harley, *William Byrd's modal practice* (Aldershot, 2005), pp. 124–7.

33 In Ellinwood's edition the abbreviated third word of the Psalm is expanded as 'we', but the full text of Parker's translation, earlier in the Psalter, gives the word as 'with'. The last line of the setting contains the phrase 'as plain as eye', but the Psalter text has 'as plain at eye'. The attraction of the canon melody has remained strong, and it has undergone a number of changes: see Nicolas Temperley, 'The adventures of a hymn tune – 1', *The Musical Times*, vol. 112 (1971), pp. 375–6. In 'Variations on a canonical theme – Elgar and the enigmatic tradition', Martin Gough added it to the list of pieces which have been

Table 9.2 Tallis's settings for Parker's Psalter

Tune	Rhyme scheme of text	Musical form	Principal cadential notes
1	aabb (lines also have internal rhymes)	ABCD	A, D, A, D
2	aabb	ABCD	D, G, F, D
3	aabb (lines also have internal rhymes)	ABCD	E, E, A, E
4	aabb	AABC	A, A, A, A
5	aabb	ABCD	F, G, C, F
6	aabb (lines also have internal rhymes)	ABCC	F, F, C, F
7	aabb	AABB	D, D, G, G
8	aa, bb, etc.	Canon	G, G, G, G
9	abcb	ABAC	C, G, C, C

in setting doggerel verse. If Tallis felt any doubts about the quality of the text, they were overcome by the perpetual fascination that musical pattern held for him. Just as Parker's translation consists of four-syllable phrases, Tallis's almost completely homophonic music is constructed from building blocks of four-note phrases.

In the original print of *God grant with grace* Tallis labelled the four voices Mean, Contratenor, Tenor and Bass. He also included 'bar lines' whose purpose is not metrical, but to separate the phrases. They are replaced in Example 9.2 by short lines in the upper staff; editorial bar lines have their usual modern meaning, and each phrase is identified by a number (just before its first note), with identical phrases bearing the same number. The tenor part is made up of six different phrases, joined together in the order 1, 2, 1, 2, 3, 4, 3, 4, 5, 4, 5, 4, 6, 4, 6, 4. The mean part begins with four free minims (0), and then sings in canon with the tenor at an octave above it, omitting the tenor's final phrase. The contratenor takes phrases 2 and 5 from the tenor, and adds phrases of its own. Similarly the bass appropriates phrases 1 and 4, and adds further phrases. (Phrase 1 has two forms, in which F is either natural or sharp.) Altogether there are 21 different phrases, plus the four free minims. Some phrases occur several times: if octave transpositions are regarded as identical, phrase 4 makes 13 appearances. Some phrases are mirror images of each other (2 and 4), or are transpositions (6 and 19), or are both (1 and 8).

The result may be no more than fortuitous, and occasioned by Tallis's method in adding two voices to a canon containing repeated phrases; but he can hardly have been unaware of what was happening, and must have allowed things to take their course. An unavoidable consequence is that sometimes (perhaps more often than he might have wished) a single note is given to two voices at the same time. But there can be no doubt that the end-product is a small but remarkably well integrated piece.

proposed as the tune underlying Elgar's Enigma Variations (*The Elgar Society Journal*, vol. 18 (2013), pp. 21–34).

Example 9.2 Tallis's canonic setting of Parker's *God grant with grace*, with the phrases identified by number

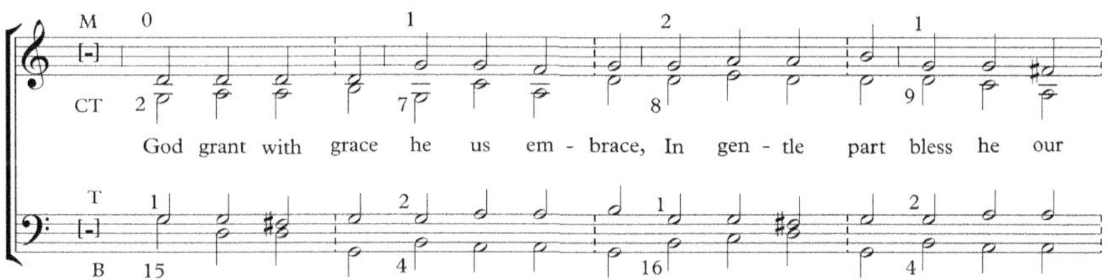
M
CT
God grant with grace he us em - brace, In gen - tle part bless he our
T
B

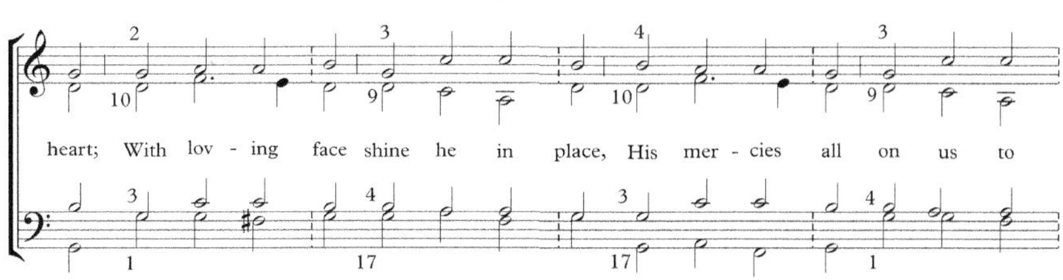
heart; With lov - ing face shine he in place, His mer - cies all on us to

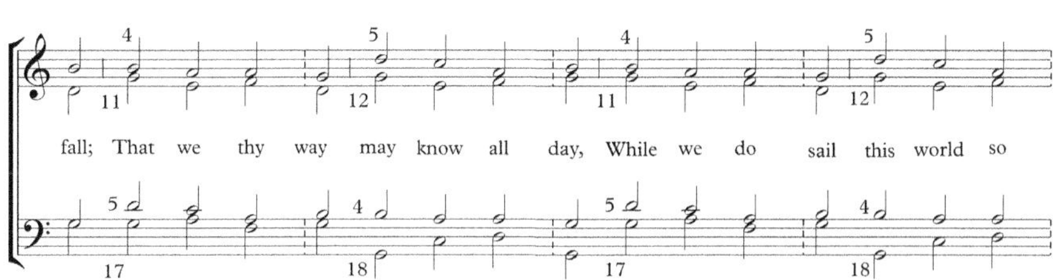
fall; That we thy way may know all day, While we do sail this world so

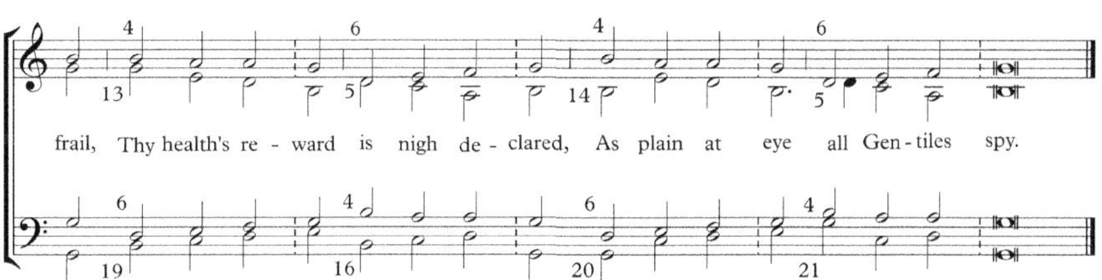
frail, Thy health's re - ward is nigh de - clared, As plain at eye all Gen - tiles spy.

Chapter 10
The Reign of Elizabeth I: Music with Latin Words, and Late Keyboard Music

The composition of music with Latin religious texts continued in England after the accession of Queen Elizabeth. Its principal exponents were the leading composers of her private chapel. Under a patent granted by the Queen on 22 January 1574/5, Tallis and Byrd published a collection of their Latin-texted music with the title *Cantiones, quae ab argumento sacrae vocantur*.

It has sometimes been suggested that Latin works by Tallis, Byrd and others might have been performed in the Elizabethan Chapel Royal (as distinct from 'by singers of the Chapel Royal'), but there is no documentary evidence to show that this ever occurred, or would have been permitted.[1] The Edwardian Act of Uniformity allowed 'anye man that understandeth the Greke Latten and Hebrewe tongue, or other straunge tongue', both to say prayers or have them said at Matins and Evensong 'in Latten or anye suche other tongue', but this related to private prayer. The use of these languages was also permitted in the chapels of the universities ('being no parish churches'), though not in 'The holie Communyon commonly called the Mass'. The provision relating to private prayer was repeated in the prefaces to the first and second Edwardian Prayer Books and the preface to the Elizabethan Prayer Book of 1559. But no mention of the Queen's chapel was made either there or in letters patent of 1560, sanctioning the use of *Liber precum publicarum*, a Latin version of the Prayer Book, at the universities and at Winchester and Eton.[2]

The language of the Elizabethan Chapel Royal was English, and although – as noted in the previous chapter (see p. 155) – the demand for new English-texted music appears not to have been great, Tallis continued to provide some pieces late into his active career. He also continued to set Latin words, presumably for friends or patrons, or simply for his own satisfaction, and very often he did so in ways which were not only unconnected with liturgical use, but which would have been unsuited to it. His work entered a phase just as experimental as the one which followed the death of Henry VIII. In writing, it may be supposed, largely for his own gratification he moved gradually into new realms of form and sound. Some

---

1 This idea appears on p. 204 of the author's *William Byrd: Gentleman of the Chapel Royal* (Aldershot, 1997, rev. 1999), but it can no longer be entertained.

2 The letters patent were printed with the 1560 edition of *Liber precum publicarum*.

of his contributions to the 1575 *Cantiones* can still strike listeners' ears as rich and strange.

Four of Tallis's pieces in the *Cantiones* (already discussed in Chapter 6) seem to have been composed before the accession of Queen Elizabeth. They are *Dum transisset sabbatum*, *Honor virtus et potestas, Candidi facti sunt* and *Sermone blando angelus–Illae dum pergunt*.[3] In the printed versions of the first three the preliminary words, which in liturgical use would have been sung as plainsong, are incorporated into the polyphonic settings. Tallis may have thought it politic not to mention this. Maybe the pieces were included because he was especially proud of them or was short of newer pieces, or because he needed pieces of a particular kind or length, or for a particular number of voices, or in a particular key. The rest of his contribution to the collection consists of 13 pieces (if we count *Suscipe quaeso* and *Si enim iniquitates* as separate works) written in the 17 years of Queen Elizabeth's reign.

Half a dozen recent pieces were left out. He must have recognized that *O salutaris hostia* was not up to scratch, and omitted it on that account – though omission did not always depend on quality. Each of his two sets of Lamentations was too long. (*Suscipe quaeso* was also long, but it fell into two parts which could be included as separate numbers.) A Magnificat probably written after 1560 was too long, and the associated Nunc dimittis made it even longer. Besides that, the Magnificat had divided voices, and would not have fitted into a collection which was probably aimed at a prospective market of small groups of amateur singers. The 40-part *Spem in alium* certainly had no place in a collection of pieces for five, six or seven voices.

The *Cantiones* collection provides a conspectus of a particular part of Tallis's work over two decades, and of Byrd's work of the same kind over a much shorter period. While the publication did not necessarily include the 'best' or the most impressive of Tallis's pieces, those which he admitted were assembled, with Byrd's, into an orderly collection. Because it was carefully planned, its contents can conveniently be treated as a group. The remainder of the present chapter is therefore divided into two parts, the first dealing with Tallis's Elizabethan pieces which were omitted from the collection, and the second (beginning on p. 186) with those which were included. A few keyboard pieces of the same period will be dealt with at the end of the chapter (see p. 206).

3 *Dum transisset*, 'if composed before 1558, certainly enjoyed a new lease of life after that date, and there is good reason to suppose that in preparing the work for publication in 1575 Tallis chose to modify it in several small details, a form of overhauling that can be seen in other motets from the Cantiones' (John Milsom, 'English polyphonic style in transition: a study of the sacred music of Thomas Tallis' (Doctoral thesis, University of Oxford, 1983), vol. 1, p. 37).

Works Not Printed in 1575

O salutaris hostia is a setting for five voices of a verse from St Thomas Aquinas's Eucharistic hymn *Verbum supernum prodiens*, written when Pope Urban IV instituted the Feast of Corpus Christi. One Elizabethan writer viewed Corpus Christi as an 'idolatrous and papisticall feast daie',[4] but the verse Tallis set had long been transformed into a devotional text expressing sentiments that were neither specifically connected with the feast nor exclusively Catholic. Tallis may have made non-liturgical settings of Latin devotional texts for domestic performance before the reign of Queen Elizabeth. Nevertheless, as *O salutaris hostia* differs from his liturgical Latin hymns, and has an obvious relationship to his works which are more certainly Elizabethan, it is sensible to consider it with his Latin-texted pieces of Elizabeth's reign – always bearing in mind that it cannot have been written very long after that reign had begun.

No source helps to determine the date of the setting The earliest surviving manuscript copies were plainly derived in different ways from Tallis's original composition, and all include errors. John Milsom's conjectural stemma suggests how they might have been transmitted.[5] The copy entered in British Library Additional manuscripts 30480–84, a set of partbooks which seems to have been started in the 1560s, was the product of perhaps four or five previous copyings. Another version occurs in King's College, Cambridge, manuscript Rowe 316, which may also have been begun about 1560, though *O salutaris* was not entered at the very beginning. In this case the scribe used a version which seems to be closer to a common ancestor than the version in Additional 30480–84, though his copy has some features of its own. Travelling by another route, a version in British Library Additional manuscript 31390 acquired other variants. It appears among a collection of wordless 'In nomines & other solfainge songs', compiled before 1578 (the date eventually added when some corrections were made), but in view of the manuscript's inclusion of numerous pieces originally setting words, there is no need to think that *O salutaris* began life as an instrumental piece.

Any copyist might introduce an error, yet the different versions of *O salutaris* contain errors that make it impossible in places to guess what Tallis originally wrote. Some stem fairly clearly from attempts by scribes, who were of necessity editors as well as copyists, to correct mistakes they perceived in the manuscripts they were working from. Other changes have the appearance of revisions which may have been made by the composer, though this remains unverifiable. Some sources begin the piece with a prolonged chord, which later sources do

4 William Harrison, *An historicall description of the Iland of Britaine*, [2nd edn] (book 2, ch. 9: 'The lawes of England'), printed in Raphael Holinshed, *The first and second* [*and third*] *volumes* of *chronicles* (London, 1587); William Harrison, *The description of England*, ed. Georges Edelen (New York, 1968), p. 180.

5 John Milsom, 'English polyphonic style in transition', vol. 2, Appendix 2.17.

not include.[6] Printing must have seemed like a godsend to composers whose music was 'spred abroade' in what Byrd called 'many untrue incorrected coppies'.[7]

O salutaris apparently enjoyed a good deal of popularity, although – or because – it was an imitative motet (a non-liturgical setting of a Latin religious text) in a style which Tallis had not previously attempted. It must have preceded *Laudate Dominum* and *Domine quis habitat*. The fact that he was not yet comfortable in the style may account for the almost predictable progress of the piece. The structure is unbroken, in the sense that it includes no cadences where all the voices pause simultaneously, and it points the way to Tallis's later 'seamless' motets and to similar pieces by Byrd; but sets of entries descending from top to bottom, with the upper voices often paired, occur too often in a piece where the tonality is almost static.

Tallis showed himself more at home in writing two 'psalm motets', both for five voices and both considerably longer than *O salutaris*. None of the manuscripts containing ***Laudate Dominum***, a setting of Psalm 117 (Vulgate 116), was compiled before the end of the sixteenth century, but the piece can probably be assigned to a period not very much later than 1560. It is evidently earlier than some of the pieces which entered the *Cantiones*, yet has features forecasting the direction Tallis's music was to take during his remaining years.

Psalm motets had a special attraction for English composers, and they often show the lingering influence of the Tudor votive antiphon. In *Laudate Dominum* it is present in the varying numbers and combinations of voices Tallis brings into play, but there is a newer influence too: continuous imitation of the kind he may have found in works reaching England from the Continent. It is now employed without the rigidity that marred *O salutaris hostia*. The notes on which voices enter are varied, and so are the distances at which they succeed one another. The first two points, setting similar words ('Laudate Dominum omnes gentes' and 'laudate eum omnes populi'), are closely akin, and are integrated into a single unit. The third point ('Quoniam confirmata est') is quickly turned into a canon by the two upper voices, and brief or extended stretches of canon are afterwards threaded through much of the piece.

The other psalm-motet, ***Domine quis habitabit–Ad nihilum deductus est*** (also probably from the early 1560s), has a quite different structure from that of *Laudate Dominum*, but there is again a Continental influence in the division into separate sections, or *partes*, of a work with a long unbroken text (as distinct from stanzas). Tallis repeated this in *Suscipe quaeso*, and for Byrd it was to be a common procedure. It is unlike the earlier practice of dividing antiphons into two

[6] The variants are discussed by John Milsom in 'English polyphonic style in transition', vol. 1, pp. 47–8, and 'Tallis's first and second thoughts', *Journal of the Royal Musical Association*, vol. 113 (1988), pp. 203–22, at 212–14.

[7] Dedication of William Byrd, *Psalmes, sonets, & songs of sadness and pietie* (London, 1588).

sections, because it does not involve a change of mensural time signature. The impression made by *Domine quis habitabit* on some leading English musicians of the eighteenth century, when Tallis's Latin-texted music was little known, appears in the decision of the Academy of Ancient Music to send a copy to the Venetian composer Antonio Lotti as a 'specimen of English music'.[8] It was accompanied by Byrd's *Tribulationes civitatum*.

The text of *Domine quis habitabit* (Psalm 15, or 14 in the Vulgate) was something of a favourite with English composers. In a large and dissonant early motet, Byrd set it for nine voices. But whereas he chose to alter the Vulgate text (if Baldwin's commonplace book is to be relied upon),[9] Tallis made no changes in the words. As always his music illuminates them and is fashioned by them. The power of the words to shape the music emerges in the grouping of voices, as it does for example in the phrases introduced by 'qui', describing those who will live in the Lord's tabernacle.

Tallis was not yet ready to embark on tonal planning of the boldest kind, but whereas the shorter *Laudate Dominum* was not allowed to stray far, or for long, from a G–D tonality, the length of *Domine quis habitabit* demanded more variety. It was restricted to a general F–C area of tonality, but its second part contains some ear-catching cadences on D (one ends each of the adjacent phrases 'qui iurat proximo suo, et non decipit' and 'qui pecuniam suam non dedit ad usuram'), and the final repetitions of 'et munera super innocentem non accepit' and 'non movebitur in aeternum' end with prominent cadences on A.

The two *partes* of *Domine quis habitabit* complement and balance each other in their use – or avoidance – of imitative counterpoint.[10] Both begin with a set of entries spaced and combined to form carefully worked expositions, but thereafter imitation comes and goes, At times it is pursued exactly by some voices, at others it is often impressionistic, and developed fitfully and loosely. Tallis performs the feat of avoiding the predictable, while holding the music firmly together by his control of melodic contours, texture, phrase length, and imprecise but balanced repetition. To end each *pars* he produces something out of the ordinary. Into the first (at 'nec fecit proximo suo') he incorporates two brief, not altogether strict, canons at the octave (two voices starting on C, and two on F), followed (at 'et opprobium non accepit') by another short, flexible and immediately repeated three-part canon between the two highest voices and the tenor. The *secunda pars*

[8] John Hawkins, *A general history of the science and practice of music* (London, 1776), vol. 5, p. 348; Academy of Ancient Musick, *Letters from the Academy of Ancient Musick at London, to Sigr Antonio Lotti of Venice* (London, 1732); Richard Turbet, 'Three glimpses of Byrd's music during its nadir', *The Consort*, vol. 65 (2009), pp. 18–28.

[9] BL R M. 24.d.2 is the sole source. For Byrd's text see William Byrd, *Latin motets I (from manuscript sources)*, ed. Warwick Edwards (The Byrd Edition, 8: London, 1984), pp. xvii, 217–18.

[10] The piece is examined at some length in Milsom, 'English polyphonic style in transition', vol. 1, pp. 166–9.

ends with a point introduced at 'Qui facit haec' and continued at 'non movebitur in aeternum'. This serves several purposes. In the upper two voices it is the basis of a canon, and of a descending sequence in which phrases sung alternately traverse a section of the circle of fifths. Material is simultaneously generated for the other voices. The unit so formed leads into a repetition of material which has preceded it (music previously used for 'non accepit' reappears in the setting of 'in aeternum'), including a slightly prolonged cadence on A. The beginning of the unit is repeated in turn, but now leads into a terminal passage and a final cadence on F.

A set of partbooks assembled by John Baldwin after 1575 is the unique source of Tallis's Latin **Magnificat** and **Nunc dimittis** for five voices.[11] The settings begin and end in the same way, and they were clearly written as a pair of related works.

Before 1549 the texts of the Magnificat and Nunc dimittis appear to have been treated as separate entities. Although an inventory of 1522 lists 'duo magni libri, Psalmorum Magnificat et Nunc Dimittis ac Antiphanarum', it need not be taken to refer to Magnificat and Nunc dimittis settings using common musical material.[12] The separation of the texts in the Sarum services of Vespers and Compline was continued by the English *Primer* of 1545.[13] They were brought into close proximity by the 1549 *Book of Common Prayer*, where due to the abridgement and conflation of the evening services they were separated only by 'a lesson of the New Testament'. Their position was not changed in the Prayer Books of 1552 and 1559, or in *Liber precum publicarum* (1560), although the first two books permitted the optional replacement of the Magnificat by 'Cantate Domino' (Psalm 98 in the English numbering, still with its Latin incipit), while the third permitted its replacement by 'Dominus regnavit' (Psalm 93).

Tallis is usually thought to have linked the traditional Latin texts after the publication of *Liber precum publicarum*, and this indeed seems probable. The *Liber* was a revision by Walter Haddon of Alexander Alesius's *Ordinatio ecclesiae* (1551), a Latin translation of the first *Book of Common Prayer*.[14] Alesius's version does not contain the words of either the Magnificat or the Te Deum, simply directing that they should be said in English, so it is unlikely to have inspired

---

11 Christ Church, Oxford, MS Mus. 979–83, originally six books (tenor missing), compiled after 1575. Concerning replacement of the absent part, see Stephen Rice, 'Reconstructing Tallis's Latin *Magnificat* and *Nunc dimittis*', *Early Music*, vol. 33 (2005), pp. 647–58.

12 W.D. Macray, ed., *A register of the members of St Mary Magdalen College, Oxford, from the foundation of the College. New series* (London, 1894–1915), vol. 2, p. 210; extracted in Frank Ll. Harrison, *Music in medieval Britain*, 4th edn (Buren, 1980), p. 431.

13 *The primer, set foorth by the Kynges Maiestie and his clergie* (London, 1545): Magnificat (for 'The evensong') at G.iii^{v}-[iv^{r}], Nunc dimittis (for 'The compline') at H.iii^{r-v}.

14 *Ordinatio ecclesiae seu, Ministerii ecclesiastici in florentissimo regno Angliae* (Leipzig, 1551).

Tallis's Latin setting.[15] It was Haddon's revision which contained the Latin texts, separated only by the turn of a page.

Gymel passages indicate that Tallis envisaged performance by a group of singers large enough to cope with divided parts, and the Chapel Royal choir springs readily to mind. But, for the reason pointed out above (see p. 169) it is unlikely that the Magnificat and Nunc dimittis were sung in Latin in the Queen's private chapel. There must be doubt, too, whether polyphonic settings of the Latin texts were sung together at the universities. When the Queen visited the chapel of King's College, Cambridge, in 1564, 'The provost began Te deum in Englishe in his cope / which was solemplye sounge in prycksonge / and thorgans playinge'.[16] Whose setting was sung is not stated; one can only say that Tallis's setting from his Short Service would probably have been available. English seems just as likely to have been used during the Queen's visit to the University Church in Oxford in 1566, when 'was theare songe & playde with Cornetts Te Deum'.[17] So how did Tallis's associated Latin settings of the Magnificat and the Nunc dimittis come into being? Maybe they were composed for some patron with sizeable musical resources, and possibly with Catholic leanings. This is not hard to imagine, since Tallis's *Spem in alium* is reported to have been sung at the Earl of Arundel's London home less than a decade after the publication of *Liber precum publicarum* (see p. 149).

Unlike the English Magnificat of his Short Service, but like his four-part Latin setting, Tallis's five-part Latin Magnificat omits passages which, in Sarum services, had customarily been chanted or played on the organ.[18] This would have fitted it for use in Queen Mary's reign, but a close association with a setting of the Nunc dimittis at that time is liturgically improbable. It is far more likely that, together, the two pieces form one of Tallis's works in which Latin texts are set in ways unsuited to the Catholic rite.

Tallis's only earlier work for five voices which relies so much on successive groups of terraced entries is *O salutaris hostia*, but the unyielding regularity of that work is rendered less prominent in the Magnificat by the separation of verses. Even-numbered verses are set one by one, in a way which prevents the long text from becoming tedious. Attention is paid to the sense of each verse, with half verses or sometimes smaller elements prompting the use of imitation. There is endless invention and variety in the way verbal phrases are characterized and contrasted by points, cadential pauses, and overlapping. To create varied textures voices are added or allowed to fall silent.

---

15 The possibility that it might seems to be entertained by Stephen Rice in 'Reconstructing Tallis's Latin *Magnificat* and *Nunc dimittis*', at p. 649.

16 *The progresses and public processions of Queen Elizabeth I : a new edition of the early modern sources*, ed. Elizabeth Goldring and others (Oxford, 2014), vol. 1, p. 402.

17 *The progresses and public processions*, ed. Goldring, vol. 1, pp. 473–4.

18 Concerning the choice of a suitable chant, see Rice, 'Reconstructing Tallis's Latin *Magnificat* and *Nunc dimittis*', at p. 650.

Example 10.1 From verse 2 of Tallis's Latin Magnificat of *c.*1560

Verse 2, the first polyphonic verse, varies both the order in which the voices enter, and the distances between them. In keeping with Tallis's habits of the 1560s and early 1570s, a series of entries repeating 'salutari meo' begins on notes traversing a segment of the circle of fifths ([A] D D G C F F B♭), before the verse works its way to a cadence on G (Example 10.1).[19] Structures of this kind were a new feature, not only in Tallis's music but in English music generally, and he

[19] The tenor part is missing, but the first note of this passage appears to be A. The tenor in the Tudor Church Music edition, followed in Example 10.1, may be the work of Sir Percy Buck.

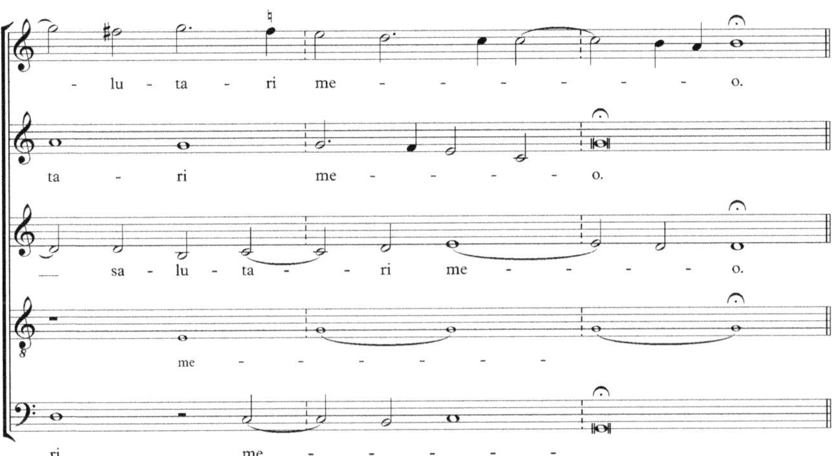

plainly thought they were to be introduced sparingly. He did not attempt another tonal excursion in the first half of the Magnificat. Verses 4 and 6 wander neither very far nor for very long from G, D or C. Verse 8 ('Esurientes implevit bonis') begins with an exposition in which the contratenor part is divided, so that there are initially six entries spread over two octaves, on D, G, G, F, C and C, though subsequent fragmentation and manipulation produces entries on notes as distant as B♭ and E. Verse 10 is less exuberant. So, for the most part, is the doxology; but at the end, from the bass upwards, it piles voices climactically one on top of another.

The much shorter Nunc dimittis sets the second and fourth verses of the text and the doxology. Its reuse of music already heard in the first polyphonic verse and the doxology of the Magnificat confirms its role as a kind of coda to the longer work.

The Lamentations of Jeremiah provided texts for many composers over a long period, both on the Continent and in England. ***Incipit lamentatio Ieremiae prophetae*** and ***De lamentatione Ieremiae prophetae*** are Tallis's settings of passages from the first chapter of the Lamentations. It has sometimes been suggested that Tallis might have extracted the verses he set from the first and second lessons read on Maundy Thursday during the Sarum rite, when that was still in use. But in *De lamentatione* (probably the first to be written) he did not reproduce exactly the words of the second lesson, omitting 'viae Syon', changing 'lugent' to 'luget', and altering the ending (see p. 181). Furthermore, in both pieces he added the conventional incipits which appear in Continental settings of the Lamentations, but which are absent from the Sarum antiphonary and breviary, as they are too from settings by English composers such as Osbert Parsley (1511–85) and Robert White (*c.*1538–74).

The incipits occur, however, in four sets of Lamentations, found only in English sources, by the Italian Alfonso Ferrabosco, who arrived at the English court in 1562 – just about the time when Tallis may have written the earlier of his sets – and was present on and off until he left England for good in 1578. The novelty of Ferrabosco's music may have been as interesting to Tallis as it was to younger English composers, including Byrd, though whether his settings of the Lamentations have any connection with Tallis's is not easy to determine (see below). Even if Ferrabosco and Tallis were composing settings of the Lamentations at the same time, the former was probably not the latter's only source of information about Continental practice. It is entirely possible that an anonymous Lamentations cycle for the Easter season, entered in slightly later manuscript partbooks from the Arundel library, exemplifies material of a kind which was at one time available more widely in England.[20]

Either because of the order in which the verses set by Tallis occur in the Bible, or because they occur in the first and second Easter lessons, his Lamentations are usually numbered 'I' and 'II', although only some musical sources (none of them very early) present the pieces together and in the order indicated by their texts.[21] For reasons shortly to be explained, the order in which Tallis's two settings are nowadays printed seems not to be the one in which they were composed. But while not written initially as companion pieces, they have certain elements in common.

[20] The partbooks are now BL Royal Appendix 12–16. They are described in Charles W. Warren, 'The music of Royal Appendix 12–16', *Music & Letters*, vol. 51 (1970), pp. 357–72, and transcribed in vol. 2 of David Timothy Flanagan, *Polyphonic settings of the Lamentations of Jeremiah by English composers* (Doctoral thesis, Cornell University, 1990). For their possible Italian origin see John Milsom, 'The Nonsuch music library', in Chris Banks and others, eds, *Sundry sorts of music books* (1993), pp. 146–82 at 166; and John Bettler, '*La compositione lacrimosa*: musical style and text selection in North-Italian Lamentations settings in the second half of the sixteenth century', *Journal of the Royal Musical Association*, vol. 118 (1993), pp. 167–202 at 201, paragraph 37.

[21] The earliest source of either (Bodleian Library, Tenbury MS 1464) contains only *De lamentatione*.

They are, naturally, divided similarly into sections; and both are written at a low pitch, leading some editors to transpose them upwards, even though the voices have ranges close to those customarily used by Tallis.[22] Their vocal colour, without the brightness of a treble, is admirably suited to the subject matter.

Another common characteristic, found more often in Tallis's Elizabethan music than in his earlier music, is the tendency of the word-setting to be syllabic, with a good deal of repetition. In this respect, both pieces are reminiscent of *Domine quis habitabit.* But *De lamentatione* additionally resembles that piece in its conservative tonal scheme, and so is probably earlier than the more adventurous *Incipit lamentatio Ieremiae prophetae*. Even so, the latter piece was early enough to influence, and perhaps inspire, Byrd's *De lamentatione Ieremiae prophetae*, which seems to have been written no later than the middle of the 1560s.[23]

Both works are superb examples of Tallis's craft as a word-setter. The emotions induced by the music match closely those conveyed by the words. In each piece he leads us at a measured pace past dark musical pictures of a city in despair. *De lamentatione* describes the affliction suffered by the priests and the people; in *Incipit lamentatio* 'She weepeth sore in the night, and her tears are on her cheeks; among all her lovers she hath none to comfort her'. The Hebrew letters inspire abstract panels between the painted scenes.

The narrower tonal range of *De lamentatione* means that it is much closer than *Incipit lamentatio* to Ferrabosco's settings.[24] Most of the principal cadences in *De lamentatione* are formed on G or its dominant, D, though there are some conspicuous exceptions. The Hebrew letters seem to have suggested the tonalities

22 See the pitches described in Roger Bowers's article 'To chorus from quartet: the performing resouces for English church polyphony, *c.*1390–1559), in John Morehen, ed., *English choral practice, 1400–1650* (Cambridge, 1995), pp. 1–47, at 42; reprinted in Bowers, *English church polyphony: singers and sources from the 14th to the 17th century* (Variorum collected studies, 633: Aldershot, 1999). There is no need for any upward transposition greater than a whole tone or third..

23 Joseph Kerman, *The masses and motets of William Byrd* (London, 1981), p. 55. An Elizabethan date for Tallis's settings has inevitably led to speculation about whether he intended them as a commentary on the condition of English Catholics: see, for example, Amelie Roper, 'Decoding Tallis's Lamentations: music for Protestant Queen or Catholic subjects?', *Brio*, vol. 47 (2010), pp. 5–20. However, restrictions on Catholics in the 1560s were not as severe as they later became; and in any case the 'Jerusalem metaphor' was not appropriated solely by Catholics: it was used most commonly 'in mainstream Church of England circles' (Kerry McCarthy, 'The personal and the political in Byrd', a talk given at All Souls College, Oxford, in March 2006). Tallis's own interpretation of the texts is of course unknown and unlikely to become known.

24 Ferrabosco, Alfonso. *Opera omnia ... II. Motets, Lamentations, an anthem and incomplete motets*, ed. Richard Charteris (Corpus mensurabilis musicae, 96: Neuhausen-Stuttgart, 1984).

of some passages: 'Gimel' is set mainly in G, 'Daleth' in D; but the prevailing tonality is dramatically disrupted by 'Heth' and the cadence on C which precedes it. The disruption follows the most anguished verse of the text: 'omnes portae eius destructae, sacerdotes eius gementes, virgines eius squalidae, et ipsa oppressa amaritudine' (*all her gates are desolate, her priests sigh, her virgins are afflicted, and she is in bitterness*). Another cadence on C occurs before the final cry of 'Ierusalem, Ierusalem, convertere ad Dominum Deum tuum'. In spite of that, the otherwise limited tonal range of the piece makes it necessary to seek other sources of variety. The opening 'De lamentatione' section relies on closely imitative writing. In the 'Migravit Iuda' section, containing very little precise imitation, the two upper voices proceed together almost throughout, continuing a partnership begun at the end of 'Gimel'. In the 'Omnes persecutores' section, which follows 'Daleth', the grouping of voices becomes a principal feature. After 'Heth' the 'Facti sunt hostes' section returns to more frequent, though not pervasive, imitation.

The settings of Hebrew letters are characterized by canon. In 'Gimel' the topmost voice and the tenor sing in canon at the octave. The intermediate voices sing the same melody in canon a fourth below; and except for their first note they are followed at a lower pitch by the bass. 'Daleth' provides only the middle voice with an extended melody. The other voices form two pairs, an octave apart, singing 'Daleth' as short musical phrases, and with one voice of each in canon with one voice of the other. 'Heth' has two free voices, but incorporates a canon begun by the highest voice and taken up an octave lower by the tenor and bass.

By the time Tallis wrote *Incipit lamentatio Ieremiae*, assuming it to be his second setting of words from Jeremiah, his ideas about tonality had taken a stride forwards and it had become a principal concern. The work's most striking feature is its tonal plan, going well beyond anything attempted in Ferrabosco's sets of Lamentations. Tallis's scheme embraces a wide sector of the circle of fifths: B♭ F C G D A E. The central note (G) does not occur as a cadential note or otherwise define a local tonality, but is the pivot on either side of which tonalities are balanced. *Incipit lamentatio* begins and ends in the Phrygian (E) mode,[25] established at the start by the first voice to enter, singing a long melody covering the whole modal octave. Byrd, whose *De lamentatione* is in the twice-transposed Phrygian, imitated Tallis by defining the mode at the outset by means of a long phrase given to the second tenor.

The first half of Tallis's piece travels from E to B♭, the longest tonal journey allowed by his chosen sector of the circle of fifths. In its course prominent cadences emphasize A and D, as well as E; but the 'Aleph' section (with conspicuous chords on A for 'Aleph') signals what is to come later. The highest voice has a Phrygian melody imitated at the interval of a fifth below, so causing B to be flattened. In the next section B♭ soon appears again, and it recurs as 'Beth' is approached. The 'Beth' section itself, placed almost exactly at the centre of the piece, ends with a

[25] As does Ferrabosco's Incipit lamentatione numbered C66 by Charteris. Apart from the setting of Samech, which ends on C, the piece sticks very much to an E–A area of tonality.

B♭ chord (perhaps inspired by the initial letter of 'Beth'). It is 'Beth' which provides the most obvious parallel with one of Ferrabosco's settings of Lamentations texts,[26] for both he and Tallis set the word with a long pedal note in the highest part. In Tallis's setting two pairs of voices sing short, gently undulating, canonic or pseudo-canonic phrases beneath a continuous F. It is a moment of quiet reflection before the heightened emotional tension of 'Plorans ploravit', and its gradual release as the music journeys back to E. The return is made by way of every available tonality except that of G, the pivotal note. The security of the return is ensured by homophonic repetitions of 'Ierusalem, Ierusalem, convertere ad Dominum Deum tuum', first with two authentic cadences on A and then with four plagal cadences on E. The importance Tallis attached to the idea expressed in this passage must be the reason why he departed from the usual words to quote Hosea 14.2.

The homophonic conclusion confirms a tendency which is present throughout the work. There are many places where two or more voices proceed in parallel, but after the incipit there is next to no consistently imitative writing. 'Aleph', which at first glance seems to consist of short canons, actually contains little in the way of imitation.

Tallis's ***Spem in alium*** is a setting for 40 separate voices of a text which, in the Sarum rite, had occurred as a response and verse during readings from the history of Judith. The setting can be dated fairly closely, since it appears to be the consequence of a challenge issued by an unnamed nobleman, most likely Thomas Howard, the fourth Duke of Norfolk.[27] If the story recounted by Wateridge is true (see p. 149), and if the challenge was connected (as it seems to have been) with Striggio's visit to England in the middle of 1567, *Spem in alium* was almost certainly first performed no later than October 1569, when Norfolk was arrested, placed in the custody of Sir Henry Nevell, and quickly committed to the Tower.

A manuscript of *Spem in alium* was once in the Lumley Library, and is listed in an inventory copied in 1609 from one made in 1596.[28] There it is described simply as 'A songe of fortie partes, made by Mr Tallys', with no indication of whether it was in the composer's hand. The work is now known from later sources, principally

---

26 C65 in Charteris's numbering.

27 There seems no need to strain after extra-musical meanings of the number 40 (examples occur in Paul Doe, 'Tallis's "Spem in alium" and the Elizabethan respond-motet', *Music & Letters*, vol. 51 (1970), pp. 1–14, at 12; and William Elders, *Symbolic scores: studies in the music of the Renaissance*, (Leiden, 1994), pp. 40–113). Denis Stevens correctly observed that 'The number 40 – whether it refers to days, nights, pounds, shillings or winks – can only extra-musically be an arbitrary one; it has long been known in the East as one of the famous "multitude" numbers' (Stevens, 'A songe of fortie partes, made by Mr. Tallys', *Early Music*, vol. 10 (1982), pp. 171–81, at 172). Note Whythorne's use of 'forty' (p. 154 above).

28 Trinity College, Cambridge, MS. O. 4. 38, forming the basis of Sears Jayne and Francis R. Johnson, eds, *The Lumley Library: the catalogue of 1609* (London, 1956), in which 'A songe of fortie partes' is no. 2605).

Egerton manuscript 3512, which is itself the source, directly or indirectly, of copies made in the seventeenth and eighteenth centuries.[29] According to Anthony à Wood, Benjamin Rogers owned a copy of 'a song of 40 parts', though Wood thought it was composed by Byrd.[30]

The copy in Egerton 3512 is a full score set out as five groups of eight similar voices, which suggests it may have been assembled from part books.[31] The highest voices are numbered, 1, 6, 11, etc., the next below are numbered 2, 7, 12, etc., and the other voices are numbered in the same way. It is thus evident that they belong to eight choirs, each made up of the customary five voices (nowadays the choirs are conventionally numbered I to VIII).[32] The score is also equipped with a thorough bass, and with English words separately praising Prince Henry and Prince Charles, the sons of King James I.[33] The thorough bass is written in the middle of each page, after the twentieth vocal part; the complete Latin text is written on f.1[r] above the thorough bass; the complete English text is immediately below the latter, and again under each part throughout. An unsuccessful attempt to underlay the music with the Latin words was made in a late eighteenth-century manuscript, British Library R. M. 4.g.1. The Latin underlay in printed editions is conjectural.

The only description we have of a performance in Tallis's lifetime, when the Latin text would have been used, is the one relayed by Wateridge, who says it took place in the long gallery of Arundel House (see p. 149).[34] Assuming this to be correct, *Spem in alium* must have been written for conditions as near to those of a

---

29 For a succinct description of Egerton 3512 and its history, see the British Library catalogue entry. See also: Bertram Schofield, 'The manuscripts of Tallis's forty-part motet', *The Musical Quarterly*, vol. 37 (1951), pp. 176–83; the preface to *Spem in alium nunquam habui: motet in forty parts by Thomas Tallis*, ed. Philip Brett (Oxford, 1966); Pamela Willetts, 'Musical Connections of Thomas Myriell', *Music and Letters*, vol. 49 (1968), pp. 39–40.

30 Bodleian Library, Oxford, MS Wood D.19(4), f.20[v]. Wood's confusion of Byrd with Tallis was noted at p. 91 above. William Mason attributed the work to John Bull in *Essays historical and critical, on English church music* (York, 1795), p. 100 (reprinted from Mason's series of 'Essays on English church music' which had appeared in *The Musical Standard*): 'Dr. Bull could produce to the astonished reader (not hearer, for the hearer would know nothing of the matter) a piece of harmony in full forty parts.'

31 Striggio's Mass is for five groups (double choirs) of eight voices.

32 In GL Gresham MS G. Mus. 420 each part is copied onto a separate page, though the manuscript is thought to derive from Egerton 3512.

33 These additions are included, with editorial figuring added to the bass, in Philip Brett's revision of the Tudor Church Music edition (Oxford, 1966).

34 Sketch plans of Arundel House published by Kingsford and Hummerson do not allow the sizes of interior spaces to be determined accurately (Charles Lethbridge Kingsford, 'Bath Inn or Arundel House', *Archaeologia*, 2nd series, vol. 72 (1922), pp. 243–77; Michael J. Hummerson, 'Excavations on the site of Arundel House in the Strand, W.C.2, in 1972', *Transactions of the London & Middlesex Archaeological Society*, vol. 26 (1975), pp. 209–51, at 211.

modern concert as any Tallis ever encountered. Performances with English words took place in the very much larger hall at Westminster, during banquets occasioned by the investitures as Prince of Wales of Henry on 4 June 1610, and of Charles on 4 November 1616.[35] The words begin 'Sing and glorify heaven's high Majesty, Author of this blessed harmony', and end with lines that allow either Henry or Charles to be addressed as 'in thy creation happy'. Nothing is said about who directed the performances, though the task could well have fallen to the organists of the Chapel Royal: John Bull in the case of the first, and Orlando Gibbons or Edmund Hooper in the case of the second. William Mason certainly associated Bull with *Spem in alium* (see p. 182), though no document is now known which confirms that he was responsible for the performance in 1610.

The first investiture banquet was described by Henry Hastings, the Earl of Huntingdon, who mentioned the performance of a piece of music in 40 parts.[36] Of the second banquet William Camden wrote that, while the Prince and his lords were dining, 'the song of 40. parts was song by the gent of the Chappell and others sitting vpon degrees ouer the Screene at the north end of the Hall which was sung agayne by the Kings commandment who stood as a spectatour in the Roome ouer the stayres ascending to the great chamber'.[37] It seems possible that on the first occasion, as on the second, the singers were at the end of the performing space, though to make the most of their antiphonal exchanges some at least may have been placed like the decani and cantoris sides of a church choir.

The musical structure of *Spem in alium* is remarkable, but it is coordinated with the structure of the Latin text, and reinforces its meaning. Although guesswork cannot be avoided in matching the Latin words to the music, the Tudor Church Music editors were largely successful in combining the two, and what they printed cannot be far adrift from Tallis's original.[38] Tallis may not have made the existing thorough bass, but it is conceivable that he devised something like it in order to control what he was writing.

---

35 Conjectures by earlier writers are overtaken by: Willetts, 'Musical Connections of Thomas Myriell'; Ian Woodfield, '"Music of forty several parts": a song for the creation of princes', *Performance Practice Review*, vol. 7 (1994), pp. 54–64; Davitt Moroney, 'Alessandro Striggio's Mass in forty and sixty parts', *Journal of the American Musicological Society*, vol. 60 (2007), pp. 1–69, note 89. See also Suzanne Cole, *Thomas Tallis and his music in Victorian England* (Woodbridge, 2008), p. 100.

36 Folger Library, V.a.277; Elizabeth Read Foster, ed., *Proceedings in Parliament 1610* (Yale historical publications, Manuscripts and edited texts, 22–3: New Haven, 1966), vol. 1, p. 98.

37 BL MS Harley 5176, f.255^{r}; quoted in John Nichols, *The progresses, processions, and magnificent festivities, of King James the First, his Royal Consort, family, and court* (London, 1828), vol. 3, p. 213.

38 This is qualified by John Milsom in his edition of Thomas Tallis and William Byrd, *Cantiones sacrae 1575* (Early English Church Music, 56: London, 2014), p. xv.

The text is divided into six sections:

Spem in alium nunquam habui
  (*I have had no hope in any*)
praeter in te, Deus Israel:
  (*other than you, God of Israel*)
Qui irasceris et propitius eris,
  (*who can be wrathful and again merciful*)
et omnia peccata hominum in tribulatione dimittis.
  (*and forgives all the sins of suffering mankind*)
Domine Deus, creator caeli et terrae:
  (*Lord God, creator of the heavens and the earth*)
respice humilitatem nostram.
  (*have regard for our lowliness*)

The avowal 'Spem in alium nunquam habui' unfolds gradually, growing in volume and moving around choirs I to IV, as they begin the first section in turn. A 20-part texture is built up from a single point, or with material that closely resembles it, and with additional material containing phrases used often enough by the different choirs to make the counterpoint seem more imitative than it actually is. Before the first section is finished, choirs V to VIII enter successively with 'praeter in te, Deus Israel', introducing a new section in which imitation is more loosely constructed. It prolongs the sideways movement around the choirs, and as it ends it is reinforced by choirs III and VI. The words are repeated by all the voices, after which movement through the choirs reverses direction.

'Qui irasceris et propitius eris' begins with a new point, first sung by choirs VII and VIII, and then taken up by other choirs working in pairs (VI and V, and IV and II). If the editorial distribution of the text is correct, the next section is begun by choirs I and II with the words 'et omnia peccata hominum', afterwards repeated and continued at the very centre of the whole composition by all 40 voices. The phrase's concluding words, 'in tribulatione dimittis', gain extra emotional force from the silence which precedes them in every part. The section is completed by a short antiphonal exchange by two pairs of choirs (V and VI, I and II), and another repetition of 'dimittis' by all the choirs together. For Tallis, we can assume, the dismissal – the forgiveness – of the sins of suffering mankind was a truth to be stated as powerfully as possible.

The last section of the piece begins with a more complex antiphonal treatment, again by choirs working in pairs, and forming a contrapuntal structure in which imitative phrases appear and disappear with great freedom. Finally, after another moment of general silence, every voice joins in an extended repetition of the prayer with which the work ends: 'respice humilitatem nostram'. We shall return to this in a moment.

Spem in alium depends for effect more upon its scoring and its melodic lines than upon dramatic changes in tonality. Each voice has an opportunity to pursue its individual melodic path. The constituent notes of each chord tend to be spread evenly through all the voices; but, with a few deliberate exceptions, the voices seldom duplicate the sounding of a note in a particular octave, or divide it in identical ways. Tallis manages at the same time to keep an eye continually on the outlines formed by the highest and lowest voices. The melodic peaks and troughs of what one choir sings are kept clear of those in the music of another choir.

The tonal scope of *Spem in alium* extends no further on either side of G than one or two fifths, but variety is achieved in other ways and for a number of purposes. It is plain from the start that this is going to be the case. In the first section of the piece choirs I to IV have similar material to sing, though during their successive introduction the notes on which their voices enter are changed. The voices of choir I enter either on G or D, but when choir II is introduced two of its voices enter on A. The voices of choir III again begin on G or D, but those of choir IV change to A and D. In the second section, 'praeter in te, Deus Israel', the tonality swings briefly and gently towards C and F, on the other side of G. Choirs V and VI end the passage on a G chord, but choirs VII and VIII end with a chord on A, sung simultaneously by choirs III and IV as they reiterate 'praeter in te'.

A more pronounced change of direction is contrived when the fifth section, 'Domine Deus, creator caeli et terrae', ends with a major chord on C, a note which is unexpectedly converted to C♯ as a major chord on A begins the final section, 'respice humilitatem nostram'. The means are simple, but their effect is heightened by the preceding silence. There could hardly be a clearer indication of the prominence Tallis wished to give to the words he was setting, and perhaps of the importance he attached to them.

On a totally different scale from *Spem in alium* is a five-part piece which appears, without text, only in a set of partbooks compiled after 1601, where it is headed 'Libera'.[39] It may have been copied for performance as a piece for viols, but it must originally have been a chant-based setting of ***Libera nos, salva nos***, an antiphon sung at Matins on Trinity Sunday in the Sarum liturgy.[40] When Sheppard made two seven-part settings of the words, presumably for Queen Mary's Chapel Royal, he anticipated that the words 'Libera nos' would be chanted. Since Tallis's cantus firmus not only follows the chant closely, but includes the notes of the initial words, it is likely that the piece is a non-liturgical setting which failed to find a place in the 1575 *Cantiones*. Its words ('Release us, save us', a prayer addressed to the Holy Trinity), and the quiet intensity of the setting, are fully in keeping with those of other Elizabethan works by Tallis.

[39] BL Additional MSS 37402–6.

[40] It has been reconstructed by Owen Rees, and recorded by Contrapunctus under his direction (Signum Classics SIGCD338).

Works Printed in 1575[41]

The printing of motets was well established on the Continent, and the title Tallis and Byrd chose for their collection resembles those of several collections published abroad. They must surely have been familiar with publications of this sort, some of which were in the Nonsuch library.[42] But *Cantiones, quae ab argumento sacrae vocantur* is no casual copy of existing anthologies. It is a carefully planned and executed collaborative work. The two composers included no exceptionally long pieces, nor any for fewer than five voices. A number of Tallis's compositions were thus ruled out, even if it crossed his mind to insert them. By counting the two *partes* of Tallis's *Suscipe quaeso* as separate pieces, and likewise the three *partes* of Byrd's *Tribue Domine*, the contributions by each composer were made to total 17, the number of years since the Queen's accession. They persuaded themselves that in these pieces the *partes* could be counted separately because they end on different notes. Pieces consisting of two or three *partes* ending on the same note (Byrd's *Libera me Domine* and *O lux beata Trinitas*) were regarded as single works.

The contents of the 1575 *Cantiones* are set out in Table 10.1 on pp. 188–9, where pieces are listed in the order in which they appear in the collection. This has little or no regard to the date of composition, but is based on considerations described in the next paragraph. An attempt to place Tallis's works in a roughly chronological order is made in Table 12.1 on pp. 224–5.

The task of arranging the pieces in order may perhaps have been undertaken by the younger of the partners, who devised still more ingenious ways of ordering the contents of his later printed collections, but there is no doubt that the result accorded with Tallis's penchant for creating patterns. Tallis's seniority was recognized by the placing of three of his pieces at the beginning of the collection, and the last of his pieces at the end. Table 10.1 (see pp. 188–9) shows the attempt that was made to take account of the keys of pieces, and in some cases to group pieces of a like kind or to place them at intervals throughout the collection. The scoring of pieces is indicated by the 'clefs' columns of the table, which of course refer to their written pitch, not necessarily to the pitch at which performers decided to sing them. It does not seem that the clef combinations played a very significant part in the organization of the *Cantiones*, as they did for instance in the organization of Byrd's song collections.[43]

---

41 The present chapter was largely completed before the publication of the Early English Church Music edition of the 1575 *Cantiones*, edited by John Milsom. What is said here should be read in conjunction with that edition.

42 Representative of such titles are *Liber cantionum sacrarum, vulgo moteta vocant* (Louvain, 1555), *Sacrae cantiones quinque vocum, vulgo moteta* (Antwerp, 1546), and *Sacrae cantiones quinque vocum Andreae Gabrielis* (Venice, 1565). See John Milsom, 'The Nonsuch music library', in Chris Banks and others, eds, *Sundry sorts of music books* (London, 1993), pp. 146–82.

43 William Byrd, *Psalmes, sonets, & songs of sadness and pietie* (London, 1588), and *Songs of sundrie natures* (London, 1589). See John Harley, *William Byrd's modal practice*

There are a few instances where the placing of pieces may have been influenced by the clefs they employ, but these could have arisen as a result of decisions made for other reasons.

Unlike Byrd's contributions to the *Cantiones*, among which several reflect a personal choice of religious words culled from various sources, most of Tallis's pieces are settings of texts connected with the Sarum rite. But it cannot be assumed that the words should be understood as referring to a lost English past, or for that matter to a foreign present. Latin liturgical texts were frequently derived from the Bible, and could be regarded in the same light as many of the English texts sung as anthems. Although the words of *In manus tuas* are those of a respond used in both the Sarum and Roman rites, they are from Psalm 30 (Vulgate numbering), and are set non-liturgically. In 1586, after the Babington plot, Henry Edyall was questioned about earlier goings-on in the home of Lord Paget, who had fled to France in 1583 after the Throckmorton plot. He could say with a clear conscience that he had never sung any 'unlawfull songe', but only 'songes of mr byrdes and mr Tallys'.[44] The pieces published by the two composers were suitable for performance in a law-abiding household.

What prompted the composition of Tallis's most recent Latin-texted works is never absolutely clear, because in his case there are none of the private letters and official documents which tell us so much about Byrd's life and music-making outside the Chapel Royal; but like much of Byrd's music, Tallis's pieces may often have been written for, or in response to requests from, members of the nobility or gentry, or the merchant or professional classes. Many lived in or visited Greenwich, its palace and its neighbourhood; and London and Westminster were a short distance upriver. The domestic pieces are songs of penitence, prayer or devotion. The political overtones which, not so long ago, it became customary to discover in the texts of Byrd's Latin pieces, and which may well exist in a good many of them, are less apparent in Tallis's pieces in the 1575 *Cantiones*, which are on the whole more personal than political. There are of course exceptions. *In ieiunio et fletu* speaks of priests praying, with fasting and weeping, for the Lord's chosen people to be spared from perdition. The sentiments are those of Byrd's *Vide, Domine, afflictionem nostram* (printed in his *Liber primus sacrarum cantionum* of 1589), and could have been read in the same way by Catholics who felt their religious beliefs to be under attack. Tallis's Catholic friends the Ropers. may have been among them.[45] But by 1575 many people in England would have thought of the words simply as drawn from the Bible (Joel 2:12 and 2:17), rather than from a long-disused respond. Tallis's intention is obscure. If we seek too closely his religious or political opinions, we are presented with a mirror.

(Aldershot, 2005), pp. 124–7.

[44] TNA SP12/193/63 (f.170r, manuscript numbering); *Calendar of state papers, domestic series ... Elizabeth, 1581–1590* (London, 1865), p. 56.

[45] John Harley, *The world of William Byrd: musicians, merchants and magnates* (Farnham, 2010), pp. 202–4.

Table 10.1 Contents of *Cantiones, quae ab argumento sacrae vocantur*

In the entry for no. 20 brackets indicate the words of the first verse, not set by Tallis. Elsewhere they enclose words which are delayed in the *Cantiones* (see p. 100).

[a] The chords on which 7 and 14 end are discussed on pp. 102–3.

S: Superius S2: Superius secundus D: Discantus CT: Contratenor CT2: Contratenor secundus T: Tenor T2: Tenor secundus B: Bassus B2: Bassus secundus

			Description	Voices	Final chord	Flats	Clefs								
							S	S2	D	CT	CT2	T	T2	B	B2
1	Tallis	*Salvator mundi salva nos* [I]		5	G	(♭♭)	C1		C3	C3		C4		F4	
2	Tallis	*Absterge Domine*		5	G	(♭♭)	C2		C3	C3		C4		F4	
3	Tallis	*In manus tuas*		5	G	(♭♭)	G2		C2	C3		C4		F4	
4	Byrd	*Emendemus in melius*		5	G	(♭♭)	G2		C2	C3		C4		F3	
5	Byrd	*Libera me Domine et pone me iuxta te*		5	G	(♭♭)	C1		C3	C3		C4		F4	
6	Byrd	*Peccantem me quotidie*		5	G	(♭♭)	G2		C2	C3		C4		C5	
7	Tallis	*Mihi autem nimis*		5	[a]D	(♭♭)	C1		C3	C3		C4		F4	
8	Tallis	*O nata lux de lumine*	Hymnus [& Canon]	5	G	(♭♭)	G2		C2	C3		C4		F4	
9	Tallis	*O sacrum convivium*		6	G		C1		C3	C3		C4		F4	
10	Byrd	*Aspice Domine quia facta est*		6	G		C1	C1	C3	C3		C4		F4	
11	Byrd	*Attolite portas*		6	G		C1	C1	C3	C3		C4		F4	
12	Byrd	*O lux beata Trinitas*	Hymnus	6	G		C1	C1	C3	C3		C4		F4	
13	Tallis	*Derelinquit impius viam suam*		5	C		C1		C3	C4		C5		C4	
14	Tallis	*[Dum transisset] sabbatum*		5	[a]E	(♭)	G1		G2	C2		C3		C4	
15	Tallis	*[Honor] virtus et potestas*		5	C		G1		C1	C1		C3		C4	

16	Tallis	[*Sermone blando angelus*] *Illae dum pergunt*	Hymnus	5	F	(♭)	C1		C3	C3		C4		F4	
17	Byrd	*Laudate pueri Dominum*		6	F	(♭)	C1		C3	C3		C4		F4	F4
18	Byrd	*Memento homo quod cinis est*		6	F	(♭)	C1		C3	C3		C4	C4	F4	
19	Byrd	*Siderum rector*	Hymnus	5	F	(♭)	C1		C2	C3		C4		F4	
20	Tallis	[*Te lucis ante terminum*] *Procul recedant somnia* (Two settings)	Hymnus	5	F	(♭♭), (♭)	C1		C3	C3		C4		F4	
21	Tallis	*Salvator mundi salva nos* [II]		5	G		C2		C3	C4		C5		F4	
22	Tallis	[*Candidi*] *facti sunt*		5	D	(♭)	C2		C4	C5		F4		F5	
23	Byrd	*Da mihi auxilium de tribulatione*		6	A		C1		C3	C3		C4		F4	F4
24	Byrd	*Domine secundum actum meum*		6	A	(♭)	C1		C3	C3		C4		F4	F4
25	Byrd	*Diliges Dominum Deum tuum*	Canon	8	F	(♭)	C1	C1		C3	C3	C4	C4	F4	F4
26	Tallis	*In ieiunio et fletu*		5	G	(♭♭)	C3		C5	C5		C4		F5	
27	Tallis	*Suscipe quaeso*		7	G		C1	C2	C4	C3		C5		F5	F4
28	Tallis	*Si enim iniquitates* (part 2 of no. 27)		7	C		C1	C2	C4	C3		C5		F5	F4
29	Byrd	*Miserere mihi Domine*	Canon	6	G		C1		C3	C3		C5		F4	F4
30	Byrd	*Tribue Domine* (part 1)		6	B♭	(♭♭)	C1		C2	C3	C4	C5		F4	
31	Byrd	*Te deprecor* (part 2 of *Tribue Domine*)		6	G	(♭♭)	C1		C2	C3	C4	C5		F4	
32	Byrd	*Gloria Patri qui creavit* (part 3 of *Tribue Domine*)		6	B♭	(♭♭)	C1		C2	C3	F4	C5		F4	
33	Byrd	*Libera me Domine*		5	G	(♭♭)	C1		C3	C3		C4		F4	
34	Tallis	*Miserere nostri Domine*	Canon	7	C	(♭)	C1	C1	C4	C4		C5		F4	F4

The first six pieces in the *Cantiones* are for five voices, and all are in G(♭♭). They begin with a setting by Tallis of ***Salvator mundi salva nos*** (customarily numbered 'I' because there is another setting later in the collection). The words occur both as a Sarum antiphon for the Exaltation of the Holy Cross and as a post-Tridentine text for Communion on Good Friday, but they occur also in a series of primers published by Wynkyn de Worde,[46] and may still have had some extra-liturgical currency later in the century. *Salvator mundi* (I) owes its position partly to its key, and perhaps also to a decision to begin the collection with a work which, although not in Tallis's very latest style, was not yet widely known. John Sadler seems to have copied *Salvator mundi* (I) soon after its publication.[47] A very rough date of composition may be suggested by its relationship to *O Lord, give thy holy spirit*, which has a text published in 1566 and was copied not long afterwards (see p. 161).

The words are set in continuous counterpoint. Only once do all the voices pause momentarily together (at 'auxiliare nobis'), and they continue without lingering. The impression of music flowing freely and uninterruptedly is, however, slightly misleading, since underlying everything is a sectionalized scheme, related to the three parts of the text: address, prayer, and concluding plea. The word-setting throughout involves a good deal of repetition, and there is a degree of determined regularity about the piece. It was used by Kerman to illustrate the manner in which, when Tallis turned from the 'flexible and unsystematic' imitation occurring in the full sections of votive antiphons, and relied increasingly on imitation as a constructional device, he tended 'to make it as rigid as possible'.[48]

The opening section sets 'Salvator mundi, salva nos' to imitative phrases which enter from top to bottom through all five voices at intervals of a fourth or fifth, and then re-enter with material added to fill the gaps which would arise from straightforward repetition. The four upper voices operate as two pairs, distinguished by the relative timing of their entries. The bass enters as though about to introduce a third pair, but continues alone, and is differentiated from the

[46] Edgar Hoskins, *Horæ Beatæ Mariæ Virginis: or Sarum and York Primers, with kindred books, and Primers of the Reformed Roman Use* (London, 1901), p. 114.

[47] Compare dates for the copying of surrounding pieces into Sadler's manuscript given by David Mateer in 'John Sadler and Oxford, Bodleian MSS Mus. e.1–5, *Music & Letters*, vol. 60 (1979), pp. 281–95, at 291. The contrafactum *With all our heart and mouth* was entered some way into BL Additional MSS 30480–4, thought to have been started in the 1560s as a set of four books, to which a fifth was added later. Differences between the music printed in 1575 and the music of the contrafactum are small, and mainly concern adjustments to accommodate a new prose text in a different language. For the contrafactum see Thomas Tallis, *English sacred music: I: Anthems*, ed. Leonard Ellinwood (Early English Church Music, 12: London, 1971, rev. Paul Doe 1973), pp. 88–94, 130–31.

[48] Joseph Kerman, 'Byrd, Tallis, and the art of imitation', in *Aspects of medieval and Renaissance music: a birthday offering to Gustave Reese*, ed. Jan LaRue and others (New York, 1966), pp. 519–37; reprinted in Kerman, *Write all these down* (Berkeley, 1994), pp. 90–105.

other voices by the long rest before its second entry. It is the bass which helps to enrich the harmonic palette by supporting chords on B♭ and E♭. A fresh set of entries begins the second section at 'qui per crucem et sanguinem'. Again the four upper voices operate as pairs, but the order of entries and their pairing is different and the bass pursues its own course until it imitates the top voice at 'auxiliare nobis'. In the third section, 'te deprecamur, Deus noster', the separation of the bass is more pronounced, and imitation occurs less predictably. It is the least rigid of the sections, and contrives to 'constantly sidestep an expected cadence'.[49]

Absterge Domine, the second piece in the *Cantiones*, has a non-liturgical penitential prose text of unknown origin. The setting may well have been circulating before it was printed, and some of it seems originally to have belonged to a different work. Where the two upper voices sing 'nam tu es Deus meus', there is a passage nine breves in length which is lifted from the two surviving parts of a piece without text, probably copied no later than 1570.[50] A larger part of that piece became the first half of *O sacrum convivium*, which occurs later in the *Cantiones*. In its final form *Absterge Domine* was copied by Sadler not long after he copied *Salvator mundi salva nos* (I). It seems to have been copied into one of the Tenbury manuscripts at about the same time, and appears also in a manuscript completed in 1578.[51] Like *Salvator mundi* (I), *Absterge Domine* was quickly adapted to English words, and the contrafactum *Wipe away my sins* was entered immediately after *With all our heart and mouth* in partbooks already mentioned.[52]

Absterge Domine is a striking contrast to the first piece in the *Cantiones*. It is twice as long as *Salvator mundi* (I), and instead of flowing with almost unbroken smoothness from start to finish it is highly sectionalized. The text falls easily into sections, although for musical purposes Tallis may repeat or link verbal phrases or parts of them, and may sometimes separate phrases conveying related ideas. Most sections are short, and each ends with a clear cadence. Tallis's skill shows in his ability to combine them into a unified composition. He does this partly by giving sections motifs which, in spite of their individual shapes and varied motion, bear a family resemblance to one another. At the same time he works within narrow tonal limits, only once ending a section with a cadence on any note other than G or D. When he does, it is with dramatic effect, switching (in modern terms) from G minor to the relative major, and intensifying with a B♭ cadence the repeated prayer at the heart of the piece: 'sis memor, Domine' (*if you are willing, Lord*).

---

[49] Paul Doe, *Tallis* (London, 1968), 2nd edn (London, 1976), p. 47.

[50] John Milsom, 'A Tallis fantasia', *The Musical Times*, vol. 126 (1985), pp. 658–62. The source is BL MS Harley 7578, ff.92r–93r. For further information on the history of *Absterge* Domine, see Thomas Tallis and William Byrd, *Cantiones sacrae 1575*, ed. John Milsom, pp. 17–20.

[51] Bodleian Library MS Tenbury 1464; BL Additional MSS 31390.

[52] BL Additional MSS 30480–4. *Absterge Domine* attracted at least six English texts: see pp. 237–8.

The off-centre placing of this passage, together with the irregular lengths of the sections, ensures that the plan of *Absterge Domine* avoids a mechanical symmetry.

In terms of length, the short ***In manus tuas Domine*** presents another contrast. But its sentiments (in essence 'you have redeemed me, Lord') follow naturally after those of *Salvator mundi* ('save us and help us') and *Absterge Domine* ('wipe away my transgressions'). Connections within the *Cantiones* are not simply musical.

In manus tuas appears in no source earlier than the *Cantiones*, from which the first surviving manuscript copy appears to have been made.[53] Superficially it has the ABB form of another short piece, *If ye love me*; but now the 'A' section merges with the first 'B' section, and the detailed organization and sound are those of a piece written some quarter of a century later. Tallis had travelled a long way. Most of the closely overlapping entries are made by two or three voices simultaneously, and voices engage in short stretches of canon (though it is seldom pursued strictly for very long). Movement through the closely knit structure has both a direction and a purpose, as a cadence at the end of the repeated second section reveals. It establishes the key after two cadences on the dominant in the first section, and re-emphasizes it on repetition. The final repetition of 'Deus veritas' is given an extra intensity by successive discords preceding the last chord.

The penitence and pleas for salvation expressed in Tallis's first three *Cantiones* pieces are continued in Byrd's first group of three. Byrd starts with an exhortation to amendment, and by the time he has reached his third piece he is begging to be saved from perpetual damnation. But there is a marked difference between the voices of the two composers. In the course of a long life Tallis has worked his way to the concise and complex contrapuntal means of expression found in *In manus tuas*. Byrd, only half Tallis's age, sets off by dispensing with counterpoint and imitation almost completely in *Emendemus in melius*. Even those purchasers of the *Cantiones* who knew Tallis's *Remember not* may have been slightly surprised to find something of that nature in the setting of a Latin text. Byrd's next two pieces would have seemed fresh but more reassuringly familiar. Whether purchasers were quite so reassured by Tallis's next group of pieces is another matter. They would certainly have remarked a change of tone. The words no longer dwell on the supplicant's sins, but contemplate the strength and grace bestowed by God.

Mihi autem nimis is not known to have circulated before its printing.[54] The originality and controlled freedom with which Tallis now wrote, even in pieces of modest conception, had become second nature to him. Freedom in this case also meant a degree of tonal ambiguity. The piece ends with a plagal G–D cadence, but its place in the *Cantiones* is at the end of a group in G(♭♭), and before two more

---

53 Another piece occurring in BL Additional MS 30480–4. On the derivation of the manuscript copy from the *Cantiones* see John Milsom, 'English polyphonic style in transition', vol. 1, p. 50.

54 For the possibility that there was an earlier versions see Thomas Tallis and William Byrd, *Cantiones sacrae 1575*, ed. John Milsom, pp. 112–13.

pieces in G(♭♭) and a group in G. No doubt Tallis (or Byrd) thought of it as centred on G, despite its final cadence. D is nonetheless emphasized in the second half of the piece, when two of the inner voices each sing D 10 or 11 times in succession.

Perhaps with its final destination in mind, the piece opens with four successive entries on D, starting in the bass; only the fifth (in the tenor) begins on G, as the first reaches its end. All describe long flowing lines. The bass then drops out briefly, as it does on four more occasions, and as from time to time other voices do too. The opening is unusual in another way, since Tallis very rarely begins a piece with a solo bass entry, and neither Tallis nor Byrd does it elsewhere in the *Cantiones*. The initial exposition is repeated in a much condensed but recognizable form, with the words 'honorati sunt' made especially prominent by the octave leap that introduces them in all but one of the voices.

The setting of the second section of the text (starting at 'nimis confortatus est') again begins with four entries on D, but this time the bass enters on G. The upper full-range tenor part likewise enters independently, ignoring the imitation of the other voices and repeatedly sounding D – something taken up a little later by the voice beneath it. Another pairing involves the treble and tenor, singing in canon at the octave. The passage is repeated with the two upper tenors exchanging parts, before the piece closes with an extended stretto setting of 'principatus eorum'.

O nata lux de lumine is the first piece in the *Cantiones* to be labelled 'Hymnus'. Pieces so designated are placed at carefully spaced points in the collection, until hymns by the two composers appear side by side. Why special attention was drawn to their inclusion is hard to fathom. The English certainly had a taste for singing hymns, but a verse like *Illae dum pergunt* is a far cry from many of the hymns printed by John Day. Whatever the reason, Tallis's *O nata lux* fits Kerman's description of Byrd's *Cantiones* hymns: 'among the most modern motets in the collection, these are concise, schematic works featuring lively syllabic declamation in homophony or half-homophony'.[55] *O nata lux* has for its text the first two verses of a hymn sung at Lauds on the Feast of the Transfiguration, but Tallis's setting is unsuited to liturgical use and makes no reference to the chant.[56] The most obvious connection with his liturgical hymns is its triple time signature (ⅽ) – though here there is no transition to duple time – and the repetition of the final bars suggests a relationship to some of Tallis's mid-century anthems. Its closer kinship is, however, with *In manus tuas*, another short work with a repeated ending.

Recent composition may also be suggested by Tallis's use of tonality. A weak cadence occurs at the end of each odd-numbered line, and there is generally a

---

[55] Joseph Kerman, *The Masses and motets of William Byrd*, p. 115. Tallis's notation is however more old-fashioned than Byrd's, and he does not employ some of the other features described by Kerman.

[56] Judith Blezzard notes the possible influence of harmonized plainsong in the repeated closing bars of *O nata lux*, where there is 'a largely static harmony around a reiterated pivot note, a device that often occurs in early English plainsong-based compositions' (Blezzard, *Borrowings in English church music 1550–1950* (London, 1990), p. 162; see also p. 23).

Example 10.2 The second verse of *O nata lux de lumine* (*You who once deigned to be made flesh for the sake of the lost, grant that we be made members of your blessed body*)

strong cadence and a rest at the end of each even-numbered line. The cadences ending the four lines of the first verse are on A, G, E♭ and B♭. The second verse ('Qui carne') stays closer to home, concluding its inital two lines with cadences on G and D before three plagal cadences on D pave the way for an affective authentic cadence on G. In the last phrase, with complete melodic and harmonic logic, discords created by passing notes and a false relation are resolved by the final

chord, a tranquil answer to the prayer 'nos membra confer effici tui beati corporis' (*grant that we be made members of your blessed body*).[57] Had Tallis needed to justify the repetition of the whole passage, he could have done so with its ending alone (Example 10.2).

There is no imitation in the usual sense, but melodic unity is created by the recurrence of short phrases, either in the original voice or another voice, and either at the same pitch or in transposition. This is another feature indicative of recent composition. The device is related to one used more intensively in the canon *God grant with grace*, probably written before the middle of 1567 (see p. 163). It is a step on the way to the creation of the 'cells', formed by two or more voices, which were to become important in Byrd's compositions.[58]

The next piece in the *Cantiones*, ***O sacrum convivium***, is one of the compositions which reveal Tallis's methods. *Ave Dei patris filia* shows him as a young man, not yet sure of himself, taking a piece by Fayrfax as his guide in writing a lengthy piece of his own. *Remember not* shows him adapting an existing work to meet more demanding circumstances. His procedures in composing *O sacrum convivium* are recorded in a rare series of snapshots that picture him selecting from music written some time before and incorporating parts of it into a new piece. They illustrate,

[57] On p. 164 of *A plaine and easie introduction to practicall musicke* (London, 1597) Thomas Morley condemns an analogous passage, saying that 'such closings have beene in too much estimation heretofore amongst the verie chiefest of our musicians'. Tallis's cadence is not exactly like Morley's example, but is close enough to suggest that 20 odd years after it was written such devices were wearing a bit thin, even though used by Morley's respected teacher William Byrd (see Harman's edition of Morley's book (London, 1952), p. 272).

[58] Kerman, *The Masses and motets of William Byrd*, p. 88.

too, the continued critical attention he gave to works he had already released for circulation.

The history of *O sacrum convivium* has been explored and described in detail.[59] In brief, its origin lies in a five-part piece of which only two parts are extant, anonymously, without text, in a manuscript apparently completed before 1570.[60] The first and second sections of the piece were joined and, with some modification, became the first half of *O sacrum convivium*, to which a new concluding section of about the same length was added. Another short section was reused in *Absterge Domine* (see p. 191). Between the original piece and the printed motet there appears to lie another version which survives without text, but to which the title *O sacra* [sic] *convivium* was added, while copies of single parts survive in other sources that are undoubtedly early even if they cannot be dated closely.

The earliest source of a further version, *I call and cry to thee* (the first of several adaptations with English words), was almost certainly copied after the *Cantiones* appeared, but it is in some details closer to the original untexted version. The coupling of its words with the music has sometimes been thought happy enough to suggest that it could have preceded the Latin version; but the music of the first half of the piece seems not to have been written originally for words in either language. Latin words – from a prose text by Thomas Aquinas, used as an antiphon at Corpus Christi – must have been fitted to it. The English text begins, like many English hymns, with four lines of verse consisting alternately of four and three iambics, in which the shorter lines are rhymed; but the attempt at verse is not sustained beyond the point at which material from the original textless piece runs out. That occurs where 'my soul doth faint' is repeated ('Passionis eius' in the Latin version), and the music arrives at a cadence on F. The succeeding few bars are taken from a later passage in the original textless piece.[61] From 'Forget my wickedness' ('et futurae gloriae') everything is freshly composed.

Although the second half of *O sacrum convivium* is new, it is matched imaginatively to the existing music. The structure of the first section of the work, up to the word 'sumitur' and the prominent cadence on G, depends on each voice repeating its initial entry without a change of pitch, and incorporating only a limited amount of additional material. The second section, up to 'passionis eius', contains little exact repetition in each voice or exact imitation between the voices, and makes its way freely to a cadence on F. The setting of 'Mens impletur gratia',

59 John Milsom, 'A Tallis fantasia', pp. 658–62, and 'Tallis's first and second thoughts', pp. 209–11. A postscript was added to the first of these articles by M.A.O. Ham ('Tallis fantasia', letter to *The Musical* Times, vol. 127 (1986), p. 74. It mentions an English version with a composite text beginning 'Deliver us O Lord our God' (in BL Additional MSS 17792–6, compiled by John Merro after 1624). The most recent account of the piece's history is in Thomas Tallis and William Byrd, *Cantiones sacrae 1575*, ed. John Milsom, pp. 128–32.

60 BL MS Harley 7578; the original number of parts is given on f.92^{v}.

61 Bars 34–40 in the transcription by Milsom in 'A Tallis fantasia'.

taken from a different part of the original composition, provides a short bridge to the newly composed material. This, like the first section of the piece, depends on repetition; but now it is a whole new section which is repeated ('et futurae gloriae, nobis pignus datur'). Only a few notes are then needed for an added plagal cadence.

O sacrum convivium completes three groups of pieces, all (broadly) in G(♭♭). The succeeding group, by Byrd, consists of pieces in G, for six voices. Tallis's next group reverts to pieces for five voices, and begins with ***Derelinquit impius***, a piece with a composite Biblical text (Isiah 55:7 and Joel 2:13)[62] and a non-liturgical form which distinguishes it from the next three pieces, all written in the previous reign. The absence of early sources suggests that it had been composed recently. *Derelinquit impius* marks a change in the tonal pattern of the *Cantiones*. It has a mobile tonality but ends on C, and so provides a useful bridge to the pieces which follow it (see Table 10.1, pp. 188–9). Tallis included other pieces ending on C, but apparently Byrd, who rarely ended any of his sacred pieces on that note, as yet had none available.

The shape of the opening point, and the melismatic treatment of 'suam', are reminiscent of Tallis's early antiphons; but the unconventional ascent of a seventh before the first rising phrase descends again, together with the irregular pitches at which other voices enter, are decidedly new and are linked to the handling of tonality.[63] They may also be part of Tallis's word-painting, illustrating the ungodly man wandering from the path of virtue. At the outset the voices start in turn on G, E, C, A and D. After a cadence on A, the next section of the piece ('et vir iniquus') begins with entries on E, C A, F♯ and D. At the point where the words from Isiah end ('et miserebitur eius'), the music pauses on D; but the pause is at once is turned into a cadence on G, which occupies the midpoint of the piece and sets 'quia', the first word of the passage from Joel. The next phrase, 'benignus et misericors est', is repeated by a series of entries, many of which contain the rising seventh from the beginning of the work; but the notes they begin on are less irregular than those in the first set of entries, and the words speak of God's loving and merciful nature. These entries lead to two cadences on A, from which Tallis moves at last towards C, where the tonality lends to 'Domine Deus noster' a certainty that suggests it was his destination all along.

Derelinquit impius is succeeded by three of Tallis's older pieces, described in Chapter 6: they are *Dum transisset sabbatum*, *Honor virtus et potestas*, and *Sermone blando angelus*. The last of them is another 'Hymnus', which leads to a group of pieces in F by Byrd. These end with another hymn, and are followed

---

62 As printed, Tallis's text subsitutes 'Derelinquit' for the Vulgate reading, 'Derelinquat'. Tallis's version means that the wicked man 'abandons his way' rather than 'should abandon his way'. Editors and commentators have sometimes restored the Vulgate reading.

63 The mean part in *Ave Dei patris filia* begins by traversing a seventh, but the first note of the treble at once turns the seventh into an octave.

at once by Tallis's two settings of ***Procul recedant somnia***, the second verse of the three-verse Compline hymn *Te lucis ante terminum*.[64] Each of the *Cantiones* partbooks displays the two settings on the same page, as one 'number', with the second below the first. The single verse works well as an independent text, and its words may even have had a popular appeal as a prayer for protection against nocturnal apparitions and the devil.

Like the hymns Tallis composed in Mary's reign, each piece has the chant melody in the highest part: in the first it is the chant for Sundays and simple feasts, and in the second it is the chant for ferias and lesser feasts. Both have the metrical signature ⊂ found in the second verses of Tallis's earlier hymns, and their rhythmic treatment of the chant is similar. Yet they have characteristics which seem to mark them out as later works. Each setting ends on an F chord, though one has a single flat and the other has two flats;[65] but both approach the final chord by way of tonalities and intermediate cadences not closely related to it. Because the chants differ, the first is harmonized with two lines ending on G (enclosing one ending on E♭), while the second is harmonized with two lines ending on D and one on G. The placing of the settings between pieces in F and G reflects the ingenuity of the *Cantiones*' organization by key. The virtually homophonic second setting is reminiscent of passages in both sets of Lamentations, and recalls Tallis's chant-based English-texted settings of Psalm 119.

Next in the group by Tallis is ***Salvator mundi*** **(II)**. Although it is not among the pieces described as canons in the index pages of the *Cantiones*, running through it from the beginning almost to the end is a canon at the octave between the highest and the tenor parts.[66] They and the free bass remained substantially unaltered during the recomposition of an original work which seems to have preceded the printed version.[67] It is impossible to say when the printed version took shape, but if we can assume that it represents Tallis's latest thoughts then an incompletely preserved work with an English text beginning 'When Jesus went into Simon the Pharisee's house' is, or is derived from, an earlier version.[68] It might be argued that

64 The pieces are so indexed in the *Cantiones*.

65 In the partbooks both settings retain the habit of including B♭ in the signature of every part, while including E♭ only in the signatures of parts where it occurs frequently. Byrd had dropped the practice in his printed books by 1591 (Harley, *William Byrd's modal practice*, pp. 102–5).

66 The canon in the third part of Byrd's *O lux beata Trinitas* is likewise ignored in the index, though it merits a label in the body of the superius, contratenor and tenor partbooks.

67 The different versions have been described in detail by John Milsom in 'English polyphonic style in transition', vol. 1, pp. 43–4, and vol. 2, App. 2.14; and 'Tallis's first and second thoughts', pp. 207–9.

68 Its entry in BL Additional MSS 30480–84 (which lack the alto part of 'When Jesus went') may pre-date the *Cantiones*: see Milsom, 'English polyphonic style in transition', vol. 1, pp. 45–6. The contratenor part is also in Shropshire Archives LB/156/1/227 (formerly 356 Mus MS 3), a single book of *c.*1597: see Alan Smith, 'Elizabethan church music at Ludlow', *Music and Letters*, vol. 49 (1968), pp. 108–21, at 118–19. The English-texted

Tallis had the Latin words in mind from the start, since the canonic voices begin with the first few notes of the chant for the antiphon *Salvator mundi salva nos*, but the likeness is very fleeting.

In neither version do the discantus and contratenor parts – the two most heavily amended before they were printed – make more than a cursory imitative gesture towards each other or the three parts which were little modified. This may be due to the lack of space available once the canon and the supporting bass were in place. The contratenor in particular has little room for movement, and is often obliged to cross with the tenor. But the true function of the 'extra' parts is to fill out and enliven the harmonies. Without them the harmonies created by the three principal voices would often be incomplete and usually benign, disturbed only by an occasional non-harmonic note resulting from a suspension or other device. Even with them things proceed pretty smoothly almost until the second half of the piece, when (in the Latin-texted version) the phrase 'auxiliare nobis, te deprecamur Deus noster' (*help us, our God, we beg you*) is urgently repeated. It is then that four successive false relations (always F against F♯) stridently intensify the fervour of the prayer.

Tallis's group of pieces containing *Salvator mundi* (II) is completed by *Candidi facti sunt*, a probably Marian choral respond already discussed (see p. 105). Since it is in D(♭) it provides a neat transition from *Salvator mundi* (in G) to Byrd's next piece, *Da mihi auxilium* (in A).

Da mihi auxilium begins a group of Byrd's pieces for a greater number of voices, ending with *Diliges Dominum*, a canon in eight-parts. It is the first of the canons which are now introduced into the collection at intervals, as hymns were previously – though Tallis's next canon does not come until the very end. After *Diliges Dominum* he resumes his contributions with a non-liturgical setting of the passionate lenten respond **In ieiunio et fletu**:

> ℟ In ieiunio et fletu orabant sacerdotes dicentes, Parce, Domine, parce populo tuo, et ne des hereditatem tuam in perditionem.
> ℣ Inter vestibulum et altare plorabant sacerdotes dicentes, Parce, Domine.
>
> (℟ *The priests shall pray with fasting and weeping, and shall say: Spare, O Lord, spare thy people, and do not give your chosen ones over to destruction.*
> ℣ *Between the porch and the altar the priests shall pray: Spare them, O Lord.*)

He treats the text with great freedom, combining the response and verse, omitting a word, repeating phrases at will, and piling on the emotion with repetitions of 'parce populo tuo':

---

version published in Ellinwood's edition of Tallis's anthems is, of necessity, based on the Latin-texted version published in the *Cantiones*.

> In ieiunio et fletu, in ieiunio et fletu orabant sacerdotes, Parce, Domine, parce populo tuo, parce populo tuo, et ne des hereditatem tuam in perditionem, hereditatem tuam in perditionem: Inter vestibulum et altare plorabant sacerdotes dicentes, Parce populo tuo, parce populo tuo, parce populo tuo, parce populo tuo, parce populo tuo.

The sense of the text is matched by the music. In writing for men alone, without the brighter sound of boys' voices, Tallis no doubt sought the rich and sombre sounds of a low pitch – though probably not quite as low as the score suggests to modern eyes. The lowest written note in his vocal music is usually *F* or *E*, but *In ieiunio* regularly includes *D*. The piece has that in common with *Candidi facti sunt*, which ended Tallis's previous group.

The text of *In ieiunio* is illustrated in other ways as well. Voices enter at unusual pitches from the start, and the tonality shifts anxiously within a segment of the circle of fifths (F C G D A E) in which G is the principal note. The remote chord of A♭ is introduced for passages describing fasting and weeping, and priests uttering their pleas in the body of the church. Not until 'Parce populo tuo' has been repeated again and again does the music settle securely into G. The piece is like a smaller companion to *Incipit lamentatio Ieremiae*, and exhibits the same careful control. Tallis's manipulation of the notes is entirely logical in terms of sixteenth-century practice, and there is unfailing attention to details such as the distinction between G♯ and A♭. *In ieiunio* illustrates superbly what Tallis was able to do after he was freed from the constraints of the liturgy and cantus firmi. He had freed himself also from the constraints of imitation, carrying further a procedure he had tried out in the shorter, and apparently slightly earlier, *In manus tuas*. In the first half of *In ieiunio* much depends on quasi-homophony and the grouping of voices, and there are few discords. The second half makes greater use of polyphony, but strict imitation is confined to short canonic phrases involving only some of the parts.

Fitting *In ieiunio et fletu* into the key scheme of the *Cantiones* may have caused some head-scratching, but it found a home after two pieces in A and one in F(♭), and before ***Suscipe quaeso Domine–Si enim iniquitates***, which at least begins on the note with which *In ieiunio* ended. Account also had to be taken of the fact that Byrd had ready for publication a good many suitable pieces for six or more voices, while almost all of Tallis's few pieces for more than five voices would have been difficult to accommodate for reasons of length or their extra-musical associations. The placing of *Suscipe quaeso*, for seven voices, depends to some extent on its division into two *partes*. It serves as a counterweight to Byrd's tri-partite *Tribue Domine*, which follows soon afterwards. The *partes* of both *Suscipe quaeso* and *Tribue Domine* are printed as though they are separate works (see p. 186). The placing of these pieces in close proximity may also have been suggested by the nature of their texts. Each is non-liturgical, and is venerable without being genuinely patristic. The words of *Suscipe quaeso* come from the writings of Isidore of Seville, and those of *Tribue Domine* are from the anonymous *Meditationes* once attributed to St Augustine of Hippo.[69]

What led Tallis to set *Suscipe quaeso* on a relatively large scale can only be guessed. There is no sign of the piece before its publication in the *Cantiones*. The number and disposition of its voices has led to the suggestion of an association with the *Puer natus est* Mass, but this is not really tenable.[70] (These works are in any case not unique in Tallis's output, and *Loquebantur variis linguis* has the same combination of voices.) Another untenable idea sometimes put forward is that *Suscipe quaeso* was written for the ceremony of national absolution in 1554. This cannot be so because its words are those of a *personal* prayer of contrition. A public prayer would have begun 'Suscipe quaesumus', like the one required by the statutes of Durham Cathedral, delivered under the great seal of Philip and Mary on 20 March 1555: 'as long as we shall survive in this life, these following collects shall be said for us at high mass, to wit *Deus in cuius manu*, etc., *Suscipe quaesumus*, etc., *Presta quaesumus*, etc.'.[71]

Whatever occasioned *Suscipe quaeso*, it has every appearance of being composed before the very latest pieces in the *Cantiones*, and has some of the characteristics of works written in the 1560s. A clue to its date may lie in the resemblance between the beginning of its *secunda pars* and the beginning of *Spem in alium*.[72] Another indication of date is its feeling for tonality, which lies between the separate boundaries outlined by Tallis's two sets of Lamentations. Cadences and cadence-like formations occur mainly on four notes (F, C, G and D), but it explores a segment of the circle of fifths (F C G D A E).

The pattern of *Suscipe quaeso*, like the patterns of many other pieces by Tallis, springs from the words it illuminates. The text consists of seven sentences, separated into two groups, the first forming the prayer of a sinner and the second reflecting on the sinful nature of all men. These groups are the basis of the *prima pars* and *secunda pars* of the motet.

---

69 Kerry McCarthy, 'Byrd, Augustine, and *Tribue, Domine*', *Early Music*, vol. 32 (2004), pp. 569–76, and 'Tallis, Isidore of Seville and *Suscipe quaeso*', *Early Music*, vol. 35 (2007), pp. 447–50.

70 The possibility of an association seems first to have been suggested by Jeremy Noble. Among references to it are: Doe, *Tallis*, p. 40; Hugh Benham, *Latin church music in England* c.*1460–1575* (London, 1977), p. 195; Nicholas Sandon, 'Paired and grouped works for the Latin rite by Tudor composers', *Music Review*, vol. 44 (1983), pp. 8–12; and Thomas Tallis, *Mass Puer natus est nobis*, ed. Sally Dunkley and David Wulstan (Oxford, 1977, rev. 1980, 2009), p. i. The idea was dismissed in Milsom, 'English polyphonic style in transition', vol. 1, pp 33–4, 182.

71 *The statutes of the cathedral church of Durham ... Mary* [ed. A. Hamilton Thompson from a Latin text prepared by J. Meade Falkner] (Surtees Society Publications, 143: Durham, 1929), pp. 160–61.

72 Milsom, 'English polyphonic style in transition', vol. 1, p. 186.

Prima pars

1. Suscipe quaeso Domine vocem confitentis. (*Receive, I beg, O Lord, the voice of one who confesses.*)
2. Scelera mea non defendo. (*I do not defend my crimes.*)
3. Peccavi, Deus, miserere mei. (*I have sinned, Lord, have mercy on me.*)
4. Dele culpas meas gratia tua. (*Blot out my offences by your grace.*)

Secunda pars

5. Si enim iniquitates recordaberis quis sustineat. (*If you should remember iniquities, who could endure it?*)
6. Quis enim iustus qui se dicere audeat sine peccato esse? (*Who is so righteous that he could say he was without sin?*)
7. Nullus est enim mundus in conspectu tuo. (*No one is pure in your sight.*)

Tallis's sense of design is in evidence from the outset. The first sentence of the text is introduced by voices entering in turn on notes which are the basis of the tonality, and in an order which has C, the key note, at its centre: G C F C G C F. The first and second entries, and the fifth and sixth, form pairs in which the second voice follows hard on the heels of the first. A similar arrangement occurs at the beginning of *Incipit Lamentatio*, and in *De lamentatione* at the words 'Facti sunt hostes eius'.

The initial subject falls into two parts, but only the first is imitated with real consistency. The second part ('vocem confitentis') is treated with a degree of freedom, though the two parts of the subject proceed together, making clear that there is a single subject and not two subjects moving in parallel. It is the kind of 'double imitation' described by Joseph Kerman as one in which 'the two parts of a single composite subject are developed flexibly together throughout a point'.[73] Tallis did not use the device again, but it was taken up and developed by Byrd, whose use of it, Kerman thought, 'owes much to the example of "Master Alfonso"'.[74]

The setting of the second sentence is brief, ending with a cadence on C. At 'peccavi' the setting of the third sentence leaps immediately to a distant major chord on E. 'Peccavi' is meant to jolt. Two steps back by way of A and D prepare for the relaxation of tension as the long phrases of 'Deus miserere mei' return to C. Two homophonic utterances of 'peccavi' are no more than a distant rumble of the thunder that accompanied its first appearance.

The fourth sentence makes its way, with multiple repetitions of 'gratia tua', to the central cadence of the piece. On more than a score of its many occurrences 'gratia' is sung to three rising notes. The emphasis on God's grace at the very centre of a major work seems to disclose a great deal about Tallis's innermost feelings. The *secunda pars* begins much as the *prima pars* began, with pairs of entries on notes representing the principal tonalities of the piece. This time the first voice to

[73] Joseph Kerman, *The Masses and motets of William Byrd*, p. 98. On p. 100 he says that 'Before Byrd, double imitation was virtually unknown in England'.

[74] Joseph Kerman, 'Byrd, Tallis, and the art of imitation'.

enter makes an additional modified entry to form a fourth pair of voices, while the last phrase of the section, 'Quis sustineat?' (*Who could endure it?*), is twice repeated homophonically. The homophony (or semi-homophony) is carried over into the next passage, which begins with another question, 'Quis enim iustus?' (*Who is so righteous?*). The questions are put plainly, and the tonality is restricted to G and C: there is no need for additional dramatic effect. No composer ever thought more carefully than Tallis about the words he was setting.

Setting the final sentence may have presented him with a puzzle. Its words answer the questions posed in the previous two sentences, but they provide a slightly curious ending. Instead of an inspirational message or the conventional words of praise which might have been expected, there is a reflection upon mankind's condition: 'Nullus est enim mundus in conspectu tuo' (*No one is pure in your sight*). First the entire sentence is sung, with repetitions of 'in conspectu tuo'. It is then repeated, and 'in conspectu tuo' is treated in the way a concluding 'Amen' might be treated in another work'. Tallis seizes on the words, writing long contrapuntal phrases until the work is brought to an end with the tenor holding an extended pedal C.

The last piece in the *Cantiones*, Tallis's canon ***Miserere nostri Domine***, is a partner for Byrd's six-voice canon *Miserere mihi Domine*, but is separated from it by the three *partes* of *Tribue Domine*.[75]

In all the surviving sets of *Cantiones* partbooks, Byrd's name, not Tallis's, appears in the discantus book at the head of *Miserere nostri* as that of the composer. This could mean that the piece was a joint composition, with Byrd contributing the subject of a canon – perhaps, as John Milsom has suggested, one resolved in four parts by Tallis, who added another, two-part, canon and a free part. The possibility that the name is a misprint is reduced by the care expended on identifying and correcting errors while printing proceeded.[76] However *Miserere nostri Domine* came about, it was most likely composed after final decisions had been taken (possibly after the Queen granted Tallis and Byrd a printing patent in January 1574/5) about the purpose and plan of a collection which, when eventually published, contained apparent references to the 17th anniversary of the Queen's accession. *Miserere nostri* is not only the 17th of the 17 contributions by Tallis, but it is for seven voices, and the first bass sings a melody of 17 long notes. This is derived from the inversion of the 12 notes (11 pitches) with which the discantus begins. (A sign over the 12th note is replaced in Example 10.3a on p. 204 by a modern *segno*, p. 205.)

The voices are those customarily required by Tallis: two trebles (superius and superius secundus), two full-range tenors (discantus and contratenor), a tenor and two basses. The index to the *Cantiones* describes *Miserere Nostri* as '6 partes

[75] The words 'Miserere nostri Domine' may have come from Psalm 122:3 (Vulgate), which seems to accord with Tallis's way of thought, but they occur often in liturgical texts.

[76] Thomas Tallis and William Byrd, *Cantiones sacrae 1575*, ed. John Milsom, p. xxv.

Example 10.3 *Miserere nostri*

a) The beginning

in duabus, cum uni parte ad placitum'. In other words, six voices take part in simultaneous canons, and one part (the tenor) is free.

Four voices begin together, but proceed at different speeds. The contratenor sings the same sequence of notes as the discantus, but they are four times as long, and by the end of the piece fewer of them have been sung. The two bass voices invert the intervals sung by the discantus and contratenor, so that a rising major third becomes a falling minor third, a rising fifth becomes a falling fourth, and so on. The second bass extends the resulting pitches to twice the length of equivalent pitches in the discantus part (occasionally breaking them into groups of shorter notes), and the first bass extends them to eight times the length. All this is described in the partbooks, so that it shall not be overlooked. The contratenor and two bass parts are labelled simply 'Canon in uni sonus', but the discantus is described more fully as taking part in a canon with three other voices: 'Quatuor partes in uni, Canon in uni sonus, Crescit in duplo, Arsim & thesim'. The last

b) The complete first *bassus* part

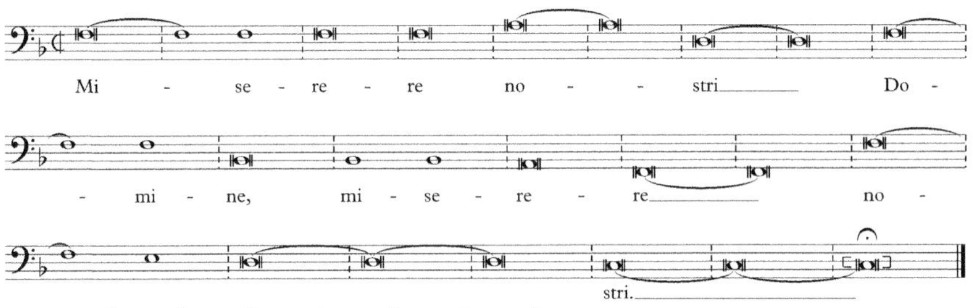

two phrases refer to the extension of note values in the three lower parts, and the inversion of intervals in two of them.[77]

The two superius parts have their own separate but parallel canon, and are labelled respectively 'Due partes in una, Canon in uni sonus' and 'Canon in uni sonus'. The first to begin, a minim later than the group of four voices, is marked

77 The use of 'arsim et thesim', or 'arsin et thesin', to describe canon by inversion seems to have been introduced by Gioseffo Zarlino in *Le istitutioni harmoniche* (Venice, 1558), which was presumably known to Tallis and Byrd.

with a sign (again replaced in the example by a *segno*) where the second enters, singing the same melody at the same speed, but a semibreve later. The free tenor part (described as 'Voluntaria pars'), starting after the first superius entry and before the second, helps to fill out the harmony. But although not engaged in canon, it is clearly related to the other parts.

Tallis achieves all this with only a few small adjustments, such as those needed to make the number of notes fit the number of syllables in the text, and to make all the voices end together. The result is a smooth and poised composition. One reason for its success is the careful choice of melodic intervals, so that the notes of individual voices combine in chords yielding a generally slow rate of harmonic change.

It cannot be certain that *Miserere nostri* was the last piece Tallis wrote for the *Cantiones*, but it seems likely that after the collection was published he wrote nothing more.

Late Keyboard Music

It was Byrd who was largely responsible for the adoption in England of popular tunes, grounds, and songs as the basis of extended and carefully crafted sets of variations for keyboard instruments. When Tallis chose to write long virtuoso keyboard works, he turned to the chant-based music he knew best. Two of his pieces based on the *Felix namque* chant are credibly dated '1562' and '1564' in the Fitzwilliam Virginal Book.[78] (The copyist had access to information or sources which enabled him also to date works by Byrd and Philips.) Some of the characteristics of the *Felix namque* pieces are apparent in a third piece, the canon *Two parts in one*, which is attributed to Bull in one source, but more convincingly to Tallis in another.

The ***Felix namque*** settings cannot have been intended for liturgical use, but belong instead to a practice of basing works on plainchant long after it had ceased to be sung during English church services. They derive from a tradition which required the organist at Lady Mass 'to play a more or less elaborate solo based

[78] Cambridge, Fitzwilliam Museum MS MU 168, traditionally thought to have been compiled by Francis Tregian in the decade after 1609 (an idea contested in Ruby Reid Thompson, 'Francis Tregian the younger as music copyist: a legend and an alternative view', *Music & Letters*, vol. 82 (2001), pp. 1–31, itself contested in David J. Smith, 'A legend? Francis Tregian the younger as music copyist', *The Musical Timezs*, vol. 143 (2002), pp. 7–16). Tallis's second *Felix namque* setting appears also in several other manuscripts, in versions suggesting that the piece underwent revision, not always necessarily by Tallis. For sources see John Caldwell, ed., *Tudor keyboard music* c.*1520–1580* (*Musica Britannica*, 66: London, 1995), where variants are recorded extensively at pp. 184–5. In 'A little-known keyboard plainsong setting in the Fitzwilliam Virginal Book: a key to Tallis's compositional process?' (*Early Music*, vol. 29 (2001), pp. 275–82), Christopher Maxim speculates about the relationship between Tallis's pieces and an anonymous fragment.

on the cantus firmus of the Offertory, *Felix namque*'.[79] The chant is a long one, but the length of Tallis's settings is remarkable. Both include the intonation and the Alleluia as well as the main body of the chant. In each of them the chant is transposed from D: in the first to G(♭♭), and in the second to A.[80] After the intonation each note of the chant is presented as a pair of semibreves, and the pieces are further lengthened by additional material. Both settings look far more like pieces intended for performance on the virginals than on the organ, and maybe not virginals of the small domestic kind.

In the first setting the intonation before the chant is transformed into an introduction, with the chant itself (initially in semibreves) in the tenor part while three other voices engage briefly in canon. In the rest of the setting the chant is in the uppermost part, but does not become clearly apparent until the third note of the chant for 'namque' (bar 18 in Caldwell's edition). The Alleluia begins at bar 141, though Tallis's figuration changes in the previous bar. Chant handled in this way no longer functions as melody, but instead provides a steady indication of time against which the speed of other notes can be measured, and determines the harmonies which are available. The method of choosing harmonies is not entirely restrictive, since each note of the chant can belong to more than one chord, and the chords are varied judiciously. The opportunities for variety are increased by the presentation of each note of the cantus firmus as two semibreves. The harmonies are not, however, the basis of the structure – if 'structure' has any meaning with regard to a piece that depends almost entirely on a constant stream of new figures. The introduction to the second *Felix namque* is based on a heavily disguised version of the chant, which in the Fitzwilliam Virginal Book text is not easily recognizable until it appears (again with the notes for 'namque') as the middle voice at the beginning of bar 15 (Caldwell's numbering), following the double bar line. The Alleluia begins at bar 143, once more without reference to a change in the figuration. Apel thought he detected some Italian influence in the second *Felix namque*, comparing its ending (bars 183–192) with closely similar passages in the keyboard works of Andrea Gabrieli (*c.*1532–1585).[81] This is by no means impossible, although we do not know what Italian keyboard music found its way to England, and Tallis's settings are a treasury of keyboard figuration that embraces virtually all the features customarily used by English organists to demonstrate their inventiveness and virtuosity. They include the simultaneous use of different proportions in different parts, so that, for example, one hand has to play what would

[79] Denis Stevens, ed., *Early Tudor organ music II. Music for the Mass* (Early English Church Music: London, 1969), p. x.

[80] The chant is given in Stevens, *Early Tudor organ music II*, pp. 135–6; Caldwell, *Tudor keyboard music* c.*1520–1580*, p. 173.

[81] Willi Apel, *The history of keyboard music to 1700*, rev. Hans Tischler (Bloomington, Ind., 1972), p. 159; John Harley, *British harpsichord music* (Aldershot, 1992–94), vol. 2, p. 15.

be written in modern notation as $\frac{9}{8}$ while the other plays $\frac{4}{4}$.[82] Tallis's invention never fails and the result is constantly astonishing, but the experience is unrelenting and overpowering rather than enjoyable. There is very little sense of progress towards a satisfying goal which informs so much of Tallis's vocal music.

Yet the impression made by the second *Felix namque* in particular was considerable. Its influence on Byrd's early fantasia in A (MB 27/13) is hardly surprising, but well into the seventeenth century John Bull seems to have been more indebted to Tallis's model than to the works of his own teacher, John Blitheman, while Thomas Tomkins placed 'mr Tallis offertori' (probably the second *Felix namque*) at the head of a list of 'lessons of worthe',[83] and he seems to have had it in mind when he wrote his own 'offertory'.[84] The second *Felix namque* was transcribed for lute, and may have influenced Dowland.[85] Even so, the future of keyboard music lay in methods being pioneered by Byrd, where organic growth was underpinned by harmonic logic.

Two parts in one is as relentless as the settings of *Felix namque*, and is placed here for that reason as much as for the fact that it is difficult to imagine it being composed in the same period as the more rewarding pieces described in Chapter 7. It is complete in a source naming the composer as John Bull, but incomplete in one ascribing it to Tallis.[86] The second attribution is consistent with Oliver Neighbour's observation that 'The dissonances between the bass and the canonic parts recall the treatment of figuration in parts of Tallis's two *Felix namque* settings'.[87] The complete copy is in the hand of Edward Bevin, whose manuscript is 'shaky in its ascriptions'; the other was probably made by Thomas Weelkes, generally regarded as a fairly reliable scribe.[88]

---

82 Passages such as this, and Redford's 'Dignare' (John Caldwell, *Early Tudor organ music: I, Music for the Office* (Early English Church Music, 6: London, 1966), p. 16), may be related to 'musica speculativa': see Roger Bray, 'Editing and performing *Musica speculativa*', in Morehen, *English choral practice 1400–1650*, pp. 48–73.

83 Bibliothèque Nationale, Paris, MS Rés. 1122.

84 No. 21 in Thomas Tomkins, *Keyboard music*, 2nd edn, ed. Stephen D. Tuttle (*Musica Britannica*, 5: London, 1964).

85 Paul O'Dette, 'Dowland's iPod: some possible models for John Dowland's lute fantasias', *Early Music*, vol. 41 (2013), pp. 306–16.

86 Complete in BL Additional MS 31403 ('Canon in subdiapente 2 pts in one with a run*n*ing Base ad placitu*m*'); incomplete in Additional MS 30485 ('A lesson of mr tallis: two partes in one'). Printed by Stevens in *Thomas Tallis ... Complete keyboard works*, ed. Denis Stevens (London, 1953) ('Lesson: Two parts in one'); and by John Steele and Francis Cameron, eds, in John Bull, *Keyboard music: I* (*Musica Britannica*, 14: London, 1960, rev. 2001), pp. 138–41 (no. 51).

87 Oliver Neighbour, *The consort and keyboard music of William Byrd* (London, 1978), p. 231.

88 Alan Brown, ed., *Elizabethan keyboard music* (*Musica Britannica*, 55: London, 1989), pp. xvi–xix.

After the first 10 breves the 'two parts', which show the composer's inventiveness lay in keyboard figuration just as much as in canon, are played entirely by the right hand, while beneath them the left hand plays an uninterrupted stream of quavers, again relying heavily on figuration. It may have been the left-hand part that led to the ascription to Bull, though the piece is not altogether typical of his work. A composer who is just as strongly recalled, however, is Thomas Preston. His *Diffusa est gratia*, for instance, and the first of his *Felix namque* settings, contain a good deal that can be compared with *Two parts in one*.[89] One might hazard a guess that Tallis's piece is an attempt to combine his own canonic skills with something of Preston's virtuoso technique and rhythmic complexity.[90]

---

[89] Preston's 'first' *Felix namque* is the first of his settings in BL Additional MS 29996; both that and his *Diffusa est gratia* are printed in Denis Stevens, ed., *Early Tudor organ music: II*, pp. 45–50, 62–5.

[90] A 'Preston' was one of two organists at St George's Chapel, Windsor, in 1559; the other was John Merbecke. It is uncertain whether he was Thomas Preston (who does not seem to have been employed elsewhere at the time), and unknown whether Tallis was acquainted with him as a fellow musician of the Queen, or was in any way responsible for his appointment. See Watkins Shaw, *The succession of organists of the Chapel Royal and the cathedrals of England and Wales* (Oxford, 1991), p. 342, and the article 'Preston, Thomas' by John Caldwell in *Grove Music Online*.

Chapter 11
The Reign of Elizabeth I: Tallis's Last Years

A letter dated 18 April 1580 was sent to Byrd by 'Richard Sugeham', telling him to expect a friend conveying information he would be glad to hear.[1] The writer was probably a Catholic who lived abroad, and who had adopted the pseudonym 'Sugeham' to prevent his identity from being discovered. He was obviously familiar with the musicians of the Chapel Royal, and asked to be remembered first to Tallis, perhaps as the most senior and respected, and to John Blitheman, John More, William Mundy, 'and the rest my good frendes'. As the letter entered the state papers, with the endorsement '1580' in a hand that was not Sugeham's, it may have been intercepted by the Elizabethan secret service. Suspicions about contacts between members of the Chapel Royal and English Catholics resident on the Continent would easily have been aroused.

Tallis's personal convictions can only be inferred, rightly or wrongly, from his will and his musical settings of religious texts. Naturally enough, the will conveys little more than the conventional ideas of his time, though the music often intimates that they were deeply held. Whatever his private thoughts may have been, in an era when people were repeatedly being told to adopt new beliefs and practices, he seems to have been content to let successive monarchs make decisions that were theirs to make, and to obey their laws. His friendship with Byrd, whose Catholic associations were well known by 1577 (if not before), seems never to have cast any shadow on him; nor does his apparent friendship with another prominent Catholic, Anthony Roper, who received a bequest from Tallis's wife.[2] Tallis's eventual burial in the high chancel of his parish church, St Alfege in East Greenwich, suggests that he was a respected member of its congregation.

On 1 June 1585 Tallis was recorded, for tax purposes, as a member of the royal household,[3] but it is unlikely that he was still active as an organist of the Chapel Royal. It is not clear who now shared Byrd's duties as organist, though Blitheman may have done so. As he was one of those to whom Sugeham wished to be remembered, his absence in Oxford may have ended by 1580 (see pp. 148–9). He went on to outlive Tallis, and died in 1591. No new organist – none of outstanding

1 TNA SP12/137/37, f.59^{r-v}; John Harley, *The world of William Byrd: musicians, merchants and magnates* (Farnham, 2010), pp. 126–7.

2 In 1561 Tallis had joined Anthony's father, William, Roper, as an overseer of Richard Bower's will.

3 TNA E115/371/121.

ability, at least – was admitted to the Chapel before Tallis's death in 1585.[4] John Bull, the organist of Hereford Cathedral, was then recruited, and was sworn in as a Gentleman in January 1585/6. He was possibly a former chorister of the Chapel Royal, and was said to have been a pupil of Blitheman, Nonetheless, he was not a straightforward replacement. The cheque book says that Henry Eveseed was appointed to Tallis's place, and that Bull filled one left vacant by the death of William Rodenhurst.

Tallis made his will on 20 August 1583, claiming that he was sound in body and mind. A codicil to the will was witnessed by Byrd, and by Thomas Fryar, who has not been identified. The overseers were Byrd and Richard Granwall (or Cranwall), who had joined the Chapel Royal shortly after Byrd, and became a close friend of the Tallises. It was the overseers' job to ensure that money or bread was given to the poor of the parish as Tallis wished, and that his bequests were duly made, including one of £3 6s 8d to the Gentlemen of the Chapel, 'towards their feast' – probably for a funeral feast, rather than the Chapel's annual feast, which is not mentioned until a later date.[5]

Tallis died in November 1585: on the 20th of the month according to a register in the Bodleian Library,[6] but on the 23rd according to the cheque book of the Chapel Royal.[7] His burial in St Alfege's high chancel is mentioned in his wife's will. The funeral service was presumably conducted by John Regatt (or Rygate), the vicar of St Alfege's since 1566.[8]

Memorials

A brass memorial plate was installed at St Alfege's church, close to one commemorating Richard Bower. It was attached to a flat stone before the chancel rails. Its inscription shows that it was placed there after Joan Tallis's death, but who was responsible is not recorded.[9] Although the plate has not survived, John Strype published the verses engraved on it 'in old Letters':

---

4 William Randall, who was an organist in the Chapel Royal by 16 July 1592, had first been sworn in as an epistler on 15 February 1584/5, but his career in the Chapel Royal was interrupted by a spell as a lay clerk at St George's Chapel, Windsor.

5 For a similar bequest, made to the Drapers' Company by Laurence Campe in 1613, see Harley, *The world of William Byrd*, p. 92.

6 Bodleian Library MS Rawlinson D318, f.27^{v}; Ashbee, *Records of English court music* (Snodland, *later* Aldershot, 1986–96), vol. 8, p. 319.

7 Dow also gives 23 November in Christ Church, Oxford, MS 988.

8 Henry H. Drake, ed., *Hasted's history of Kent: corrected, enlarged and continued ... The hundred of Blackheath* (London, 1886), p. 99.

9 Burney and Hawkins both say that Henry Aldrich was later responsible for the repair of the stone (Charles Burney, *A general history of music from the earliest ages to the present time* (London, 1776–89), vol. 3, p. 75; John Hawkins, *A general history of the science and practice of music* (London, 1776), vol. 3, p. 266).

Enterred here doth ly a worthy Wyght
Who for long Tyme in Musick bore the Bell:
His Name to shew, was Thomas Tallys hyght
In honest vertuous Lyff he dyd excell.
He serv'd long Time in Chappell with grete prayse,
Fower Sovereygnes Reygnes (a Thing not often seen)
I mean Kyng Henry and Prynce Edward's Dayes,
Queene Mary, and Elizabeth our Quene.
He maryed was, though Children he had none,
And lyv'd in Love full thre and thirty Yeres,
Wyth loyal Spowse, whose Name yclypit was Jone,
Who here entomb'd, him Company now bears.
As he dyd lyve, so also did he dy,
In myld and quyet Sort (O! happy Man)
To God ful oft for Mercy, did he cry,
Wherefore he lyves, let Death do what he can.[10]

William Byrd marked Tallis's passing with a deeply felt song, *Ye sacred muses*, for a treble voice and four viols. The words are translated from a lament on the death of Josquin:[11]

Ye sacred Muses, race of Jove,
  Whom Music's lore delighteth,
Come down from crystal heav'ns above
  To earth where sorrow dwelleth,
In mourning weeds, with tears in eyes:
  Tallis is dead, and Music dies.

Robert Dow, who outlived Tallis by only three years, wrote verses praising Tallis in his music books. One appears to have been written before Tallis's death:

Talis es et tantus Tallisi musicus, ut si
fata sene*m* auferrent musica muta foret.

[10] John Stow, *A survey of the cities of London and Westminster ... brought down from the year 1633 ... by John Strype* (London, 1720), vol. 2, appendix, pp. 91–2. The reference to the 'thre and thirty Yeres' of Tallis's marriage is not quite correct, as Joan's previous husband did not die until 1554. Eighteenth-century musical settings of the epitaph by Benjamin Cooke and William Crotch are discussed by Suzanne Cole in her book *Thomas Tallis and his music in Victorian England* (Woodbridge, 2008).

[11] The original words are 'Musae, Jovis ter maximi | proles canora, plangite', attributed by Franciscus Sweertius (*Athenae belgicae, sive nomenclator Infer. Germaniæ scriptorum* (Antwerp, 1628)) to Gerardus Avidius of Nijmegen (alias Jean Geerhart). It was set to music by both Benedictus Appenzeller and Nicolas Gombert, whose settings were printed by Tylman Susato in his 1545 collection of Josquin's chansons.

The other was written after Tallis's death, and parallels the memorial brass in referring to his service under four sovereigns:

> Quatuor illustris vixit sub Regibus iste
> Tallisius magno dignus honore senex.
> Sub quibus eximius si musicus esset habendus
> Talliisius semper gloria prima fuit.[12]

Since Dow's father was a London merchant who almost certainly knew members of William Byrd's family,[13] it is possible that the younger Dow had direct or indirect contact with Byrd (he certainly had access to pre-publication versions of some of Byrd's works), and may have known the esteem in which Tallis was held by Byrd. Tallis's reputation during the next three centuries was nevertheless often little more than symbolic, and was usually based on a very incomplete knowledge of his works.[14]

The church where Tallis was buried was replaced after its roof collapsed in 1710, and the memorial plate may have been lost at that time. A Tallis memorial fund was set up in 1874, and after a shaky start was successful in raising money for a new brass plate, which was installed in 1876.[15] It was inscribed, again in 'old Letters', mixed with red roman capitals:

✠ In memory of
THOMAS TALLIS
the Father of English Church Music
He died on the twenty-third day of
November in the year of Our Lord fifteen
hundred and eighty-five aged sixty five and
with his wife was buried in this Church
This Brass
was set up in the year of Our Lord
1876

---

12 Christ Church, Oxford, Music MSS 984–8, bass book (f.20^{r}) and tenor book (f.42^{v}); translated as follows in Morrison Comegys Boyd, *Elizabethan music and musical criticism*, 2nd edn (Philadelphia, 1962), pp. 74–5: 'Thou art so renowned and great a musician, Tallis, that if fate should carry thee away in thine old age, music would be mute', and 'Renowned Tallis lived under four monarchs, an aged man deserving of great honour. If in their time any one musician had been singled out as exceptional, Tallis would always have been their chief glory'. Another translation, by Leofranc Holford-Strevens, is given in the introductory volume of *The Dow partbooks: Oxford, Christ Church Mus. 984–988* (DIAMM facsimiles: Oxford, 2010).

13 Harley, *The world of William Byrd*, p. 99.

14 It has been described in Cole, *Thomas Tallis and his music in Victorian England*.

15 Letters from H. Walter Miller in *The Musical Times and Singing Class Circular*, vol. 16 (1 May 1874), pp. 491–2, and vol. 17 (1 June 1876), p. 504.

Although the day given for Tallis's death agrees with that in the cheque book of the Chapel Royal (and was probably taken from Rimbault's transcription, published in 1872), it cannot possibly be right about Tallis's age when he died.[16]

A service commemorating the tercentenary of Tallis's death took place at St Alfege's on 23 November 1885, with music performed by the church's choir and singers from neighbouring churches.[17] In November 1935 the memorial of 1876 was supplemented by another, of bronze, with the inscription which had been on the first memorial. It was dedicated by the musical scholar Edmund H. Fellowes, who had been ordained as an Anglican priest in 1895.[18]

Visual representations of Tallis began in the eighteenth century with an engraving of a probably imaginary portrait of Tallis, published with another of Byrd. The engraving is signed 'N. Haym delin. G. VanderGucht fecit'.[19] Since it shows Tallis holding a pen in his left hand, Haym's original drawing may have been reversed in the process of printing from the engraved plate, though it is not easy to tell this from the book of music which Tallis's pen is touching. As the subject's name ('Tomaso Tallis Inglese Compositore') is not reversed, it may have been engraved separately. A sculptural representation of Tallis by Henry Hugh Armstead is among the figures at the base of the Albert Memorial, unveiled in 1872.[20]

A memorial window, depicting Tallis seated at the organ, was installed at St Alfege's, and unveiled in 1925 along with one commemorating General Gordon. They did not survive the Second World War, but pictures of them are reproduced in

---

[16] This was probably taken from Bumpus: see note 23 below.

[17] BL 3408.g.12(2.): St Alfege Church, Greenwich, *Order of service: "Tallis" commemoration service ... November 23rd, 1885* (Greenwich, 1885). This, as noted in Cole, *Thomas Tallis and his music in Victorian England*, p. 86, contains an evidently inaccurate version of the wording on the memorial plate. See also 'Tallis Commemoration Service', *The Musical Times and Singing Class Circular*, vol. 26 (1885), pp. 722–3. Among the pieces performed, the *Order of service* lists Tallis's *Litany* and his Te Deum (perhaps from the Short Service), his *Hear the volice and prayer*, and 'Glory to thee, my God, this night' sung to 'Tallis's canon'. *All people that on earth do dwell*, sung to 'The old hundredth', is listed with an erroneous attribution to Tallis. The opening processional hymn 'The son of God goes forth to war' (the words of which were written by Reginald Heber in 1812) also appears to be attributed to Tallis, suggesting that whoever compiled the *Order of service* had been provided with rough notes which he did not understand.

[18] Edmund H. Fellowes, *Memoirs of an amateur musician* (London, 1946), pp. 72, 145.

[19] Reproduced as a frontispiece in John Harley, *William Byrd: Gentleman of the Chapel Royal* (Aldershot, 1997, rev. 1999). Nicola Francesco Haym, who was born in Rome, arrived in England in 1700 or 1701, and was employed by the second Duke of Bedford. He was a cellist, literary editor, librettist, composer and antiquarian. Gerard Vandergucht (1696/7–1776) was in England by July 1688, and by 1734 was advertising himself as a dealer in historical portraits.

[20] The process by which images of Tallis came to be formed is described in Cole, *Thomas Tallis and his music in Victorian England*, pp. 62–5, 81–3.

pamphlets published by the church.[21] (Figure 11.1, p. 217 shows the Tallis window.) The same pictures, possibly made directly from the original photographic plates or film, are preserved with a few documents concerning the windows.[22] In the Tallis window, on the floor to the composer's left, is a sheet of music headed 'LITANY', while to his right is a partly unrolled scroll headed 'MOTTETTS'. Beneath the figure of Tallis is pictured a plaque bearing a representation of music headed 'CANON' and signed 'Thomas Tallis'.

One of the church's pamphlets reads:

> Greenwich Parish Church. Order of service at the unveiling and dedication of two stained-glass windows at 3 p.m., Saturday, 21st November, 1925 ... The window commemorating the burial of Thomas Tallis in this church, will be unveiled by E. S. Roper ... organist and composer at His Majesty's Chapels Royal ... The windows have been erected under the will of the late Mr. Frederic Fountain, a parishioner and sometime churchwarden ...

Before the proceedings began, Roper played *Choral prelude on a theme of Tallis* by Harold Darke, one of his preludes op. 20. Several pieces of Tallis's Anglican music were performed during the service. After it was over, Roper played pieces by Rheinberger, Oldroyd, and Franck. The other pamphlet is entitled *St. Alfege Church, Greenwich. Gordon & Tallis memorial windows. November 21st, 1925.* It contains pictures of both windows, and records that they were 'designed and the work carried out in the Studios of Messrs. Jas. Powell & Sons (Whitefriars) Ltd., 98, 100 Wigmore St., London, W.1'. The order for the Tallis window is copied into the firm's order book, now in the Victoria and Albert Museum's Archive of Art and Design. James Powell and Sons, later known as Whitefriars Glass Ltd, was purchased by Caithness Glass in 1981.

Pictures of the Tallis and Gordon windows were included again in *Greenwich parish church: St. Alfege. A short history of the church and its environs* (1951). The biographical notes about Tallis are inaccurate,[23] but correctly observe: 'Death conquered Tallis, but was powerless to kill his music'.

---

[21] BL 3408.ee.38, two pamphlets bound together, and catalogued under the heading 'Two pamphlets relating to the dedication of the Gordon and Tallis memorial windows'. Each has 12 unnumbered pages; the first has no separate cover, while the second has a stiff paper cover and is printed on art paper. Both pamphlets were printed by Henry Richardson, Ltd., of 4 Church Street, Greenwich.

[22] LMA DS/F/1925/033/1–10, mainly letters, etc., approving the installation of the windows.

[23] They were probably taken from John Skelton Bumpus, *The organists and composers of S. Paul's Cathedral* (London, 1891), p. 264, where it is said that Tallis was 'Born c. 1520. Chorister of S. Paul's and the Chapel Royal'. It is quite possible that Bumpus relied on information originating with Maria Hackett and her circle: see Harley, *The world of William Byrd*, p. 25, note 33.

Figure 11.1 The Tallis memorial window installed at St Alfege Church, Greenwich, in 1925, and destroyed in the Second World War (image by permission of the vicar, the Reverend Christopher Moody)

In March 1941 St Alfege Church was badly damaged in an air raid. Both Tallis memorial plates survived, and were installed again when St Alfege's was rebuilt once more. Restoration work was carried out in the 1950s, with Sir Albert Richardson as the supervising architect. The church's large east window, unveiled in 1953, was designed by Francis Spear, and he was asked to design smaller memorial windows for the aisles. He began work on them early in 1954, and his designs were approved by the Parochial Church Council in the following year. In February 1956 an order for the smaller windows was placed with Lowndes and Drury, of Fulham, who in July 1957 submitted an invoice for £184 12s 6d – which less than 60 years later seems an unbelievably small price for six panels. The dedication of the completed windows took place in April 1956.[24] Spear's design is clearly based on Vandergucht's engraving, and seen from inside the church, therefore, the window depicts Tallis as left-handed (Figure 11.2).

The memorial window of 1925 showed Tallis seated at an organ; in the second he is shown standing before one. Although there is no record of Tallis ever having played the organ of his parish church, it seems unlikely that he never did so. The instrument listed in a church inventory of 1552,[25] having survived the roof collapse, was subsequently enlarged, and was finally destroyed in 1941. Its keyboard is reputed to be the one now displayed in a glass case in the church, adjacent to the Tallis memorial plates.[26]

Joan Tallis

Joan Tallis's will, made on 12 June 1587, described her as 'in good helthe and perfecte memorie', although she signed it (as the probate copy discloses) only by making her mark alongside the seal. The passage about her health may have been merely conventional, since it is hard to believe that the widow of two educated

[24] Alan Brooks, *The stained glass of Francis Spear* (London, 2012), pp. 34–5, very kindly supplemented by a number of generous personal communications. The records of Lowndes and Drury are at the Victoria and Albert Museum's Archive of Art and Design, catalogued under the collective numerical prefix AAD/2008/1. Jonathan Partington of the Greenwich Heritage Centre has helpfully located 'The Restoration of the Church of St Alfege, Greenwich' in the Centre's collections; it is an item of fund-raising literature, published by the vicar of St Alfege's in March 1956, and includes a 'Synopsis of Restoration' noting that 'the very fine East Window was by Mr Francis Spear, who is also providing six cartouche windows for the side aisles'.

[25] TNA E117/3/43, m.16, church inventory for 'Estgrenewych', dated 16 November 1552, listing 'j paire of organes'; transcribed in Mackenzie E. Walcott, E. P Coates, and W. A. Scott Robertson, 'Inventories of parish church goods in Kent, A. D. 1552', *Archaeologia Cantiana*, vol. 8 (1872), pp. 74–163. The article is continued in *Archaeologia Cantiana*, vols. 9 (1874), 10 (1876), 11 (1877), and 14 (1882).

[26] St Alfege Church, Greenwich, *Greenwich parish church: St. Alfege. A short history of the church and its environs* (Greenwich, 1951), p. 9.

Figure 11.2 Francis Spear's design for the present Tallis memorial window at St Alfege Church, Greenwich. The completed window was dedicated in April 1956 (image by permission of Simon and John Spear)

men had never learned to write her name. (Bury appears to have been schooled at Eton). As her will says she was 'very olde and unhable to take care for thing*es*', its reference to 'the chamber wheare I nowe lye' may mean that she was confined to bed.

The first page of the will, where her beliefs and hopes are set out, suggests that she was sincerely religious – as she may have been, though whether the expression of her beliefs was entirely her own, or inserted by a lawyer, is another matter. It contains nothing which could not have been uttered by any pious Protestant.

Anthony Roper received from Joan Tallis 'one guilte bowle with the cover therunto belonginge', and William Byrd received 'one grate guilte cuppe withe the cover for the same'. These may have been substantial gifts, representing a part of Joan's savings, and may previously have been kept securely in the barred chest with two locks which is also mentioned in her will. Among the most splendid examples of covered cups was the one William Lambarde gave in 1578 to the Drapers' Company (of which the musician Byrd's brother John was a leading light), as a token of gratitude for the Company's agreement to assume trusteeship of his almshouses.[27] It was made by the (apparently unrelated) goldsmith John Byrd, who was the father of the first William Byrd to settle in Virginia.[28]

Before the bequests to her family, Joan listed one to Richard Granwall, who had cared for her 'rather as a naturall childe … then otherwise'. He got a 'cupp guilte withe the cover therunto belonginge and one guilte bowle'. Joan Tallis was obviously not hard up. Granwall also received many of Joan's household goods and a house occupied by Thomas Palmer, probably one adjacent to the house Joan lived in. The goods Granwall did not get were left to Joan Payre and her children, or 'for default of suche issue' to William Byrd.

Joan's charitable bequests included one of 10 shillings, which continued 'yearly for ever' a payment to the almshouses set up by Lambarde. This appears to have been paid until 1856.[29] Joan Payre was the executrix of the will; the overseers were Byrd, Granwall and Justice Graeme (or Greames), a local inhabitant who at one time sold property to Anthony Roper.[30]

---

27 For the different kinds of such cups, see Philippa Glanville, *Silver in England* (London, 1987), pp. 37–41. For the Lambarde cup, see M.A. Greenwood, *The ancient plate of the Drapers' Company* (London, 1930), pp. 13–19 and frontispiece.

28 The goldsmith was descended (like the musician Byrd's namesake, William Burd of the Mercer's Company) from the Byrds of Cheshire.

29 'Report on the Charities of the Drapers' Company: Part II', in Royal Commission on the Livery Companies of the City of London, *Report and appendix* (London, 1884), vol. 4, pp. 146–60.

30 For Graeme, see indexed entries in Drake, *Hasted's history of Kent*. For Roper, see p. 90 above.

Chapter 12
Reflections

Outside a few formal documents, sixteenth-century references to Thomas Tallis are rare. Those which exist are united in admiring him but reveal little of him as a person. He was praised, together with William Byrd, in the prefatory matter of the 1575 *Cantiones*. There Richard Mulcaster wrote that each of the composers deserved an honoured name, while Ferdinando Richardson described Tallis as an old man deserving of great honour, and Byrd as lending further honour to so great a master. In Robert Dow's music books (compiled 1581–88) Tallis received unsolicited praise of a kind accorded also to White, Parsons, Mundy, Ferrabosco, and inevitably Byrd. John Baldwin, who added two pieces to Dow's manuscripts,[1] included Tallis's name in a poem he inscribed in his own commonplace book (*c.*1586–*c.*1605). It was, however, Byrd, whom he knew and whose keyboard music he copied into My Ladye Nevells Booke in 1591 (apparently under the composer's supervision), who was praised at length. In about 1593, Tallis and Byrd were the first to come to Thomas Whythorne's mind when he was listing the most famous English musicians of recent times who were 'uncommenced' (not masters or doctors of music). Afterwards he added Sheppard's name.[2] In another list, published in 1598, Francis Meres named Tallis as one of 16 'excellent' English musicians.[3] Thomas Morley mentioned Tallis in *A plaine and easie introduction to practicall musicke* (1597), but either as one of the composers of the *Cantiones* or as someone whose works exemplified points Morley wished to make. It was for similar reasons that, in the next century, Charles Butler mentioned Tallis's *Miserere nostri*, *Absterge Domine* and *Dum transisset sabbatum*.[4]

The portrait we can paint of Tallis is therefore sketchier than that of Byrd, his pupil and friend, whose life is recorded in considerable detail in genealogies,

[1] David Mateer, 'Oxford, Christ Church MSS 984–8: an index and commentary', [*Royal Musical Association*] *Research Chronicle*, vol. 20 (1986–87), pp. 1–18, at 4.

[2] Thomas Whythorne, *The autobiography of Thomas Whythorne*, ed. James M. Osborn (Oxford, 1961), p. 302.

[3] Francis Meres, *Palladis Tamia. Wits treasury being the second part of Wits commonwealth* (London, 1598), p. 288^{v}. Meres's full list, which includes some unexpected names, is '*Maister Cooper, Maister Fairfax, Maister Tallis, Maister Tauerner, Maister Blithman, Maister Bird, Doctor Tie, Doctor Dallis, Doctor Bull, M. Thomas Mud,* sometimes fellow of *Pembrook hal* in *Cambridge, M. Edward Iohnson, Maister Blankes, Maister Randall, Maister Philips, Maister Dowland, and M. Morley*'.

[4] Charls [*sic*] Butler, *The principles of musik, in singing and setting* (London, 1636), pp. 41, 85, 91; reprinted in facsimile New York,1970, with an introduction by Gilbert Reaney (New York, 1970).

church and legal records, official papers and private letters. Byrd's signature is appended to numerous documents, some of which he wrote himself. Byrd is also the first major English composer of whose work we have anything like a fairly complete picture – partly because he took care to ensure that much of it was preserved in copies of which he sought to ensure the accuracy. (The manuscript keyboard music in My Ladye Nevells Booke was corrected in his own hand.) Most of the printed books of Byrd's music contain prefaces expressing at least a few of his ideas about composition and performance.

By contrast with Byrd, we probably have a smaller proportion of Tallis's output, and we certainly know less about his life and thoughts. We cannot estimate how much of Tallis's music has been lost, but since several works exist as single copies it seems possible that others have perished completely. We assuredly have no more than a handful of his early works, and insufficient evidence about when he wrote them. We have only one signature presumed to be his. We have no writings which can be attributed to him with certainty. Who composed his will? Possibly an attorney. Who composed the dedication of the 1575 *Cantiones*, and the subsequent petition to the Queen? There is a strong probability that Byrd was chiefly responsible.

We may conjecture that, as a boy, Tallis was a chorister of Canterbury Cathedral, but the notion is not backed up by documentary evidence. Some of his early compositions show the influence of Fayrfax and Taverner, though there is no indication that he had any personal contact with either. We nevertheless know the names of musicians whom Tallis worked with at St Mary-at-Hill, and Canterbury Cathedral and the Chapel Royal; and we know of others such as Sebastian Westcote of St Paul's, who may have sent Byrd to him as a pupil, and John Heywood, whom he probably knew not only as a musician of St Paul's and the court, but as a prominent parishioner of St Mary-at-Hill. We know too that Tallis's music contains borrowings from other composers, especially in the Mass for four voices, and references to their works, although it is not always easy to know what to make of these. The insertion of a phrase of Taverner's into the final revision of *Dum transisset sabbatum* could hardly be anything but a tribute, and other references to pieces by Taverner – in the Benedictus of the 'Salve intemerata' Mass for instance – may fall into the same category. Quotations from others may sometimes have been intended as friendly acknowledgements, to be recognized by the original composer or those in the know. If so, they suggest that music was circulating freely enough and was sufficiently well known for quotations to be worth including, or that Tallis's musical memory was so full of quotable phrases that they occasionally slipped out by accident. Perhaps all these things were true. It would be interesting to know whether quotations from Continental composers occur in Tallis's music, but so far none seems unequivocally to have been identified.[5]

---

[5] See, however, John Milsom: 'Crecquillon, Clemens, and four-voice fuga', in Eric Jas, ed., *Beyond contemporary fame: reassessing the art of Clemens non Papa and Thomas Crecquillon. Colloquium Proceedings, Utrecht, April 24–26, 2003* (Turnhout, 2005),

Other names occurring in connection with Tallis's musical activities, like those of Henry Fitzalan and Thomas Howard, suggest that associations formed at court led him into circles beyond it, but nothing indicates whether he mixed socially with the nobility or received their friendship and patronage to the extent that Byrd did. This could be due simply to the absence of records, or it could reflect a temperament less thrusting and less socially ambitious than Byrd's. Tallis may have been satisfied with professional success.

It may easily be correct to suppose that the relationship between Tallis and Byrd cannot have been that of chalk and cheese, but we should remember the errors made by others who have tried to portray aspects of Tallis's inner life.[6] We have no information about Tallis's interests beyond music. Unlike Byrd, he has left no records relating to legal disputes or religious dissent. Byrd's active involvement in both is attested by his repeated appearances in courts of law, and his friendship with the Catholic Earl of Worcester and members of the Paget and Petre families. And his interest in both law and religion is evident from books surviving from his personal library. Tallis's concern with the law, on the other hand, is not known to have gone beyond the signing of wills and documents relating to property. He and William Roper, a leading lawyer and prominent Catholic, were jointly overseers of Richard Bower's will, but neither that nor Joan Tallis's bequest to Roper's son Anthony is compelling evidence of Thomas Tallis's religious inclinations. Nor is his probable association with Catholics such as Fitzalan and Howard. The way in which Tallis set religious texts offers some reason for supposing that he adhered sincerely and strongly to the commonly held beliefs of his time, but it provides no clue to his views on matters which were in dispute.

There is no reason to doubt that Tallis lived 'In myld and quyet Sort', though the main evidence is provided by the words of his epitaph. Besides that, his name heads those of the men to whom, in a letter to Byrd, 'Richard Sugeham' asked to be remembered. And there is some indication that he was a man with whom his colleagues could engage comfortably on a personal level. It may not be too much to read into his marriage to Thomas Bury's widow, Joan, the existence of a particular friendship with one colleague and his family. Certainly, after their marriage, Thomas and Joan Tallis both enjoyed a close friendship with Byrd, to whose younger son Tallis was godfather and, in the event of Joan's death, left his share of any profits from the music printing monopoly granted by Queen Elizabeth.

All the same, however mild Tallis's disposition and behaviour may have been, his make-up must have included a streak of determination. In the absence of any reference to pushiness or patronage, we must assume that he rose to the top of his profession through application, skill and experience. And, when he was considered for a senior position in the Chapel Royal, an air of authority and a reputation for diligence and reliability must have been as important as his musical capacity.

---

pp. 293–345; and Thomas Tallis and William Byrd, *Cantiones sacrae 1575*, ed. John Milsom (Early English Church Music, 56: London, 2014), p. 1.

6 Surveyed in Suzanne Cole, *Thomas Tallis and his music in Victorian England* (Woodbridge, 2008), pp. 87–96.

Tallis was active continuously as a composer from the 1520s, if not before, until the 1570s: that is, from the time of Fayrfax to the time of Byrd. The difficulty of attaching accurate dates to Tallis's works has often been mentioned in previous chapters, but Table 12.1 is an attempt to list the bulk of his surviving music in a very broad chronological order. References are given to pages where the dates of pieces are discussed.

Table 12.1 Hypothetical chronology of selected works by Tallis

Works	Events
	***c.*1505 Tallis born**
Magnificat for four voices (pp. 22ff.)	
Ave Dei patris filia (pp. 25ff.)	
Ave rosa sine spinis (pp. 27ff.)	
Salve intemerata Before 1530 (p. 30)	
	1530–31 Accounts of Dover Priory list Tallis as organist
	1535 Surrender of Dover Priory
	1537–38 Tallis a conduct at St Mary-at-Hill
	1538?–40 Tallis employed at Waltham Abbey
	1540 (March) Surrender of Waltham Abbey
Mass *Salve intemerata* By *c.*1540 (p. 39)	
	1541 (April) Canterbury Cathedral refounded
	1541–42 Tallis a vicar choral at Canterbury Cathedral
	1543/4 First evidence of Tallis at of the Chapel Royal
Sancte Deus, sancte fortis 1543–47? (p. 38)	
Solo responds 1543–47? (p. 53)	
Audivi vocem	
Hodie nobis caelorum Rex	
In pace in idipsum	
Mass for four voices 1545–46 (p. 48)	
When shall my sorrowful sighing slack Before 1547? (p. 86)	
	1546/7 (January) Death of Henry VIII, accession of Edward VI
Hear the voice and prayer Before 1550 (p. 69)	
Remember not (first version) Before 1550 (p. 63)	
If ye love me Before 1550 (pp. 63–4)	
*Blessed are those c.*1547–1552 (p. 73)	
*Benedictus c.*1547–52 (p. 77)	
*Te Deum 'for means' c.*1549–52 (pp. 79–80)	
*Short Service c.*1552 (p. 82)	
*Service 'Five Parts Two in One' c.*1552 (p. 85)	
	1553 (July) Death of Edward VI, accession of Mary I
Gaude gloriosa Dei mater 1553? (p. 121)	
Mass *Puer natus est* 1554? (p. 127)	
Like as the doleful dove Mid–1550s? (p. 88)	

Choral responds Mid–1550s? (p. 98)

Dum transisset sabbatum

Candidi facti sunt

Honor virtus et potestas

Homo quidam fecit cenam

Videte miraculum

Loquebantur variis linguis

Hymns Mid-1550s? (p. 112)

Quod chorus vatum–Haec Deum caeli

Salvator mundi Domine–Adesto nunc propitious

Iam Christus astra ascenderat–Solemnis urgebat dies

Sermone blando angelus–Illae dum pergunt

Jesu salvator saeculi verbum–Tu fabricator omnium

1558 (November) Death of Mary I, accession of Elizabeth I

Litany, Preces and responses 1558–62? (p. 156)

Remember not (expanded version) By 1560 (p. 68)

Verily, verily I say unto you 1560s? (p. 161)

Salvator mundi I 1560s? (p. 190)

Psalm 119, verses 9–16 Early 1560s? (pp. 159–60)

Psalm 119, verses 17–24 Early 1560s? (pp. 159–60)

Absterge Domine Early 1560s (p. 191)

Domine quis habitat Early 1560s (p. 172)

Laudate Dominum Early 1560s (p. 172)

Mihi autem nimis Early 1560s (p. 192)

O sacrum convivium Early 1560s (p. 196)

O salutaris hostia Early 1560s (p. 171)

Magnificat and Nunc dimittis After 1560 (p. 174)

Salvator mundi II 1560s? (p. 198)

*De lamentatione c.*1562 (pp. 178–9)

Felix namque I 1562 (p. 206)

Fellix namque II 1564 (p. 206)

*Suscipe quaeso c.*1565? (p. 201)

Derelinquit impius Mid 1560s (p. 197)

Tunes for Parker's Psalter Mid 1560s? (p. 163)

*Incipit lamentatione c.*1565–66? (pp. 178–80)

O lord, give thy holy spirit 1566–70 (pp. 161–3)

Spem in alium 1567–69 (pp. 149–51)

Psalm 119, verses 25–32 1570–75? (p. 160)

In manus tuas After 1570 (p. 192)

O nata lux After 1570 (pp. 193–5)

In ieiunio et fletu After 1570 (pp. 199–200)

Miserere nostri 1574–75 (p. 203)

1575 (November?) Publication of *Cantiones sacrae*

1585 (November) Death of Tallis

Table 12.1 omits most of Tallis's keyboard music, his works for viols, several of his lesser vocal pieces, and another dozen or more pieces which are known only from single parts. But in spite of these omissions, and the faults it must undoubtedly have, the table serves some useful purposes. It makes clear that most of the works by which we judge Tallis's achievement were written during a period of some 30 years, from about 1545 to 1575. Unless the table is seriously wrong about the 1530s and early 1540s, that period was either one which was not conducive to composition, or almost everything Tallis wrote has been lost. Even if, say, it were to be supposed that his solo responds were not written for the Chapel Royal but for singers at St Mary-at-Hill or Waltham Abbey, there would still be a good many years to which no music can be attributed. Some music may – and, indeed, must – have perished after the surrender of Waltham Abbey, but we know neither the amount nor its nature. The *Salve intemerata* Mass stands out among his earlier compositions, but it survives in only one source, and nothing tells us if it was written for a particular institution. The idea that it may have been prepared for the prospective refounding of Canterbury Cathedral is attractive, but is not backed by evidence. It is clear, nevertheless, that Tallis's extant music includes little which was certainly written, and not much which was possibly written, in a large part of Henry VIII's reign. This does not diminish the importance of works such as *Salve intemerata* and the Mass derived from it, but almost all the pieces we possess were composed when Tallis was more than 40 years old.

A respect in which the table may be misleading is the emphasis it places on Elizabethan works with Latin texts compared with works of the same period with English texts. This could result both from losses and from a limited demand for new music for the Chapel Royal. It may also be due to the unsuitability of some English-texted music for domestic singing and its consequent absence from the manuscripts of private collectors. It is more obviously due to the preservation of over a dozen Latin pieces in copies of the *Cantiones*.

Tallis appears to have stopped writing only at the beginning of his last decade. If he wrote anything after the publication of the *Cantiones* it seems not to have been preserved. Perhaps his health failed, even though in his will he claimed to be both 'whole in bodye' and 'of good and perfect memorye'.

His music is without doubt the work of a man who was both thoughtful and inventive. His ownership of a book containing musical treatises, which he took with him from Waltham Abbey (see p. 28), suggests a curiosity about the history and theory of his craft which went beyond daily needs. He was a master, whose skill in manipulating musical materials was barely approached in England during the middle years of the sixteenth century. Between the late works of Taverner, written before 1540,[7] and Byrd's first mature works, the quality of his Latin-texted compositions was rivalled only by those of Nicholas Ludford (*d.*1557) and John

[7] Taverner appears to have withdrawn from musical activities in the late thirties (Hugh Benham, *John Taverner: his life and music* (Aldershot, 2003), pp. 12–13).

Sheppard (*d.*1558). Before the advent of Byrd his works for the Anglican church were not rivalled at all. What he wrote is notable for its variety, ranging from the simple to the complex and the modest to the majestic. It is often deeply affecting.

Yet there were some kinds of music which Tallis never or rarely essayed, or of which examples are now entirely or almost entirely lost. If he shared Byrd's interest in popular tunes and dance music, there is no sign of it. Nor is there any sign that he ever wrote more than a few pieces of music with secular English words, although our view may be distorted by the survival of his religious works while secular pieces have largely vanished.

While we have some of Tallis's instrumental music, there is not enough to indicate that he wrote a great deal. Almost always, in his surviving works, Tallis was concerned with setting words to music. He read his texts carefully, and reflected on them. His attention to their pattern, argument and meaning is plain, not simply in word-painting but in the sensitive treatment of single words, emphasizing their implications. For four or five decades of his long working life Tallis fashioned music to suit whatever officially authorized vision of the church prevailed at any time, but nothing he wrote is entirely routine or perfunctory. Although the changing demands of his employers led him to write in what seems superficially to have been a variety of styles, there is a continuity in his work. Throughout his career he was engaged with recurring problems of musical construction and expression, and his music therefore exhibits recurrent and recognizable features, gestures and behaviour.[8] Towards the end of his career, in semi-retirement, he apparently wrote mainly for private performance, thus enjoying greater freedom to explore. As has happened with other composers, advancing years led him into a new world of sound.

The days are happily past when a severely limited knowledge of Tallis's music caused him to be thought of primarily as 'The Father of English cathedral music' or the 'Father of English church music',[9] and when, if his originally Latin-texted pieces were remembered at all, it was as contrafacta. The enthusiasm of Protestants, who found their ideal in his English-texted church music, and the later enthusiasm of Catholics who tended to champion his Latin-texted music at the expense of his Anglican music, made it difficult for his works to be assessed and appreciated as a whole. It was not until 1928 that most of his music with Latin words became

[8] A similar appreciation is to be found in Peter Phillips, 'Sign of contradiction: Tallis at 500', *The Musical Times*, vol. 146 (Summer 2005), pp. 7–15.

[9] Suzanne Cole, *Thomas Tallis and his music in Victorian England*, pp. 56, 86, etc. See also Suzanne Cole's articles 'Who is the father? Changing perceptions of Tallis and Byrd in late nineteenth-centuury England', *Music & Letters*, vol. 89 (2008), pp. 212–26; and 'Father of English church music 1505–2005', *Choral Journal*, vol. 47 (2006), pp. 8–17.

available in a single edition.[10] His keyboard works were collected in 1953,[11] an edition of his English-texted music followed in 1971,[12] and his three pieces for viols were included in a collection of consort music in 1979.[13] Only at the end of 2014 did an exemplary edition of *Cantiones, quae ab argumento sacrae vocantur* allow the modifications Tallis made in some of his works to be seen clearly.[14]

More than four centuries after Tallis's death, it is still not easy to become thoroughly acquainted with all his surviving works. And we have the added difficulty of hearing them in conditions which Tallis could never have imagined. Few were created as entities having only a musical purpose and existence, and many were intended for church services in which they were combined with speech, drama and spectacle. Parted from their original circumstances, and the beliefs that went with them, they have had to assume a new identity.[15] Fortunately the musical construction and content of Tallis's pieces have given them the strength to withstand a frequent transformation into free-standing concert items. In recent years recordings have multiplied (though usually of the Latin-texted pieces), providing opportunities for unlimited private listening.[16] If for a full understanding they demand an imaginative effort, it is well worth making.

---

[10] Thomas Tallis, *Tudor church music ... Volume VI: Thomas Tallis c.1505–1585* (London, 1928): editorial committee: P.C. Buck, E.H. Fellowes, A. Ramsbotham, and S. Townsend Warner. Amendments to volume VI were published in *Tudor church music. Appendix with supplementary notes by Edmund H. Fellowes.* (London, 1948), pp. 22–7.

[11] Thomas Tallis, *Complete Keyboard Works*, ed. Denis Stevens (London, 1953). Much of Tallis's keyboard music is now available in later collections edited by John Caldwell: see p. 262.

[12] *Thomas Tallis, English sacred music I: Anthems*, ed. L. Ellinwood (Early English Church Music, 12: London, 1971; rev. Paul Doe, 1973); *English sacred music II: Service music*, ed. L. Ellinwood (Early English Church Music, 13: London, 1971; rev. Paul Doe, 1974).

[13] Doe, Paul, ed. *Elizabethan consort music: I* (*Musica Britannica*, 44: London, 1979), nos 23, 24 and 36, the last of which is *A solfinge songe*, 'for voyces or instrumentes'.

[14] Tallis and Byrd. *Cantiones sacrae 1575*, ed John Milsom (Early English Church Music, 56: London, 2014).

[15] Changing assessments of Tallis's works and views of his historical position are explored in Cole, *Thomas Tallis and his music in Victorian England.*

[16] The most comprehensive collection to date is 'Thomas Tallis: The complete works, performed by Alistair Dixon, Chapelle du Roi, and instrumentalists and soloists (Signum Records, 1997–2004: SIGCD001–003, SIGCD010, SIGCD016, SIGCD022, SIGCD029, SIGCD036, SIGCD042; reissued in 2011 as the boxed set Brilliant Classics 94268).

Appendix A
The Wills of Thomas and Joan Tallis

Thomas Tallis

[From a loose copy at TNA PROB 10, box 116.[1]]

In the name of god amen. I Thomas Tallis of Est Greenwich in the County of Kente. one of the gentlemen of her Maiesties Chappell beinge the xxth daye of August in the yeare of oure Lorde 1583 whole in bodye of good and perfect memorye doe make and ordeine This my last will and Testament in mann*er* and fourme followinge ffirst I bequeath my soule vnto Allmightie god ou^{r} lorde and saviou^{r} Jesus Christ the only Redeemer of the worlde, and my bodye to be buried in the Churche of Sayncte Alphe*ge* within the aforesaide Est Greenwich. and that there be giuen and distributed the day of my buriall to the poore people of the same p*ar*ishe xl^{s}. in mony or the value thereof in breade by the hand*es* of those whom Joane my wieffe shall thinke good. Also I will that the said Joan mye wieffe doe giue or cause to be giuen after my departure euery ffryday duringe her Naturall lieffe sixe pence in mony or as much bread as it cometh to to six poore people Besides that I geue vnto my cozen John Sayer dwelling in the Ile of Thanett within the aforesaid county of Kent xl^{s}. of good and lawfull mony of Englande. Lykewise I giue vnto Joane Peare[2] my wieffes sisters daughter xl^{s}. Moreouer I giue & bequeathe to my company the gentlemen of her Maties. chappell toward*es* their feaste iij^{li}. vj^{s}. viij^{d}. / ffurthermore I giue and bequeath to Joane my wieffe my moyety for the printinge of musicall book*es*, song*es*, and Ruled paper duringe the Terme of the yeares to come, the which the Queenes Matie. gave ioyntly betweene M^{r}. Will*ia*m Birde one of the gentlemen of her Maties. chappell & mee. And if it soe happen the saide Joane my wieffe to depart this worlde before the expirac*i*on of the yeares I will that the saide moyetye duringe the yeares yett to come doe remayne to the vse and proffitt of Thomas Bird my godson the sonne of the aforesaid Will*ia*m Birde / Yf it please god to take to his mercy the saide Thom*as* Birde my godsonne

1 It seems that Tallis's original will no longer exists. The copy in the probate register, TNA PROB 11/68/662, differs in spelling, etc., from the copy used here, and omits a word (see note 4 below). It is not always possible to tell whether the loose copy's scribe intended to begin a word with a capital letter. He made no distinction between capital and miinuscule 'c' at the beginnings of words. He always began 'william' with a letter like his lower case 'w', though other Christian names in the will begin with a capital. His random placing of full points after abbreviations is regularized here.

2 'Payre' or 'Payer' in Joan Tallis's will, which was proved by 'Joane Paire'.

before the yeares are fully ended I will that the saide moyety doe appertaigne wholye to the vse and disposic*i*on of the aforesaid Will*ia*m Bird whilest the yeares doe laste The Rest of all my good*es* my debt*es* being paid and funerall discharged I giue fully and wholye moveables and vnmoveables whatsoeu*er* vnto Joane my wieffe whom I ordeine and make my sole Executrix of this my laste will and Testament Also W*i*lliam Birde[3] and Richard Cranwall gentlemen of her Maties. chappell my ouerseers and for their paines taken herein, I giue to eyther of them xx^{s} apeece In wittnes whereof I haue to theis p*rese*nt*es* sett to my hand and seale the yeare and daye aboue written in the p*rese*nt*es* of theis parties whose names are heare subscribed

By me Thom*as* Tallis

Also wheras I haue giuen afore in my will to my cozen John Sayer xl^{s}. my will is that[4] the same be made iij^{li}. vj^{s}. viij^{d}. And I will also that Joane Peare shall haue the xl^{s}. which I gaue her in my will made also iij^{li}. vj^{s}.viij^{d} And also I will that my ouerseers shall haue xx^{s}. apeece more than is mentioned in my will / Sealed and deliu*er*ed as his last will in the pr*ese*nc*e* of vs vnderwritten

By me Thom*as* ffryar

By me Will*ia*m Birde

[Proved 29 November 1585 by Joan Tallis]

Joan Tallis

[From the probate register, TNA PROB 11/74/51.[5]]

In the name of god amen the tweluethe of June in the nine and twentithe yeare of the raigne of our soueraigne Ladye Elizabethe by the grace of god of England ffraunce and Ireland queene defendor of the faiethe &c And in the Yeare of our Lorde god one thousand five hundred eightie seaven I Joane Tallis of East Greenewiche in the Countie of Kent widowe late wife to Thomas Tallis somtimes one of the gent of her maiesties chappell now deceased beinge at this present in good helthe and perfecte memorie god be thanked for it and carryinge a mynde and purpose to dispose of theis small thing*es* whiche god hathe lent me in this worlde so that after my deathe no disquiet contention or dislyke may growe amongest my kinsfolk*es* and frendes in or aboute the same or any parte therof and that every one maye accordinge to my intent and meaninge quietly enioye suche

3 An 'i' is blotted in 'William'.

4 The probate register omits 'that'.

5 The original will is not known to have survived. The probate register is followed here.

portion therof as I shall limitt and appoynte to him or them doe make and ordeyne this my last will and testament in manner and forme followinge ffirst in the dutie and profession of a christian I humbly com*m*end my sowle into the handes of almightie god creator redeemer and comforter of the wholl worlde stedfastly hopinge throughe the meritt*es* passian and pretius bludsheddinge of our Lord and saviour Jhesus christ to be made partaker of eternall life and coheier withe him in his fathers kingedome. Item I will that my bodye shall be buried in the highe chauncell of the churche of East Greenewiche aforesaide by the bodye of my late husband Thomas Tallis deceased Item I giue and bequeathe to m[r] Anthony Roper esquier one guilte bowle with the cover thervnto belonginge in respect of his good favors shewed to my late husband and mee Item I giue and bequeathe to William Bird one of the gent of her maiesties chappell one greate guilte cuppe withe the cover for the same Item I giue and bequeathe to Thomas Birde sonne to William Birde aforesaide my husbandes godsonne thre siluer spoones Item as well for and in consideration of the greate goodwill and frendshipp whiche was betwene my late husband deceased and Richard Granwall an other of the gentlemen of her maiesties chappell as also for and in consideration of the continuall and tender care he hathe had of me ever synce my husbandes deathe I beinge then verye olde and unhable to take care for thing*es* my selfe whearin I haue founde him to deale rather as a naturall childe towardes me then otherwise I giue and bequeathe to him the saide Richard Granwall one cupp guilte withe the cover thevnto belonginge and one guilte bowle Item thre siluer spoones Item one Bedsted standinge in the parlour and five curteynes belonginge to the same, one featherbed one bowlster twoe pillowes fower pillowbeers twoe rugg*es* one coverlett of tapisterie of the storye of a shepheard twoe fustian blankett*es* thre payer of hollande sheet*es* and twoe payer of flaxen sheet*es* of myne owne spyninge Item a wool mattrice beinge in the same parlour Item twoe tableclothes of flaxen the one longe and the other shorter a longe flaxen towell and a shorter syx flaxen napkins the standinge cupborde by the chimnye withe twoe cupbord clothes belonginge to the same the one of Venice[6] and the other of flaxen one bason and ewer of pewter standinge uppon the same cupbord one courte table standinge behinde the parlor dore withe a cupborde cloth therto belonginge Item one chiste of firr standinge in the same parlor by the bedside Item the paynted clothes hanginge and beinge in the parlour Item one longe table withe the frame and twoe Venice carpett*es* belonginge to the same fower ioyned stooles six cushions [of greene clothe twoe velvet cushens][7] twoe wrought cushions of needle worke one windowe curteyne in the parlour and one scrine Item the settells and waynscott twoe landirons twoe creepers[8] one payer of tong*es* one fyre shovell fower flower pott*es* of pewter Item a barred chest withe twoe lock*es* standinge in the chamber wheare I nowe lye withe a square table withe a cupbord in the same standinge in the same chamber Item a close chayer

6 Lace.

7 The bracketed words are written in the margin.

8 Small iron 'dogs' placed on a hearth between the andirons.

of ioyned worke in the same chamber Item one brasse pott twoe spitt*es* Item the greatest kettell savinge one Item an other kettell somwhat lesser then that Item a cuple of bell candlestick*es* a cupple of plates a brode plate and a lesser Item a wine quarte and a wine pynte of the new fashion makinge Item one greate charger twoe platters five dishes twoe sowcers and twoe poringers Item I giue and bequeathe fortie shilling*es* to be bestowed in bread and[9] to be distributed amongest the pore vppon the daye of my buriall by the discretion of my executors and overseers Item I giue and bequeathe for dischardge of the churche duties twentie shilling*es* Item to be bestowed vppon a din*n*er for my neighbors and lovinge frendes vppon the daye of my buriall fortie shillinges Item I giue to m^r^ William Birde m^r^ Richard Granwall and m^r^ Justice Greames[10] my overseers xl^s^ a peece for their paines takinge Item I giue and bequeathe to the hospitall provided for the pore in Greenew*i*ch and the pore therin beinge x^s^ yearly for euer v^s^ therof to be paide out of the howse I now dwell in and v^s^ out of the howse whearin Thomas Palmer now dwellethe whiche Richard Granwall hathe of my gifte which howse also I giue and bequeathe to the saide Richarde his heiers and assignes for euer by this my Last will and testament[11] Item I giue and bequeathe the rest of all my goodes moveables and vnmoveables herein before not bequeathed to my coozen Joane Payre Item I give and bequeathe the howse whiche I now dwell in w*hi*ch I lately purchased of Mr Lambert[12] to the saide Joane Payer for and duringe her naturall life and after her decease to her son ffraunces and the heiers of his bodye Lawfully begotten and for default of suche issue the remainder to Elizabethe daughter of the saide Joane and the heiers of her bodye lawfully begotten and for default of suche issue to the residue of the children of the saide Joane successiuely accordinge to their age and prioritie and to the heiers of their bodyes Lawfully begotten and for default of suche issue the remainder to the saide William Birde one of the gentlemen of ber maiesties chappell and his heiers and assignes for euer Item of this my Last will and testament I doe ordeyne constitute and appoynte my sayde cosen Joane Paire my sole executrix And overseers therof they before named William Bird Richard Granwall and m^r^ Justice Greames Provided alwayes that if the saide Joane Payer my executrix of this my Last will and testament doe not within one monethe next after my deathe prove fulfill keepe and performe this my Last will[13] and testament in all poyntes accordinge to the tenor purport and trew meaninge hereof that then all the power libertie and authoritie vnto her giuen as executrix by this my last will and testament shall surcease and become vtterly voyde and of none effect to all

---

9 'to be bestowed in bread and' repeated.

10 See Henry H. Drake, ed. *Hasted's history of Kent: corrected, enlarged and continued ... The hundred of Blackheath* (London, 1886), entries indexed under 'Graeme'.

11 When Granwall made his own will in February 1606/7, he left all his houses and lands to his nephew 'Richard Clarke son of Wyllyam Clarrk late of London Taylor deceased' (TNA PROB 11/109/225).

12 William Lambarde: see p. 94.

13 'will' repeated.

intent*es* and purposes and that then and from thence forthe all and euery Legacie and Legacies bequest and bequest*es* to her or her children or any of them by this my Last will and testament giuen or bequeathed shall remaine and be utterly frustrate thenceforthe the saide howse whearein I now dwell shall remaine and be to the saide William Birde Richard Granwall and m[r] Justice Greames their heiers and assignes to sell and dispose of the same as they thinck good for the payment of my debts and Legacies accordinge to my appoyntment in this my Last will and testament whom also imediatly after suche defaulte made by my cosen Joane Paire as aforesaide I doe appoynt make and ordeyne my executors of this my Last will and testament to see the same performed in all poynt*es* accordinge to the purporte trew meaninge and intent hereof In witnes whearof I the saide Joane Tallis to theis present*es* have sett to my hand and seale the daye and yeare first above written This is m*ist*ris Tallis marke Sealed and deliuered as the last will and testament of the sayde m*ist*ris Tallis in presence of vs

Richard Granwall Thomas Palmer This is Richard Yeomans marke John Browne

[Proved 10 June 1589 by Joane Paire]

Appendix B
Adaptations and Pieces of Mistaken or Doubtful Authorship

During Tallis's lifetime a number of his works were subjected to partial or extensive revision or alteration, or to adaptation to meet new needs, either at his own hands or at the hands of others. Changes affected the music, or the words, or both. The expansion of *Remember not* has already been described (see p. 68). Mention has also been made (see p. 191) of the possibility that *Absterge Domine* and *O sacrum convivium* derive from a single earlier work, and that before Latin words were fitted to any of the music some of it may have accommodated the English words 'I call and cry'. Another version of *O sacrum convivium*, in partbooks compiled after 1624, has words beginning 'Deliver us O Lord our God';[1] and yet another begins 'Have mercy upon me, O God'.[2] There is not enough information to show exactly the original form and words of every piece which was revised or adapted, or how far Tallis was himself responsible, though there is a good deal of evidence to suggest that he often returned to works which he had already allowed to be copied.

Adaptation, as distinct from revision or alteration, has most frequently stemmed from the replacement of Latin words by English words. But not always. No textual change at all was needed when Thomas Causton transferred part of Tallis's English *Te Deum* 'for means' into his own four-voice Service 'for children' (see p. 80). In another case the language remained unchanged but the sentiments of the words were altered. 'Purge me O Lord' and 'Fond youth is a bubble' appear to have been sung to the same music, quite probably while Tallis was still alive (see p. 87).

Adaptations continued to be made after Tallis's death. A good many pieces which originally had Latin texts were adapted to meet the needs of the Anglican church. When, in 1641, John Barnard published *The first book of selected church musick*,[3] he included Tallis's Short Service, his preces, responses, litany and three psalm settings, together with five more pieces presumably sung as anthems. Among the last group was *O Lord give thy holy spirit*, Tallis's setting of words from Henry Bull's collection *Christian prayers* (1566), but the other four pieces had been published with Latin words in the *Cantiones* of 1575. They were *I call*

[1] BL Additional MSS 17792–6 (M.A.O. Ham, letter to *The Musical Times*, vol. 127 (1986), p. 74).

[2] Queens' College, Cambridge MS G.4.17.

[3] John Barnard, *The first book of selected church musick, consisting of services and anthems, such as are now used in the cathedrall, and collegiat churches of this kingdome* (London, 1641).

and cry (mentioned above), *Blessed be thy name* (*Mihi autem nimis*), *Wipe away my sins* (*Absterge domine*), and *With all our heart and mouth* (*Salvator mundi* [I]).[4] Since Barnard's collection was clearly intended for use in Anglican churches, he was offering its users English religious texts in complex settings which reformers of Tallis's own time might well have found objectionable. Three of the adaptations published by Barnard were included in a manuscript collection made by Thomas Tudway in the years 1714–20,[5] but the music of *Absterge Domine* was now equipped with English words beginning 'Discomfit them, O Lord'.

All the pieces adapted along these lines were Elizabethan, and most of them came from the 1575 *Cantiones*. A particular favourite for adaptation was *Absterge Domine*. Some adaptations (*With all our heart and mouth* is an example) found their way into an unusually large number of collections. Adaptations made from Tallis's Latin-texted works before 1800 are listed in Table B.1, with their earliest sources, and the English words provided for them. A more detailed account, covering a longer period, has been given by Suzanne Cole.[6] Many, but not all, adaptations of Tallis's works are listed, with the sources containing them, in the EECM Primary Source Database. (Dates in Table B.1 sometimes differ slightly from those in the database.)

Table B.1 does not include the adaptations and arrangements made by Henry Aldrich (1648–1710), Dean of Christ Church, Oxford. These are listed in Table B.2 on p. 238, which is based on information given more completely in the online music catalogue of Christ Church Library. Aldrich's adaptations are the subject of an article by Robert Shay.[7]

Pieces of Mistaken or Doubtful Authorship

Tallis's reputation is reflected in the numerous pieces which have been attributed to him erroneously or without sufficient evidence. The systematic study of manuscript sources which began in the nineteenth century led to a reduction in the number of misattributed pieces, and the Tudor Church Music edition of Tallis's Latin-texted works published in 1928, though not quite complete, contained only

---

4 'With all our heart and mouth' is evidently the original text of the contrafactum, drawn from Romans 10:9–10. The words appear thus in BL Additional MSS 30480–4; 'hearts and mouths' is a later amendment.

5 BL MSS Harley 7337–42.

6 Suzanne Cole, *Thomas Tallis and his music in Victorian England* (Woodbridge, 2008), pp.13–61. The scores of a number of adaptations are included in Thomas Tallis and William Byrd, *Cantiones sacrae 1575*, ed. John Milsom (Early English Church Music, 56: London, 2014).

7 Robert Shay, '"Naturalizing" Palestrina and Carissimi in late seventeenth-century Oxford: Henry Aldrich and his recompositions', *Music & Letters*, vol. 77 (1996), pp. 368–400.

Table B.1 Adaptations made before 1800 of Tallis's Latin-texted works, with early sources

Absterge Domine (*Cantiones* 1575)
Discomfit them, O Lord New York Public Library Mus. Res. *MNZ (*c*.1618–33)
Forgive me, Lord, my sin[a] Bodleian Library, Tenbury 1023 (late 17th century)
O God, be merciful[a] Cambridge University Library, Peterhouse 35–44 (*c*.1635)
Wipe away my sins[a] King's College, Cambridge, Rowe 316 (medius) (*c*.1560–90)

Mihi autem nimis (*Cantiones* 1575)
Blessed be thy name[a] Essex Record Office MS D/DP Z6/1 (*c*.1590)

O sacrum convivium (*Cantiones* 1575)
Deliver us O Lord our God[a] British Library Additional 17792–6 (after 1624)[b]
Have mercy upon me, O God[a] Queens' College, Cambridge, G.4.17 (after 1630)
I call and cry to thee[a] British Library Additional 22597 (after 1580)[c]
O sacred and holy banquet British Library Additional 29372–7 (1616)

O salutaris hostia
O praise the Lord, all ye heathen[a] Royal College of Music, Mus 1051 (1625)

***Salvator mundi* [I]** (*Cantiones* 1575)
Arise O Lord and hear Durham Cathedral Library A3 (*c*.1635–65)
With all our heart and mouth[a] British Library Additional 30480–4 (*c*.1565–1600)

***Salvator mundi* [II]** (*Cantiones* 1575)
When Jesus went into Simon the Pharisee's house British Library 30480–4 (*c*.1565–1600)

Spem in alium
Sing and glorify[d] (1610?)

[a] The English words are included in James Clifford's *The divine services and anthems* (1663, enlarged 1664). *Forgive me, Lord, my sin* is included only in the 1664 edition.
[b] See the letter from M. A. O. Ham in *The Musical Times*, vol. 127 (1986), p. 74.
[c] John Milsom, 'A Tallis fantasia', *The Musical Times*, vol. 126 (1985), pp. 658–62.
[d] See p. 183 above, and Bertram Schofield, 'The manuscripts of Tallis's forty-part motet', *The Musical Quarterly*, Vol. 37 (1951), pp. 176–83.

two pieces which are now accepted as the work of other composers: *Domine Deus* (by Tye) and *Hic nempe* (by Sheppard).

The reasons for misattributions are many. Some mistakes no doubt arose when a scribe was obliged to work from a copy without a composer's name and had to guess who he might have been. In some instances different early sources attribute a work to different composers. *O sing unto the Lord a new song* is thus attributed to Sheppard in one Bodlleian Library manuscript (Tenbury 791), but to Tallis in

Table B.2 Adaptations and arrangements by Henry Aldrich

From *Absterge Domine*

I look for the Lord Mus. 11, no 19; Mus. 16, no. 31; Mus. 510–14, nos. 1 and 2; Mus. 614, no. 22; Mus. 1220–4, nos. 212 and 263; Mus. 1230, no. 19.

I will magnify Thee Mus. 11, no 20; Mus 16, no. 32; Mus. 1220–4, nos. 204 and 262; Mus. 1230, no 20.

From *In manus tuas* and *O nata lux* (combined)

O pray for the peace of Jerusalem Mus. 510–14, no. 3.

Litany

Mus. 9, no. 4; Mus. 510–14, no. 4 (words omitted), and no. 5 ('O God the Father', words largely missing).

Arrangement for four voices Mus. 48, no. 30.

As *Pater de caelis Deus* Mus. 468–72, no. 102; Mus. 1205(C), no. 4.

Mus. 48, no. 29, is a 'Litany-service, For men', possibly an arrangement by Aldridge, spuriously attributed to Tallis.

another (Mus. Sch. e.423).[8] A piece attributed to both Tallis and Byrd is *As Caesar wept* (see p. 86). In neither case is Tallis thought likely to be the composer, but sometimes there is insufficient evidence to enable a guess to be made about the accuracy of an attribution. Only one part survives of *O Lord God of hosts*, with Tallis's name attached to it (in Additional MS 29289). It does not appear to belong to a contrafactum, but its words refer to 'Charles, our king', so it must have been copied at least 40 years after Tallis's death. All one can do is to treat it with caution. In the case of another piece, *The simple sheep that went astray*, there is even less to go on. The words alone survive, in Bodleian Library manuscript Rawl. Poet. 23, a book of *c.*1635 containing the texts of pieces sung in the Chapel Royal, and in a manuscript of the Restoration period derived from it, British Library Harley 6346.[9]

Sometimes confusion has arisen because two composers set the same words, or words that are similar. One example is *Christ rising again–Christ is risen again*, attributed to both Tallis and Byrd (see p. 75). Another example concerns Tallis's *A new commandment give I unto you* and Sheppard's *I give you a new commandment* (see p. 72). Such confusions can have a surprisingly long life. When Vaughan Williams was editing *The English hymnal* (1906) he printed, as no. 153, a version of 'Veni Creator' with the English words 'Come Holy Ghost' by John Cosin, and

8 Bray, *The sixteenth century*, p. 331, note 104.

9 [G.E.P. Arkwright], 'The Chapel Royal anthem book of 1635', *The Musical Antiquary*, II (1910–11), pp. 108–13; Wyn K. Ford, 'The Chapel Royal at the Restoration', *The Monthly Musical Record*, vol. 90 (1960), pp. 99–106.

a tune (in C minor) which he cautiously described as 'Attributed to T. Tallis'. The tune (in D minor) had been printed in 1803 by William Crotch, together with 'The Latin Litany by Tallis with additions by D^r^. Aldrich Adapted for the Organ'.[10] The beginning of the tune had appeared in 1633 in the tenor part of a setting of *Veni Creator* attributed to Thomas Ravenscroft.[11] Crotch probably attributed it to Tallis because he knew that Tallis had set Parker's words beginning 'Come Holy Ghost'. Crotch was not however party to another persistent misattribution to Tallis: that of *All people that on earth do dwell*. In his publication containing the Litany he said that the hymn was 'usually attributed to M: Luther, Germany'.[12]

Lists or discussions of wrongly attributed pieces (only a few of which are discussed or indexed in this book) can be found in a variety of sources. Among them are (a) Paul Doe, *Tallis*, 2nd edn (London, 1976), pp. 70–71;[13] (b) the list of Tallis's works in *Grove Music Online*; (c) Thomas Tallis, *English Sacred Music II: Service music*, ed. L. Ellinwood (Early English Church Music, 13: London, 1971; rev. Paul Doe, 1974), pp. xi–xii;[14] (d) Roger Bray, ed., *Music in Britain: the sixteenth century* (Blackwell history of music in Britain, 2: Oxford, 1995), pp. 107–11; and (e) Suzanne Cole, *Thomas Tallis and his music in Victorian England* (Woodbridge, 2008), indexed under 'Spurious compositions'.

A note here about *Out from the deep* may be helpful, since it is included in Ellinwood's collected edition of Tallis's English sacred music.[15] The anthem sets an anonymous metrical rendering of Psalm 130. Two manuscripts in the same hand, and probably completed *c.*1630–35, assign the piece to Tallis: they are the partbooks New York Public Library Mus. Res. *MNZ, whose attributions

10 William Crotch, ed., *Tallis's Litany, adapted to the Latin words by Dr Aldrich ... and Tallis's "Come Holy Ghost"* (London, 1803).

11 Thomas Ravenscroft, *The whole booke of psalmes ... Newly corrected and enlarged* (London, 1633).

12 Concerning *Come Holy Ghost*, and *All people that on earth do dwell* (sung to the tune known as the 'Old Hundredth') see Cole, *Thomas Tallis and his music in Victorian England*, pp. 44–55. The online *Oxford dictionary of music*, ed. Michael Kennedy (2006), says the history of the Old Hundredth 'goes back to Marot and Béza's Genevan Psalter of 1551, in which it is attached to the 134th psalm. An even earlier form of the tune appears in the Antwerp collection *Souter Liederkens* (1540).'

13 On p. 34 Doe notes additionally that *Deus tuorum militum* may be by Sheppard. The piece is unlike Tallis's hymn settings.

14 Ellinwood printed some pieces thought not to be by Tallis, but made clear their doubtful authorship in his notes: (1) *Out from the deep* (Tallis, *English sacred music: I. Anthems* (Early English Church Music, 12: London, 1971, rev. Paul Doe 1973), pp.35–39, 126; (2) *Christ rising again*, in Tallis, *English sacred music: II. Service music* (Early English Church Music, 13: London, 1971, rev. Paul Doe 1974), pp. viii, 63–77, 203–4; (3) *Offertory sentence*, in *English sacred music: II*, pp. 190–91, 209.

15 Tallis, *English sacred music: I*, pp.35–9.

are not always secure, and the organ book Christ Church, Oxford, Mus MS 6.[16] It is more convincingly attributed to William Parsons (*fl.* 1545–63) in partbooks from Gloucester Cathedral, compiled after 1641 (since they contain copies made from Barnard's *The first book of selected church musick*).[17] *Out from the deep* is a competent setting, and has the ABB form of Tallis's *If ye love me* and *Fond youth is a bubble*, but it lacks the quality of sound and the imaginative touches which might identify it readily as a work by Tallis.[18]

[16] See Peter le Huray, 'The Chirk Castle partbooks', *Early Music History*, vol. 2 (1982), pp. 17–42, at 21, 26, 31.

[17] See note 35 on p. 75 above concerning manuscripts at Gloucester Cathedral. Parsons was a vicar choral at Wells Cathedral in 1555, but payments made to him between 1552 and 1560 are noted in the Communar's Paper Book, and suggest that he was also employed by the cathedral as a composer and copyist. He appears to have been responsible for a large number of the settings in *The whole psalmes in foure partes*, published by John Day in 1563.

[18] David Evans suggested that it may have been subjected to some rearrangement in order to maintain four parts throughout, and his edition in *Three Chirk Castle miniatures* (Bangor, 2012) provides an ending in five parts.

Appendix C
The Modes

Matthew Parker's *The whole Psalter translated into English Metre, which contayneth an hundreth and fifty Psalmes*, for which Tallis provided some musical settings (see pp. 163–4) was registered with the Stationers' Company by John Day in 1567. Included in it, before the psalms, is a page (signature Ei[v]) occupied by a description and a table of the musical modes (or 'tunes' as they were known in England) making up the eight-mode system (Figure C.1, p. 242). The placing of the description in Parker's *Psalter* is hard to explain, since it is not closely connected with the subjects dealt with on adjacent pages, but with Tallis's psalm settings and related material at the end of the book.

There is no indication of the origin of the description. Nor is there anything to show whether Tallis subscribed to the characterization of the modes conveyed by the table, which reflects ideas of a sort that were current in the middle ages or even antiquity. Tallis was undoubtedly familiar with the notion that there were eight modes or tunes, but may have thought it somewhat out of date by the 1560s. After setting a psalm in each of them (headed 'The first Tune', 'The second Tune', etc.), he added a setting of Parker's 'Come Holy Ghost', possibly representing the Ionian mode, which Glarean claimed in his *Δωδεκαχορδον* (1547) to have restored to the modal system.

The description and table of the modes are as follows:

> Veteres quatuor ta*n*tum musicos modos (quos tropos sive tonos vocarunt) celebres habuerunt. Scilicet Prothum: Dentrum: Tritum & tetradum, quibus recentiores superinstruxeru*n*t alios quatuor quasi collaterales, & hos ex gentium peculiaribus affectibus sic vocabulis notarunt ut Dorium, Phrigium, Lydium &c. quibus modis maxime trahebantur. Nam morum similitudine molliores in molliore gaudent tono, & natura hilares, Iucundioribus, tristes gravioribus modis delectantur, iuxta innatam quandam proportionem affectuum animorum, cum diversitate consonantiarum quibus occulta familiaritate excitantur.

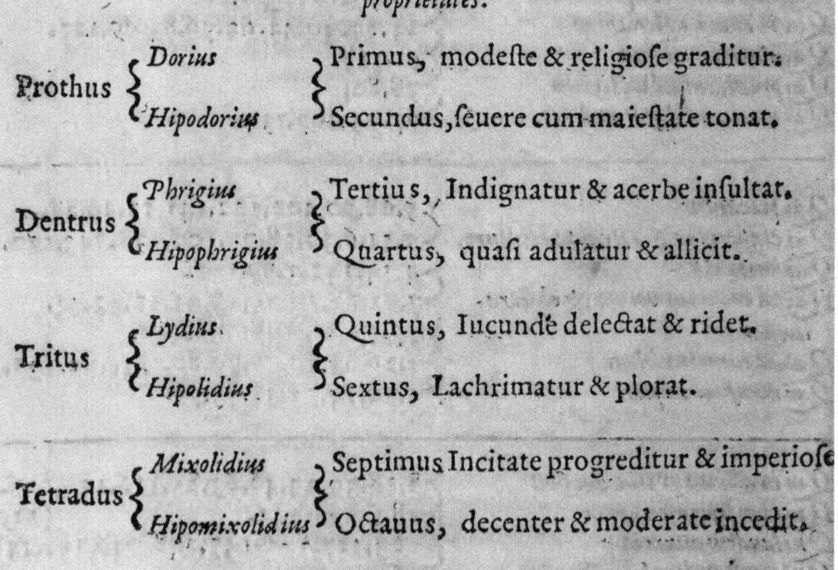

VEteres quatuor tãtum muſicos modos(quos tropos ſiue tonos vocarunt)celebres habuerunt. Scilicet Prothum: Dentrum : Tritum & tetradum,quibus recentiores ſuperinſtruxerũt alios quatuor quaſi collaterales,& hos ex gentium peculiaribus affectibus ſic vocabulis notarunt vt Dorium, Phrigium, Lydium &c. quibus modis maxime trahebantur. Nam morum ſimilitudine molliores in molliore gaudent tono,& natura hilares , Iucundioribus,triſtes grauioribus modis delectantur,iuxta innatam quandam proportionem affectuum animorum,cum diuerſitate conſonantiarum quibus occulta familiaritate excitantur.

¶ *Octo tonorum diſtinctiones & proprietates.*

Prothus	*Dorius*	Primus, modeſte & religioſe graditur.
	Hipodorius	Secundus,ſeuere cum maieſtate tonat.
Dentrus	*Phrigius*	Tertius, Indignatur & acerbe inſultat.
	Hipophrigius	Quartus, quaſi adulatur & allicit.
Tritus	*Lydius*	Quintus, Iucundè delectat & ridet.
	Hipolidius	Sextus, Lachrimatur & plorat.
Tetradus	*Mixolidius*	Septimus Incitate progreditur & imperioſe
	Hipomixolidius	Octauus, decenter & moderate incedit.

Figure C.1 A description of the eight modes, from Matthew Parker's *The whole Psalter translated into English Metre* (London, 1567?) (by permission of the Princeton Theological Seminary)

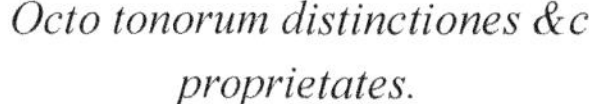
Octo tonorum distinctiones &c proprietates.

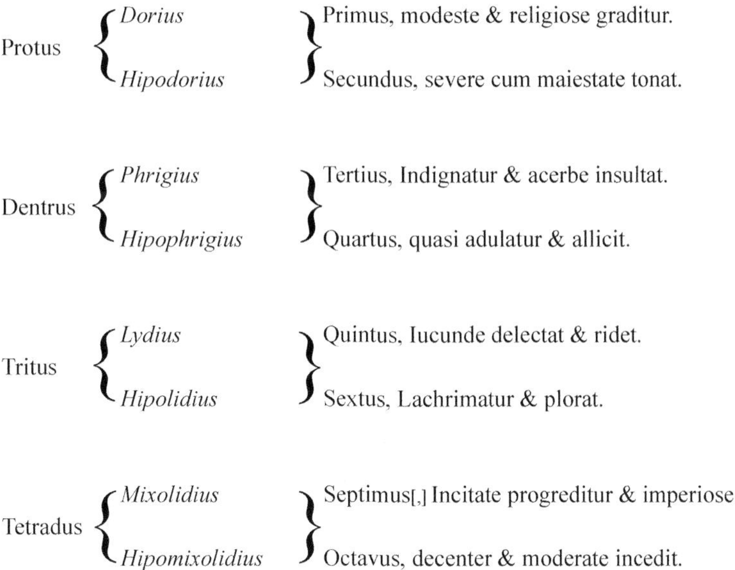

Protus	*Dorius*	Primus, modeste & religiose graditur.
	Hipodorius	Secundus, severe cum maiestate tonat.
Dentrus	*Phrigius*	Tertius, Indignatur & acerbe insultat.
	Hipophrigius	Quartus, quasi adulatur & allicit.
Tritus	*Lydius*	Quintus, Iucunde delectat & ridet.
	Hipolidius	Sextus, Lachrimatur & plorat.
Tetradus	*Mixolidius*	Septimus[,] Incitate progreditur & imperiose.
	Hipomixolidius	Octavus, decenter & moderate incedit.

The description may be translated as follows:

> The ancients distinguished only four modes (which they called tropes[1] or tones), namely protus, deuterus, tritus and tetrardus: to which more recent generations added four other auxiliary modes, and they named the modes according to the peculiar dispositions of the nations, with terms such as Dorian, Phrygian, Lydian, etc., from which modes of temperament the musical modes were chiefly derived. For softer men rejoice in a softer sound by the similarity of character, and those who are cheerful by nature delight in more pleasant tones, those who are sad in more serious tones, according to a certain innate proportion in the affection of souls, with the diversity of harmonies by which they are stirred up in hidden familiarity.

The characters of the modes given in the table are translated in verses which precede Tallis's pieces at the end of the Psalter. The translator could well have been Parker himself.

---

[1] 'Trope' was used much less than 'mode' or 'tone' during the Renaissance (Frans Wiering, *The language of the modes: studies in the history of polyphonic modality* (New York, 2001), p.74).

The first is méeke; devout to sée,
The second sad: in maiesty.
The third doth rage: and roughly brayth.
The fourth doth fawne: and flattry playth,
The fyfth deligth: and laugheth the more,
The sixt bewayleth: it wéepeth full sore,
The seventh tredeth stoute: in froward race,
The eyghte goeth milde: in modest pace.

Bibliography

This bibliography lists:

- books, articles, printed documents and theses
- printed editions and collections of music
- archival material.

Music manuscripts mentioned in the pages of this book are listed in the subject index.

Books, Articles, Printed Documents and Theses

If there is more than one place of publication, only the first is given.

Academy of Ancient Musick. *Letters from the Academy of Ancient Musick at London, to Sigr Antonio Lotti of Venice* (London, 1732).

An acte for the repeale of certayne actes made in the tyme of King Edwarde the sixte (London, 1553).

Acts of the Privy Council of England SEE Privy Council.

Allinson, David [*or* David John]. 'The rhetoric of devotion: some neglected elements in the context of the early Tudor votive antiphon' (Doctoral thesis, University of Exeter, 1998).

Antiphonale Sarisburiense SEE Frere, Walter Howard.

Apel, Willi. *The history of keyboard music to 1700*, rev. Hans Tischler (Bloomington, Ind., 1972).

Aplin, John. 'The survival of plainsong in Anglican music: some early English Te-Deum settings', *Journal of the American Musicological Society*, vol. 32 (1979), pp. 247–75.

——— '"The fourth kind of faburden": the identity of an English four-part style', *Music & Letters*, vol. 61 (1980), pp. 245–65.

——— 'The origins of John Day's "Certaine notes"', *Music & Letters*, vol. 62 (1981), pp. 295–9.

——— 'Cyclic techniques in the earliest Anglican services', *Journal of the American Musicological Society*, vol. 35 (1982), pp. 409–35.

Arber, Edward SEE Stationers' Company.

[Arkwright, G.E.P.] 'The Chapel Royal anthem book of 1635', *The Musical Antiquary*, II (1910–11), pp. 108–13.

Ashbee, Andrew. *Records of English court music* (Snodland, *later* Aldershot, 1986–96).

——— and John Harley. *The cheque books of the Chapel Royal* (Aldershot, 2000). For addenda and errata see the following article.

——— and John Harley. 'Records of the English Chapel Royal', *Fontes Artis Musicae*, vol. 54 (2007), pp. 481–521.

——— and David Lasocki. *A biographical dictionary of English court musicians* (Aldershot, 1998).

Aston, T.H. SEE Corpus Christi College, Oxford.

Banks, Chris, and others, eds. *Sundry sorts of music books: essays on the British Library collections, presented to O. W. Neighbour on his 70th birthday* (London, 1993).

Benham, Hugh. 'The formal design and construction of Taverner's works', *Musica Disciplina*, vol. 26 (1972), pp. 189–209.

——— *Latin church music in England* c.*1460–1575* (London, 1977).

——— *John Taverner: his life and music* (Aldershot, 2003).

Bennett, John. 'A Tallis patron?', [*Royal Musical Association*] *Research Chronicle*, 21 (1988), pp. 41–4.

Bettler, John. '*La compositione lacrimosa*: musical style and text selection in North-Italian Lamentations settings in the second half of the sixteenth century', *Journal of the Royal Musical Association*, vol. 118 (1993), pp. 167–202.

Bible, New Testament SEE *In Novum Testamentum*.

Blezzard, Judith. *Borrowings in English church music 1550–1950* (London, 1990).

Boemus, Johannes. *The fardle of facions*, trans. William Waterman (London, 1555).

Book of Common Prayer:

The Booke of the Common Praier and administracion of the sacramentes, and other rites and ceremonies of the Churche: after the use of the Churche of Englande (London, 1549). Variant title-pages.

The Boke of Common Praier, and administracion of the sacramentes, and other rites and ceremonies in the Churche of Englande (London, 1552). Variant title-pages.

The Boke of Common Praier, and administration of the sacramentes, and other rites and ceremonies in the Churche of Englande (London, 1559). Variant title-pages.

Liber Precum Publicarum, seu ministerii ecclesiasticae administrationis Sacramentorum, aliorumque rituum et caeremoniarum in Ecclesia Anglicana [London, 1560]. Revised by Walter Haddon from the translation of Alexander Alesius.

The first and second Prayer Books of Edward VI (Everyman's Library, 448: London, 1968).

The Book of Common Prayer 1559, ed. John E. Booty (Washington, DC, 1976).

Bowers, Roger. 'To chorus from quartet: the performing resource for English church polyphony, *c.*1390–1559', in John Morehen, ed., *English choral* *practice, 1400–1650* (1995), pp. 38–9. Reprinted in Roger Bowers, *English church polyphony* (1999).

——— 'The vocal scoring, choral balance and performing pitch of Latin church polyphony in England, c.1500–58', *Journal of the Royal Musical Association*, 112 (1987), pp. 38–76. Reprinted in Roger Bowers, *English church polyphony* (1999).

——— *English church polyphony: singers and sources from the 14th to the 17th century* (Variorum collected studies, 633: Aldershot, 1999).

——— 'The Chapel Royal, the first Edwardian Prayer Book, and Elizabeth's settlement of religion, 1559', *The Historical Journal*, 43 (2000), pp. 317–44.

——— 'Sounding pitch in Thomas Tallis, Mass "Puer natus est nobis"', *Early Music Review*, 197 (2014), pp. 11–14.

Boyd, Morrison Comegys. *Elizabethan music and musical criticism*, 2nd edn (Philadelphia, 1962).

Boynton, Susan, and Eric Rice, eds. *Young choristers 650–1700* (Woodbridge, 2008).

Bray, Roger. 'Editing and performing *musica speculativa*', in John Morehen, ed., *English choral practice, 1400–1650* (Cambridge, 1995), pp. 48–73.

——— 'Music and the quadrivium in early Tudor England', *Music & Letters*, vol. 76 (1995), pp. 1–18.

——— ed., *Music in Britain: the sixteenth century* (Blackwell history of music in Britain, 2: Oxford, 1995).

Brett, Philip. 'Homage to Taverner in Byrd's Masses', *Early Music*, vol. 9 (1981), pp. 169–76. Reprinted in Philip Brett, *William Byrd and his contemporaries* (2007), pp. 8–21.

——— *William Byrd and his contemporaries: essays and a monograph* (Berkeley, 2007).

Breviarium ad usum insignis Ecclesiae Sarum SEE Procter, Francis, and Christopher Wordsworth.

Brooks, Alan. *The stained glass of Francis Spear* (London, 2012).

Brown, Alan, and Richard Turbet, eds. *Byrd studies* (Cambridge, 1992).

Brown, Rawdon SEE *Calendar of state papers ... Venice.*

Buck, P.C. SEE (1) Taverner, John. *Tudor church music ... Volume I*, (2) Tallis, Thomas. *Tudor church music ... Volume VI.*

Bukofzer, Manfred F. *Studies in medieval and Renaissance music* (London, 1961).

Bull, Henry, ed. *Christian prayers and holy meditations* (London, 1566). Reprinted, Parker Society (Publications, 38: Cambridge, 1842), with 'the praiers commonly called Lidleys praiers'.

Bumpus, John Skelton. *The organists and composers of S. Paul's Cathedral* (London, 1891).

Burney, Charles. *A general history of music from the earliest ages to the present time* (London, 1776–89).

Butler, Charls [*sic*]. *The principles of musik, in singing and setting* (London, 1636). Reprinted in facsimile, with an introduction by Gilbert Reaney (New York, 1970).

Byrne, Muriel St. Clare, ed. *The Lisle letters* (Chicago, 1981).

Caldwell, John. 'Keyboard plainsong settings in England, 1500–1660', *Musica Disciplina*, vol. 19 (1965), pp. 129–53

——— *English keyboard music before the nineteenth century* (Oxford, 1973).

——— *The Oxford history of English music* (Oxford, 1991–98).

Calendar of state papers and manuscripts, relating to English affairs, existing in the archives and collections of Venice, and in other libraries of northern Italy, ed. Rawdon Brown (London, 1864–1947).

Calendar of state papers, domestic series ... Elizabeth, 1581–1590 (London, 1865).

Calendar of the manuscripts of ... the Marquis of Salisbury SEE Historical Manuscripts Commission.

Calendar of the patent rolls preserved in the Public Record Office ... Philip and Mary vol. I, A. D. 1553–1554 (London, 1937).

——— *Philip and Mary, vol. IV, A. D. 1557–1558* (London, 1939).

——— *Elizabeth I, volume IV, 1566–1569* (London, 1964).

——— *Elizabeth I, volume VI, 1572–1575* (London, 1973).

——— *Elizabeth I, volume VII, 1575–1578* (London, 1982).

Carley, James P. *The libraries of King Henry VIII* (Corpus of British medieval library catalogues, 7: London, 2000).

——— *The books of Henry VIII and his wives* (London, 2004).

Carlisle Cathedral. *The statutes of the cathedral church of Carlisle. Translated ... by J.E. Prescott* (London, 1903).

Charles, Sydney Robinson. 'The provenance and date of the Pepys MS 1236', *Musica Disciplina*, vol. 16 (1962), pp. 57–71.

Chronicle of the Grey Friars of London, ed. John Gough Nichols (Camden Society, 1st series, 53: London, 1852).

Church of England, General Synod. *Talent and Calling. A review of the law and practice regarding appointments to the offices of suffragan bishop, dean, archdeacon and residentiary canon* (GS 1650: London, 2007).

Clifford, James, ed. *The divine services and anthems usually sung in the cathedrals and collegiate choires in the Church of England* (London, 1663).

——— *The divine services and anthems usually sung in his Majesties Chappell, and in all cathedrals and collegiate choires in England and Ireland. The second edition, with additions* (London, 1664). Alternative title: ' ... with large additions'.

Cockeram, Henry. *The English dictionarie: or interpreter of hard English words* (London, 1623).

Cole, Suzanne. 'Father of English church music 1505–2005', *Choral Journal*, vol. 47 (2006), pp. 8–17.

——— *Thomas Tallis and his music in Victorian England* (Woodbridge, 2008).

——— 'Who is the father? Changing perceptions of Tallis and Byrd in late nineteenth-century England', *Music & Letters*, vol. 89 (2008), pp. 212–26.

Collins, H.B. 'Thomas Tallis', *Music & Letters*, 10 (1929), pp. 152–66.

Collinson, Patrick, and others, eds. *A history of Canterbury Cathedral, 598–1982* (Oxford, 1995).

Copernicus, Nicolaus. *De revolutionibus orbium coelestium* (Nuremberg, 1543).

Corpus Christi College, Oxford. *Annual report and The Pelican* (Oxford, 1978–79). A note by T.H. Aston on the discovery of the college's manuscript 566 is at pp. 10–11.

Coussemaker, Charles-Edmund-Henri, ed. *Scriptorum de musica medii aevi novam seriem a Gerbertina alteram collegit nuncque primum edidit E. de Coussemaker* (Paris, 1864–76).

Cranmer, Thomas. *A Letanie with suffrages to be sayd or songe in the tyme of ... processions* (London, 1544). Facsimile in Eric J. Hunt, ed., Cranmer's first Litany (1939).

——— *Miscellaneous writings and letters of Thomas Cranmer* (Parker Society publications, 24: Cambridge, 1846).

Crowley, Robert. *The Psalter of Dauid newely translated into Englysh metre* (London, 1549).

Daniel, Ralph T., and Peter le Huray, compilers. *The sources of English church music, 1549–1660* (Early English church music, supplementary volume 1, parts 1 and 2: London, 1972). Now embodied in the EECM Primary Source Database, hosted by Trinity College, Dublin.

Davey, Henry. *History of English music*, 2nd edn (London, 1921).

Davison, Nigel. 'Structure and unity in four free-composed Tudor Masses', *Music Review*, 34 (1973), pp. 328–38.

Dickinson, F.H., ed. *Missale ad usum insignis et praeclarae Ecclesiae Sarum* (Burntisland, 1861–83).

Dictionary of national biography, ed. Leslie Stephen and Sidney Lee (London, 1885–1900).

——— SEE ALSO *Oxford dictionary of national biography*.

Doe, Paul. 'Latin polyphony under Henry VIII', *Proceedings of the Royal Musical Association*, vol. 95 (1968/69), pp. 81–96.

——— 'Tallis's "Spem in alium" and the Elizabethan respond-motet', *Music & Letters*, vol. 51 (1970), pp. 1–14.

——— *Tallis* (London, 1968). 2nd edn (London, 1976).

Drake, Henry H., ed. *Hasted's history of Kent: corrected, enlarged and continued ... The hundred of Blackheath* (London, 1886).

Duffy, Eamon., *The stripping of the altars: traditional religion in England* c.*1400*-c.*1580* (New Haven, Ct, 1992).

Durham Cathedral. *The statutes of the cathedral church of Durham. With other documents relating to its foundation and endowment by King Henry the Eighth and Queen Mary* [ed. A. Hamilton Thompson from a text prepared by J. Meade Falkner] (Surtees Society: Durham and London, 1929).

Eccles, Mark. 'Bynneman's books', *The Library*, 5th series, vol. 12 (1957), pp. 81–92.

[Edwards, Richard]. *The paradise of dainty devices (1576–1606)*, ed. Hyder Edward Rollins (Cambridge, Mass., 1927).

Edwards, Warwick [*or* Warwick Anthony]. 'The sources of Elizabethan consort music' (Doctoral thesis, University of Cambridge, 1974).

Elder, John. *The copie of a letter sent in to Scotlande* (London, 1555).

Elders, William. *Symbolic scores: studies in the music of the Renaissance* (Leiden, 1994).

Ellinwood, Leonard. 'Tallis' tunes and Tudor psalmody', *Musica Disciplina*, vol. 2 (1948), pp. 189–203.

Erasmus, Desiderius SEE (1) *In Novum Testamentum*, (2) Froude, James Anthony.

Evenden, Elizabeth. *Patents, pictures and patronage: John Day and the Tudor book trade* (Aldershot, 2008).

Fallows, David. 'English song repertories of the mid-fifteenth century', *Proceedings of the Royal Musical Association*, vol. 103 (1976–77), pp. 61–79.

Faulkner, Ann E. 'The Parker–Tallis psalter collaboration: the untold story', in *Abstracts of papers read at the fifteenth annual meeting of the American Musicological Society meeting jointly with the with the Society for Music Theory, Philadelphia, Pennsylvania, October 25–28, 1984*, ed. Anne Dhu Shapiro and Peter Breslauer (Philadelphia: American Musicological Society, 1984), p. 68.

Fellowes, Edmund H., *Memoirs of an amateur musician* (London, 1946).

——— *William Byrd*, 2nd edn (London, 1948).

Fenlon, Iain, ed. *Cambridge music manuscripts, 900–1700* (Cambridge, 1982).

——— and John Milsom. '"Ruled paper imprinted": music paper and patents in sixteenth-century England', *Journal of the American Musicological Society*, vol. 37 (1984), pp. 139–63.

Feuillerat, Albert, ed. *Documents relating to the Office of the Revels in the time of Queen Elizabeth* (W. Bang, Materialien zur Kunde des älteren englischen Dramas, 21: Louvain, 1908).

——— ed. *Documents relating to the revels at court in the time of King Edward VI and Queen Mary (the Loseley manuscripts)* (W. Bang, Materialien zur Kunde des älteren englischen Dramas, 44: Louvain, 1914).

Flanagan, David Timothy. 'Polyphonic settings of the Lamentations of Jeremiah by English composers' (Doctoral thesis, Cornell University, 1990).

Flynn, Jane. 'The education of choristers in England during the sixteenth century', in John Morehen, ed., *English choral practice* (Cambridge, 1995), pp. 180–99.

——— 'Thomas Mulliner: an apprentice of John Heywood?', in Susan Boynton and Eric Rice, eds, *Young choristers 650–1700* (Woodbridge, 2008), pp. 173–94.

Ford, Wyn K. 'The Chapel Royal at the Restoration', *The Monthly Musical Record*, vol. 90 (1960), pp. 99–106.

Foster, Elizabeth Read, ed. *Proceedings in Parliament 1610* (Yale historical publications, Manuscripts and edited texts, 22–3: New Haven, 1966).

Frere, Walter Howard, ed. *The Use of Sarum* (Cambridge, 1898–1901): vol. 1, *The Sarum customs as set forth in the consuetudinary and customary*; vol. 2, *The ordinal and tonal.*

——— 'Edwardine vernacular services before the first Prayer Book', *The Journal of Theological Studies*, vol. 1 (1899–1900), pp. 229–46.

——— ed. *Antiphonale Sarisburiense. A reproduction in facsimile of a manuscript of the thirteenth century, with a dissertation and analytical index* (London, 1901–25).

——— and William Waugh McClure Kennedy, eds. *Visitation articles and injunctions of the period of the Reformation* (Alcuin Club Collections, 14–16: London, 1910).

Froude, James Anthony. *Life and letters of Erasmus*, new edn (London, 1894).

Glanville, Philippa. *Silver in England* (London, 1987).

Glarean, Heinrich. *Δωδεκαχορδον* (Basle, 1547).

Goldring, Elizabeth SEE Nichols, John.

Gough, Martin. 'Variations on a canonical theme – Elgar and the enigmatic tradition', *The Elgar Society Journal*, vol. 18 (2013), pp. 21–34.

Greenwich Parish Church SEE St Alfege Church, Greenwich.

Greenwood, M.A. *The ancient plate of the Drapers' Company* (London, 1930).

Greg, W.W. *Some aspects and problems of London publishing between 1550 and 1650* (Oxford, 1956).

Griffiths, David. *A catalogue of the music manuscripts in York Minster Library* ([York], 1981).

Grove, George, ed., *A dictionary of music and musicians ... with appendix*, ed. J.A. Fuller Maitland (London, 1879–90).

Grove's dictionary of music and musicians, 3rd edn, ed. H.C. Colles (London, 1927–40).

———, 5th edn, ed. Eric Blom (London, 1954).

Haines, Charles Reginald. 'The library of Dover priory', *The Library*, 4th series, vol. 10 (1927), pp. 73–118.

——— *Dover priory* (Cambridge, 1930).

Ham, M.A.O. 'Tallis fantasia', letter to *The Musical Times*, vol. 127 (1986), p. 74.

Harington, John. *Nugae antiquae* (London, 1769).

Harley, John. *British harpsichord music* (Aldershot, 1992–94).

——— 'New light on William Byrd', *Music & Letters*, vol. 79 (1998), pp. 475–88.

——— *William Byrd: Gentleman of the Chapel Royal* (Aldershot, 1997, rev. 1999).

——— *William Byrd's modal practice* (Aldershot, 2005).

——— *The world of William Byrd: musicians, merchants and magnates* (Farnham, 2010).

Harper, John. *The forms and orders of western liturgy from the tenth to the eighteenth century* (Oxford, 1991).

Harrison, Frank Ll. 'Faburden in pratice', *Musica Disciplina*, vol. 16 (1962), pp. 11–34.

——— *Music in medieval Britain*, 4th edn (Buren, 1980).

Harrison, William. *An historicall description of the Iland of Britaine*, [2nd edn], in Raphael Holinshed, *The first and second* [*and third*] *volumes of chronicles* (London, 1587).

——— *The description of England*, ed. Georges Edelen (New York, 1968).

Hasted, Edward SEE Drake, Henry H.

Hawkins, John. *A general history of the science and practice of music* (London, 1776).

Henry VIII, King of England SEE (1) *The inventory of King Henry VIII*, (2) *A necessary doctrine*, (3) *The primer*.

Hentzner, Paul. *Paul Hentzner's travels in England* (London, 1797).

Hilsey, John. *Manual of prayers, or the prymer in Englishe* (London, 1539).

Historical Manuscripts Commission. *Calendar of the manuscripts of ... the Marquis of Salisbury* (London, 1899–1970)

Hofman, May, and John Morehen, compilers. *Latin music in British sources,* c.*1485*–c.*1610* (Early English church music, supplementary volume 2: London, 1987). Now embodied in the EECM Primary Source Database, hosted by Trinity College, Dublin.

Holinshed, Raphael. *The first and second [and third] volumes of chronicles* (London, 1587).

Hoskins, Edgar. *Horæ Beatæ Mariæ Virginis: or Sarum and York Primers, with kindred books, and Primers of the Reformed Roman Use* (London, 1901).

Howard, Henry, Earl of Surrey. *Songes and sonettes, written by the ryght honorable Lorde Henry Haward late Earle of Surrey, and other* (London, 1557).

Hummerson, Michael J. 'Excavations on the site of Arundel House in the Strand, W.C.2, in 1972', *Transactions of the London & Middlesex Archaeological Society*, vol. 26 (1975), pp. 209–51.

Humphreys, David. [Letter concerning the *Puer natus est* Mass and *Suscipe quaeso*], *Early Music*, 28 (2000), pp. 508–9.

Hunt, Eric J., ed. *Cranmer's first Litany* (London, 1939).

In Novum Testamentum, primum ad Graecam veritatem ... adnotationes Erasmi Roterodami (Basel, 1516).

The institution of a Christen man (London, 1537).

An introduction of the eyght partes of speche, and the construction of the same, compiled and sett forthe by the commau[n]dement of our most gracious soverayne lorde the king (London, 1542).

The inventory of King Henry VIII: Society of Antiquaries MS 129 and British Library MS Harley 1419. The transcript, ed. David Starkey (London, 1998).

James, Montague Rhodes. *The ancient libraries of Canterbury and Dover* (Cambridge, 1903).

Jas, Eric, ed. *Beyond contemporary fame: reassessing the art of Clemens non Papa and Thomas Crecquillon. Colloquium Proceedings, Utrecht, April 24–26, 2003* (Turnhout, 2005).

Jayne, Sears, and Francis R. Johnson, eds. *The Lumley Library: the catalogue of 1609* (London, 1956).

Johnstone, Andrew. 'Tallis's service "of Five Parts Two in One" re-evaluated', in Katelijne Schiltz and Bonnie J. Blackburn, eds, *Canons and canonic techniques, 14th–16th centuries: theory, practice, and reception history. Proceedings of the International Conference, Leuven, 4–6 October 2005* (Analysis in Context, Leuven Studies in Musicology, 1: Leuven, 2007), pp. 381–405.

Kerman, Joseph. 'Byrd, Tallis, and the art of imitation', in *Aspects of medieval and Renaissance music: a birthday offering to Gustave Reese*, ed. Jan LaRue and others (New York, 1966), pp. 19–37; reprinted in Joseph Kerman, *Write all these down* (Berkeley, 1994), pp. 90–105.

——— *The masses and motets of William Byrd* (London, 1981).

——— 'The *Missa Puer natus est* by Thomas Tallis', in Chris Banks and others, eds, *Sundry sorts of music books* (1993), pp. 40–53; revised in Joseph Kerman, *Write all these down* (1994), pp. 125–38.

——— *Write all these down* (Berkeley, 1994).

John Kimbell. *An account of the legacies, gifts, rents, fees &c ... of the parish of St. Alphege Greenwich* (Greenwich, 1816).

Kingsford, Charles Lethbridge, ed. 'Two London chronicles from the collection of John Stow', in *Camden miscellany*, 12 (Camden, 3rd series, 18: London, 1910).

——— 'Bath Inn or Arundel House', *Archaeologia*, 2nd series, vol. 72 (1922), pp. 243–77.

Kisby, Fiona [*or* Fiona Louise]. 'The royal household chapel in early Tudor London, 1484–1547' (Doctoral thesis, University of London, 1996).

——— 'Officers and office-holding at the English court: a study of the Chapel Royal, 1485–1547', [*Royal Musical Association*] *Research Chronicle*, vol. 32 (1999), pp. 1–61.

——— ' "When the King goeth a procession": chapel ceremonies and services, the ritual year, and religious reforms at the early Tudor court, 1485–1547', *Journal of British Studies*, vol. 40 (2001), pp. 44–75.

——— 'Religious ceremonial at the Tudor court: extracts from the royal household regulations', in *Religion, politics and society in sixteenth-century England*, ed. Ian W. Archer and others (Camden, 5th series, 22: Cambridge, 2003), pp. 1–33.

Kitching, C.J., ed. *London and Middlesex chantry certificate, 1548* (London Record Society publications, 16: London, 1980).

Knowles, David and R. Neville Hadcock. *Medieval religious houses: England and Wales* (London, 1971).

LaRue, Jan, and others, eds. *Aspects of medieval and Renaissance music: a birthday offering to Gustave Reese* (New York, 1966).

Legg, J. Wickham, and W.H. St John Hope, eds. *Inventories of Christchurch Canterbury* (Westminster, 1902).

le Huray, Peter. *Music and the Reformation in England 1549–1660* (London, 1967; rev. Cambridge, 1978).

——— 'The Chirk Castle partbooks', *Early Music History*, vol. 2 (1982), pp. 17–42.

Leland, John. *De rebus Britannicis collectanea*, ed. T. Hearne (London, 1774).

A Letanie with suffrages to be sayd or songe in the tyme of ... processions (London, 1544).

Letters and papers, foreign and domestic of the reign of Henry VIII (London, 1864–1932).

Liber precum publicarum SEE *Book of Common Prayer*.

Littlehales, Henry, ed. *The medieval records of a London city church (St Mary at Hill) A.D. 1420–1559* (Early English Text Society, original series, 125, 128: London, 1904–05).

Loewenstein, David, and Janet Mueller, eds. *The Cambridge history of early modern English literature* (The new Cambridge history of English literature: Cambridge, 2002).

McCarthy, Kerry. 'Byrd, Augustine, and *Tribue, Domine*', *Early Music*, vol. 32 (2004), pp. 569–76.

——— 'William Mundy's "Vox patris caelestis" and the assumption of the Virgin Mary', *Music & Letters*, vol. 85 (2004), pp. 353–67.

——— 'Tallis, Isidore of Seville and *Suscipe quaeso*', *Early Music*, vol. 35 (2007), pp. 447–50.

MacCulloch, Diarmaid. *Thomas Cranmer: a life* (New Haven, Ct, 1996).

Machyn, Henry. *The diary*, ed. John Gough Nichols (Camden Society, old series, 42: London, 1848).

Macray, W.D., ed. *A register of the members of St Mary Magdalen College, Oxford, from the foundation of the College. New series* (London, 1894–1915).

Maskell, William, ed. *Monumenta ritualia ecclesiae Anglicanae* (London, 1846–7).

Mason, William. *Essays historical and critical, on English church music* (York, 1795). Reprinted from Mason's series of 'Essays on English church music' which appeared in *The Musical Standard*.

Mateer, David. 'John Sadler and Oxford, Bodleian MSS Mus. e.1–5', *Music & Letters*, vol. 60 (1979), pp. 281–95.

——— 'Oxford, Christ Church MSS 984–8: an index and commentary', [*Royal Musical Association*] *Research Chronicle*, vol. 20 (1986–87), pp. 1–18.

——— 'The compilation of the Gyffard partbooks', [*Royal Musical Association*] *Research Chronicle*, vol. 26 (1993), pp. 19–43.

——— 'The Gyffard partbooks: composers, owners, date and provenance', [*Royal Musical Association*] *Research Chronicle*, vol. 28 (1995), pp. 21–50.

Maxim, Christopher. 'A little-known keyboard plainsong setting in the Fitzwilliam Virginal Book: a key to Tallis's compositional process?', *Early Music*, vol. 29 (2001), pp. 275–82.

Meres, Francis. *Palladis Tamia. Wits treasury being the second part of Wits commonwealth* (London, 1598).

Miller, Walter H. [Letters concerning the Tallis memorial brass plate], *The Musical Times and Singing Class Circular*, vol. 16 (1 May 1874), pp. 491–2, and vol. 17 (1 June 1876), p. 504.

Milsom, John [*or* John Ross]. 'Songs, carols and *contrafacta* in the early history of the Tudor anthem', *Proceedings of the Royal Musical Association*, vol. 107 (1980–81), pp. 34–45.

——— 'A new Tallis contrafactum', *The Musical Times*, vol. 123 (1982), pp. 429–31.

——— 'English polyphonic style in transition: a study of the sacred music of Thomas Tallis' (Doctoral thesis, University of Oxford, 1983).

——— 'The masses and motets of William Byrd', [*Royal Musical Association*] *Research Chronicle*, no. 19 (1983–85), pp. 85–95. Review of Joseph Kerman's book.

——— 'A Tallis fantasia', *The Musical Times*, vol. 126 (1985), pp. 658–62.

——— 'Tallis's first and second thoughts', *Journal of the Royal Musical Association*, vol. 113 (1988), pp. 203–22.

——— 'The Nonsuch music library', in Chris Banks and others, eds, *Sundry sorts of music books* (1993), pp. 146–82.

——— 'Tallis, Byrd and the "incorrected copy": some cautionary notes for editors of early music printed from movable type', *Music & Letters*, vol. 77 (1996), pp. 348–67.

——— 'Crecquillon, Clemens, and four-voice fuga', in Eric Jas, ed., *Beyond contemporary fame* (2005), pp. 293–345.

——— 'Caustun's contrafacta', *Journal of the Royal Musical Association*, vol. 132 (2007), pp. 1–31.

——— 'William Mundy's "Vox patris caelestis" and the accession of Mary Tudor', *Music & Letters*, vol. 91 (2010), pp. 1–38.

Missale ad usum insignis et praeclare Ecclesiae Sarum SEE Dickinson, F.H.

Monson, Craig. 'The preces, psalms and litanies of Byrd and Tallis: another "virtuous contention in love"', *Music Review*, vol. 40 (1979), 257–71.

——— '"Throughout all generations": intimations of influence in the Short Service styles of Tallis, Byrd and Morley', in Alan Brown and Richard Turbet, eds, *Byrd studies* (1992), pp. 83–111.

Morehen, John, ed. 'The "Burden of proof": the editor as detective, in John Morehen, ed., *English choral practice, 1400–1650* (Cambridge, 1995), pp. 200–20.

——— *English choral practice, 1400–1650* (Cambridge, 1995).

——— 'English church music', in Roger Bray, ed., *Music in Britain: the sixteenth century* (Blackwell history of music in Britain, 2: Oxford, 1995), pp. 94–146.

Morgan, Nigel. 'The introduction of the Sarum calendar into the dioceses of England in the thirteenth century', in Michael Prestwich and others, eds, *Thirteenth century England VIII* (2001), pp. 179–206.

Morley, Thomas. *A plaine and easie introduction to practicall musicke* (London, 1597). Reprinted, ed. R. Alec Harman (London, 1952).

Moroney, Davitt [*or* Michael Davitt]. 'Under fower sovereigns: Thomas Tallis and the transformation of English polyphony' (Doctoral thesis, University of California, Berkeley, 1980).

——— 'Alessandro Striggio's Mass in forty and sixty parts', *Journal of the American Musicological Society*, vol. 60 (2007), pp. 1–69.

A necessary doctrine and erudition for any Christen man, sette furthe by the kynges maiestie of Englande (London, 1543).

Neighbour, Oliver [*or* Oliver Wray]. *The consort and keyboard music of William Byrd* (London, 1978).

Nichols, John. *The progresses, processions, and magnificent festivities, of King James the First, his Royal Consort, family, and court* (London, 1828).

——— *The progresses and public processions of Queen Elizabeth I : a new edition of the early modern sources*, ed. Elizabeth Goldring and others (Oxford, 2014).

Nichols, John Gough, ed. *Literary remains of King Edward the Sixth* (Roxburghe Club: London, 1857).

Nixon, Howard M. 'Day's *Service Book*, 1560–1565', *British Library Journal*, vol. 10 (1984), pp. 1–31.

North, John. *The ambassadors' secret*, revised edn (London, 2004).

O'Dette, Paul. 'Dowland's iPod: some possible models for John Dowland's lute fantasias', *Early Music*, vol. 41 (2013), pp. 306–16.

The order of the Communion, 1548. A facsimile of the British Museum copy C.25, f.15, ed. H.A. Wilson (Henry Bradshaw Society, 34: London, 1908).

Ordinatio ecclesiae seu, Ministerii ecclesiastici in florentissimo regno Angliae (Leipzig, 1551).

Orme, Nicholas. *Medieval schools from Roman Britain to Renaissance England* (New Haven, Ct, 2006).

Oxford dictionary of national biography, ed. H.C.G. Matthew and Brian Harrison (Oxford, 2004).

Page, Daniel Bennett. 'Uniform and Catholic: church music in the reign of Mary Tudor (1553–1558)' (Doctoral thesis, Brandeis University, 1996).

Parker, Matthew. *The whole Psalter translated into English Metre, which contayneth an hundreth and fifty Psalmes* (London, Day, 1567?). Includes Tallis's 'eyght tunes'.

——— *Correspondence of Matthew Parker ... from A.D. 1535 to his death A.D. 1575*, ed. John Bruce and Thomas Thomason Perowne (Parker Society: Cambridge, 1853).

Patent rolls SEE *Calendar of the patent rolls*.

Payne, Ian. 'A tale of two counties: the biography of Thomas Tallis (*c.*1505–85) revisited', *The Leicestershire Archaeological and Historical Society: Transactions*, vol. 88 (2014), pp. 85–100.

Pfaff, Richard W. *The liturgy in medieval England: a history* (Cambridge, 2009).

Phillips, Peter. *English sacred music 1549–1649* (Oxford, 1991).

——— 'Sign of contradiction: Tallis at 500', *The Musical Times*, vol. 146 (2005), pp. 7–15.

Prestwich, Michael, and others, eds. *Thirteenth century England VIII: proceedings of the Durham Conference 1999* (Woodbridge, 2001).

The primer, set foorth by the Kynges Maiestie and his clergie (London, 1545). Reprinted in *Three Primers put forth in the reign of Henry VIII,* [ed. Edward Burton] (Oxford, 1834).

Privy Council. *Acts of the Privy Council of England. New series, ed. John Roche Dasent* [and others] (London, 1890–1964).

Processionale ad vsus insignis eccl[es]ie Sar[um] (Antwerp, 1545).

Procter, Francis, and Christopher Wordsworth, eds. *Breviarium ad usum insignis Ecclesiae Sarum ... Juxta editionem maximam pro Claudio Chevallon et Francisco Regnault, A.D. MDXXXI, in alma Parisiorum academia impressam* (Cambridge, 1879–86).

Rankin, Susan, and David Hiley, eds. *Music in the medieval English liturgy* (Oxford, 1993).

Rapson, Penelope. *A technique for identifying textual errors and its application to the sources of music by Thomas Tallis* (Outstanding dissertations in music from British universities: New York, 1989).

Rees, Owen. 'The English background to Byrd's motets: textual and stylistic models for *Infelix ego*', in Alan Brown and Richard Turbet, eds, *Byrd studies* (1992), pp. 24–50.

Reese, Gustave, and Robert J. Snow, eds. *Essays in musicology in honor of Dragon Plamenac on his 70th birthday* (Pittsburgh, Pa, 1969).

Religion, politics and society in sixteenth-century England, ed. Ian W. Archer and others (Camden, 5th series, 22: Cambridge, 2003),

Renwick, William SEE *Sarum rite*.

Respublica. An interlude for Christmas 1553. Attributed to Nicholas Udall, ed. W.W. Greg (Early English Text Society, original series, 226: London, 1952).

Rice, Stephen. 'Reconstructing Tallis's Latin *Magnificat* and *Nunc dimittis*', *Early Music*, vol. 33 (2005), pp. 647–58.

Ringler, William A. *Bibliography and index of English verse in manuscript 1501–1550 ... prepared and completed by Michael Rudick and Susan J. Ringler* (New York, 1992).

Robinson, Hastings, ed. *Original letters relative to the English Reformation* (Parker Society, 37–38: Cambridge, 1846–47).

Roper, Amelie. 'Decoding Tallis's Lamentations: music for Protestant Queen or Catholic subjects?', *Brio*, vol. 47 (2010), pp. 5–20.

Rose, Malcolm. 'The history and significance of the Lodewijk Theewes claviorgan', *Early Music*, 32 (2004), pp. 577–93.

Royal Commission on the Livery Companies of the City of London. *Report and appendix* (London, 1884). 'Report on the Charities of the Drapers' Company: Part II', in vol. 4, pp. 146–60.

St Alfege Church, Greenwich. *Order of service: "Tallis" commemoration service ... November 23rd, 1885* (Greenwich, 1885).

——— *Gordon & Tallis memorial windows. November 21st, 1925* (Greenwich, 1925).

——— *Greenwich Parish Church. Order of service at the unveiling and dedication of two stained-glass windows at 3 p.m., Saturday, 21st November, 1925* ... (Greenwich, 1925).

——— *Greenwich parish church: St. Alfege. A short history of the church and its environs* (Greenwich, 1951).

St Laurence, Thanet. *The register book of St Laurence in Thanet, from 1560 to 1653. Transcribed by Kenyon Wood Wilkie ... completed and indexed by ... Christopher Hales Wilkie* (Canterbury, 1902);

St Mary-at-Hill SEE Littlehales, Henry.

Sandon, Nicholas [*or* Nick *or* Nicholas John]. 'The Henrician partbooks at Peterhouse, Cambridge', *Proceedings of the Royal Musical Association*, vol. 103 (1976–77), pp. 106–40.

——— 'The Henrician Partbooks belonging to Peterhouse, Cambridge (Cambridge, University Library, Peterhouse Manuscripts 471–474): a study, with restorations of the incomplete compositions contained in them' (Doctoral thesis, University of Exeter, 1983).

——— 'Paired and grouped works for the Latin rite by Tudor composers', *Music Review*, vol. 44 (1983), pp. 8–12.

——— 'The manuscript London, British Library Harley 1709', in Susan Rankin and David Hiley, eds, *Music in the medieval English liturgy* (Oxford, 1993), pp. 355–79.

The Sarum Missal, ed. J. Wickham Legg (Oxford, 1916).

The Sarum rite: breviarium Sarisburiense cum nota, ed. William Renwick (Hamilton, Ontario, 2010). Online at http://www.sarum-chant.ca.

Schiltz, Katelijne and Bonnie J. Blackburn, eds. *Canons and canonic techniques, 14th–16th centuries: theory, practice, and reception history. Proceedings of the International Conference, Leuven, 4–6 October 2005* (Analysis in Context, Leuven Studies in Musicology, 1: Leuven, 2007).

Schofield, Bertram. 'The manuscripts of Tallis's forty-part motet', *Musical Quarterly*, vol. 37 (1951), 176–83.

Scot, Stefan [*or* Stefan Anthony]. 'The Prayer Book in practice: textual anomalies and their implications in Tudor musical settings of the first Book of Common Prayer', *Brio*, vol. 34 (1997), pp. 81–9.

——— 'Text and context: the provision of music and ceremonial in the services of the first Book of Common Prayer (1549)' (Doctoral thesis, University of Surrey, 1999).

Shaw, Watkins. *The succession of organists of the Chapel Royal and the cathedrals of England and Wales* (Oxford, 1991).

Shay, Robert. '"Naturalizing" Palestrina and Carissimi in late seventeenth-century Oxford: Henry Aldrich and his recompositions', *Music & Letters*, vol. 77 (1996), pp. 368–400.

Sheppard, H. Fleetwood. 'Tallis and his song of forty parts', *The Musical Times and Singing Class Circular*, vol. 19 (1878), pp. 97–8.

Shirley, Timothy Francis. *Thomas Thirlby* (London, 1964).

Skelton, John. *The complete English poems...*, rev. edn, ed John Scattergood (Liverpool, 2015).

Skinner, David. 'The Marian anthem in late medieval England', in R.W. Swanson, ed., *The church and Mary* (2004), pp. 169–80.

Smith, Alan. 'Elizabethan church music at Ludlow', *Music & Letters*, vol. 49 (1968), pp. 108–21.

Smith, David J. 'A legend? Francis Tregian the younger as music copyist', *The Musical Times*, vol. 143 (2002), pp. 7–16.

Smith, Jeremy L. '"Unlawful song": Byrd, the Babington plot and the Paget choir', *Early Music*, vol. 38 (2010), pp. 497–508.

Society of Antiquaries. *A collection of ordinances and regulations for the government of the Royal Household, made in divers reigns, from King Edward III. to King William and Queen Mary* (London, 1790).

State papers SEE (1) *Calendar of state papers ... Venice*, (2) *Calendar of state papers, domestic series*.

Stationers' Company. *A transcript of the registers of the Company of Stationers*, ed. Edward Arber (London, 1875–94).

Statutes of the colleges of Oxford [ed. E.A. Bond] (London, 1853).

Statutes of the realm (London, 1810).

Stevens, Denis. 'A musical admonition for Tudor schoolboys', *Music & Letters*, vol. 39 (1957), pp. 49–52.

——— 'A songe of fortie partes, made by Mr. Tallys', *Early Music*, vol. 10 (1982), pp. 171–81.

Stoneman, William P., ed., *Dover priory* (Corpus of British medieval library catalogues, 5: London, 1999).

Stow, John. *A survey of the cities of London and Westminster ... brought down from the year 1633 ... by John Strype* (London, 1720).

Strunk, Oliver. *Source readings in music history from classical antiquity to the Romantic era* (London, 1952).

Strype, John. *Memorials of the most reverend father in God, Thomas Cranmer* (London, 1694).

——— *Historical memorials, chiefly ecclesiastical ... under King Henry VIII, King Edward VI and Queen Mary the First* (London, 1721).

——— SEE ALSO Stow, John.

Swanson, R.W., ed. *The church and Mary* (Studies in Church History, 39: London, 2004).

Sweertius, Franciscus. *Athenae belgicae, sive nomenclator Infer. Germaniæ scriptorum* (Antwerp, 1628).

'Tallis Commemoration Service', *The Musical Times and Singing Class Circular*, vol. 26 (1885), pp. 722–3.

Temperley, Nicolas. 'The adventures of a hymn tune—1', *The Musical Times*, vol. 112 (1971), pp. 375–6.

Thompson, Ruby Reid. 'Francis Tregian the younger as music copyist: a legend and an alternative view', *Music & Letters*, vol. 82 (2001), pp. 1–31.

Three Primers put forth in the reign of Henry VIII. viz. I. A Goodly Prymer, 1535. II. The Manual of Prayers or the Prymer in English, 1539. III. King Henry's Primer, 1545 [ed. Edward Burton] (Oxford, 1834).
Thurley, Simon. *The royal palaces of Tudor England: architecture and court life 1460–1547* (New Haven, Ct, 1993).
——— *Whitehall Palace: an architectural history of the royal apartments, 1240–1698* (New Haven, Ct, 1999).
——— *Hampton Court: a social and architectural history* (New Haven, Ct, 2003).
Tinctoris, Johannes. *Liber de natura et prorietate tonorum* [1476], in Charles-Edmund-Henri Coussemaker, ed., *Scriptorum de musica medii aevi* (1864–76), vol. 4, pp. 16b–41a.
Trowell, Brian. 'Faburden and fauxburden', *Musica Disciplina*, vol. 13 (1959), pp. 43–78.
Turbet, Richard. *William Byrd: a guide to research* (New York, 1987).
——— 'The consort music of William Byrd', *The Viol*, vol.1 (2005–6), pp. 18–19.
——— 'Three glimpses of Byrd's music during its nadir', *The Consort*, vol. 65 (2009), pp. 18–28
——— *William Byrd: a research and information guide. Third edition* (New York, 2012).
——— 'Music by Byrd and his British contemporaries in European libraries', *The Musical Times*, vol. 154 (2013), pp. 33–42.
Udall, Nicholas SEE *Respublica.*
Valor ecclesiasticus temp. Henr. VIII auctoritate regis institutus (London, 1810–34).
Vesalius, Andreas. *De humani corporis fabrica libri septem* (Basel, 1543).
The Victoria history of the county of Kent, ed. William Page (London, 1908–).
Walcott, Mackenzie E.C. 'Inventory of Waltham Holy Cross', *Transactions of the Essex Archaeological Society*, [original series] 5 (1873).
———, E.P. Coates and W.A. Scott Robertson. 'Inventories of parish church goods in Kent, A.D. 1552', *Archaeologia Cantiana*, vol. 8 (1872), pp. 74–163. Continued in vols. 9 (1874), 10 (1876), 11 (1877) and 14 (1882).
Ward, John M. 'Spanish musicians in sixteenth-century England', in Gustave Reese and Robert J. Snow, eds, *Essays in musicology in honor of Dragon Plamenac* (Pittsburgh, Pa, 1969), pp. 353–64.
Warren, Charles W. 'Music at Nonesuch', *Musical Quarterly*, vol. 54 (1968), pp. 47–57.
——— 'The music of Royal Appendix 12–16', *Music & Letters*, vol. 51 (1970), pp. 357–72.
Waterhouse, Ellis. *Painting in Britain 1530 to 1790*, [5th edn] (New Haven, Ct, 1994).
Wesley, Samuel Sebastian. *A few words on cathedral music and the musical system of the Church, with a plan of reform* (London, 1849). Facsimile edn, with introduction and notes by W. Francis Westbrook and Gerald W. Spink (London, 1961).

Whythorne, Thomas. *The autobiography of Thomas Whythorne*, ed. James M. Osborn (Oxford, 1961).
Wiering, Frans. *The language of the modes: studies in the history of polyphonic modality* (New York, 2001).
Willetts. Pamela, 'Musical Connections of Thomas Myriell', *Music & Letters*, vol. 49 (1968), pp. 39–40.
Williams, C.H. *English historical documents 1485–1558* (English historical documents, 5: London, 1967).
Williamson, Magnus. '*Pictura et scriptura*: the Eton Choirbook in its iconographical context', *Early Music*, vol. 28 (2000), pp. 359–80.
——— 'Affordable splendour: editing, printing and marketing the Sarum Antiphoner (1519–20)', *Renaissance Studies*, vol. 26 (2012), pp. 60–87.
Woodfield, Ian. '"Music of forty several parts": a song for the creation of princes', *Performance Practice Review*, vol. 7 (1994), pp. 54–64.
Wood-Legh, K.L., ed. *Kentish visitations of Archbishop Warham and his deputies, 1511–1512* (Maidstone, 1984).
Woodruff, C.E, 'Canterbury Cathedral: a contemporary list of the members of King Henry VIII's new foundation', *Canterbury Cathedral Chronicle*, no. 37 (1941), pp. 9–13.
Wrightson, James. *The 'Wanley' manuscripts: a critical commentary* (Outstanding Dissertations in Music from British Universities: New York, 1989).
Wriothesley, Charles. *A chronicle of England during the reigns of the Tudors, from A. D. 1485 to 1559* (Camden Society, new series, 11, 20: London, 1875–77).
Wulstan, David. *Tudor music* (London, 1985).
Zarlino, Gioseffo. *Le istitutioni harmoniche* (Venice, 1558).

Printed Editions and Collections of Music

If there is more than one place of publication, only the first is given.

Barnard, John, ed. *The first book of selected church musick, consisting of services and anthems, such as are now used in the cathedrall, and collegiat churches of this kingdome* (London, 1641).
Blezzard, Judith, ed. *The Tudor church music of the Lumley books* (Recent Researches in the Music of the Renaissance, 65: Madison, Wis., 1985).
Brown, Alan, ed., *Elizabethan keyboard music* (*Musica Britannica,* 55: London, 1989).
Bull, John, *Keyboard music: I*, ed. John Steele and Francis Cameron (*Musica Britannica* 14: London, 1960, rev. 2001).
Byrd, William. *Psalmes, sonets, & songs of sadness and pietie* (London, 1588).
——— *Liber primus sacrarum cantionum* (London, 1589).
——— *Songs of sundrie natures* (London, 1589).

——— *Consort songs for voice and viols*, ed. Philip Brett (The Byrd Edition, 15: London, 1970).

——— *Consort music*, ed. Kenneth Elliott (The Collected Works of William Byrd [later redesignated The Byrd Edition], 17: London, 1971).

——— *The English services*, ed. Craig Monson (The Byrd Edition, 10a: London, 1980).

——— *The English anthems*, ed. Craig Monson (The Byrd Edition, 11: London, 1983).

——— *Latin motets I (from manuscript sources)*, ed. Warwick Edwards (The Byrd Edition, 8: London, 1984).

——— SEE ALSO (1) Tallis, Thomas, and William Byrd. *Cantiones, quae ab argumento sacrae vocantur* (London, 1575); and (2) Tallis, Thomas, and William Byrd. *Cantiones sacrae 1575*, ed. John Milsom (Early English Church Music, 56: London, 2014).

Caldwell, John, ed. *Early Tudor organ music: I. Music for the Office* (Early English Church Music, 6: London, 1966).

——— *Tudor keyboard music* c.*1520–1580* (*Musica Britannica*, 66: London, 1995).

——— *The Mulliner book, newly transcribed and edited* (*Musica Britannica*, 1: London, 2011). SEE ALSO Stevens, Denis.

Charles, Sydney Robinson, ed. *The music of the Pepys MS 1236* (Corpus mensurabilis musicae, 40: Dallas, Tex.,1967).

Crotch, William, ed. *Tallis's Litany, adapted to the Latin words by Dr Aldrich ... and Tallis's 'Come Holy Ghost'* (London, 1803).

Day, John, printer. *Certaine notes set forth in foure and three parts* (London, 1560). Bassus book only; completed as *Mornyng and euenyng prayer* (1565).

——— *The whole booke of psalmes, collected into Englysh metre by T. Sternhold I. Hopkins & others ... with apt notes to synge the[m] withal* (London, 1562).

——— *The whole psalmes in foure partes, whiche may be song to al musicall instrumentes, set forth for the encrease of vertue: and abolishyng of other vayne and triflyng ballades* (London, 1563).

——— *Mornyng and euenyng prayer and communion* (London, 1565).

Doe, Paul, ed. *Elizabethan consort music: I* (*Musica Britannica*, 44: London, 1979).

The Dow partbooks: Oxford, Christ Church Mus. 984–988 (DIAMM facsimiles: Oxford, 2010). Introduction and indexes by John Milsom.

Evans, David, ed. *Three Chirk Castle miniatures* (Bangor, 2012).

Ferrabosco, Alfonso. *Opera omnia ... II. Motets, Lamentations, an anthem and incomplete motets*, ed. Richard Charteris (Corpus mensurabilis musicae, 96: Neuhausen-Stuttgart, 1984).

Gyffard SEE Mateer, David.

Hughes, Andrew, ed., *Fifteenth-century liturgical music* (Early English Church Music, 8: London, 1968).

Lumley SEE Blezzard, Judith.

Mateer, David, ed. *The Gyffard partbooks* (Early English Church Music, 48, 51: London, 2007–09).

McPeek, Gwynn S., ed. *The British Library manuscript Egerton 3307* (London, 1963).

Merbecke, John. *The Boke of Common Praier noted* (London,1550).

Mulliner SEE (1) Caldwell, John, (2) Stevens, Denis.

Parker, Matthew. *The whole Psalter translated into English Metre, which contayneth an hundreth and fifty Psalmes* (London, Day, 1567?). Includes Tallis's 'eyght tunes'.

Ravenscroft, Thomas. *The whole booke of psalmes ... Newly corrected and enlarged* (London, 1633).

Stevens, Denis, ed. *The Mulliner Book (Musica Britannica, 1* (1951, rev. 1954). SEE ALSO Caldwell, John.

——— *Early Tudor organ music II. Music for the Mass* (Early English Church Music: London, [1969]).

Tallis, Thomas. *Tudor church music ... Volume VI: Thomas Tallis c.1505–1585* (London, 1928). Editorial committee: P.C. Buck, E.H. Fellowes, A. Ramsbotham, and S. Townsend Warner.

——— *Tudor church music. Appendix with supplementary notes by Edmund H. Fellowes.* (London, 1948). Amendments to volume VI on pp. 22–7.

——— *Complete keyboard works*, ed. Denis Stevens (London, 1953).

——— *Spem in alium nunquam habui: motet in forty parts* (Oxford, 1966). Reissued from *Tudor church music*, vol.VI, and rev. Philip Brett.

——— *English sacred music I: Anthems*, ed. L. Ellinwood (Early English Church Music, 12: London, 1971; rev. Paul Doe, 1973).

——— *English sacred music II: Service music*, ed. L. Ellinwood (Early English Church Music, 13: London, 1971; rev. Paul Doe, 1974).

——— *Ave rosa sine spinis*, ed. Nicholas Sandon (Antico Edition RCM136: Moretonhampstead, 1995).

——— *Salve intemerata* [and] *Missa Salve intemerata*, ed. Nicholas Sandon (Antico Edition RCM134: Moretonhampstead, 1995).

——— *Ave Dei patris filia*, ed. David Allinson (Antico Edition RCM20: Moretonhampstead, 1996).

——— *Mass Puer natus est nobis*, ed. Sally Dunkley and David Wulstan (Oxford, 1977, rev. 1980, 2009).

——— and William Byrd. *Cantiones, quae ab argumento sacrae vocantur* (London, 1575).

——— and William Byrd. *Cantiones sacrae 1575*, ed. John Milsom (Early English Church Music, 56: London, 2014).

——— SEE ALSO Parker, Matthew.

Taverner, John. *The Mean Mass*, ed. Nicholas Sandon (Antico Edition RCM24: Moretonhampstead, 2001).

——— *Tudor church music ... Volume I: John Taverner c.1495–1545* (London, 1923). Editorial committee: P.C. Buck, E.H. Fellowes, A. Ramsbotham, and S. Townsend Warner.

Tomkins, Thomas. *Keyboard music*, ed. Stephen D. Tuttle: 3rd revised edn prepared by John Irving (*Musica Britannica*, 5: London, 1964).

Tudor church music SEE (1) Tallis, Thomas, (2) Taverner, John.

Wrightson, James, ed., *The Wanley manuscripts* (Recent researches in the music of the Renaissance, 99–101: Madison, Wisc., 1995).

Archival Material

Bodleian Library

Rawl. Poet. 23. A Chapel Royal word-book, *c.*1635. Related to BL Harley 6346.

British Library manuscripts

Additional 25107. Accounts of Dover priory, Michaelmas to Michaelmas 1530–31.

Additional 27404. A collection of miscellaneous accounts, etc., some relating to the household of Henry VIII.

Additional 46348, vols A and B. The first part of an inventory of the effects of Henry VIII, made by a commission appointed in September 1547. Another copy is Society of Antiquaries MS 129. The second part is Harley MS 1419 A and B.

Additional 59900. Chamber receipt and issue book of Henry VIII, Michaelmas to Michaelmas 1543–44.

Additional MS 71009. Descriptions of early Tudor court ceremonial, probably by John Norris, a Gentleman Usher.

Arundel 97. Payments by the Treasurer of the King's Household, 1537–42.

Cotton, Vitellius F.V. The chronicle of Henry Machyn, 1550–63.

Harley 239. An account of lands leased by Queen Mary during her reign.

Harley 610. Household regulations of Edward IV (*Liber Niger*) and Henry VIII (*Statuta Regis*).

Harley 1419, vols A and B. Part of the probate inventory of Henry VIII. See the entry above for Additional MS 46348.

Harley 5176. A composite volume of state tracts, papers and speeches.

Harley 6346. A Chapel Royal word-book of the Restoration period, largely derived from Bodleian Library Rawl. Poet. 23.

Lansdowne 763. A collection of writings about music, assembled by John Wylde of Waltham Abbey.

Stowe 571. Lists of royal servants, etc., from the reign of Edward VI to the reign of Elizabeth I.

Canterbury Cathedral Archives

CCA-DCc-DE/164. List of members of the foundation, 1541–42.

Kent History and Library Centre

DRb/Pwr 1. Wills, Consistory Court of Rochester; containing (f.254) the will of Thomas Bury.

Corpus Christi College, Cambridge

MS 106, p.493c–d. Edward Seymour, Duke of Somerset and Lord Protector, letter to Cambridge University, 4 September 1548. Online at http://parkerweb.stanford.edu.

Folger Shakespeare Library

V.a.277. Henry Hastings, Earl of Huntingdon, 'A book of those things that passeth or was done in this present session of Parliament in the higher house', 1609–10.

London Metropolitan Archives

DS/F/1925/033/1-10. Documents concerning the installation at St Alfege's Church in 1925 of windows commemorating General Gordon and Thomas Tallis, with photographs of the windows.

P69/MRY4/B/005/MS01239/001/003 (formerly Guildhall Library MS 1239/1, part 3). St Mary-at-Hill, churchwardens' accounts, 1527–1559.

The National Archives

C66/929. Patent roll, 1557–58.

C66/1037. Patent roll, 1566–67.

E25/42. Acknowledgement by the monks of Dover Priory of the King's supremacy in matters of religion, December 1534.

E101/427/6. Warrants etc. relating to the funeral of Edward VI.

E115/368/132. Certificate of residence, Thomas Tallis, 1563.

E115/369/133. Certificate of residence, Thomas Tallis, 1568.

E115/369/146. Certificate of residence, Thomas Tallis, 1571.

E115/371/121. Certificate of residence, Thomas Tallis, 1585.

E117/3/43. Inventories of church goods, Kent, 1547–58.

E117/11/24. Inventory of Waltham Abbey at its dissolution in 1540.

E179/69/36. Lay subsidy roll, 1543/4.

E179/69/58. Lay subsidy roll, 1549.

E179/69/60. Lay subsidy roll, 1551.

E301/88. The 'brief' London and Middlesex chantry certificate, 1548.

E315/160. Household book of Sir Anthony Denny, Keeper of the Palace of Westminster, completed 24 April 1542, with additional entries to January 1548/9.

E322/78. Surrender of Dover Priory, 16 November 1535.

E322/252. Surrender of Waltham Abbey, 23 March 1540.

LC2/2. Lord Chamberlain's papers, funeral of Henry VIII.

LC2/3/1. Lord Chamberlain's papers, coronation of Edward VI.

LC2/3/2. Lord Chamberlain's papers, coronation of Edward VI.

PROB 10. Prerogative Court of Canterbury, bundles of original wills.

PROB 11. Prerogative Court of Canterbury, registers of wills and probate.
SP1/98. State papers, report on Dover Priory by Richard Layton, 1535.
SP1/208. State papers, letter from Thomas Cranmer to Henry VIII, 1544 (at f.169).
SP1/246. State papers, including part songs (ff.18^{r}–32^{v}).
SP10/1/17. State papers, burial of Henry VIII, 1547.
SP12/137/37. State papers, Letter to William Byrd, signed by 'Richard Sugeham', 1580.
SP12/193/63. Evidence of Henry Edyall, 1586.

Society of Antiquaries of London
MS 125. Fees and offices, 1553.
MS 129. A second copy of the inventory contained in BL Additional MS 46348.

Index of Tallis's Works

Contrafacta mentioned in earlier pages are included below.

For sources of Tallis's works see:

- editions listed in the Bibliography
- the Index of Names and Subjects, under 'music manuscripts'
- the EECM database.

Index of Names and Subjects

Printed in Great Britain
by Amazon

18267576R00169